SCOTT FORESMAN • ADDISON WESLEY

Mathematics

Grade 5

Homework Workbook

PEARSON
Scott Foresman

Editorial Offices: Glenview, Illinois • Parsippany, New Jersey • New York, New York

Sales Offices: Parsippany, New Jersey • Duluth, Georgia • Glenview, Illinois
Coppell, Texas • Ontario, California • Mesa, Arizona

ISBN 0-328-07560-4

5 6 7 8 9 10 V011 09 08 07 06 05

Name ______________________________

Place Value Through Billions

R 1-1

Place-value chart:

Billions period			Millions period			Thousands period			Ones period		
hundred billions	ten billions	billions	hundred millions	ten millions	millions	hundred thousands	ten thousands	thousands	hundreds	tens	ones
		6,	3	9	2,	5	8	0,	1	0	1

Expanded form: 6,000,000,000 + 300,000,000 + 90,000,000 + 2,000,000 + 500,000 + 80,000 + 100 + 1

Standard form: 6,392,580,101

Word form: six billion, three hundred ninety-two million, five hundred eighty thousand, one hundred one

Write the word name for each number and tell the value of the underlined digit.

1. 3,552,308,725 ______________________________

____

____

____

2. 843,208,732,833 ______________________________

____

____

____

3. Write 2,000,000,000 + 70,000,000 + 100,000 + 70,000 + 3,000 + 800 + 10 in standard form.

____

4. **Number Sense** What number is 100,000,000 more than 5,438,724,022?

____

Name ____________________

Place Value Through Billions

P 1-1

Write the word form for each number and tell the value of the underlined digit.

1. 34,23<u>5</u>,345 ____________________

____

____

2. 1<u>9</u>,673,890,004 ____________________

____

____

3. Write 2,430,090 in expanded form.

____

Write each number in standard form.

4. 80,000,000 + 4,000,000 + 100 + 8 ____________________

5. twenty-nine billion, thirty-two million ____________________

6. **Number Sense** What number is 10,000 less than 337,676? ____________________

Test Prep

7. Which number is 164,502,423 decreased by 100,000?

A. 164,402,423 **B.** 164,501,423 **C.** 164,512,423 **D.** 264,502,423

8. **Writing in Math** Explain how you would write 423,090,709,000 in word form.

____

____

____

____

Name ____________________

Comparing and Ordering Whole Numbers

R 1-2

Order these numbers from least to greatest: 4,752,213; 5,829,302; 4,234,295; 4,333,209.

Step 1: Write the numbers, lining up places. Begin at the left to find the greatest or least number.

4,752,213
5,829,302
4,234,295
4,333,209

5,829,302 is the greatest.

Step 2: Write the remaining numbers, lining up places. Find the greatest and least of these.

4,**7**52,213
4,**2**34,295
4,**3**33,209

4,752,213 is the greatest of these.

4,**2**34,295
4,**3**33,209

4,234,295 is the least.

Step 3: Write the numbers from least to greatest.

4,234,295
4,333,209
4,752,213
5,829,302

Complete. Write >, <, or = in each ○.

1. 7,642 ○ 7,843

2. 2,858,534 ○ 2,882,201

Order these numbers from least to greatest.

3. 768,265 769,205 739,802

____

____

4. Write the areas of each country in order from greatest to least.

____

____

____

____

Country	Area in Square Miles
Albania	28,748
Burundi	27,830
Solomon Islands	28,450
Haiti	27,750

Name ____________________

Comparing and Ordering Whole Numbers

P 1-2

Complete. Write >, <, or = for each ◯.

1. 23,412 ◯ 23,098

2. 9,000,000 ◯ 9,421,090

Order these numbers from least to greatest.

3. 7,545,999 7,445,999 7,554,000

____

4. **Number Sense** What digit could be in the ten millions place of a number that is less than 55,000,000 but greater than 25,000,000? ____________

5. Put the trenches in order from the least depth to the greatest depth.

____

____

____

____

Depths of Major Ocean Trenches

Trench	Depth (in feet)
Philippine Trench	32,995
Mariana Trench	35,840
Kermadec Trench	32,963
Tonga Trench	35,433

Test Prep

6. These numbers are ordered from greatest to least. Which number could be placed in the second position?

2,643,022 1,764,322 927,322

A. 2,743,022 **B.** 1,927,304 **C.** 1,443,322 **D.** 964,322

7. **Writing in Math** Explain why 42,678 is greater than 42,067.

____

____

____

Name ______________________________

Place Value Through Thousandths

R 1-3

Here are different ways to represent 1.753.

Place-value chart:

Ones	Tenths	Hundredths	Thousandths
1 .	7	5	3

Expanded form: 1 + 0.7 + 0.05 + 0.003

Standard form: 1.753

Word form: one and seven hundred fifty-three thousandths

The following decimals are equivalent to 0.9.

0.9 = 0.90 and 0.9 = 0.900

Why? Because 9 tenths have 90 hundredths or 900 thousandths.

Write the word name for each number and tell the value of the underlined digit.

1. 6.0<u>2</u> ______________________________

____

2. 5.<u>3</u>19 ______________________________

____

Write each number in standard form.

3. 7 + 0.7 + 0.04 + 0.005 __________

4. four and five hundred fifty-eight thousandths __________

Write two decimals that are equivalent to each number.

5. 0.80 __________

6. 0.300 __________

Name ____________________

Place Value Through Thousandths

P 1-3

Write the word form for each number and tell the value of the underlined digit.

1. 4.34<u>5</u> ____________________

____

2. 7.<u>8</u>80 ____________________

____

Write each number in standard form.

3. 6 + 0.3 + 0.02 + 0.001 ____________

4. seven and five hundred thirty-three thousandths ____________

Write two decimals that are equivalent to each number.

5. 0.68 ____________________

6. 0.9 ____________________

7. **Number Sense** Explain why 0.2 and 0.020 are not equivalent.

____

____

____

8. Cheri's time in the bobsled race was 1 min, 38.29 sec. Write the word form and the value of the 9 in Cheri's time.

____

Test Prep

9. Which is the word form of the underlined digit in 46.<u>5</u>04?

A. 5 ones **B.** 5 tenths **C.** 5 hundredths **D.** 5 thousandths

10. **Writing in Math** Write the value for each digit in the number 1.639. ____________

Name ______________________________

Comparing and Ordering Decimals

R 1-4

List the numbers in order from least to greatest: 6.943, 5.229, 6.825, 6.852, 6.779.

Step 1: Write the numbers, lining up places. Begin at the left to find the greatest or least number.

6.943
5.229
6.825
6.852
6.779

5.229 is the least.

Step 2: Write the remaining numbers, lining up places. Find the greatest and least.

6.**9**43
6.**8**25
6.**8**52
6.**7**79

6.779 is the least.
6.943 is the greatest.

6.8**2**5
6.8**5**2

6.852 is greater.

Step 3: Write the numbers from least to greatest.

5.229
6.779
6.825
6.852
6.943

Complete. Write >, <, or = for each ◯.

1. 7.539 ◯ 7.344 **2.** 9.202 ◯ 9.209 **3.** 0.75 ◯ 0.750

Order these numbers from least to greatest.

4. 3.898 3.827 3.779

____

5. 5.234 5.199 5.002 5.243

____

Which had the faster speed?

6. Driver A or Driver D

____

7. Driver C or Driver A

____

Car Racing Winners

Driver	Average Speed (mph)
Driver A	145.155
Driver B	145.827
Driver C	147.956
Driver D	144.809

Name ______________________________________

Comparing and Ordering Decimals

Write >, <, or = for each ◯.

1. 5.424 ◯ 5.343 **2.** 0.33 ◯ 0.330 **3.** 9.489 ◯ 9.479

4. 21.012 ◯ 21.01 **5.** 223.21 ◯ 223.199 **6.** 5.43 ◯ 5.432

Order these numbers from least to greatest.

7. 8.37, 8.3, 8.219, 8.129 ______________________

8. 0.012, 0.100, 0.001, 0.101 ______________________

9. Number Sense Name three numbers between 0.33 and 0.34. ______________________

10. Which runner came in first place?

____

11. Who ran faster, Amanda or Steve?

____

12. Who ran for the longest time?

____

Half Mile Run

Runner	Time (minutes)
Amanda	8.016
Calvin	7.049
Liz	7.03
Steve	8.16

Test Prep

13. Which number is less than 28.43?

A. 28.435 **B.** 28.34 **C.** 28.430 **D.** 29.43

14. Writing in Math Explain why it is not reasonable to say that 4.23 is less than 4.13.

____

____

____

Name ______________________________

Place-Value Patterns

R 1-5

You can name the number 30,000 in several different ways.

3 ten thousands (or 3 × 10,000)

30 thousands (or 30 × 1,000)

300 hundreds (or 300 × 100)

3,000 tens (or 3,000 × 10)

30,000 ones (or 30,000 × 1)

Ten Thousands	Thousands	Hundreds	Tens	Ones
3	0	0	0	0
3	**0**	0	0	0
3	**0**	**0**	0	0
3	**0**	**0**	**0**	0
3	**0**	**0**	**0**	**0**

Notice the pattern as you describe 30,000 in terms of ten thousands, thousands, hundreds, tens, and ones. The bold digits show how many ten thousands, thousands, hundreds, tens, and ones there are in 30,000. You can see, for example, that 3 ten thousands is the same as 3,000 tens.

Tell how many tens, hundreds, and thousands are in each number.

1. 50,000 ____________ tens ____________ hundreds

____________ thousands

2. 15,000,000 ____________ tens ____________ hundreds

____________ thousands

What number makes each statement true?

3. 97,000 = 970 × ____________ **4.** 8 = 0.8 × ____________

Name ____________________

Place-Value Patterns

P 1-5

Tell how many *tens, hundreds,* and *thousands* are in each number.

1. 12,000 ____________________

____

2. 9,000,000 ____________________

____

What number makes each statement true?

3. $9{,}000 = 900 \times$ ______ **4.** $600{,}000 = 60 \times$ ______

5. $4 = 0.4 \times$ ______ **6.** $60 = 0.6 \times$ ______

Name each number in two different ways.

7. 90,000,000 ____________________

8. 40,000 ____________________

9. **Number Sense** How many thousands are in 5,000,000? ______

10. The volume of Fort Peck Dam is $96{,}050 \times 1{,}000\ m^3$. Suppose the state of Montana decides to increase the volume of the dam. After the improvements, Fort Peck will hold 10 times as many cubic meters. How many cubic meters will Fort Peck hold after the improvements?

____

Test Prep

11. Which is the correct product for $1{,}000 \times 0.4$?

A. 4,000 **B.** 400 **C.** 4.000 **D.** 0.0004

12. **Writing in Math** Complete the missing information in this sentence:

Twenty-nine ____________________ is equal to $29 \times 1{,}000$.

Name ____

PROBLEM-SOLVING SKILL **R 1-6**

Read and Understand

Anniversary James's parents celebrated their 25th wedding anniversary in 1999. In what year did they get married?

Read and Understand

Step 1: What do you know?

- Tell the problem in your own words. James's parents got married during a certain year.
- Identify key details and facts. James's parents had been married for 25 years in 1999.

Step 2: What are you trying to find?

- Tell what the question is asking. You want to know the year that James's parents were married.
- Show the main idea.

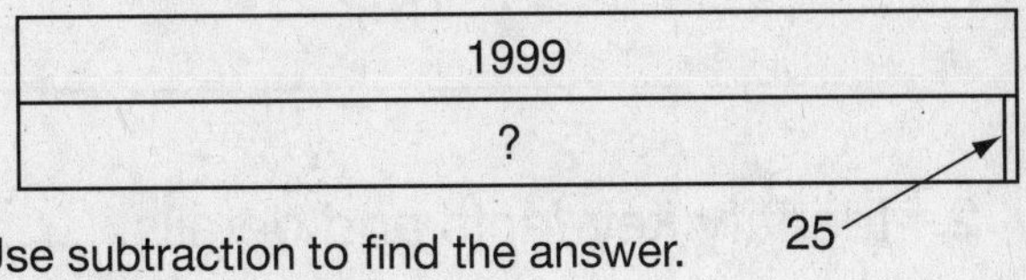

Use subtraction to find the answer.
1999 − 25 = 1974

Female Athletes In a certain year at Pembrook High School, 24 out of every 500 female students played on the volleyball teams, and 34 played on the soccer teams. If there were 1,000 female students at the high school that year, how many more athletes played on the soccer teams than the volleyball teams?

1. Identify key facts and details.

____

____

____

____

2. Solve the problem. Write your answer in a complete sentence.

____

____

____

Name ____________________

PROBLEM-SOLVING SKILL **P 1-6**

Read and Understand

The day a new manufacturing plant opened, the population of Sunny Grove was 13,731 people. In its first year of operation, 2,950 new residents moved into Sunny Grove. In the second year, double that number moved in. What was the population of Sunny Grove by the end of the second year of the plant's operation?

1. Tell the problem in your own words. ____________________

2. Identify key facts and details. ____________________

3. Tell what the question is asking. ____________________

4. Show the main idea.

5. Solve the problem. Write the answer in a complete sentence.

Name______________________________________

Adding and Subtracting Mentally

There are several ways that you can add and subtract numbers mentally to solve a problem.

Commutative Property of Addition

You can add two numbers in any order.

15 + 27 = 27 + 15

Associative Property of Addition

You can change the groupings of addends.

17 + (13 + 10) = (17 + 13) + 10

Compatible numbers are numbers that are easy to compute mentally.

25 + 93 + 75

25 and 75 are compatible because they are easy to add.

25 + 93 + 75 = (25 + 75) + 93
= 100 + 93 = 193

With **compensation**, you adjust one number to make computations easier and compensate by changing the other number.

320 − 190
+ 10 + 10
⇓ ⇓
330 − 200 = 130

Add or subtract mentally.

1. 265 + 410 + 335 = __________

2. 885 − 155 = __________

3. 2,500 + 1,730 + 70 = __________

4. 1,467 − 397 = __________

Strikeout Data

Pitcher	Number of Strikeouts
A	372
B	293
C	220
D	175
E	205

5. How many more strikeouts did Pitcher A have than Pitcher C?

____

6. How many strikeouts did Pitcher B and Pitcher E have altogether?

____

7. How many strikeouts were recorded by all five pitchers?

____

Name ____________________

Adding and Subtracting Mentally

P 1-7

Show how you can add or subtract mentally.

1. 70 + 90 + 30 = ______ **2.** 350 − 110 = ______

National Monuments

Name	State	Acres
George Washington Carver	Missouri	210
Navajo	Arizona	360
Fort Sumter	South Carolina	200
Russell Cave	Alabama	310

3. How many more acres are there at Navajo monument than at George Washington Carver monument? ______

4. How many acres are there at Fort Sumter and Russell Cave combined? ______

Test Prep

5. Fresh Market bought 56 lb of apples in August from a local orchard. In September, the market purchased an additional 52 lb of apples and 32 lb of strawberries. How many pounds of fruit did the market buy?

A. 108 lb **B.** 140 lb **C.** 150 lb **D.** 240 lb

6. **Writing in Math** Write the definition and give an example of the Commutative Property of Addition.

____

____

Name ____________________

R 1-8

Rounding Whole Numbers and Decimals

Look at the numbers listed below. You can use the number line to tell if 8,237,650 is closer to 8,000,000 or 9,000,000.

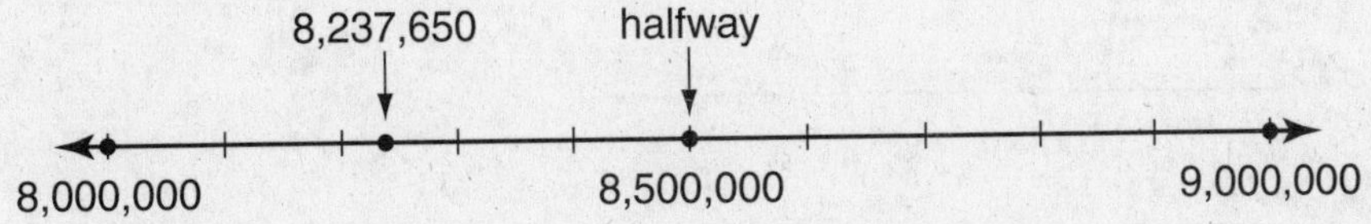

8,237,650 is closer to 8,000,000.

The number line can also help you determine if 7.762 is closer to 7.7 or 7.8.

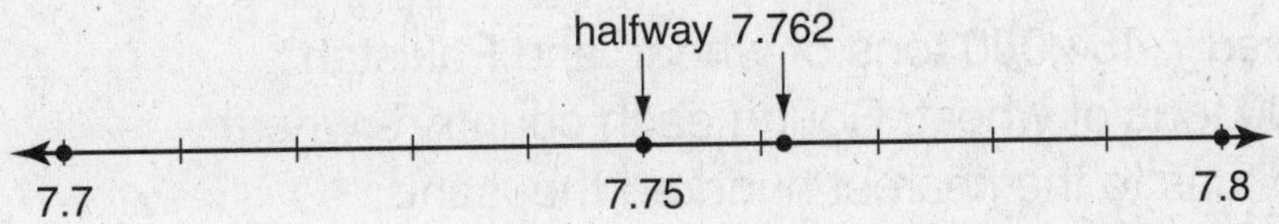

7.762 is closer to 7.8.

Round each number to the place of the underlined digit.

1. 4,725,806 ____________________

2. 7.049 ____________________

3. 165,023,912 ____________________

4. 18.692 ____________________

5. Round the number of connected computers in Year 2 to the nearest ten million. ____________________

Number of Computers Connected to the Internet

Year 1	30,979,376
Year 2	42,199,279
Year 3	63,592,854

6. Number Sense Marc earned $9.37 per hour working at the library. Round his wage to the nearest ten cents. ____________________

Name ______________________

Rounding Whole Numbers and Decimals

P 1-8

Round each number to the place of the underlined digit.

1. 32.<u>6</u>0 ______________

2. 48<u>9</u>,334,209 ______________

3. 32<u>4</u>,650 ______________

4. 32.<u>0</u>73 ______________

5. Reasoning Name two different numbers that round to 30 when rounded to the nearest ten. ______________

In 2000, Italy produced 7,464,000 tons of wheat, and Pakistan produced 21,079,000 tons of wheat. Round each country's wheat production in metric tons to the nearest hundred thousand.

6. Italy ______________

7. Pakistan ______________

The price of wheat in 1997 was $3.38 per bushel. In 1998, the price was $2.65 per bushel. Round the price per bushel of wheat for each year to the nearest tenth of a dollar.

8. 1997 ______________

9. 1998 ______________

Test Prep

10. Which number rounds to 15,700,000 when rounded to the nearest hundred thousand?

A. 15,000,000 **B.** 15,579,999 **C.** 15,649,999 **D.** 15,659,999

11. Writing in Math Write a definition of rounding in your own words.

____

____

Name ____________________

Estimating Sums and Differences

R 1-9

During one week, Mr. Graham drove a truck to five different towns to make deliveries. About how far did he drive in all?

Mr. Graham's Mileage Log

Cities	Mileage
Mansley to Mt. Hazel	243
Mt. Hazel to Perkins	303
Perkins to Alberton	279
Alberton to Fort Maynard	277
Fort Maynard to Mansley	352

You can round each number to the nearest hundred mile.

$$\begin{array}{rcr} 243 & \Rightarrow & 200 \\ 303 & \Rightarrow & 300 \\ 279 & \Rightarrow & 300 \\ 277 & \Rightarrow & 300 \\ \underline{+352} & \Rightarrow & \underline{+400} \\ & & 1{,}500 \text{ mi} \end{array}$$

Mr. Graham drove about 1,500 mi.

You can estimate differences in a similar way.

Estimate 7.25 – 4.98.

You can round to the nearest whole number.

$$\begin{array}{rcr} 7.25 & \Rightarrow & 7 \\ \underline{-4.98} & \Rightarrow & \underline{-5} \\ & & 2 \end{array}$$

The difference is about 2.

Estimate each sum or difference.

1. 19.7 – 6.9

____

2. 59 + 43 + 95

____

3. 582 + 169 + 23

____

4. 87.99 – 52.46

____

5. Estimation Brigid worked 16.75 hr. Kevin worked 12.50 hr. About how many more hours did Brigid work than Kevin?

____

Name ______________________________

Estimating Sums and Differences

P 1-9

Estimate each sum or difference.

1. 5,602 − 2,344 __________ **2.** 7.4 + 3.1 + 9.8 __________

3. 2,314 + 671 __________ **4.** 54.23 − 2.39 __________

5. Number Sense Wesley estimated 5.82 − 4.21 to be about 2. Is this an overestimate or an underestimate? Explain.

____

____

Average Yearly Precipitation of U.S. Cities

City	Inches	Days
Asheville, North Carolina	47.71	124
Wichita, Kansas	28.61	85

6. Estimate the total precipitation in inches and in days for Asheville and Wichita.

____

7. In inches and in days, about how much more average yearly precipitation is there in Asheville than in Wichita?

____

Test Prep

8. Which numbers should you add to estimate the answer to this problem: 87,087 + 98,000?

A. 88,000 + 98,000 **B.** 87,000 + 98,000

C. 85,000 + 95,000 **D.** 80,000 + 90,000

9. Writing in Math You want to estimate 5.25 − 3.3. Why would using front-end estimation and adjusting tell you more about the answer than rounding?

____

____

Name ____

PROBLEM-SOLVING SKILL **R 1-10**

Plan and Solve

Car Sales During March through May, Mr. Matthews sold cars at a dealership. Each month after March, he sold 6 more cars than the previous month. How many cars did he sell during these three months if he sold 8 cars in March?

Here are the steps to follow when you plan and solve a problem.

Step 1: Choose a strategy.

- **Show what you know:** Draw a picture, make an organized list, make a table or chart, use objects/act it out.
- **Look for a pattern.**
- **Try, check, and revise.**
- **Use logical reasoning.**
- **Solve a simpler problem.**
- **Work backward.**
- **Write an equation.**

Step 2: Stuck? Don't give up. Try these.

- Reread the problem.
- Tell the problem in your own words.
- Tell what you know.
- Identify key facts and details.
- Try a different strategy.
- Retrace your steps.

Step 3: Answer the question in the problem.

What strategy can be used to solve the Car Sales problem?

A chart can organize the information and make the problem easier to solve.

Mr. Matthews's Car Sales

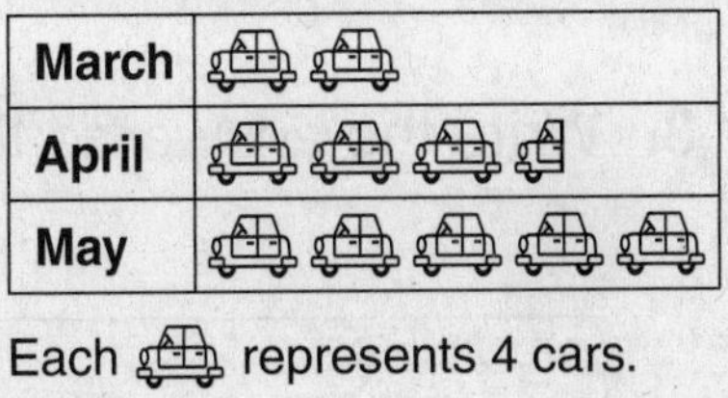

The answer to the problem: Mr. Matthews sold 42 cars in three months.

Reading Lynesia read 2 books during the first week of school. She read 3 books each week after that. How many weeks did it take Lynesia to read 18 books?

1. What strategy might work to solve this problem?

____

____

2. Give the answer to the problem in a complete sentence.

____

____

Name ______________________________

PROBLEM-SOLVING SKILL **P 1-10**

Plan and Solve

Yarn Wade and his mother bought four colors of yarn at the craft store. The blue yarn was longer than the green yarn but shorter than the red yarn. The yellow yarn was shorter than the green yarn. Order the colored yarns from the shortest to the longest.

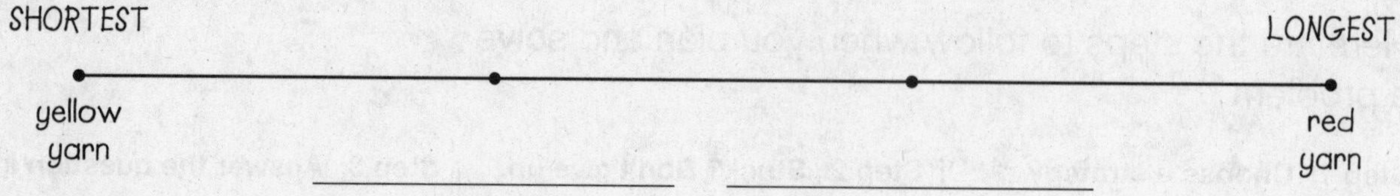

1. Finish the picture to help solve the problem.

2. What strategy was used to solve the problem?

3. Write the answer to the problem in a complete sentence.

Basketball Juanita's team is playing in a basketball competition. Each of the seven teams in the competition play all the other teams once. How many games are played in the competition?

4. What strategy did you use to solve this problem?

5. Give the answer in a complete sentence.

Name ____________________

Adding and Subtracting Whole Numbers

R 1-11

Find 35,996 + 49,801.

Step 1: Write the numbers, lining up places. Add the ones and then the tens.

$$\begin{array}{r} 35{,}996 \\ +\ 49{,}801 \\ \hline 97 \end{array}$$

Step 2: Continue adding hundreds, thousands, and ten thousands. Regroup as needed.

$$\begin{array}{r} 1\,1 \\ 35{,}996 \\ +\ 49{,}801 \\ \hline 85{,}797 \end{array}$$

So 35,996 + 49,801 = 85,797.

Find 35,996 − 17,902.

Step 1: Write the numbers, lining up places. Subtract the ones, tens, and hundreds.

$$\begin{array}{r} 35{,}996 \\ -\ 17{,}902 \\ \hline 094 \end{array}$$

Step 2: Continue by subtracting thousands. Regroup as needed.

$$\begin{array}{r} 2\,15 \\ \not{3}\not{5}{,}996 \\ -\ 17{,}902 \\ \hline 18{,}094 \end{array}$$

So 35,996 − 17,902 = 18,094.

Add or subtract.

1. $\begin{array}{r} 7{,}502 \\ +\ 9{,}909 \\ \hline \end{array}$

2. $\begin{array}{r} 64{,}782 \\ -\ 33{,}925 \\ \hline \end{array}$

3. $\begin{array}{r} 835{,}029 \\ -\ 26{,}332 \\ \hline \end{array}$

4. $\begin{array}{r} 85{,}926 \\ +\ 17{,}938 \\ \hline \end{array}$

5. $\begin{array}{r} 734{,}588 \\ -\ 141{,}672 \\ \hline \end{array}$

6. $\begin{array}{r} 901{,}633 \\ +\ 22{,}459 \\ \hline \end{array}$

Myronville School District has 23,081 students, and Saddleton School District has 45,035 students.

7. Number Sense How many more students are there in Saddleton than in Myronville?

____

Name______________________________________

Adding and Subtracting Whole Numbers

Add or subtract.

1. 29,543 + 13,976

2. 93,210 − 21,061

3. 369,021 − 325,310

4. 893,887 + 22,013

5. 971,234 + 55,423 = ______________

6. **Number Sense** Is 4,000 a reasonable estimate for the difference of 9,215 − 5,022? Explain.

____

7. How many people were employed as public officials and natural scientists?

____

8. How many more people were employed as university teachers than as lawyers and judges?

____

People Employed in U.S. by Occupation in 2000

Occupation	Workers
Public officials	753,000
Natural scientists	566,000
University teachers	961,000
Lawyers and judges	926,000

Test Prep

9. Which is the difference between 403,951 and 135,211?

A. 200,000 **B.** 221,365 **C.** 268,740 **D.** 539,162

10. **Writing in Math** Issac is adding 59,029 and 55,678. Should his answer be greater than or less than 100,000? Explain how you know.

____

____

____

Name

Adding Decimals

R 1-12

Miss Solade bought 2.4 lb of ground beef and 1.692 lb of chicken. How many pounds of meat did she buy altogether?

Step 1: Write the numbers. Line up the decimal points. Include the zeros to show place value.

$$\begin{array}{r} 2.400 \\ +\ 1.692 \\ \hline \end{array}$$

Step 2: Add as you would with whole numbers. Bring the decimal point straight down in the answer.

$$\begin{array}{r} \scriptstyle 1 \quad\quad \\ 2.400 \\ +\ 1.692 \\ \hline 4.092 \end{array}$$

Miss Solade bought 4.092 lb of meat.

Add.

1. 2.97 + 0.35 = ________

2. 13.88 + 7.694 = ________

3. 39.488 + 26.7 = ________

4. 88.8 + 4.277 + 78.95 = ________

5. **Number Sense** Is 16.7 a reasonable sum for 7.5 + 9.2? Explain.

____

6. How much combined snowfall was there in Milwaukee and Oklahoma City?

____

City	Snowfall (inches) in 2000
Milwaukee, WI	87.8
Baltimore, MD	27.2
Oklahoma City, OK	17.3

Name ______________________________

Adding Decimals

Add.

1. $58.0 + 3.6$

2. $40.5 + 22.3$

3. $34.587 + 21.098$

4. $43.1000 + 8.4388$

5. 16.036 + 7.009 = ____________

6. 92.30 + 0.32 = ____________

7. **Number Sense** Reilly adds 45.3 and 3.21. Should his sum be greater than or less than 48? Tell how you know.

____

____

____

In science class, students weighed different amounts of tin. Carmen weighed 4.361 g, Kim weighed 2.704 g, Simon weighed 5.295 g, and Angelica weighed 8.537 g.

8. How many grams of tin did Carmen and Angelica have combined?

____

9. How many grams of tin did Kim and Simon have combined?

____

Test Prep

10. In December the snowfall was 0.03 in. and in January it was 2.1 in. Which was the total snowfall?

A. 3.2 in. **B.** 2.40 in. **C.** 2.13 in. **D.** 0.03 in.

11. **Writing in Math** Explain why it is important to line up decimal numbers by their place value when you add or subtract them.

____

____

Name ____________________

Subtracting Decimals

Julie ran 2.67 mi and Caitlin ran 1.586 mi. How much farther did Julie run than Caitlin?

Estimate: 2.67 rounds to 3 and 1.586 rounds to 2.

So, 3 − 2 = 1.

Step 1: Write the numbers, lining up the decimal points. Write zeros to show place value.

$$\begin{array}{r} 2.67\mathbf{0} \\ -\ 1.586 \\ \hline \end{array}$$

Step 2: Subtract the thousandths. Decide if you need to regroup. Regroup 7 hundredths as 6 hundredths and 10 thousandths.

$$\begin{array}{r} {\scriptstyle 6\,10} \\ 2.67\!\!\!/0\!\!\!/ \\ -\ 1.586 \\ \hline \mathbf{4} \end{array}$$

Step 3: Subtract the hundredths. Regroup 6 tenths as 5 tenths and 10 + 6 hundredths. Continue subtracting as with whole numbers. Place the decimal in the answer.

$$\begin{array}{r} {\scriptstyle 5\,16\,10} \\ 2.6\!\!\!/7\!\!\!/0\!\!\!/ \\ -\ 1.586 \\ \hline \mathbf{1.084} \end{array}$$

The difference is close to the estimate so the answer is reasonable.

Check: 1.084 + 1.586 = 2.670

Julie ran 1.084 more miles than Caitlin.

Subtract.

1. 18.6 − 13.8

2. 63.7 − 12.66

3. 8.76 − 4.945

4. 82.7 − 5.59

5. 43.3 − 12.82

6. 7.28 − 4.928

7. Reasonableness Dylan subtracted 5.6 from 17.28 and got 14.68. Is his answer reasonable? Why or why not?

____

____

____

Name ____________________

Subtracting Decimals

Subtract.

1. 92.1 − 32.6

2. 52.7 − 36.9

3. 85.76 − 12.986

4. 32.7 − 2.328

5. 8.7 − 0.3 = ________

6. 23.3 − 1.32 = ________

7. **Number Sense** Kelly subtracted 2.3 from 20 and got 17.7. Explain why this answer is reasonable.

____

____

At a local swim meet, the second place swimmer of the 100 m freestyle had a time of 9.33 sec. The first place swimmer's time was 1.32 sec faster than the second place swimmer. The third place time was 13.65 sec.

8. What was the time for the first place swimmer? ________

9. What was the difference in time between the second and third place swimmers? ________

Test Prep

10. Miami's annual precipitation in 2000 was 61.05 in. Albany's was 46.92 in. How much greater was Miami's rainfall than Albany's?

A. 107.97 in. **B.** 54.31 in. **C.** 14.93 in. **D.** 14.13 in.

11. **Writing in Math** Explain how to subtract 7.6 from 20.39.

____

____

____

____

Name ____________________

PROBLEM-SOLVING SKILL **R 1-14**

Look Back and Check

Lunch Cost Anthony bought a pretzel for $0.57 and a box lunch, which cost $3.00. He paid $0.29 for tax. How much did Anthony spend for his lunch? How much change did he get back if he paid with a $5 bill?

Donald's Work

```
   1              9
 $0.57          4̶1010
  3.00          $5.0̸0̸
+ 0.29        -  3.86
 $3.86          $2.14
```

Anthony spent $3.86 on lunch and received $2.14 in change.

Step 1: Check your answer.
Did Donald answer the right questions?
Yes, he found the total cost for the lunch and the amount of change Anthony should get back.

Step 2: Check your work.
Donald could use subtraction and addition to check if his answers are correct. The amount Anthony paid for the lunch is correct, but the amount of change he received should be $1.14 instead of $2.14. Donald forgot to change $5 to $4 when he regrouped the dollars into ten cents.

Order by Age Five students want to line up according to the order of their births. Bradley is the oldest. Jerry's birthday is 5 days after Katie's birthday. Mattison's birthday is on December 31 and is the only birthday in December. Hank's birthday is the closest birthday to Bradley's. In what order would the students line up? Look back and check Colin's work on this problem.

YOUNGEST ——— OLDEST

Mattison — Hank — Jerry — Katie — Bradley

In order, the students are Bradley, Katie, Jerry, Hank, and Mattison.

1. Is Colin's work correct? Explain.

____

____

____

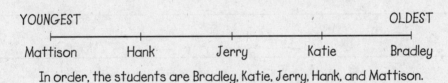

Name ______________________________

PROBLEM-SOLVING SKILL **P 1-14**

Look Back and Check

Art Collection The Collector's Museum is home to lots of great art. The most valuable item is a painting finished in 1840 called *The Mirror.* Its estimated value is $1,202,450. The piece titled *A Summer Memory* is valued at $100,000 less than the value of *The Mirror.* The entire art collection is estimated to be worth $13,000,000. Overall there are 45 works of art in the museum. What is the total estimated value of the other 43 works of art?

Jacques solved the Art Collection problem. Check his work.

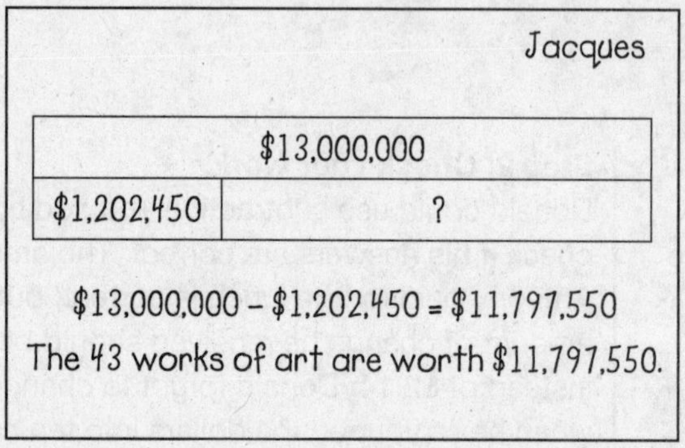

Jacques
$13,000,000
$1,202,450
?
$13,000,000 – $1,202,450 = $11,797,550
The 43 works of art are worth $11,797,550.

1. Did Jacques answer the right question? Explain.

____

____

2. Is his answer correct? Explain.

____

____

____

Solve the problem. Then, look back and check your work.

3. An empty jar weighs 39 g. A jar that is full of water weighs 207 g. What does the water in the jar weigh?

____

Name

PROBLEM-SOLVING APPLICATION **R 1-15**

It's Elemental!

Platinum is a metal element used in chemical equipment, electrical wires, and jewelry. The following data chart shows the demand for platinum in different areas of the world for the years 1998 to 2001. The demand chart shows the areas that use the most platinum in *thousands* of ounces.

Platinum Demand (in thousands of ounces)

	1998	1999	2000	2001
Europe	910	995	1,150	1,490
Japan	1,795	1,820	1,410	1,250
North America	1,325	1,080	1,225	1,285

Which area had the lesser platinum demand in 2001, Japan or North America?

Step 1: Write the numbers, lining up places. Begin at the left and compare.

1,250,000

1,285,000

Step 2: Find the first place where the digits are different and compare.

1,2**5**0,000

1,2**8**5,000

Since 5 is less than 8, then 1,250,000 is less than 1,285,000. So, Japan had a lesser platinum demand in 2001.

1. In which year did Japan have a greater platinum demand, 1998 or 1999?

____

2. If Europe's platinum demand is 10 times larger in 2011 as in 2001, what will the platinum demand be?

____

Name ______________________________

Champions

At a gymnastics meet, Karl took first place. Karl scored 9.836 on the vault, Yao received a score of 9.772 on the parallel bars, and Quincy scored 9.672 on the vault.

1. How much higher was Karl's vault score than Quincy's vault score? ______________

2. What information did you not need to answer the question?

____

____

Four weight lifters competed in the state tournament. Barney lifted 205 kg, Eddie lifted 290 kg, Pierre lifted 305 kg, and Nathan lifted 325 kg.

3. How much more did Eddie lift than Barney? ______________

4. How much more did Eddie and Pierre lift combined than Barney and Nathan combined? ______________

Six runners competed in a race. Kathryn finished third. Salma finished ahead of Kathryn and Marita. Jackie finished before Lara but after Nikki. List the runners in the order they finished.

5. Draw a picture to help you solve the problem.

6. Write your answer in a complete sentence.

____

____

Name ____________________

Multiplication Patterns

R 2-1

Commutative Property of Multiplication	Associative Property of Multiplication
You can multiply two factors in any order. $15 \times 9 = 9 \times 15$	You can change the grouping of factors. $(8 \times 20) \times 5 = 8 \times (20 \times 5)$

You can also use patterns to multiply mentally.

Fact: $5 \times 7 = 35$

$50 \times 7 =$ **35**0 $\quad 5 \times 70 =$ **35**0

$500 \times 7 =$ **3,5**00 $\quad 50 \times 70 =$ **3,5**00

$5{,}000 \times 7 =$ **35,**000 $\quad 500 \times 70 =$ **35,**000

$50{,}000 \times 7 =$ **35**0,000 $\quad 5{,}000 \times 70 =$ **35**0,000

Pattern: Notice that the product is always 35 with the different number of zeros that are in the factors.

Find $30 \times 3 \times 50$.

Use the Associative Property of Multiplication to regroup.

$(30 \times 50) \times 3$

$1{,}500 \times 3 = 4{,}500$

Find each product. Use patterns and properties to compute mentally.

1. $80 \times 90 =$ ____________ **2.** $40 \times 800 =$ ____________

3. $5 \times 10 \times 20 =$ ____________ **4.** $4 \times 30 \times 25 =$ ____________

5. Number Sense You know that $6 \times 7 = 42$. How can you find 60×700?

____

____

____

Name ______________________________

Multiplication Patterns

P 2-1

Find each product. Use patterns and properties to compute mentally.

1. $40 \times 20 =$ ________

2. $50 \times 700 =$ ________

3. $20 \times 2 \times 30 =$ ________

4. $2 \times 50 \times 30 =$ ________

5. $250 \times 37 \times 4 =$ ________

6. $20 \times 65 \times 5 =$ ________

Calories in Fruit

Fruit (1 piece)	Calories
Apple	80
Orange	60
Peach	35

7. How many calories are in 10 peaches? ________

8. How many calories are in 5 apples? ________

9. Callie ate 3 oranges each day for 10 days. How many calories did all of these oranges have? ________

10. **Algebra** $m \times n = 6{,}300$. If m and n are 2-digit multiples of 10, what numbers could m and n be?

____

Test Prep

11. Which of the following has a product of 1,600?

A. $4{,}000 \times 400$ **B.** 4×400 **C.** 400×400 **D.** 40×400

12. **Writing in Math** Write a definition for the Associative Property of Multiplication in your own words and explain how you would use it to compute $4 \times 27 \times 25$ mentally.

____

____

____

Name ____________________

Estimating Products

R 2-2

A bus service drives passengers between Milwaukee and Chicago every day. They travel from city to city a total of 8 times each day. The distance between the two cities is 89 mi. In the month of February, there are 28 days. The company's budget allows for 28,000 total miles for February. Is 28,000 mi a reasonable budget mileage amount?

One Way to Estimate

Estimate $28 \times 8 \times 89$.

You can round 89 to 100 and 8 to 10. Then multiply.

$28 \times 10 \times 100 = 280 \times 100 = 28{,}000$

Because this is an overestimate, there are enough miles.

Another Way to Estimate

Estimate $28 \times 8 \times 89$.

Adjust 28 to 30, 8 to 10, and 89 to 90.

$(30 \times 10) \times 90 = 300 \times 90 = 27{,}000$

Because all the numbers were adjusted higher, there are enough miles.

28,000 total miles is a reasonable budget amount.

Estimate each product.

1. $42 \times 5 \times 90$ ____________
2. $27 \times 98 \times 4$ ____________
3. $9 \times 55 \times 10$ ____________
4. $22 \times 19 \times 100$ ____________
5. **Number Sense** What are two different ways to estimate $9 \times 299 \times 10$?

____

Mrs. Carter ordered new supplies for Memorial Hospital.

Supplies	
Electronic thermometers	$ 19 each
Pulse monitors	$189 each
Pillows	$ 17 each
Telephones	$ 19 each

6. About how much will it cost to purchase 48 electronic thermometers?

____

7. About how much will it cost to purchase 96 pillows?

____

Name ___________________________________

Estimating Products

Estimate each product.

1. $36 \times 12 \times 9 =$ ____________ **2.** $16 \times 7 \times 34 =$ ____________

3. $2 \times 82 \times 26 =$ ____________ **4.** $56 \times 11 \times 2 =$ ____________

5. $44 \times 67 \times 7 =$ ____________ **6.** $22 \times 69 \times 4 =$ ____________

7. $53 \times 78 \times 21 =$ ____________ **8.** $6 \times 12 \times 42 =$ ____________

9. **Number Sense** Give three numbers whose product is about 9,000. ____________

10. About how much would it cost to buy 4 CD/MP3 players and 3 MP3 players?

____

Electronics Prices	
CD player	$74.00
MP3 player	$99.00
CD/MP3 player	$199.00
AM/FM radio	$29.00

11. Estimate to decide whether 8 AM/FM radios or 3 CD players cost less. Explain.

____

____

____

Test Prep

12. Which is the closest estimate for the product of $2 \times 15 \times 5$?

A. 1,150 **B.** 150 **C.** 125 **D.** 50

13. **Writing in Math** Explain how you know whether an estimate of a product is an overestimate or an underestimate.

____

____

____

Name ____________________

Mental Math: Using the Distributive Property

R 2-3

Mr. Braxton bought 26 boxes of bathroom tissue for his company. Each box contains 6 rolls of tissue. How many rolls of tissue did he order altogether?

You can find 6×26 using the distributive property with addition or subtraction.

Use Addition	Use Addition	Use Subtraction
Split 26 into 20 + 6.	Split 26 into 25 + 1.	Split 26 into 30 − 4.
$6 \times 26 = 6 \times (20 + 6) =$	$6 \times 26 = 6 \times (25 + 1) =$	$6 \times 26 = 6 \times (30 - 4) =$
$(6 \times 20) + (6 \times 6) =$	$(6 \times 25) + (6 \times 1) =$	$(6 \times 30) - (6 \times 4) =$
$120 + 36 =$	$150 + 6 =$	$180 - 24 =$
156	156	156

Use the distributive property to multiply mentally.

1. $8 \times 19 =$ ____________ **2.** $7 \times 61 =$ ____________

3. $23 \times 101 =$ ____________ **4.** $9 \times 26 =$ ____________

5. $40 \times 17 =$ ____________ **6.** $5 \times 350 =$ ____________

7. There are 16 oz in every pound. How many ounces are there in 5 lb?

____

____

____

8. **Algebra** If $10 \times 198 = (10 \times m) - (10 \times 2)$, what is the value of m?

____

Name ______________________________

Mental Math: Using the Distributive Property

P 2-3

Use the Distributive Property to multiply mentally.

1. $5 \times 607 =$ __________
2. $16 \times 102 =$ __________
3. $7 \times 420 =$ __________
4. $265 \times 5 =$ __________
5. $44 \times 60 =$ __________
6. $220 \times 19 =$ __________
7. $45 \times 280 =$ __________
8. $341 \times 32 =$ __________

9. **Number Sense** Fill in the blanks to show how the Distributive Property can be used to find 10×147.

   $10 \times (150 - 3) = (10 \times 150) - ($ __________ $\times 3) =$

   $1{,}500 -$ __________ $=$ __________

10. In 1990, there were 1,133 tornadoes in the U.S. If there were the same number of tornadoes for the next 10 years, what would have been the 10-year total? __________

11. There were 1,071 tornadoes in the U.S. in 2000. What is the number of tornadoes multiplied by 20? __________

Test Prep

12. If $4 \times 312 = (4 \times (300 + n)$, which is the value of n?

   A. 4 **B.** 12 **C.** 48 **D.** 300

13. **Writing in Math** Margaret said that she used the Distributive Property to solve 4×444. Is her answer shown below correct? Explain.

   $4 \times 444 = 4 \times (400 + 40 + 4) =$

   $(4 \times 400) + (4 \times 40) + (4 \times 4) =$

   $1{,}600 + 160 + 16 = 1{,}776$

____

Name _____

Multiplying Whole Numbers

Find 128 × 23. Estimate: 100 × 20 = 2,000

	Step 1 Multiply the ones. Regroup as needed.	**Step 2** Multiply the tens. Regroup as needed.	**Step 3** Add the products.

$$
\begin{array}{r} 128 \\ \times\ 23 \\ \hline {}^{1}384 \\ +\ 2{,}560 \\ \hline 2{,}944 \end{array}
\qquad
\begin{array}{r} 128 \\ \times\ 3 \\ \hline 384 \end{array}
\qquad
\begin{array}{r} 128 \\ \times\ 20 \\ \hline 2{,}560 \end{array}
$$

Because the answer is close to the estimate, the answer is reasonable.

Find the product. Estimate to check if your answer is reasonable.

Problem	Multiply Ones	Multiply Tens	Add Products
1. $\begin{array}{r}282\\ \times\ 19\\ \hline 2{,}538\\ +\\ \hline\end{array}$	$\begin{array}{r}282\\ \times\ 9\\ \hline 2{,}538\end{array}$	$\begin{array}{r}282\\ \times\ 10\\ \hline\end{array}$	
2. $\begin{array}{r}538\\ \times\ 46\\ \hline\end{array}$			

3. **Reasonableness** Is 2,750 a reasonable answer for 917 × 33? Explain.

Name ____________________

Multiplying Whole Numbers

Find each product. Estimate to check that your answer is reasonable.

1. $543 \times 4 =$ ________

2. $254 \times 6 =$ ________

3. $756 \times 6 =$ ________

4. $560 \times 34 =$ ________

5. $424 \times 76 =$ ________

6. $513 \times 13 =$ ________

7. $107 \times 51 =$ ________

8. $816 \times 52 =$ ________

9. 15×29

10. 876×4

11. 55×44

12. 89×65

13. 235×32

14. Show how you can use the distributive property to multiply 22×85.

____

15. Player A's longest home run distance is 484 ft. If Player A hits 45 home runs at his longest distance, what would the total distance be?

____

16. Player B's longest home run distance is 500 ft. There are 5,280 ft in 1 mi. How many home runs would Player B need to hit at his longest distance for the total to be greater than 1 mi?

____

Test Prep

17. Which is a reasonable answer for the product of $96 \times 7 \times 34$?

A. 672 **B.** 3,264 **C.** 22,848 **D.** 28,800

18. **Writing in Math** Why is 2,482 not a reasonable answer for 542×6?

____

____

____

Name ________________________________

Choose a Computation Method

R 2-5

Use mental math when the numbers are easy to multiply in your head, such as 15 × 3.

Use paper and pencil when the numbers are not easy to multiply mentally, such as 18 × 24.

Use a calculator when the numbers are large and you want an exact answer, such as 327 × 56.

Find each product. Tell what computation method you used.

1. 800 × 25 = ____________________

2. 99 × 71 = ____________________

3. 243 × 598 = ____________________

4. What is the cost of three baseball mitts?

____

____

Sporting Goods Sale

Item	Price
Baseball mitt	$49
Soccer ball	$32
In-line skates	$104
Softball	$9
Running shoes	$28

5. What is the cost of two pairs of in-line skates?

____

____

6. Writing in Math Explain how to use mental math to find the product of 20 × 49.

____

____

____

Name ______________________

Choose a Calculation Method

P 2-5

Find each product. Tell what computation method you used.

1. 200 × 50 = ______________________

2. 57 × 7 = ______________________

3. 34 × 22 = ______________________

4. 60 × 17 = ______________________

5. 455 × 309 = ______________________

6. 250 × 200 = ______________________

7. **Number Sense** Find 77 × 96. Explain the method you used.

____

____

8. If Reneé rode her bicycle every day last year for 7 mi each day, how many miles did she ride altogether? ______________

9. Jason went to school 180 days last year. If he walked 2 mi each way, how many miles did he walk to and from school in all? ______________

Test Prep

10. Eli used mental math to solve 6 × 32. Which answer shows how he could find the correct solution?

A. (3 × 3) + (6 × 2)

B. 6 × (9 × 4)

C. (6 × 30) + (6 × 2)

D. (6 × 30) + 2

11. **Writing in Math** Explain why mental math would not be the best way to multiply 309 × 399.

____

Name ____________________

Make an Organized List

Coin Toss Jan and Linda thought of a coin tossing game that uses a quarter. If the coin lands "heads" up, the player receives 10 points. If it lands "tails" up, the player receives 9 points. Each player gets 3 tosses. What scores are possible for one game for one player?

Read and Understand

What do you know? In each round, a player can score either 10 or 9 points. There are 3 rounds.

What are you trying to find? The scores that are possible for one game for one player.

Plan and Solve

What strategy will you use? **Strategy:** Make an organized list.

Scores per Round	Total Score	
10, 10, 10	30	First, find the combinations
10, 10, 9	29	with a "heads" flip or 10.
10, 9, 9	28	Then, find the combinations
9, 9, 9	27	with a "tails" flip or 9.

Answer: Possible scores are 30, 29, 28, and 27.

Look Back and Check

Is your work correct? Yes, each possible point combination was listed.

1. The sandwich shop sells tuna, egg, and peanut butter sandwiches. You can have your sandwich on whole wheat, rye, or a bagel. How many different sandwiches are possible?

____

____

Name ____________________

PROBLEM-SOLVING STRATEGY **P 2-6**

Make an Organized List

Solve each problem. Write the answer in a complete sentence.

1. The mystery first name of a student in class does not begin with A, B, C, D, E, or F. The name's first letter comes before S, T, U, V, and W. The students whose names start with J, K, L, M, and N are not it. All letters from O through Q are not it. X, Y, Z and G, H, I are not it. What is the first letter of the mystery name?

____

____

2. Evan is thinking of a 3-digit odd number that uses the digit 7 twice. The digit in the tens place is less than one. What is the number?

____

____

3. In the Laser Bowl Tournament, the judges take away 50 points for a gutter ball. Players score 30 points for a red head pin strike, 20 points for a blue pin strike, and 15 points for a green pin strike. Two red head pin strikes in a row earns a one-time bonus of 50 points. How many points would you score if you earned 2 red head pin strikes in a row, 2 blue pin strikes, 0 green pin strikes, and 2 gutter balls?

____

4. Writing in Math Explain how you completed the list in Exercise 1.

____

____

____

Name______________________________

Decimal Patterns

R 2-7

You can use patterns to multiply decimals mentally by 10, 100, and 1,000.

Look at what happens to the decimal when you multiply decimals by 10.

Multiplying by 10	What happens to the decimal?
32.5 × 10 = 325	The decimal moves one place to the right.
5.936 × 10 = 59.36	The decimal moves one place to the right.

Now look at multiplying decimals by 100 and 1,000.

Multiplying by 100	What happens to the decimal position?
32.5 × 100 = 3,250	The decimal moves two places to the right.

Multiplying by 1,000	What happens to the decimal position?
5.9362 × 1,000 = 5,936.2	The decimal moves three places to the right.

Find the product. Use mental math.

1. 3.7 × 10 = __________ **2.** 1.828 × 1,000 = __________

3. 56 × 1,000 = __________ **4.** 100 × 39.9 = __________

5. Mr. Williams invests $125 in a stock. After three years, the stock's value is 10 times greater. What is the value of the stock after three years? __________

6. At birth, the length of a snake is 0.087 ft. After three years, the length is 100 times greater than at birth. What is the length of the snake after three years? __________

7. **Algebra** What is *m* if 163.25 × *m* = 163,250? __________

Name ____________________

Decimal Patterns

Find each product. Use mental math.

1. $0.31 \times 10 =$ ________

2. $100 \times 7.000 =$ ________

3. $0.02 \times 1{,}000 =$ ________

4. $1{,}000 \times 5.1 =$ ________

5. $45.6 \times 100 =$ ________

6. $30.3 \times 1{,}000 =$ ________

7. $10 \times 102.2 =$ ________

8. $100 \times 0.312 =$ ________

9. $10 \times 7.522 =$ ________

10. $0.002 \times 10 =$ ________

11. $578.31 \times 100 =$ ________

12. $9.50 \times 1{,}000 =$ ________

Student	Art Size
Jade	0.25 mm
Willa	0.24 mm
Jess	0.05 mm
Mae	0.37 mm

13. Which student will enlarge her art to 5 mm if she enlarges it 100 times?

____

14. How many millimeters will Mae's art be if she enlarges it 100 times?

____

15. Algebra What is the value of n if $23.2 \times n = 2{,}320$? ________

Test Prep

16. Which is the product of 0.225×100?

A. 2.25 **B.** 22.5 **C.** 225 **D.** 2,250

17. Writing in Math Write a word problem using the number sentence $4.23 \times 10 = 42.3$.

____

____

Name________________________________

Estimating Decimal Products

R 2-8

Bonnie wants to buy 3.7 lb of cashews for a recipe. The cashews cost $8.95 per pound. About how much will the cashews cost?

Two Ways for Bonnie to Estimate the Cost of the Cashews

Estimating by rounding

You can estimate 3.7 × $8.95 by rounding both numbers.

3.7 is close to 4.
$8.95 is close to $9.

4 × $9 = 36
3.7 × $8.95 is about $36.

So the cashews will cost about $36.

This is an overestimate since both numbers were rounded up. The exact answer is less than $36.

Estimating by using compatible numbers

Another way to estimate is to adjust one or both numbers to compatible numbers that are easy to multiply.

3.7 × $8.95
⇓
3.7 × $10
3.7 × $10 = $37
3.7 × $8.95 is about 37.

So the cashews will cost about $37.

Estimate each product.

1. 6.3 × $17.59

____

2. 29 × 2.002

____

3. 88.8 × 6.908

____

4. 7.94 × 51.25

____

5. **Number Sense** Estimate 6.7 × 11 using two different ways. Tell how you found each estimate.

____

____

6. Which product is greater, 35.34 × 6.4 or 35.47 × 6.4? Explain your answer.

____

____

Name ______________________

Estimating Decimal Products

P 2-8

Estimate each product.

1. $43 \times 2.1 =$ ______

2. $5.40 \times 7 =$ ______

3. $2.23 \times 15.9 =$ ______

4. $250 \times 5.1 =$ ______

5. $0.02 \times 96 =$ ______

6. $2.65 \times 7.4 =$ ______

7. $435.22 \times 2 =$ ______

8. $781.93 \times 13 =$ ______

9. $1.90 \times 526.8 =$ ______

10. James has $65 to spend at the clothing sale. Does James have enough money to buy one of each item?

Clothing Sale	
Sweater	$19.99
Pants	$29.99
Shirt	$12.99
Socks (1 pair)	$2.99

____

____

____

11. Algebra A reasonable estimate for n is 1,000. Complete the problem to make it true.

$n \times$ ______ $= 6{,}350$

Test Prep

12. Which is a reasonable estimate for 41.3×8.78?

A. 36 **B.** 360 **C.** 3,600 **D.** 36,000

13. Writing in Math Explain how you know that 200 is not a reasonable estimate for 19.6×20.

____

____

Name________________________________

Multiplying Whole Numbers and Decimals

R 2-9

A human can walk a long distance at an average rate of 4.2 mi per hour. A high-speed train can travel the same distance 48 times faster. What is the speed of the high-speed train?

Step 1: Estimate, then multiply as with whole numbers.

4.2 × 48 is about
4 × 50 = 200.

```
    48
 × 4.2
    96
  1920
  2016
```

Step 2: Write the decimal point in the product. First, count the number of decimal places in both factors.

```
    48 ← 0 decimal places
 × 4.2 ← 1 decimal place
    96
  1920
 201.6
```

Since there is a total of 1 decimal place in the factors, there is 1 decimal place in the product.

Your answer is reasonable. It is close to 200.

1. 6.3 × 8

2. 21 × 2.5

3. 0.002 × 4

4. 35 × 5.3 = ____________

5. 17.6 × 40 = ____________

6. Mrs. Bilda bought six cans of orange juice at a cost of $1.33 per can, including tax. How much change did she get from a $10 bill? ____________

7. **Algebra** If 0.3 × *n* = 0.24, what is the value of *n*? ____________

8. **Writing in Math** John is multiplying two factors, each with one decimal place. He says that the product should also have only one decimal place. Is his explanation correct? Explain.

____

____

____

Name ____________________

Multiplying Whole Numbers and Decimals

P 2-9

Find each product.

1. 5.4×3

2. 3.8×4

3. 0.55×8

4. 8.19×5

Insert a decimal point in each answer to make the equation true.

5. $5 \times 6.3 = 315$ ____________

6. $3.001 \times 9 = 27009$ ____________

Average Desert Rainfall in August

Reno	0.19 mm
Sahara	0.17 mm
Mojave	0.1 mm
Tempe	0.24 mm

7. Which desert accumulates the least amount of rain in August?

____

8. If each month in Reno had the same average rainfall as in August, what would the total number of millimeters be after 12 months?

____

Test Prep

9. **Algebra** If $4n = 3.60$, which is the value of n?

A. 0.09 **B.** 0.9 **C.** 9 **D.** 90

Use the desert rainfall table to answer Exercise 10.

10. **Writing in Math** In December, the average rainfall in all of the deserts is 0.89 mm. Use the figures from the table to write a comparison of average desert rainfall in August and December.

____

____

____

Name ______________________________

Using Grids to Multiply Decimals by Decimals

R 2-10

0.9 × **0.5** = **0.45**

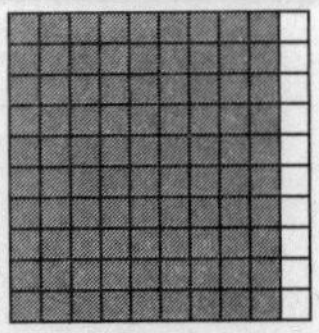

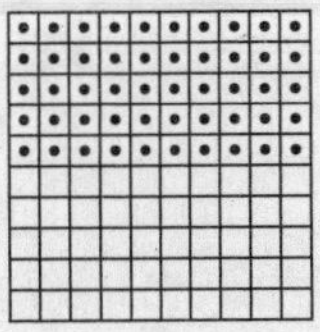

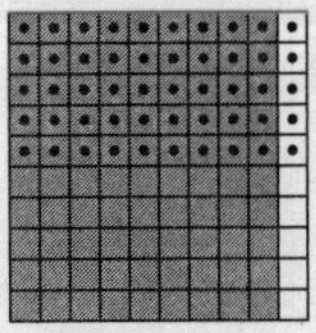

90 squares are shaded.
This is 90 hundredths — 0.90
or
9 tenths — 0.9.

50 squares are dotted.
This is 50 hundredths — 0.50
or
5 tenths — 0.5.

The squares that are shaded and dotted represent the product of 0.9 and 0.5.

So, 0.9 × 0.5 = 0.45.

Write a multiplication sentence that describes the shaded and dotted areas of each grid.

1.

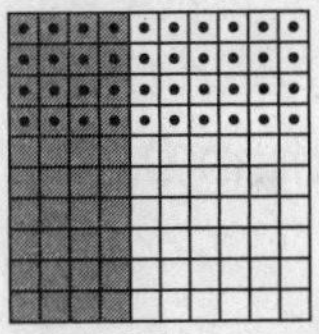

____

2.

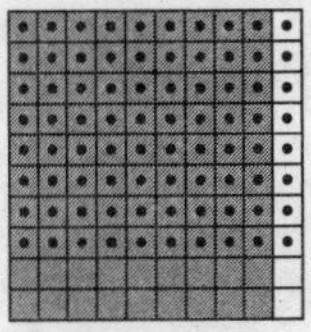

____

3.

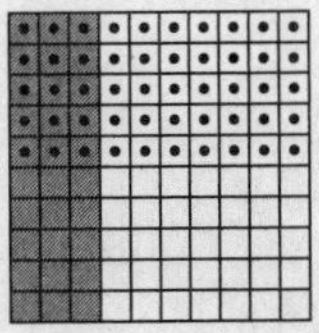

____

4.

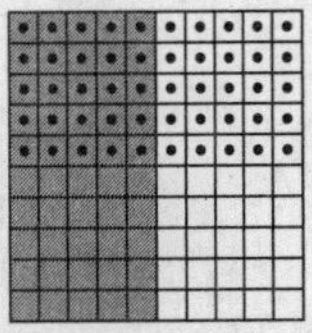

____

Find each product. You can use a 10 × 10 grid to help.

5. 0.5 × 0.2 = ______________

6. 0.8 × 0.8 = ______________

7. **Number Sense** Which product is greater, 0.8 × 0.2 or 0.8 × 0.3? Explain.

____

____

Name________________________________

Using Grids to Multiply Decimals by Decimals

P 2-10

Write a multiplication sentence that describes the shaded areas of each grid.

1. 

2. 

_______________________ _______________________

Find each product. You can use 10 × 10 grids to help.

3. 0.3 × 0.4 = ______ **4.** 0.2 × 0.7 = ______ **5.** 0.6 × 0.6 = ______

6. 0.5 × 0.5 = ______ **7.** 0.7 × 0.8 = ______ **8.** 0.6 × 0.3 = ______

9. Write two numbers whose product is 0.56.

____

10. Number Sense Is 0.4 × 0.8 greater than or less than 0.3 × 0.9?

____

Test Prep

11. Which 10 × 10 grid shows the product of 0.6 × 0.2?

A. 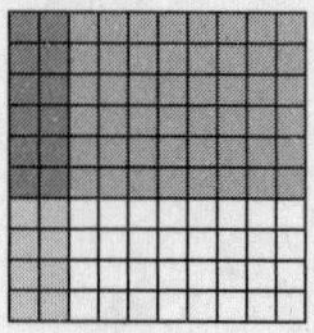

B. 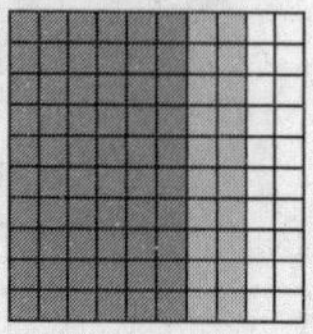

C. 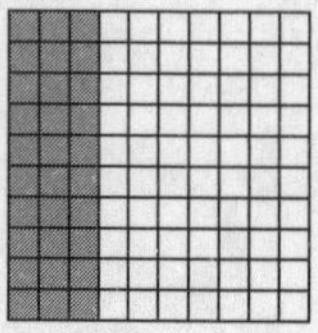

D. 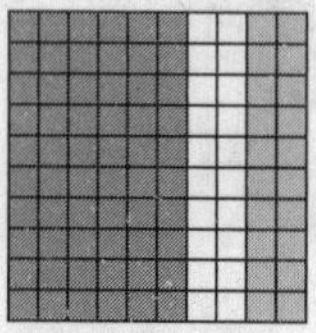

12. Writing in Math Explain why 0.2 × 0.4 equals 0.08 and not 0.8.

____

____

____

____

Name________________________

Multiplying Decimals by Decimals

R 2-11

Multiplying two decimal numbers is nearly the same as multiplying two whole numbers. The only difference is deciding where to place the decimal point in the answer.

Where do you place the decimal point in the answer?

First, multiply as with whole numbers.
Then, count the decimal places in both factors.

$$\begin{array}{r} 0.77 \\ \times \quad 4.8 \\ \hline 616 \\ 3080 \\ \hline 3.696 \end{array}$$

0.77 ⟶ 2 decimal places
4.8 ⟶ 1 decimal place

3.696 — 3 decimal places

There are a total of 3 decimal places in the factors, so you need the same number in the answer.

When should you add extra zeros to the answer?

$$\begin{array}{r} 0.09 \\ \times \quad 0.25 \\ \hline 45 \\ 180 \\ \hline 225 \end{array}$$

0.09 ⟶ 2 decimal places
0.25 ⟶ 2 decimal places

Since there are 4 decimal places in the factors, you need 4 decimal places in the answer.

0.0225

The product only has 3 decimal places, so annex 1 zero.

Find each product.

1. $\begin{array}{r} 8.7 \\ \times \ 0.4 \\ \hline \end{array}$

2. $\begin{array}{r} 2.28 \\ \times \ 0.7 \\ \hline \end{array}$

3. $\begin{array}{r} 92.3 \\ \times \ 0.2 \\ \hline \end{array}$

4. **Estimation** Which is greater, 8.2 × 0.015 or 8.2 × 0.15? Explain.

____

____

5. Noelle found the product of 4.28 × 0.9. Her answer was 38.52. How do you know her answer was incorrect?

____

____

____

____

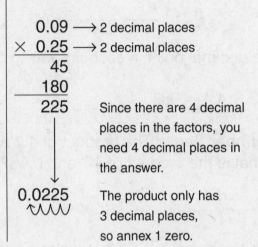

Name ______________________________

Multiplying Decimals by Decimals

P 2-11

Find each product.

1. 3.7 × 0.3

2. 4.4 × 0.2

3. 0.61 × 6.8

4. 1.9 × 0.005

5. 0.61 × 6.8 = ____________

6. 0.79 × 0.005 = ____________

Insert a decimal point in each answer to make the equation true.

7. 0.2 × 4.4 = 088 ____________

8. 8.81 × 5.2 = 45812 ____________

9. **Number Sense** The product of 4.7 and 6.5 equals 30.55. What is the product of 4.7 and 0.65? 4.7 and 65?

____________ ____________

10. What is the gravity in relation to Earth that is 3.4 times the gravity of Mercury?

____

11. What is the product of the gravity of Pluto and Neptune?

____

Relative (to Earth) Surface Gravity

Planet	Gravity
Mercury	0.37
Neptune	1.22
Pluto	0.06

Test Prep

12. How many decimal places are in the product of a number with decimal places to the thousandths multiplied by a number with decimal places to the hundredths?

A. 2 **B.** 3 **C.** 4 **D.** 5

13. **Writing in Math** Explain how you know the number of decimal places that should be in the product when you multiply two decimal numbers together.

____

Name ______________________

Variables and Expressions

R 2-12

An algebraic expression is a mathematical phrase that uses variables, numbers, and operations, such as addition and multiplication. Here are some other examples of algebraic expressions.

Addition	**Subtraction**	**Multiplication**	**Division**
$7 + e$	$f - 33$	$5 \times g$ or $5g$	$h \div 2$ or $\frac{h}{2}$

You can evaluate an algebraic expression by replacing the variable with a number, then performing the computation.

Evaluate $a + 7$ if $a = 6.5$.

Replace a with 6.5 in the expression.

$a + 7$

⇓

$6.5 + 7 = 13.5$

Evaluate $d \times 9.9$ if $d = 4$.

Replace d with 4 in the expression.

$d \times 9.9$

⇓

$4 \times 9.9 = 39.6$

Evaluate each expression for $p = 9$ and $p = 11$.

1. $p - 7 =$ ______________

2. $5.8 + p =$ ______________

3. $p \times 5 =$ ______________

4. $99 \div p =$ ______________

5. Representation What is another way to write the expression $82p$? ______________

6. Write an algebraic expression to represent the cost of a dog d with an additional tax of \$20. ______________

7. Algebra Jim is going to give away 7 of the t baseball cards in his collection and wonders how many cards he will have left. Does the algebraic expression $7 - t$ correctly represent this situation? Why or why not?

____

____

____

Name ______________________________

Variables and Expressions

P 2-12

1. Write an algebraic expression to represent the cost of a concert ticket, *h*, with a service charge of \$6.75.

____

2. Write an algebraic expression to represent the cost of *m* gallons of gasoline if each gallon costs \$1.45.

____

Evaluate each expression for $n = 3$ and $n = 6$.

3. $0.2 \times n$ ________ ________

4. $n - 2.1$ ________ ________

5. $\frac{12}{n}$ ________ ________

6. $35 + n$ ________ ________

Complete each table.

7.

n	$0.9 + n$
0.5	
0.2	
0.15	
0.1	

8.

n	$96 \div n$
1	
2	
3	
4	

9. Representations What is another way to write the expression $44n$? $44 \div n$?

____

Test Prep

10. Which is the correct product of $n \times 7$ if $n = \$0.25$?

A. \$3.25 **B.** \$2.75 **C.** \$2.25 **D.** \$1.75

11. Writing in Math Write a situation that can be represented by the algebraic expression \$3.25*d*.

____

Name ______________________________

PROBLEM-SOLVING SKILL **R 2-13**

Translating Words into Expressions

You can use the word clues below to write algebraic expressions.

Words or Phrases	Operation	Example	Algebraic Expression
plus sum of more than increased by	addition	15 more than a number	$n + 15$
minus difference less than decreased by	subtraction	a number decreased by 7	$n - 7$
times multiplied by product	multiplication	8 times a number	$8 \times n$, $8 \bullet n$, $8n$
divided by quotient	division	a number divided by 13	$n \div 13$, $\frac{n}{13}$

Write each word phrase as an algebraic expression.

1. 10 less than the number of shoes ______________

2. the quotient of y and 70 ______________

3. 15 more than the number of days ______________

4. the product of 14.2 and f ______________

5. **Number Sense** Write two word phrases for $18 + n$.

____

____

____

Name ____________________

PROBLEM-SOLVING SKILL **P 2-13**

Translating Words into Expressions

Write each word phrase an as algebraic expression.

1. the product of 5 and *n* ____________

2. a height divided by 3 ____________

3. $200 less than *n* ____________

4. a number of books plus 30 ____________

5. **Number Sense** Explain what the expression $6x$ means.

____

____

6. Dan is 12 in. taller than Jay. Use x for Jay's height. Which expression shows Dan's height, $x + 12$, $x - 12$, or $12x$? ____________

7. There are 60 min in a hour. If there are y hr in a day, what expression shows the number of minutes in a day, $60y$, $60 + y$, or $\frac{y}{60}$? ____________

8. Write two word phrases for the expression $\frac{t}{30}$.

____

____

9. **Writing in Math** Explain the difference between the expressions $x - 3$ and $3 - x$.

____

____

____

Name ______________________________

Find a Rule

R 2-14

Looking for a pattern in a table can help you find a rule for it.

When you add 3 to each input number, you get the output number.

Input	7	12	19	30
Output	10	15	22	33

7 + 3 = 10
12 + 3 = 15
19 + 3 = 22
30 + 3 = 33

The rule for this table is **Add 3.**

How to find a rule for a table:

1. Look at the input numbers. Think about how they relate to the output numbers.
2. Ask yourself what operation and what number have been used to change the input number to the output number.
3. Test it on each pair of numbers in the table. If it works for each pair of numbers, it is the rule.

Write a rule for each table. Write the rule in words.

1.

Input	7	9	11	15
Output	15	17	19	23

____

2.

Input	3	8	9	12
Output	9	24	27	36

____

3.

Input	25	28	30	35
Output	20	23	25	30

____

4.

Input	4	8	10	13
Output	36	72	90	117

____

5. Number Sense The rule is **Add 15.** If the input number is 18, what will the output number be? ______________

Name ______________________

Find a Rule

P 2-14

Find a rule for each table. Write the rule in words.

1.

Input	Output
6	18
24	36
48	60
72	84

____

2.

Input	Output
5	30
9	54
12	72
15	90

____

3.

Input	Output
19	9
54	44
78	68
24	14

____

Representations Write a rule with a variable for

4. Exercise 1. ______________

5. Exercise 2. ______________

6. Find a rule for the table. Write the rule in words.

Roses	Cost
12	\$24
24	\$48
36	\$72

____

____

7. How much would 72 roses cost?

____

Test Prep

8. Which is the rule with a variable for the table?

Input	Output
3	81
5	135
7	189
9	243

A. Add 78; $n + 78$

B. Multiply by 17; $17n$

C. Multiply by 27; $27n$

D. Add 86; $n + 86$

9. **Writing in Math** Explain how you find a rule from a table.

____

____

Name ______________________

Solving Equations

R 2-15

To solve equations, you find the value of the variable that makes the equation true. This value is called the solution. You can use mental math or test different values for the variable.

Use Mental Math

Solve $y - 8 = 14$.

- Ask yourself, "What number minus 8 equals 14?"
- $22 - 8 = 14$ Use mental math.
- $14 = 14$ Check that the equation is true.
- Solution: $y = 22$

Test Different Values for the Variable

Solve $8n = 48$.

- Think of some numbers you can substitute for n, such as 5, 6, or 7.
- Try $n = 5$: $8 \times 5 = 40$ No
  Try $n = 6$: $8 \times 6 = 48$ Yes
  Try $n = 7$: $8 \times 7 = 56$ No
- Solution: $n = 6$

Solve each equation by using mental math.

1. $b + 11 = 19$ ____________ **2.** $12 \times n = 24$ ____________

3. $62 - c = 42$ ____________ **4.** $75 \div b = 25$ ____________

5. $144 - f = 124$ ____________ **6.** $r \times 10 = 140$ ____________

Solve each equation by testing the given values for the variable.

7. $g - 7 = 14$ $g = 21, 24,$ or 28 ____________

8. $11d = 88$ $d = 7, 8,$ or 9 ____________

9. Reasonableness Bernie solved $w \div 12 = 12$. He wrote $w = 24$. Is he correct? Explain your answer.

____

____

____

____

Name ______________________________

Solving Equations

P 2-15

Solve each equation by using mental math.

1. $a + 3 = 35$ ________

2. $1 + e = 21$ ________

3. $3.18n = 31.8$ ________

4. $\frac{45}{p} = 5$ ________

5. $7m = 56$ ________

6. $17x = 51$ ________

Solve each equation by testing the given values for a variable.

7. $y - 9 = 11$

$y = 18, 19, \text{ or } 20$ ________

8. $25k = 50$

$k = 1, 2, \text{ or } 3$ ________

9. $\frac{z}{4} = 12$

$z = 48, 49, \text{ or } 50$ ________

10. $29 - p = 13$

$p = 14, 15, \text{ or } 16$ ________

11. Reasoning Write an equation that has a solution of $x = 4.3$.

____

____

Test Prep

12. Which is the written equation represented by the picture at the right?

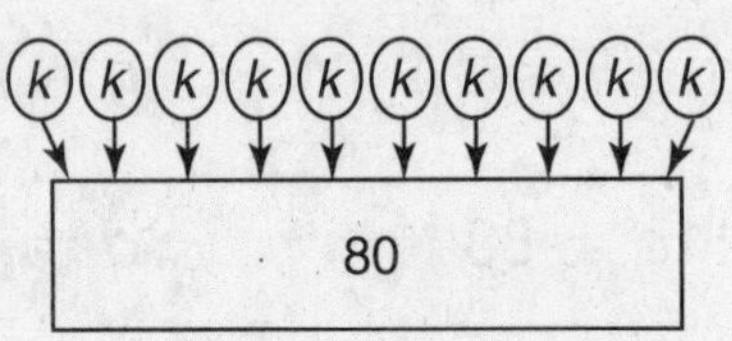

A. $10k = 80$ **B.** $5k = 80$ **C.** $k = 80$ **D.** $2k = 80$

13. Writing in Math Write a description of how mental math can be used to solve the equation $7 = x - 3$.

____

____

____

Name ______________________________

PROBLEM-SOLVING APPLICATION **R 2-16**

Let's Eat!

Food	Amount	Calories	Protein (g)	Saturated Fats (g)
Cheddar cheese	1 oz	115	7	6.0
Hard-boiled egg	1	75	6	1.6
Banana	1	105	1	0.2
Raw clams	3 oz	65	11	0.3
Spaghetti and meatballs	1 c	330	19	3.9

How many calories are in 9 oz of raw clams?

There are 65 calories in 3 oz of raw clams. To find the number of calories in 9 oz, multiply by 3.

$$\begin{array}{r} {}^{1}\\ 65 \\ \times\ \ 3 \\ \hline 195 \end{array}$$

So, there are 195 calories in 9 oz of raw clams.

1. Which contains more grams of protein, 6 oz of raw clams or 3 oz of cheddar cheese?

   ____

2. There are 10 bananas in the bunch. How many total grams of saturated fats are there? ____________

3. Rhoda ate 3.5 hard-boiled eggs. How many grams of saturated fats did she consume? ____________

4. **Algebra** Write an algebraic expression to represent *m* calories of bananas. ____________

Name ______________________

Fast Flights

How Fast Do Birds Fly?

Bird	Speed (miles per hour)
Peregrine falcon	168
Hummingbird	71
Mallard	40.6
Wandering albatross	33.6

1. How fast would a hummingbird be flying if it doubled its maximum speed? ______

2. If a wandering albatross doubled its maximum speed, could it fly as fast as a hummingbird?

______

______

______

3. **Estimation** Which bird flies about four times as fast as a mallard? ______

4. How fast would a wandering albatross be flying if its maximum speed was multiplied by 1.8? ______

5. A mallard is flying at a speed of 2.8 mph. If it then flies 1.2 times faster, how fast is it flying? ______

6. A certain bird can fly twice as fast as a hummingbird. Write an equation to express this. ______

Name ____________________

The Meaning of Division

R 3-1

To find out how many are in each group when an amount is shared equally, you use a type of division called sharing.

Example:

Suppose there are 22 books being given to a class of 11 students. How many books can each student receive if each student gets the same amount of books?

What you think: 22 separated into equal groups of 11 students.

What you write: $22 \div 11 = 2$.

Each student can receive 2 books.

Draw a picture or use objects to show each division situation. Then find the quotient.

1. James has 28 pennies. He makes 4 equal groups of pennies. How many pennies are in each group?

Find $28 \div 4 = p$. (Hint: Think $4 \times p = 28$.)

____

2. There are 4 times as many regular cars as trucks in an auto lot. If the lot has 24 regular cars, how many trucks are in the lot?

Find $24 \div 4 = x$.

____

Name

The Meaning of Division

P 3-1

Draw a picture or use objects to show each division situation. Then find the quotient.

1. How many groups of 6 can be formed if there are 36 students in the class?

2. In a theater with 108 seats, there are 12 times as many seats as there are rows. How many rows does the theater hold?

3. Ann and Bill need to arrange 36 coins from their collection on a page. If they use 4 rows, how many coins will be in each row?

Name the operation needed to solve each problem. Then solve.

4. At the airport, 72 people are waiting to board 9 different planes. If an equal number of people board each plane, how many people get on each plane?

5. At the halftime show during a football game, a band with 7 people in 8 rows marches out onto the field to entertain the crowd. How many people are in the band?

Test Prep

6. A high school volleyball team has 20 members. If there is an equal number of members from each of the 4 grades, how many students from each grade are on the team?

A. 3 **B.** 4 **C.** 5 **D.** 6

7. **Writing in Math** If there are 50 students in the fifth grade and the entire grade had to take the same language class, which language would have 10 different classes? Explain.

Language	Class Size
French	7
Italian	6
Russian	5
Spanish	10
German	6

Name ____________________

Division Patterns

R 3-2

You can use math facts and patterns to help you divide mentally.

What is 480 ÷ 6?

You already know that 48 ÷ 6 = 8.

So, 48<u>0</u> ÷ 6 = 8<u>0</u>.

What is 60,000 ÷ 6?

60 ÷ 6 = 10

So, 60,<u>000</u> ÷ 6 = 10,<u>000</u>.

Find each quotient. Use mental math.

1. 32 ÷ 8 = ________

2. 320 ÷ 8 = ________

3. 560 ÷ 7 = ________

4. 6,400 ÷ 8 = ________

5. 720 ÷ 9 = ________

6. 3,500 ÷ 7 = ________

7. 15,000 ÷ 3 = ________

8. 4,500 ÷ 5 = ________

9. **Number Sense** Explain how dividing 720 by 9 is like dividing 72 by 9.

____

____

Newspapers Arlo has a newspaper delivery job. He wants to wrap each of his newspapers in a plastic bag to protect them from the rain. The newspapers are in bundles.

Arlo's Newspaper Delivery	
Number of bundles	12
Number of newspapers per bundle	9

Use mental math to answer the following questions.

10. How many bags will he use for 5 bundles? ________

11. How many bags will he use for 7 bundles? ________

12. How many bags will he use for all 12 bundles? ________

Name ______________________________

Division Patterns

P 3-2

Find each quotient. Use mental math.

1. $27 \div 9 =$ ______ **2.** $270 \div 9 =$ ______ **3.** $2{,}700 \div 9 =$ ______

4. $24 \div 4 =$ ______ **5.** $240 \div 4 =$ ______ **6.** $2{,}400 \div 4 =$ ______

7. $720 \div 9 =$ ______ **8.** $140 \div 7 =$ ______ **9.** $2{,}100 \div 3 =$ ______

10. If a bike race covers 120 mi over 6 days and the cyclists ride the same distance each day, how many miles does each cyclist ride each day? ______

Use mental math to answer the following questions.

Dealership Vehicle Storage	
Sections of vehicles	4
Vehicles for sale	1,200
Rows per section	10

11. If the vehicles are divided evenly between the sections, how many vehicles are in each section?

______

12. If the vehicles are divided evenly between the rows in each section, how many vehicles are in each row? ______

13. **Algebra** If $160{,}000 \div n = 4$, find n. ______

Test Prep

14. Find $32{,}000 \div 8$ mentally.

A. 4,000 **B.** 400 **C.** 40 **D.** 4

15. **Writing in Math** Solve the equation $n \times 50 = 5{,}000$. Explain your solution.

______

______

______

Name ______________________________

Estimating Quotients

R 3-3

There are several ways to adjust whole numbers to estimate quotients.

Example:

There are 216 students. The school has 8 classrooms. How many students will be in each classroom?

Estimate 216 ÷ 8.

Rounding	Compatible Numbers	Multiplication
Round 216 to 200. 200 ÷ 8 = 25 25 students per room is an underestimate because 216 was rounded down to 200.	Substitute 240 for 216, because 24 is a multiple of 8. 24 ÷ 8 = 3 240 ÷ 8 = 30 30 students per class is an overestimate because 216 was rounded up to 240.	Think: 8 times what number is about 216? 8 × 25 = 200 8 × 30 = 240 216 is between 200 and 240. So a good estimate is a little more than 25 and a little less than 30 students per classroom.

Estimate each quotient. Tell what method you used.

1. 162 ÷ 4 ______________

2. 925 ÷ 9 ______________

3. $53.54 ÷ 6 ______________

4. 5,845 ÷ 9 ______________

5. Number Sense If you estimate 342 ÷ 7 by using 350 ÷ 7 = 50, is 50 greater than or less than the exact answer? How did you decide? Is 50 an overestimate or an underestimate?

____

____

6. Mr. Delahunt earned $5,985 during a 4-week period at work. About how much did he earn each week?

____

Name ____________________

Estimating Quotients

Estimate each quotient. Tell which method you used.

1. 195 ÷ 4 ______ ____________
2. 283 ÷ 5 ______ ____________
3. 766 ÷ 8 ______ ____________
4. 179 ÷ 2 ______ ____________
5. \$395.20 ÷ 5 ______ ____________
6. \$31.75 ÷ 8 ______ ____________
7. \$247.80 ÷ 5 ______ ____________
8. **Reasoning** If you use \$63.00 ÷ 9 to estimate \$62.59 ÷ 9, is \$7.00 greater than or less than the exact answer? Explain.

____

____

9. A band playing a 3-night concert earned \$321.00. Estimate how much the band earned each night.

____

10. At a department store, a woman's total was \$284.00 for 7 items. Estimate the cost of each item.

____

Test Prep

11. Which is the closest estimate for 213 ÷ 4?

A. 50 **B.** 40 **C.** 30 **D.** 20

12. **Writing in Math** Explain how to estimate 524 ÷ 9.

____

____

Name ______________________

PROBLEM-SOLVING STRATEGY **R 3-4**

Look for a Pattern

You can look for a pattern to solve problems.

Look for a pattern in each row. Write the missing numbers.

2, 7, 12, ____, ____, ____

15, 19, 23, ____, ____, ____

In the first row, you added 5 to each number to get the next number. The completed row would be 2, 7, 12, 17, 22, and 27. In the second row, 4 is added to each number. The completed row would be 15, 19, 23, 27, 31, and 35.

Look for a pattern. What would the next figure look like?

1st 2nd 3rd 4th 5th

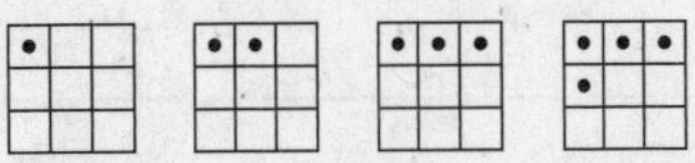

Once a row is filled in with dots, a new row begins. The next figure would look like this:

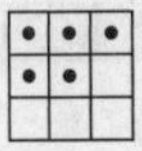

Look for a pattern. Write the missing numbers or draw the missing figures.

1. 5, 10, 15, 20, ______, ______, ______

2. 100, 92, 84, ______, ______, ______

3.

1st 2nd 3rd 4th ?

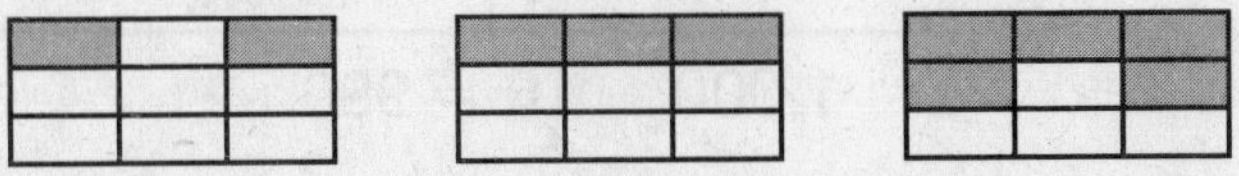

____

Look for a pattern in each chart. Write the missing number.

4.

$8 \div 4 = 2$

$80 \div 4 = 20$

$800 \div 4 = 200$

⋮

$80{,}000 \div 4 = ?$

____

Name ____

PROBLEM-SOLVING STRATEGY **P 3-4**

Look for a Pattern

Look for a pattern. Write the missing numbers, or draw the missing figures.

1. 20, 35, 50, ________, ________, ________

2. 32, 28, 24, ________, ________, ________

3. 4, 12, 20, ________, ________, ________

4. 56, 49, 42, ________, ________, ________

5. 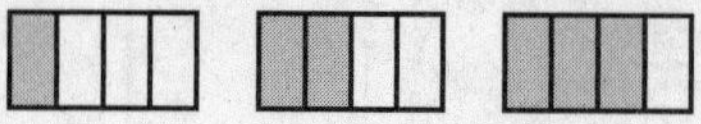

6. 

7. 

8. 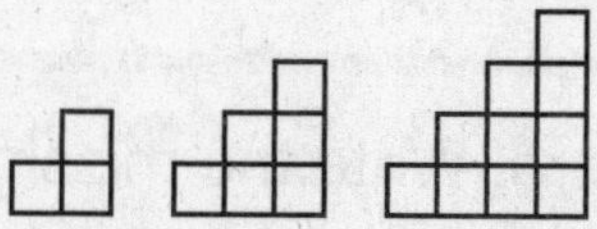

Look for a pattern. Write the missing number sentence.

9. $3 \times 2 = 6$

   $3 \times 22 = 66$

   $3 \times 222 = 666$

   ____

10. $10{,}000 - 10 = 9{,}990$

    $1{,}000 - 10 = 990$

    $100 - 10 = 90$

    ____

11. A banana-nut muffin recipe calls for 3 tbsp of nuts. The recipe makes 4 muffins. For 8 muffins the recipe calls for 6 tbsp of nuts. How many muffins can you make if you use 24 tbsp of nuts?

    ____

12. Complete the pattern.

    \$40.00, \$39.00, \$37.00, \$34.00, ________, ________, ________

Name ____________________

Understanding Division

R 3-5

Three people want to share $642 equally. How can they divide the money so that each person gets the same amount?

What You Show	What You Think	What You Write
	Share the $100 groups (five $20 bills in each group). Each person gets two $100 groups. Two $100 groups have been shared. → Zero $100 groups are left. →	2 3)642 −6 0
	Share four $10 bills. 3 of four $10 bills have been shared. → One $10 bill is left to be shared. → Trade a $10 bill for ten $1 bills.	21 3)642 −6↓ 04 − 3 1
	Share the $1 bills. Twelve $1 bills are left. → Twelve $1 bills have been shared. → No $1 bills are left. →	214 3)642 −6 4 − 3↓ 12 − 12 0

Each person gets two $100 groups, one $10 bill, and four $1 bills or $214.

1. Three people share $225 equally. The $20 bills are replaced with twenty $10 bills.

a. How many $10 bills are there after the $20 bills are replaced? ____________________

b. How many $10 bills does each person get? ____________________

Name ____

Understanding Division

P 3-5

After mowing lawns for one week, John put the money he earned on the table. There were four $100 bills, three $10 bills, and five $1 bills.

1. If John's brother borrowed one of the $100 bills and replaced it with ten $10 bills,

a. how many $100 bills would there be? ____________

b. how many $10 bills would there be? ____________

2. If John needed to divide the money evenly with two other workers, how much would each person receive? ____________

3. If John needed to divide the money evenly with four other workers, how much would each person receive? ____________

Complete each division problem. You may use play money to help.

4.

□□
4) 1 3 6
− □□
□ 6
− □□
□

5.

□□
3) 1 6 2
− □□
□ 2
− □□
□

Test Prep

6. If $644.00 is divided equally between 7 people, how much will each person receive?

A. $82.00 **B.** $92.00 **C.** $93.00 **D.** $103.00

7. Writing in Math Write a story problem using two $100 bills, nine $10 bills, and seven $1 bills.

____

____

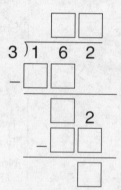

Name ____________________

Dividing Whole Numbers

Find 882 ÷ 6.

Step 1

Divide the hundreds. Multiply and subtract.

```
   1
6)882
 -6
  2
```

Divide.
$8 \div 6 = 1$

Multiply.
$1 \times 6 = 6$

Subtract.
$8 - 6 = 2$

Compare.
$2 < 6$

Step 2

Bring down the tens. Divide the tens. Multiply and subtract.

```
   14
6)882
 -6↓
  28
 -24
   4
```

Divide.
$28 \div 6 = 4$

Multiply.
$4 \times 6 = 24$

Subtract.
$28 - 24 = 4$

Compare.
$4 < 6$

Step 3

Bring down the ones. Divide the ones. Multiply and subtract.

```
   147
6)882
 -6
  28
 -24↓
   42
 - 42
    0
```

Divide.
$42 \div 6 = 7$

Multiply.
$7 \times 6 = 42$

Subtract.
$42 - 42 = 0$

Compare.
$0 < 6$

Divide. Check by multiplying.

1. 7)249

2. 8)863

3. 2)499

4. 5)365

5. 8)448

6. 6)396

7. Number Sense How can you tell before you divide 425 by 9 that the first digit of the quotient is in the tens place?

____

Name ______________________________

Dividing Whole Numbers

P 3-6

Find each quotient. Check your answers by multiplying.

1. $2\overline{)586}$ **2.** $3\overline{)565}$ **3.** $5\overline{)718}$ **4.** $4\overline{)599}$

5. $5\overline{)642}$ **6.** $6\overline{)354}$ **7.** $9\overline{)210}$ **8.** $8\overline{)927}$

The Paez family lives in Louisville, Kentucky, and has decided to take a road trip for their summer vacation.

9. How many miles will the Paez family drive each day if they decide to take 5 days to drive 865 mi to Dallas?

____

10. The Paez family decides they want to drive 996 mi to Boston in 6 days. How many miles will they drive each day?

____

Test Prep

11. If a staff of 9 had to clean a hotel with 198 rooms, how many rooms would each person have to clean if they divided the rooms equally?

A. 29 **B.** 25 **C.** 23 **D.** 22

12. **Writing in Math** Explain how to check the quotient from a division problem.

____

____

____

Name

Zeros in the Quotient

Find 823 ÷ 4.

Step 1	Step 2	Step 3	Step 4
Estimate. Decide where to place the first digit in the quotient. 800 ÷ 4 = 200 The first digit in the quotient is in the hundreds place.	Divide the hundreds. $4\overline{)823}$ quotient 2 -8 0 8 ÷ 4 = 2 2 × 4 = 8 8 − 8 = 0 0 < 4	Bring down the tens. Divide the tens. $4\overline{)823}$ quotient 20 $-8\downarrow$ 02 There are just 2 tens. You cannot divide 2 tens by 4. Write 0 in the tens place.	Bring down the ones. Divide the ones. $4\overline{)823}$ quotient 205 $-8\downarrow$ 023 -20 3 23 ÷ 4 = 5 5 × 4 = 20 23 − 20 = 3 3 < 4

Find each quotient. Check your answers by multiplying.

1. $8\overline{)640}$ **2.** $3\overline{)322}$ **3.** $8\overline{)909}$

4. $15\overline{)225}$ **5.** $3\overline{)873}$ **6.** $4\overline{)179}$

7. Writing in Math Is 593 ÷ 6 a little less than 10, a little more than 10, a little less than 100, or a little more than 100? Explain.

Name ____________________

Zeros in the Quotient

P 3-7

Find each quotient. Check your answers by multiplying.

1. $490 \div 7 =$ ________
2. $326 \div 3 =$ ________
3. $916 \div 3 =$ ________
4. $720 \div 2 =$ ________
5. $2\overline{)941}$
6. $9\overline{)982}$
7. $7\overline{)740}$
8. $5\overline{)703}$

9. If there are 505 seats in an auditorium divided equally into 5 sections, how many seats are in each section? ________

10. A book company publishes 749 copies of a novel and distributes them to 7 bookstores. If each bookstore were to receive the same amount of novels, how many novels would be sent to each store? ________

Test Prep

11. In one year Dolores and Tom's 4 children saved $420 by recycling cans. When they divided the money equally, how much money did each child receive?

A. $50 **B.** $100 **C.** $105 **D.** $1,500

12. **Writing in Math** Explain why estimating before you divide $624 \div 6$ helps you place the first digit in the quotient.

____

____

____

Dividing Larger Dividends

You can divide larger numbers using the same method you used with smaller numbers.

Find $5,776 \div 8$.

Step 1	Step 2	Step 3	Step 4	Step 5
Estimate first.	Divide the hundreds.	Bring down the tens.	Bring down the ones.	Check by multiplying.
Use compatible numbers.	Multiply and subtract.	Divide the tens.	Divide the ones.	
$5,600 \div 8 = 700$		Multiply and subtract.	Multiply and subtract.	
The first digit will be in the hundreds place.				

Step 2:
$$\begin{array}{r} 7 \\ 8\overline{)5,776} \\ -56 \\ \hline 1 \end{array}$$

Step 3:
$$\begin{array}{r} 72 \\ 8\overline{)5,776} \\ -56\downarrow \\ \hline 17 \\ -16 \\ \hline 1 \end{array}$$

Step 4:
$$\begin{array}{r} 722 \\ 8\overline{)5,776} \\ -56 \\ \hline 17 \\ -16\downarrow \\ \hline 16 \\ -16 \\ \hline 0 \end{array}$$

Step 5:
$$\begin{array}{r} 722 \\ \times\ 8 \\ \hline 5,776 \end{array}$$

1. $6\overline{)3,457}$ **2.** $8\overline{)7,283}$ **3.** $4\overline{)9,942}$ **4.** $2\overline{)1,392}$

5. Number Sense In the year 2000, the population of Galax, Virginia, was 6,837. The town covers 8 sq mi. About how many people were there in each square mile?

Name ____________________

Dividing Larger Dividends

Find each quotient. Check your answers by multiplying.

1. $6\overline{)3{,}681}$ **2.** $5\overline{)6{,}346}$ **3.** $8\overline{)7{,}258}$ **4.** $6\overline{)2{,}325}$

5. $4{,}773 \div 3 =$ ________ **6.** $8{,}340 \div 9 =$ ________

7. $5{,}228 \div 7 =$ ________ **8.** $6{,}574 \div 3 =$ ________

9. Students at Belle School are collecting box tops to get books for their library. Five classes need to collect 7,505 box tops. How many tops must each class collect if the classes collect the same amounts? ________

10. **Estimation** There are 5 days in a school week. How many school weeks will it take a class from Belle School to collect their tops if it takes them 145 days? ________

Test Prep

11. 1,504 divided by 4 is

A. equal to 40. **B.** less than 40. **C.** less than 400. **D.** more than 400.

12. **Writing in Math** Predict the number of digits in the quotient for 9,010 divided by 8. Explain.

____

____

____

____

Name ____________________

Dividing Money

R 3-9

Mrs. Hayes bought 8 lb of meat for $17.76, including tax. Find the price per pound for the meat.

Step 1	Step 2	Step 3	Step 4	Step 5
Estimate. Use compatible numbers. $16 ÷ 8 = $2 The first digit in the quotient is the ones digit.	Place the decimal point in the quotient.	Divide the ones.	Bring down the tenths. Divide the tenths. Multiply and	Bring down the hundredths. Divide the hundredths. Multiply and
	. 8)17.76	2. 8)17.76 −16 1	2.2 8)17.76 −16↓ 17 − 16 1	2.22 8)17.76 −16 17 − 16↓ 16 − 16 0

The meat cost $2.22 per pound.

1. 3)$5.46   **2.** 7)$34.79   **3.** 8)$93.44   **4.** 6)$238.92

5. The Mixons went to an amusement park. Each entrance ticket cost $8.50. They also spent $28.90 on food. If there are 4 people in the family, about how much did they spend on each person?

____

Name ____________________

Dividing Money

P 3-9

Find each quotient. Check your answers by multiplying.

1. \$9.03 ÷ 7 = __________ **2.** \$8.24 ÷ 4 = __________

3. \$0.75 ÷ 5 = __________ **4.** \$17.55 ÷ 5 = __________

5. 8)\$93.76 **6.** 9)\$34.65 **7.** 7)\$94.15 **8.** 8)\$744.48

For 9 and 10, write the dollar amount the farmer received for each pound of potatoes. Then write the year.

9. A farmer received \$165.75 for 75 lb of potatoes.

__________ __________

10. A farmer received \$402.05 for 473 lb of potatoes.

__________ __________

Average Potato Prices

Year	\$ per Pound
1940	0.85
1950	1.50
1960	2.00
1970	2.21
1980	6.55
1990	6.08
2000	4.95

Test Prep

11. Use what you know about patterns and find the missing number. If \$25.75 divided by 5 = \$5.15, then \$257.50 divided by 5 = *n*.

A. *n* = \$51.50 **B.** *n* = \$51.55 **C.** *n* = \$515.00 **D.** *n* = \$515.50

12. Writing in Math Explain how dividing \$6.75 by 9 is like dividing 675 by 9. How is it different?

____

____

Name____

Factors and Divisibility

R 3-10

A number is divisible by:	**Example:**
2 → If the number is even.	16, 20, 300, 568
3 → If the sum of the digits of the number is divisible by 3.	**99** 9 + 9 = 18 18 ÷ 3 = 6
4 → If the last two digits are divisible by 4.	**1,024** 24 ÷ 4 = 6
5 → If the last digit is 0 or 5.	30; 105; 645; 10,100
6 → If the number is divisible by BOTH 2 and 3.	**996** 9 + 9 + 6 = 24 24 ÷ 3 = 8 Divisible by 3. Even number, so divisible by 2.
9 → If the sum of the digits is divisible by 9.	**9,585** 9 + 5 + 8 + 5 = 27 27 ÷ 9 = 3
10 → If the last digit is 0.	200; 1,000; 46,000

1. Is 4,400 divisible by 10? How do you know?

____

2. Is 234 divisible by 9? How do you know?

____

Find all the factors of each number.

3. 12 ____

4. 35 ____

5. 45 ____

6. 49 ____

7. Writing in Math Explain how to find all the factors of 72. List all the factors.

____

____

Name ____________________

Factors and Divisibility

Find all the factors of each number.

1. 36 ____________________
2. 27 ____________________
3. 30 ____________________
4. 75 ____________________
5. 90 ____________________
6. 84 ____________________

Number Sense A number is divisible by 4 if the last two digits are divisible by 4. Write yes on the line if the number is divisible by 4 and no if it is not.

7. 324 ________ 8. 634 ________ 9. 172 ________

10. A class of 80 students is graduating from elementary school. The teachers need help figuring out how to line up the students for the ceremony. One row of 80 students would be too long. What other ways could the students be arranged for the ceremony?

____

____

11. A number is divisible by another number when the ____________ is 0.

Test Prep

12. What factor pair is missing for 45 if you already know 1 and 45, 5 and 9?

A. 7 and 6 **B.** 8 and 6 **C.** 3 and 15 **D.** 4 and 12

13. **Writing in Math** Explain how to find all the factor pairs of 40.

____

____

Prime and Composite Numbers

Numbers such as 2, 3, 5, 7, and 11 are prime numbers. A prime number has *only* two factors, itself and 1. A whole number greater than 1 that has *more than two* factors is called a composite number.

3 is an example of a prime number. Its only factors are 1 and 3.

◯ ◯ ◯ $1 \times 3 = 3$

8 is a composite number. Its factors are 1, 2, 4, and 8.

◯ ◯ ◯ ◯ ◯ ◯ ◯ ◯ $1 \times 8 = 8$

◯ ◯ ◯ ◯
◯ ◯ ◯ ◯ $2 \times 4 = 8$

How to use a factor tree.

12 ⟵ Think of two numbers whose product is 12. You can use 2×6 or 3×4.

2×6 ⟵ 6 is not prime, so keep dividing.

$2 \times 2 \times 3$ ⟵ All the factors are prime, so you can stop dividing.

Write whether each number is prime or composite.

1. 17 _____ **2.** 47 _____

3. 68 _____ **4.** 266 _____

Find the prime factors of each number.

5. 28 _____

6. 24 _____

7. Number Sense The prime factorization of a number is $2 \times 3 \times 3$. What is the number? _____

Name ______________________________

Prime and Composite Numbers

P 3-11

Write whether each number is prime or composite.

1. 21 __________ **2.** 36 __________ **3.** 31 __________

4. 87 __________ **5.** 62 __________ **6.** 23 __________

Use factor trees to find the prime factorization of each number.

7. 44 ______________ **8.** 63 ______________

9. 13 ______________ **10.** 54 ______________

11. Number Sense Audrey says that the prime factorization of 42 is 21×2. Is she correct? If not, tell why.

____

____

12. Is 4,564,282 prime or composite? Explain how you determined your answer.

____

____

Test Prep

13. Which of the following is a prime number?

A. 105 **B.** 27 **C.** 19 **D.** 9

14. Writing in Math Does it matter what two factors you select to complete a factor tree? Explain.

____

____

____

Name ______________________________

PROBLEM-SOLVING SKILL **R 3-12**

Interpreting Remainders

Elron has 159 CDs. He is going to purchase CD cases for the CDs. Each case holds 12 CDs.

Question 1	Question 2	Question 3
How many cases will he need to hold all of his CDs?	How many cases will be filled?	How many extra CDs are in the case that is not filled?
Plan and Solve $159 \div 12 = 13$ R3 14 cases are needed.	***Plan and Solve*** $159 \div 12 = 13$ R3 13 cases will be filled.	***Plan and Solve*** $159 \div 12 = 13$ R3 There are 3 extra CDs in the case that is not filled.
Look Back and Solve One more case is needed for the 3 extra CDs. So, $13 + 1 = 14$ cases are needed.	***Look Back and Solve*** 13 cases will have 12 CDs. An additional one will have less than 12.	***Look Back and Solve*** The remainder of 3 tells us there are 3 extra CDs.

1. Sadee has 139 quarters. She wants to put them in paper rolls. Each roll holds 20 quarters.

   a. How many rolls will be completely filled? ______________

   b. How many quarters will be in the unfilled roll? ______________

2. Bukka has 983 paperback books. He wants to put his paperback books on storage shelves. Each shelf can hold 50 paperback books.

   a. How many shelves will be completely filled? ______________

   b. How many paperback books will be on the shelf that is not completely filled? ______________

Name ____________________

PROBLEM-SOLVING SKILL **P 3-12**

Interpreting Remainders

A fifth-grade project was to make something representative of the United States and send it to an address outside the United States. The shipping prices for weight are at the right.

Shipping Prices

Pounds	Price
1–5	$3.00
6–10	$7.00
11–15	$10.00
16–20	$15.00
More than 20	$20.00

1. One group of four students pooled their money. They had $24.00. Three out of the 4 packages fell into the same weight category. Give one example of that weight category. What would the other weight category be?

____

____

____

____

____

Another group of four students all had boxes in the same weight category. This group had a total of $30.00 for shipping.

2. Give one example of weight category they might choose.

____

____

____

3. After they have paid for their packages, how much money will be left over? ____________________

4. If divided equally, how much money will each person get back?

____

Name ____________________

Order of Operations

R 3-13

Order of Operations | **Example**

First, do the operations inside the parentheses. → $36 - (3 + 2) \times 5$

↓

Then, multiply and divide from left to right. $36 - 5 \times 5$

↓

Finally, add and subtract from left to right. → $36 - 25 = 11$

How to insert parentheses to make a statement true:

$7 + 2 \times 3 = 27$

By placing parentheses around 7 + 2, you would do this operation first:

$(7 + 2) \times 3 = 27$

↓

$9 \times 3 = 27$

Use the order of operations to evaluate each expression.

1. $2 + 3 \times 5 =$ ____ **2.** $5 \times (2 + 7) =$ ____

3. $6 + 2 \times 2 \times (1 + 1) =$ ____ **4.** $10 \times 4 - (9 + 11) =$ ____

Insert parentheses to make each statement true.

5. $17 - 8 - 5 = 14$ ____________________

6. $88 \div 2 + 6 - 7 = 4$ ____________________

7. Number Sense Felix bought 3 bags of oranges with 12 oranges per bag and 5 bags of apples with 10 apples per bag. Write an expression with sets of parentheses for the total amount of fruit that Felix bought.

____

Name ______________________

Order of Operations

P 3-13

Use the order of operations to evaluate each expression.

1. $4 \times 4 + 3 =$ ______

2. $3 + 6 \times 2 \div 3 =$ ______

3. $24 - (8 \div 2) + 6 =$ ______

4. $(15 - 11) \times (25 \div 5) =$ ______

5. $26 - 4 \times 5 + 2 =$ ______

6. $15 \times (7 - 7) + (5 \times 2) =$ ______

7. $(8 \div 4) \times (7 \times 0) =$ ______

8. $5 \times (6 - 3) + 10 \div (8 - 3) =$ ______

9. Number Sense Which is a true statement, $5 \times 4 + 1 = 25$ or $3 + 7 \times 2 = 17$? ______

Insert parentheses to make each statement true.

10. $25 \div 5 - 4 = 25$ ______

11. $7 \times 4 - 4 \div 2 = 26$ ______

12. $3 + 5 \times 2 - 10 = 6$ ______

13. Insert parentheses in the expression $6 + 10 \times 2$ so that:

a. the expression equals 32. ______

b. the expression equals $(12 + 1) \times 2$. ______

Test Prep

14. Solve $(25 - 7) \times 2 \div 4 + 2$.

A. 6 **B.** 11 **C.** 5 **D.** 18

15. Writing in Math Write two order of operation problems. Then trade with a classmate and solve the problems.

______

______

Name ____________________

Graphing Ordered Pairs

R 3-14

How to locate a point on a grid.

The ordered pair (5, 7) describes the location of point *A*.

(5, 7)

The first number tells how far to move to the right from zero.

The second number tells how far to move up.

Step 1: Start at zero.

Step 2: Move 5 spaces to the right.

Step 3: Move 7 spaces up.

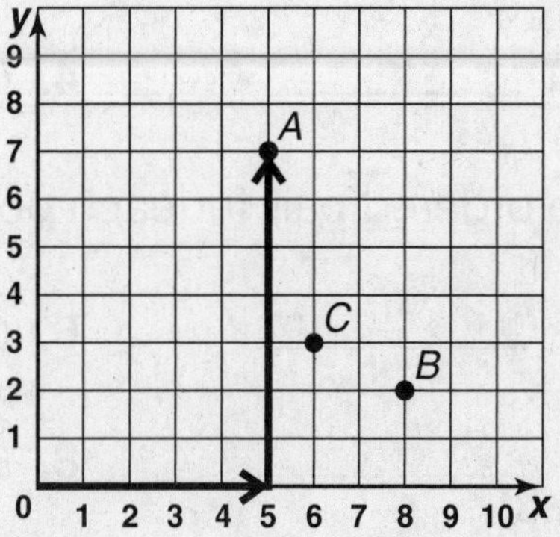

The ordered pair for point *B* is (8, 2).

The ordered pair for point *C* is (6, 3).

Name the point that is located by each ordered pair.

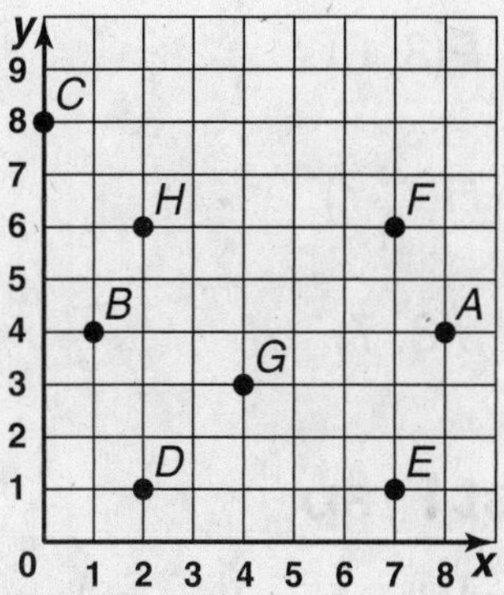

1. (7, 1) ____ **2.** (2, 6) ____

3. (0, 8) ____ **4.** (4, 3) ____

Write the ordered pair for each point.

5. *F* ________ **6.** *B* ________ **7.** *D* ________ **8.** *A* ________

Graph each point on the grid at the right. Label each point.

9. *J*(3, 5) **10.** *K*(5, 10)

11. *L*(4, 3) **12.** *M*(7, 7)

13. *N*(8, 2) **14.** *P*(2, 9)

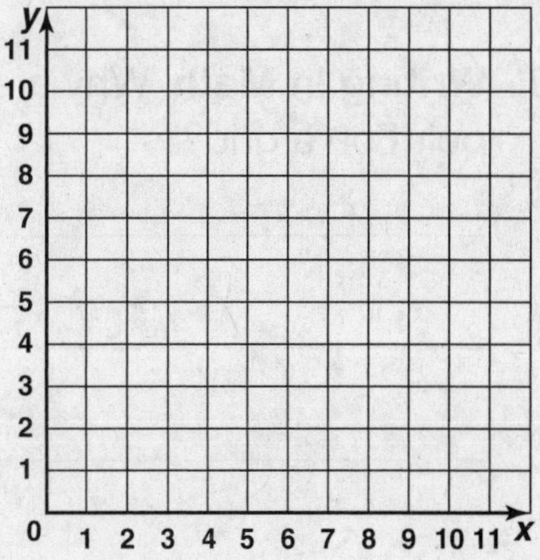

Name ______________________________

Graphing Ordered Pairs

P 3-14

Name the point that is located by each ordered pair.

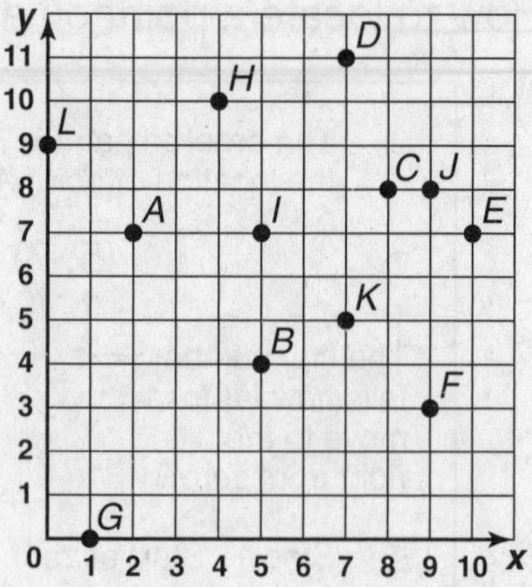

1. (9, 3) ________ **2.** (1, 0) ________

3. (7, 5) ________ **4.** (5, 7) ________

Write the ordered pair for each point.

5. *D* ________ **6.** *C* ________

7. *E* ________ **8.** *L* ________

Graph each point on the grid to the right. Label each point.

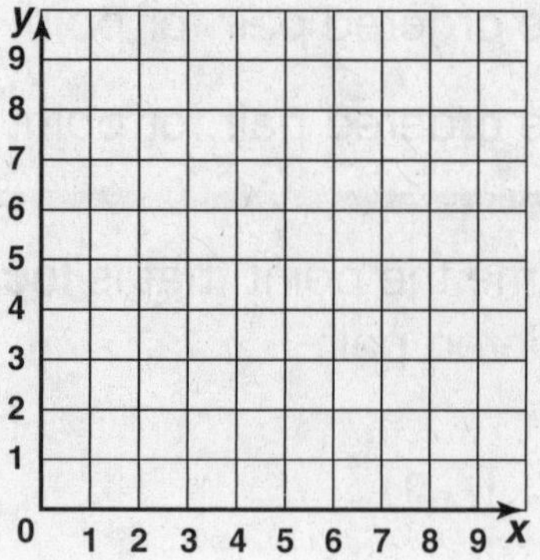

9. *M*(3, 4) **10.** *Z*(6, 5)

11. *T*(0, 9) **12.** *X*(4, 4)

13. *P*(3, 0) **14.** *A*(2, 8)

15. *H*(7, 7) **16.** *B*(2, 9)

17. *J*(3, 7) **18.** *L*(1, 6)

Test Prep

19. Which is the ordered pair for a point 7 units to the right of the *y*-axis and 8 units above the *x*-axis?

A. (8,7) **B.** (7,8) **C.** (1,7) **D.** (1,8)

20. **Writing in Math** Why are (4, 6) and (6, 4) not at the same point on a grid?

____

____

____

____

Name

Rules, Tables, and Graphs

R 3-15

How to make a table of values from a rule:

Rule in words: Multiply by 4, then add 2.

Rule using a variable: $4n + 2$.

Step 1

Draw a table.
Write in the rule.

n	$4n + 2$
1	
2	
3	
4	
5	

Select five values for n and write them in the table.

Step 2

Evaluate the expression $4n + 2$ using 1, 2, 3, 4, and 5 for n.

n	$4n + 2$	
1	6	← For $n = 1$, $4n + 2 = 4 \times 1 + 2 = 6$
2	10	← For $n = 2$, $4n + 2 = 4 \times 2 + 2 = 10$
3	14	← For $n = 3$, $4n + 2 = 4 \times 3 + 2 = 14$
4	18	← For $n = 4$, $4n + 2 = 4 \times 4 + 2 = 18$
5	22	← For $n = 5$, $4n + 2 = 4 \times 5 + 2 = 22$

Write the answer in the right column of the chart.

Create a table of values for each rule. Use at least four values for n.

1. Subtract 9: $n - 9$

2. Multiply by 2, then add 1: $(n \times 2) + 1$

3. **Writing in Math** Write this rule in words: $8v + 7$.

Name ______________________________

Rules, Tables, and Graphs

P 3-15

Create a table of values for each rule. Use at least four values for *x*.

1. Multiply by 3, then add 2: $3x + 2$

2. Divide by 3, then add 1: $x \div 3 + 1$

On separate grids, make a graph for each table in Exercises 1 and 2.

3.

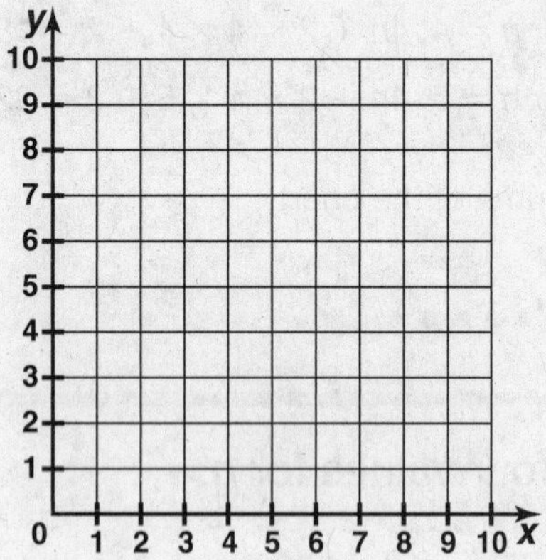

4.

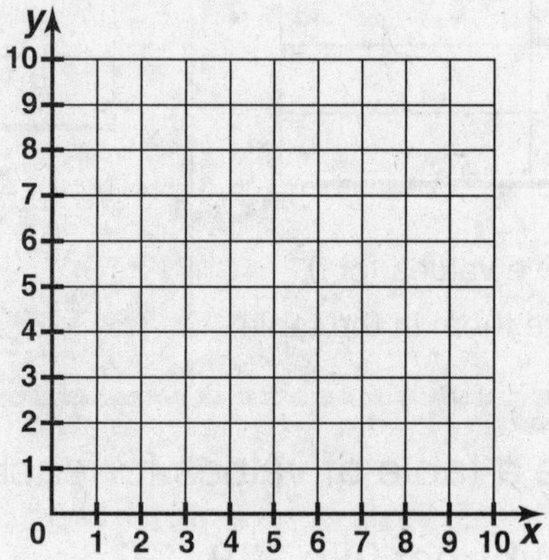

Test Prep

5. Which of the following coordinates does not belong in the table of values for the rule: Multiply by 2, then add 1: $2x + 1$.

A. (2, 5) **B.** (3, 6) **C.** (4, 9) **D.** (0, 1)

6. **Writing in Math** Make a table of values for the following rule: Multiply by 3, then subtract 2. Explain.

____

____

____

Name ____________________

PROBLEM-SOLVING APPLICATION **R 3-16**

Writers

During a 9-year period, Jack London wrote 135 short stories. About how many short stories did he write each year?

First estimate. Use compatible numbers.

$150 \div 10 = 15$

Then divide using these steps:

Step 1

Divide the tens.

The first digit of the quotient will go in the tens place.

$$\begin{array}{r} 1 \\ 9\overline{)135} \\ -\ \underline{9} \\ 4 \end{array}$$

Multiply 1×9, then subtract.

Step 2

Bring down the ones.

Divide the ones.

$$\begin{array}{r} 15 \\ 9\overline{)135} \\ -\ \underline{9\downarrow} \\ 45 \\ -\ \underline{45} \\ 0 \end{array}$$

Multiply 5×9, then subtract.

London wrote about 15 short stories each year for 9 years.

1. Mark Twain is another famous American author. *The Complete Short Stories of Mark Twain* contains all of Twain's short stories. The last 5 stories are printed on a total of 153 pages. About how long is each story?

____

2. Writing in Math Explain the meaning of the remainder in Exercise 1.

____

____

____

Name ____________________

PROBLEM-SOLVING APPLICATION **P 3-16**

Hit Parade

Motown Records is one of the most famous African American owned music companies. During the 1960s and 1970s, Motown artists wrote, recorded, and produced a large number of No. 1 rhythm-and-blues songs and records.

Smokey Robinson was one of Motown's most famous songwriters, singers, producers, and musicians.

1. If Smokey Robinson wrote a total of 176 songs in an 8-year period, how many songs did he write per year?

   ____

2. **Writing in Math** Smokey Robinson wrote about 24 No. 1 hits for Motown artists. Explain how you know that the numbers 3 and 4 are both factors of 24.

   ____

   ____

   ____

3. If you paid $53.94 for 6 Smokey Robinson CDs, how much did you pay for each CD? ____________

Stevie Wonder is another famous original Motown songwriter and recording artist.

4. Nine of Stevie Wonder's CDs have a total of 107 songs. About how many songs are on each CD?

   ____

5. Robbie bought 7 Stevie Wonder CDs. 4 CDs cost $8.00 each. 2 CDs cost $9.00 each. 1 CD costs $7.00. He gave the cashier $70.00. To calculate his change, Robbie correctly wrote the following equation: Change $= 70 - 4 \times 8 - (2 \times 9 + 7)$. How much change did he get? ____________

Name ____________________

Dividing by Multiples of 10

R 4-1

You can use basic facts and patterns to divide mentally.

Using basic facts

What is 350 ÷ 70?

Think: 350 ÷ 70 is the same as 35 tens ÷ 7 tens.

35 ÷ 7 = 5

So, 350 ÷ 70 = 5.

Using patterns

What is 5,400 ÷ 60?

5,400 ÷ 60 is the same as 540 ÷ 6.

54 ÷ 6 = 9, so 540 ÷ 60 = 9.

So, 5,400 ÷ 60 = 90.

Find each quotient. Use mental math.

1. 280 ÷ 70 = ________

2. 320 ÷ 40 = ________

3. 360 ÷ 60 = ________

4. 7,200 ÷ 80 = ________

5. 9,000 ÷ 30 = ________

6. 4,800 ÷ 80 = ________

7. 2,000 ÷ 40 = ________

8. 5,600 ÷ 70 = ________

9. Number Sense How is dividing 250 by 50 the same as dividing 2,500 by 500?

____

____

____

____

____

10. Writing in Math Explain how you can mentally determine that 35,000 ÷ 70 = 500.

____

____

Name ____________________

Dividing by Multiples of 10

P 4-1

Find each quotient. Use mental math.

1. $480 \div 60 =$ ________ **2.** $8{,}100 \div 90 =$ ________

3. $32{,}000 \div 40 =$ ________ **4.** $15{,}000 \div 30 =$ ________

5. $4{,}900 \div 70 =$ ________ **6.** $16{,}000 \div 40 =$ ________

Solve for *n*.

7. $n \div 20 = 60$ **8.** $n + (400 \div 20) = 27$ **9.** $420 \div n = 70$

________ ________ ________

The vegetable farm is planning the summer harvest layout.

Vegetable Farm Layout
Plants harvested: 60,000
Sections: 20
Rows in each section: 30

10. How many plants will be harvested from each section?

____

11. How many plants will grow in each row?

____

Test Prep

12. Using the data above, determine how many plants would be harvested in each row if 30,000 plants were harvested and only 10 sections were used.

A. 10 **B.** 100 **C.** 1,000 **D.** 10,000

13. **Writing in Math** Explain the steps you took to figure out your answer for Exercise 12.

____

____

____

Name ______________________________

Estimating with Two-Digit Divisors

There are different ways to estimate quotients.

Estimating with compatible numbers:

Estimate 1,750 ÷ 32.

Substitute 1,800 for 1,750 and 30 for 32.

1,800 ÷ 30 = 60

So, a good estimate is about 60.

Estimating using rounding and multiplication:

Estimate 1,750 ÷ 32.

32 × ? is about 1,750.

Round 32 to 30.

Round 1,750 to 1,800.

30 × 60 = 1,800

So, a good estimate is about 60.

Estimating with decimals and money:

Estimate $78.60 ÷ 41.

Round $78.60 to $80.

Round 41 to 40.

$80 ÷ 40 = 2

When estimating with money, it is good to find an overestimate. Round the dividend up and the divisor down.

Estimate each quotient. Tell which method you used.

1. 298 ÷ 25 ______________________________

2. 5,391 ÷ 77 ______________________________

3. 24,303 ÷ 12 ______________________________

4. 43.44 ÷ 85 ______________________________

5. $63.75 ÷ 59 ______________________________

6. 397.86 ÷ 31 ______________________________

At Elmer Elementary School, fifth-grade students are saving money for a summer trip to Washington, D.C.

7. About how many times more money has Percy saved than James?

____

8. About how many times more money has Bertha saved than Emily?

____

Student	Amount Saved
Percy	$125
Emily	$80
George	$202
James	$41
Bertha	$159

Name ______________________

Estimating with Two-Digit Divisors

P 4-2

Estimate each quotient. Tell which method you used.

1. $269 \div 33$ ______________________

2. $158 \div 52$ ______________________

3. $\$910 \div 85$ ______________________

4. $\$250 \div 48$ ______________________

5. $200 \div 29$ ______________________

6. $1{,}950 \div 94$ ______________________

The Town Traveling Club has 19 members. Estimate each member's share of each trip expense.

7. transportation $195

____

8. jet ski rentals $635

____

9. food $385

____

10. Estimate the total expense for each member of the Town Traveling Club.

____

Test Prep

11. Which is a reasonable estimate for $378 \div 87$?

A. 1 **B.** 3 **C.** 4 **D.** 7

12. **Writing in Math** Which quotient is greater? Explain how you know without finding the answer.

$\$37.68 \div 15$ or $\$35.25 \div 15$

____

____

____

Name

PROBLEM SOLVING STRATEGY: **R 4-3**

Try, Check, and Revise

Heights David is 10 in. taller than his sister Katie. The sum of their heights is 104 in. What is each of their heights?

Read and Understand

Step 1: What do you know?

- Tell the problem in your own words.

When you add David's and Katie's heights, they total 104 in.

- Identify key facts and details.

David is 10 in. taller than Katie.

Step 2: What are you trying to find?

- Tell what the question is asking.

You want to know the height of each person.

- Show the main idea.

David's height + Katie's height = 104 inches

Plan and Solve

Step 3: What strategy will you use?

Strategy: Try, Check, and Revise

Try: David = 50 in., Katie = 40 in.

Check: 50 + 40 = 90

Revise: 90 is too low. Their heights must equal 104. Increase each height.

Try: David 57 in., Katie 47 in.

Check: 57 + 47 = 104

Answer: David is 57 in., Katie is 47 in.

Mr. Caine filled a large container with 129 qt of water. (4 qt = 1 gal) He wants to pour the water into gallon containers. He does this without spilling any water. How many gallon containers will be needed?

1. Identify key facts and details.

____

2. Solve the problem. Write the answer in a complete sentence.

____

Name ____________________

PROBLEM-SOLVING STRATEGY **P 4-3**

Try, Check, and Revise

Solve. Write your answer in a sentence.

1. Bryan needs to build a fence around his rectangular vegetable garden. The length will be 2 ft longer than the width. If he uses 16 ft of fencing, what will be the length and width?

____

2. Bryan plans on building a larger garden next year. He would like to keep the length the same but extend the width of his garden so that it is square. If Bryan extends the width to make a square, how much fencing will he need to surround the garden?

____

3. The school district has 294 basketballs to distribute to 36 different teams in the intramural basketball league. If the basketballs are equally distributed, how many basketballs can each team have for practice? How many basketballs will be remaining?

____

____

4. Hannah is 8 in. taller than her brother Quinn. If their combined height is 80 inches, how tall is Quinn?

____

5. The area of a rectangle is 50 ft. The length is two times the width. What are the length and the width? (Hint: The area of a rectangle is $l \times w$.)

____

____

Name______________________________

Dividing Whole Numbers by Two-Digit Divisors

Find 437 ÷ 39.

	What You Think	What You Write
Step 1 Estimate. Decide where to place the first digit in the quotient. \$437 ÷ 39 is about \$440 ÷ 40 or 11.	Start dividing tens.	
Step 2 Divide the tens. Multiply and subtract.	1 group of 39 or 1 × 39 = 39. This leaves 4 left over.	1 39)437 −39 4
Step 3 Divide the ones. Multiply and subtract.	1 group of 39 or 1 × 39 = 39. This leaves 8 left over.	11 39)437 −39 47 −39 8
Step 4 Compare and write the answer.	Since 39 > 8, I do not have to divide again.	437 ÷ 39 = 11 R8

Complete.

1. 77)283 = 3 R☐

2. 49)197 = 4 R☐

3. 58)418 = ☐ R12

Find each quotient. Check by multiplying.

4. 18)179

5. 94)835

6. 67)356

Name ________________________________

Dividing Whole Numbers by Two-Digits P 4-4

Complete. Find each missing remainder or quotient.

1. 37)120 = 3 R ☐

2. 39)342 = ☐ R30

3. 14)413 = 29 R ☐

Find each quotient. Check by multiplying.

4. 25)768

5. 34)264

6. 19)401

7. 62)338

8. 599 ÷ 37 = ____________

9. 9,227 ÷ 83 = ____________

10. The school student council sponsored a Switch Day where students were able to switch classes every 20 min. The students are in school for 7 hr. If each student switched the same number of times, how many times did each student get to visit another classroom? (Hint: There are 60 min in 1 hr.) ____________

11. 456 students participated in Switch Day. The students raised money for a charity so that the principal would approve of the day. If the total amount of money raised was $912 and each student brought in the same amount of money, how much did each student raise? ____________

Test Prep

12. Which is 458 ÷ 73?

A. 5 R19 **B.** 5 R20 **C.** 6 R19 **D.** 6 R20

13. **Writing in Math** If you have a two-digit divisor and a three-digit dividend, does the quotient always have the same number of digits? Explain.

____

____

Name____________________

Dividing Larger Numbers

R 4-5

Find 899 ÷ 19.

Step 1

Estimate. Decide where to place the first digit in the quotient.

899 ÷ 19 is about 900 ÷ 20 = 45 or 4 tens, 5 ones.

Start dividing tens.

Step 2

Divide the tens. Multiply and subtract.

$$\begin{array}{r} 4 \\ 19\overline{)899} \\ -76 \\ \hline 13 \end{array}$$

Multiply:
4 × 19 = 76

Subtract:
89 − 76 = 13

Compare:
13 < 19

Step 3

Bring down the ones. Divide the ones. Multiply and subtract.

$$\begin{array}{r} 47 \\ 19\overline{)899} \\ -76\downarrow \\ \hline 139 \\ -133 \\ \hline 6 \end{array}$$

Multiply:
7 × 19 = 133

Subtract:
139 − 133 = 6

Compare:
6 < 19

Step 4

Check:

$$\begin{array}{r} 47 \\ \times 19 \\ \hline 423 \\ 47 \\ \hline 893 \\ +\quad 6 \\ \hline 899 \end{array}$$

So, 899 ÷ 19 = 47 R6.

Find each quotient. Check your answer by multiplying.

1. $48\overline{)3,796}$
2. $41\overline{)2,588}$
3. $85\overline{)4,346}$
4. $47\overline{)7,492}$
5. $94\overline{)8,203}$
6. $43\overline{)2,374}$

Name______________________________

Dividing Larger Numbers

P 4-5

Find each quotient. Check your answers by multiplying.

1. $53\overline{)6,324}$ **2.** $52\overline{)6,348}$ **3.** $86\overline{)31,309}$ **4.** $33\overline{)3,455}$

5. 17,496 ÷ 91 = __________ **6.** 25,214 ÷ 47 = __________

7. 2,312 ÷ 26 = __________ **8.** 4,895 ÷ 83 = __________

The Humphrey family decided to fly from San Francisco, California, to Tokyo, Japan. There were 3 stops along the way.

9. It took the Humphrey family 6 hr to travel from San Francisco to New York. How many kilometers did they travel per hour?

____

Distances by Plane	
San Francisco to New York	4,140 km
New York to Rome	6,907 km
Rome to New Delhi	5,929 km
New Delhi to Tokyo	5,857 km

10. During the flight from New Delhi to Tokyo, the children played some games. If they switched games every 575 km, how many games did they play?

____

Test Prep

11. Use the data from Exercises 9–10. When the family arrived in New Delhi from Rome, the youngest son asked the pilot how fast he was flying the plane. The pilot told him about 847 km per hour. How many hours did it take the family to fly from Rome to New Delhi?

A. 5 hr **B.** 6 hr **C.** 7 hr **D.** 8 hr

12. Writing in Math Write a word problem that would require you to use 5,621 ÷ 23.

____

Name ____________________

Dividing: Choose a Computation Method

R 4-6

You can divide using mental math, paper and pencil, or a calculator.

What You Think	Find 50,000 ÷ 10. This is easy to do in my head, so I will use **mental math.**	Find 58,560 ÷ 80. Both numbers are multiples of 10, so 58,560 ÷ 80 is the same as 5,856 ÷ 8. One digit divisors are easy to do with **paper and pencil.**	Find 93,279 ÷ 37. There are no basic facts or zeros, so using a **calculator** is the easiest way to find the quotient.
What You Do	50,000 ÷ 10 is the same as 5,000 ÷ 1. Since 50 ÷ 10 = 5, 5,000 ÷ 10 must be 500. So, 50,000 ÷ 10 = 5,000.	732 8)5,856 −56 25 − 24 16 So, 58,560 ÷ 80 = 732.	93279 [÷] 37 [=] 2521.054 So, 93,279 ÷ 37 is a little greater than 2,521.

Divide and check. Tell what computation method you used.

1. $25\overline{)500}$

2. $100\overline{)3,000}$

3. $82\overline{)735}$

4. $50\overline{)6,450}$

5. $85\overline{)859}$

6. $16\overline{)32,000}$

Name ____________________

Dividing: Choose a Computation Method

Divide and check. Tell which computation method you used.

1. 40)24,000 **2.** 40)6,440 **3.** 22)4,818 **4.** 46)9,936

5. 37,800 ÷ 90 = __________ **6.** 18,000 ÷ 30 = __________

7. 24,000 ÷ 60 = __________ **8.** 350,000 ÷ 35 = __________

The summer-sale paper was delivered to everyone in the neighborhood.

9. Toni and Bill saw the sale paper and thought they could share the cost of the speed boat with their 4 brothers and sisters. If they divide the cost equally, how much will each person pay?

____

Summer Sale

Speed boat $18,000

Pontoon boat $9,672

Jet ski $2,100

Test Prep

10. Use the data from Exercise 9. Four different families decided to share the cost of the pontoon boat. There would be a total of 8 people sharing the cost of the boat. How much did each person have to pay?

A. $2,418.00 **B.** $1,209.00 **C.** $806.00 **D.** $604.50

11. **Writing in Math** Describe when it is helpful to use a calculator in dividing. When is it better to use another method?

____

____

____

Name

Dividing with Zeros in the Quotient

R 4-7

Sometimes when you bring down the next digit in dividing, you get a number less than the divisor. You need to place a zero in the quotient and bring down the next digit.

Step 1

Find 9,286 ÷ 89.

Estimate. Decide where to place the first digit in the quotient.

Think: 9,000 ÷ 90 = 100.

Start dividing hundreds.

Step 2

Divide hundreds. Multiply, subtract, and bring down.

$$\begin{array}{r} 10 \\ 89\overline{)9{,}286} \\ -89 \\ \hline 38 \end{array}$$

Since 38 < 89, you cannot divide. Write a zero in the quotient. Bring down the next digit.

Step 3

Continue to divide.

$$\begin{array}{r} 104 \\ 89\overline{)9{,}286} \\ -89 \\ \hline 38 \\ -0 \\ \hline 386 \\ -356 \\ \hline 30 \end{array}$$

So, 9,286 ÷ 89 = 104 R30.

Find each quotient. Check your answer by multiplying.

1. $59\overline{)641}$

2. $32\overline{)3{,}354}$

3. $53\overline{)5{,}777}$

4. $58\overline{)6{,}326}$

5. $79\overline{)8{,}299}$

6. $49\overline{)5{,}358}$

7. **Number Sense** Is 5,309 ÷ 26 greater than 20, less than 20, greater than 200, or less than 200?

Name ____________________

Dividing with Zeros in the Quotient

Find each quotient. Check your answers by multiplying.

1. $60\overline{)6,360}$ **2.** $84\overline{)8,750}$ **3.** $14\overline{)9,828}$ **4.** $57\overline{)36,485}$

5. 12,925 ÷ 19 = ______ **6.** 22,348 ÷ 37 = ______

7. 9,523 ÷ 28 = ______ **8.** 16,451 ÷ 81 = ______

9. If 75 players hit 7,950 baseballs at the batting cages, how many hits were there for each player? ______

Find each quotient.

10. 3,030 ÷ 30 = ______ **11.** 4,242 ÷ 42 ______ **12.** 5,050 ÷ 50 = ______

13. Number Sense Explain the reason for the pattern in the quotients in Exercises 10–12.

______

______

Test Prep

14. Which is 17,889 ÷ 88?

A. 203 **B.** 203 R25 **C.** 204 R1 **D.** 205

15. Writing in Math Write a problem with a two-digit divisor, a five-digit dividend, and a quotient of 308. Explain how you did it.

______

______

______

Name____

PROBLEM-SOLVING SKILL

Multiple-Step Problems

Law Firm Mr. Barnett earned about $98,000 last year at his law firm. He had to pay about $19,000 in taxes. He also had to pay about $6,000 for office supplies. About how much did he make each month?

Read and Understand

Step 1: What do you know?

$98,000 was Mr. Barnett's income. He had to pay $19,000 and $6,000.

Step 2: What are you trying to find?

How much money he earned each month

Plan and Solve

To solve problems that involve multiple steps, ask yourself what hidden questions are in the problem.

- **Hidden question 1:** What were Mr. Barnett's total expenses?

  $19,000 + $6,000 = $25,000

- **Hidden question 2:** How much did he earn after expenses?

  $98,000 − $25,000 = $73,000

$73,000 ÷ 12 is about $6,000. So, Mr. Barnett made about $6,000 each month.

Write and answer the hidden question or questions and then solve the problem.

1. Leslie bought 3 posters that were priced at $9.98 each, including tax. The store had a special sale that day. For each 3 posters you buy, you get the third one for half price. Leslie gave the cashier $30.00. How much change did she receive?

____

____

____

____

____

Name ____________________

PROBLEM-SOLVING SKILL **P 4-8**

Multiple-Step Problems

Write and answer the hidden question or questions in each problem and then solve the problem. Write your answer in a complete sentence.

Storewide Sale	
Jeans	$29.95 for 1 pair OR 2 pairs for $55.00
T-shirts	$9.95 for 1 OR 3 T-shirts for $25.00

1. Sue bought 2 pairs of jeans and a belt that cost $6.95. The tax on the items was $5.85. Sue paid the cashier $70.00. How much money did Sue receive in change?

2. A recreation department purchased 12 T-shirts for day camp. The department does not have to pay sales tax. It paid with a $100.00 bill. How much change did it receive?

3. When Mrs. Johnson saw the sale, she decided to get clothes for each child in her family. She bought each of her 6 children a pair of jeans and a T-shirt. She paid $14.35 in sales tax. How much was Mrs. Johnson's total bill?

4. **Writing in Math** Write a two-step problem about buying something at the mall that has a hidden question. Tell what the hidden question is and solve your problem. Use $8.95 somewhere in your equation. Write your answer in a complete sentence.

Name ______________________________

Dividing Decimals by 10, 100, and 1,000

R 4-9

Understanding place value makes it easy to divide decimals by 10, 100, and 1,000.

Dividing a number by 10 moves the decimal point one place to the left.

Example: 317 ÷ 10 = 31.7

Dividing a number by 100 moves the decimal point two places to the left.

Example: 317 ÷ 100 = 3.17

Dividing a number by 1,000 moves the decimal point three places to the left.

Example: 317 ÷ 1,000 = 0.317

Find each quotient. Use mental math.

1. 87.3 ÷ 10 = ______________

2. 56.2 ÷ 100 = ______________

3. 77.78 ÷ 100 = ______________

4. 275 ÷ 100 = ______________

5. 38.93 ÷ 1,000 = ______________

6. 128.75 ÷ 10 = ______________

7. 66.28 ÷ 1,000 = ______________

8. 1.85 ÷ 1,000 = ______________

9. **Writing in Math** 87.5 divided by 100 is the same as 87.5 multiplied by what decimal? Explain your answer.

____

____

Algebra Write 10, 100, or 1,000 for each *n*.

10. 14.7 ÷ *n* = 0.147 ______________

11. 6.4 ÷ *n* = 0.64 ______________

12. 325.67 ÷ *n* = 0.32567 ______________

Name ______________________________

Dividing Decimals by 10, 100, and 1,000

Find each quotient. Use mental math.

1. $86.6 \div 10 =$ __________

2. $192.5 \div 100 =$ __________

3. $1.99 \div 100 =$ __________

4. $0.87 \div 10 =$ __________

5. $228.55 \div 1{,}000 =$ __________

6. $0.834 \div 100 =$ __________

7. $943.35 \div 1{,}000 =$ __________

8. $1.25 \div 10 =$ __________

Algebra Write 10, 100, or 1,000 for each *n*.

9. $78.34 \div n = 0.7834$ __________

10. $0.32 \div n = 0.032$ __________

11. $(75.34 - 25.34) \div n = 5$ __________

12. There are 145 children taking swimming lessons at the pool. If 10 children will be assigned to each instructor, how many instructors need to be hired? __________

13. The instructors must pass a test before getting the job. The instructors must swim 2 mi. If it takes Jane 5 min every half mile, how long should it take her to finish? __________

Test Prep

14. Ronald ran 534.3 mi in 100 days. If he ran an equal distance each day, how many miles did he run per day?

A. 5 **B.** 5.13 **C.** 5.343 **D.** 6.201

15. **Writing in Math** Carlos says that $17.43 \div 100$ is the same as 174.3×0.01. Is he correct? Explain.

____

____

Name ______________________

Dividing Money by Two-Digit Divisors

R 4-10

You buy a 22 oz box of granola for \$2.86. How much do you pay per ounce?

Step 1

Write the decimal point in the quotient directly above the decimal point in the dividend.

$$\begin{array}{r} . \\ 22\overline{)\$2.86} \end{array}$$

Step 2

22 is greater than 2, so place a zero above the 2.

$$\begin{array}{r} 0. \\ 22\overline{)\$2.86} \end{array}$$

Start dividing tenths.

$$\begin{array}{r} 0.1 \\ 22\overline{)\$2.86} \\ -\ 2\ 2 \\ \hline 6 \end{array}$$

Step 3

Bring down the hundredths. Continue dividing.

$$\begin{array}{r} 0.13 \\ 22\overline{)\$2.86} \\ -\ 2\ 2 \\ \hline 66 \\ -\ 66 \\ \hline 0 \end{array}$$

You paid \$0.13 for 1 oz of granola.

Find each quotient. Check your answers by multiplying.

1. $13\overline{)\$8.71}$ **2.** $59\overline{)\$36.58}$ **3.** $87\overline{)\$167.91}$

Decide if each quotient is greater than or less than \$1.00.

4. $7\overline{)\$11.55}$ **5.** $11\overline{)\$8.25}$ **6.** $16\overline{)\$17.95}$

__________ __________ __________

7. Writing in Math Suppose 2.1 lb of ham costs \$6.30. Is it reasonable to state that the price per pound of ham is \$3.00? Why or why not?

____

____

Name ____________________

Dividing Money by Two-Digit Divisors

P 4-10

Find each quotient. Check your answers by multiplying. (Round to the nearest cent, if necessary.)

1. 11)$8.91 **2.** 61)$43.92 **3.** 12)$84.24 **4.** 28)$4.20

5. $87.08 ÷ 82 = ________ **6.** $93.49 ÷ 59 = ________

7. $17.83 ÷ 5 = ________ **8.** $114.38 ÷ 19 = ________

Number Sense Decide if each quotient is greater than or less than $1.00.

9. $76.65 ÷ 73 ____________________

10. $9.30 ÷ 62 ____________________

11. **Estimation** Is the quotient you get when you divide $550.81 by 70 closer to $0.80, $8.00, or $80.00? ________

Test Prep

12. If 6 people split a dinner bill of $180.30, how much will each person pay?

A. $30.05 **B.** $30.15 **C.** $30.50 **D.** $30.55

13. **Writing in Math** Explain why $46.50 ÷ 30 could not be $15.00.

____

____

____

____

Name ____________________

Dividing Decimals by Whole Numbers

R 4-11

Dividing decimals by whole numbers

Find 1.64 ÷ 4.

Step 1: Place the decimal point in the quotient above the decimal point in the dividend.

Step 2: Divide the same way you would with whole numbers.

$$\begin{array}{r} 0.41 \\ 4\overline{)1.64} \\ -1\,6 \\ \hline 04 \\ -\quad 4 \\ \hline 0 \end{array}$$

Answer: 0.41

Check: 0.41 × 4 = 1.64

Dividing decimals by multiples of 10, 100, and 1,000

36 ÷ 90 = 0.4

3.6 ÷ 90 = 0.04

0.36 ÷ 90 = 0.004

Notice the pattern. When you move the decimal one place to the left and then divide by the same number, you move the decimal point in the previous answer one more place to the left. To do this, you often have to add zeros as decimal place holders.

Find each quotient. Check by multiplying.

1. $14\overline{)6.3}$ **2.** $77\overline{)2.31}$ **3.** $89\overline{)2.492}$

Choose the best estimate for each.

4. 34.61 ÷ 16

A. 2.2 **B.** 0.22 **C.** 20.2

5. 16.3 ÷ 17

A. 1 **B.** 0.1 **C.** 0.01

6. 59.4 ÷ 65

A. 0.9 **B.** 9.1 **C.** 0.09

7. Reasonableness Is 61.5 ÷ 15 a little less than 4, a little more than 4, a little less than 40, or a little more than 40?

Name ____________________

Dividing Decimals by Whole Numbers

Find each quotient. Check by multiplying.

1. $13\overline{)68.9}$ **2.** $35\overline{)412.3}$ **3.** $90\overline{)14.4}$ **4.** $60\overline{)53.4}$

5. 123.08 ÷ 34 = __________ **6.** 0.57 ÷ 30 = __________

7. 562.86 ÷ 59 = __________ **8.** 24.4 ÷ 80 = __________

9. If a package of granola bars with 12 bars costs $3.48, how much does each granola bar cost? __________

10. John paid $7.99 for 3 boxes of cereal. The tax was $1.69. Excluding tax, how much did John pay for each box of cereal if they all were the same price? __________

Test Prep

11. 64.82 ÷ 11 is

A. a little more than 6. **B.** a little less than 6.

C. a little more than 60. **D.** a little less than 60.

12. Writing in Math Explain how to divide 0.12 by 8.

____

____

____

____

Name ____________________

Cable TV

In the year 2000, the number of American homes that had cable television was 68,544,000. What is 68,544,000 ÷ 10?

Remember, to divide a number by 10, you can move the decimal point one place to the left.

68,544,000.

So, 68,544,000 ÷ 10 = 6,854,400.

Cable Television There were 10,929 cable television systems in the United States in the year 2000.

Find each quotient. Use mental math.

1. 10,929 ÷ 10 = ____________

2. 10,929 ÷ 100 = ____________

3. 10,929 ÷ 1,000 = ____________

4. The Jameson Cable Television Company is housed in a building that takes up 9,400 sq yd. Suppose the building is divided into 25 separate departments. How big is each department?

____

5. The company sold a total of 15 cable TV systems for $9,285. How much does each system cost?

____

Name ____________________

PROBLEM-SOLVING APPLICATION **P 4-12**

Listen to This

The Federal Communications Commission (FCC) reported that there were 12,615 radio stations in the United States in 1999.

1. The FCC reported that there were 4,783 AM radio stations in the United States in 1999. Round 4,783 to the nearest hundred.

____

2. Use that number to determine the average number of AM radio stations per state in the United States. (Hint: There are 50 states in the United States.)

____

____

3. There were 5,766 FM radio stations in the United States in 1999. Find the average number of FM radio stations per state in the United States. Round your answer to the nearest one.

____

____

4. In a 30-year period between 1970 and 2000, 6,108 new radio stations were started in the United States. If the number of radio stations started was the same each year, about how many radio stations were started per year?

____

____

5. During a 20 hr broadcast day, the average United States radio station broadcasts about 280 min of commercials. About how many minutes of commercials are broadcast each hour? (Remember: There are 60 min in 1 hr.)

____

Name ____________________

Collecting Data from a Survey

R 5-1

You ask survey questions to gather information called data. Data can be facts or opinions.

A fact is actual information. Here are some facts:

Cars use gasoline.

Cats have whiskers.

An opinion is what a person likes or dislikes. Here are some opinions:

Steak is the tastiest food.

Football is a better sport than soccer.

Data that are gathered can be shown in a line plot or frequency table.

Survey Question:
What color is your school folder?

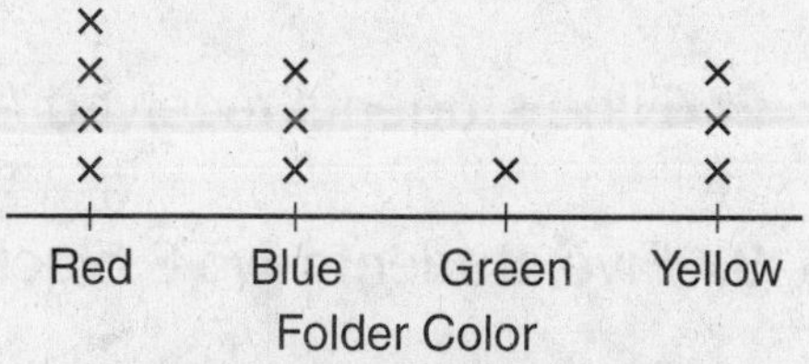

Survey Question:
What is your favorite animal?

Favorite Animals	
Animal	**Number**
Pig	3
Elephant	9
Ram	4

Identify each statement as a fact or an opinion.

1. The racetrack is 1.5 mi long. ____________

2. The president is doing a good job with foreign policy. ____________

Write a survey question that might gather the following information.

3. The favorite day of the week of 4 people is Friday.

____

4. How many people responded to the favorite sports survey?

____

Favorite Sports	
Sport	**Number**
Soccer	7
Football	3
Track	1

5. **Writing in Math** Describe how you might pick a sample of 50 minivan owners that represents the minivan owners of your state.

____

____

Name ____________________

Collecting Data from a Survey

P 5-1

Identify each statement as either a fact or an opinion.

1. Dogs are the best pets to own. ____________

2. Nine students received As on their tests. ____________

3. Five students live 3 blocks from school. ____________

4. Three people is a good number for a team. ____________

5. Spaghetti is the tastiest meal. ____________

Music Bought in Class B

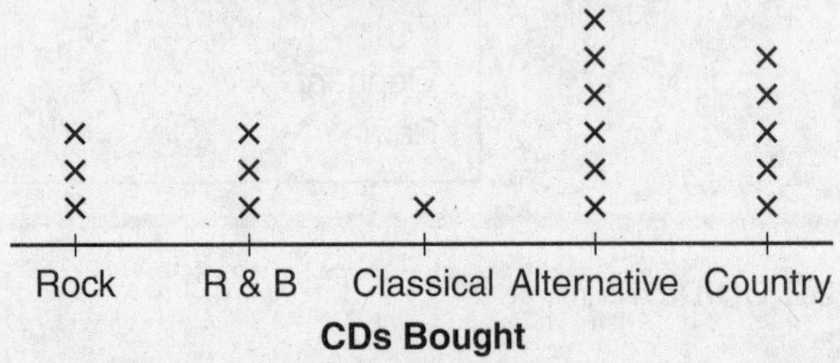

6. If the entire class responded to the survey, how many students are in the class? ____________

7. What information was collected about music?

____

Test Prep

8. Use the line plot above. Which type of CDs did students buy most often?

A. Alternative **B.** Classical **C.** Country **D.** Rock

9. **Writing in Math** Write a survey question that might gather the following information.

In one school there are 6 sets of twins, 2 sets of triplets, and 1 set of quadruplets.

____

____

Name ______________________________

Bar Graphs

R 5-2

How to make a bar graph

Step 1 Decide on a scale and its intervals. Draw the graph. Label the axes.

Step 2 Write a key for the two bars.

Step 3 Graph the data by drawing bars of the correct length or height.

Step 4 Title your graph.

Conference Baseball Champions

High School	Freshmen	Varsity
Smith	2	4
Phillips	3	3
Dominican	5	2

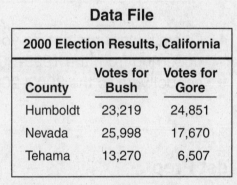

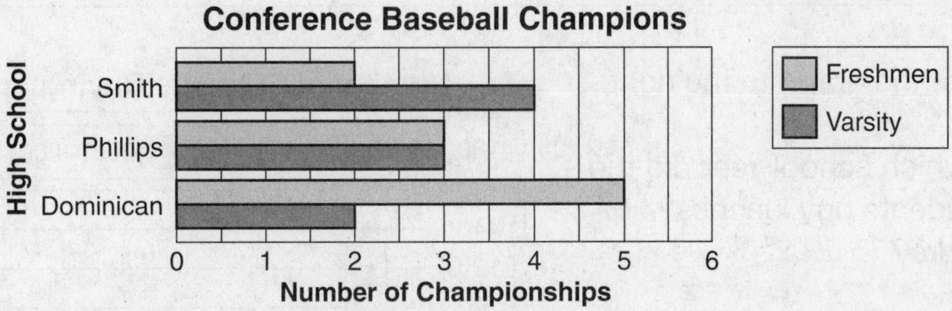

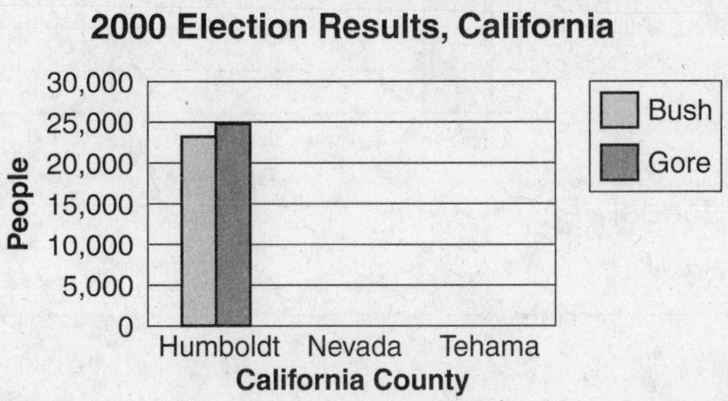

Data File

2000 Election Results, California

County	Votes for Bush	Votes for Gore
Humboldt	23,219	24,851
Nevada	25,998	17,670
Tehama	13,270	6,507

1. Complete the graph. Write a sentence about the data represented.

____

2. Representations Explain why you need to use a double bar graph and not a single bar graph to represent this data.

____

____

Name ____________________

Bar Graphs

P 5-2

The data at the right shows the number of students who bought lunch the first week of school during the 1999–2000 and 2000–2001 school years. The data has been rounded to the nearest ten.

Students Buying Lunch

Days	1999–2000	2000–2001
Mon.	90	140
Tue.	60	70
Wed.	120	160
Thur.	130	140
Fri.	100	120

1. Which data would have the shortest bar on a graph?

____

2. Complete the graph to the right.

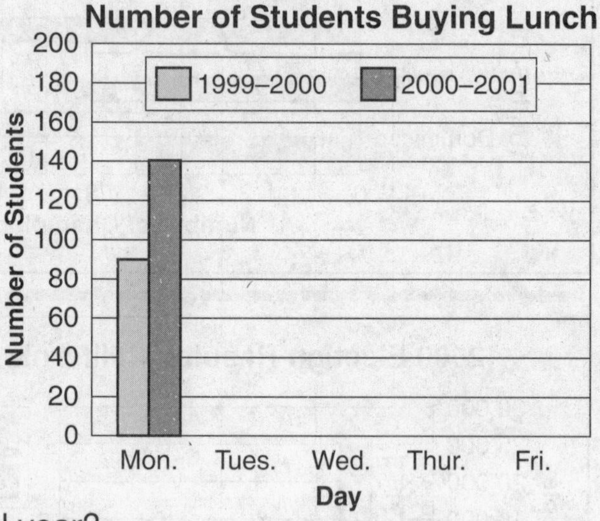

3. During which school year did the most students buy lunches? How many more?

____

____

4. Overall, what pattern do you see occurring from the 1999–2000 school year to the 2000–2001 school year?

____

Test Prep

5. Use the graph above. On which day of the week was an average of 100 lunches sold?

A. Tuesday **B.** Wednesday **C.** Thursday **D.** Friday

6. **Writing in Math** Is a data file needed to make a bar graph? Explain.

____

____

Name ____________________

Line Graphs

A line graph is often used to show a **trend** in data. By looking at the graph, you can tell if the data is increasing or decreasing.

The trend on this graph shows that there is a steady increase in the amount of weight Dave lifted over time.

Dave's Weightlifting

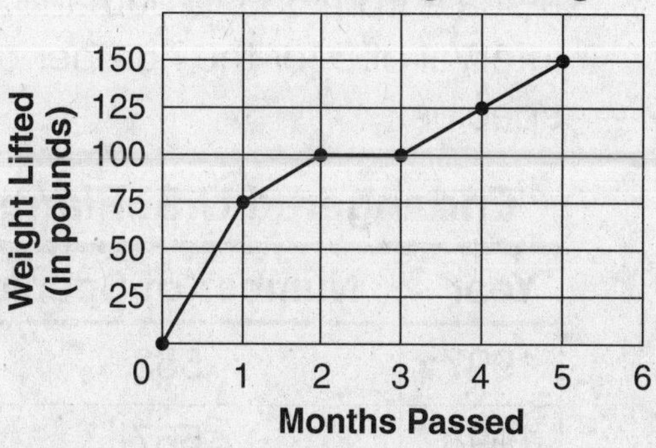

How to make a line graph

Step 1

Decide on a scale and its intervals. Draw the graph. Label the axes.

Step 2

Graph the data by plotting the points.

Step 3

Connect the points for each set of data.

Step 4

Title your graph.

Ron's Earnings					
Time	0 hr	1 hr	2 hr	3 hr	4 hr
Earnings	$0	$4.50	$9.00	$13.50	$18.00

Ron's Earnings

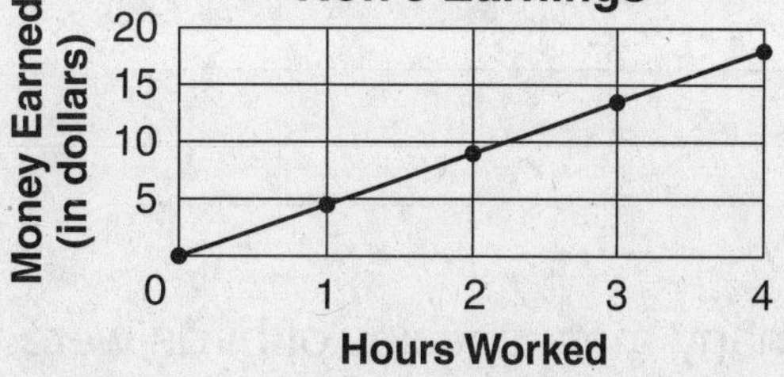

1. Make a line graph of the data. Use a scale from 0–450 and an interval of 50 for people donating blood.

Data File

Blood Drive	
Week	**Number of Donors**
1	73
2	162
3	257
4	399

Name ___________

Line Graphs

1. Make a line graph of the data. Use a scale from 550 to 600 and an interval of 5 for the number of species.

Endangered U.S. Plants

Year	Number of Species
1997	553
1998	567
1999	581
2000	592
2001	595

2. What is the trend in the data in the graph to the right?

____

____

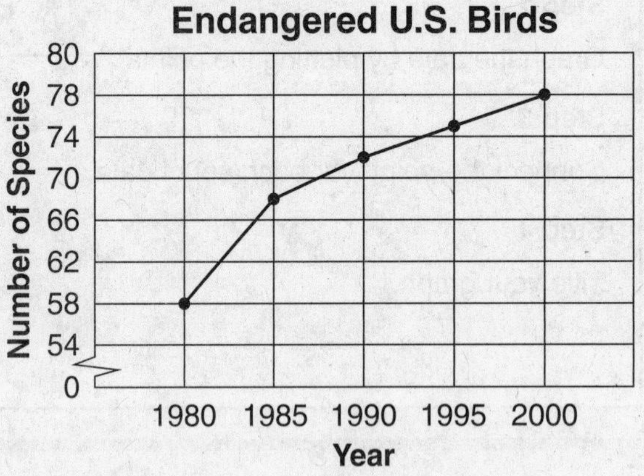

3. How many more species of birds were endangered in 2000 than in 1980?

____

Test Prep

4. Which is the trend if the line on a graph is rising from left to right?

A. Staying the same　　**B.** Increasing

C. Decreasing　　**D.** Doubling

5. **Writing in Math** The numbers in a data file are 71, 56, 62, 77, and 38. What scale would you use to graph the data? Explain your choice.

____

____

Name

Stem-and-Leaf Plots

R 5-4

To make a stem-and-leaf plot, first write the data in order from least to greatest:

12, 14, 23, 27, 32, 36, 38, 38, 39, and 41

Stems	Leaves
1	2

Begin with the lowest value, 12. Place the tens digit in 12, or 1, under the Stems heading. Then place the ones digit, or 2, under the Leaves heading.

Use the same method to fill in the remaining values in order. Leaves for each stem have the same tens digit.

Stems	Leaves
1	2 4
2	3 7
3	2 6 8 8 9
4	1

Use the following data to complete Exercises 1–4.

13, 63, 53, 59, 33, 18, 67, 58, 55, 33, 43, 22, 69, 61, 33

1. Make a stem-and-leaf plot of the data.

2. What is the range of the data? ______

3. How many numbers are in the fifties? ______

4. **Writing in Math** How does this stem-and-leaf plot make it easy to tell which values occurred most frequently?

______

______

Name ____________________

Stem-and-Leaf Plots

The data file below shows the ages of people in a movie theater.

Ages of People at the Movie Theater
25, 16, 42, 34, 65, 54, 10, 18, 45, 34, 23, 33, 51, 36, 21, 19, 18, 34, 15, 50

1. Make a stem-and-leaf plot of the data. Title the plot "Ages of People at the Movie Theater."

2. What is the range of the data? How do you know?

____

____

3. How many people over 20 years old watched the movie? ____________

4. How many people under 20 years old watched the movie? ____________

5. What age was most frequent at this movie theater? ____________

Test Prep

6. Which age group had the most people at the movie?

   A. People under twenty
   B. People in their twenties
   C. People in their thirties
   D. People in their forties

7. **Writing in Math** Is Bill's explanation correct? If not, tell why.

____

____

____

> Bill's Explanation
>
> How do you make a stem-and-leaf plot?
>
> First, you list all the first digits on the left in the plot.
>
> Then you list all the second digits on the right in the plot.

Name ____

PROBLEM-SOLVING STRATEGY **R 5-5**

Make a Graph

Book Reading Two classrooms had a contest to see how many extra books the students could read during a two-month period. Which class won the contest?

Mrs. Blane's Class

Books	9	10	11	12	13	14	15	16
Students	2	3	0	2	3	4	4	5

Mr. Parker's Class

Books	9	10	11	12	13	14	15	16
Students	3	6	5	4	0	2	0	2

Read and Understand

Step 1: What do you know?

You know how many students read each number of books.

Step 2: What are you trying to find?

Find which class won the contest.

Plan and Solve

Step 3: What strategy will you use?

Strategy: Make a graph

Mrs. Blane's Class

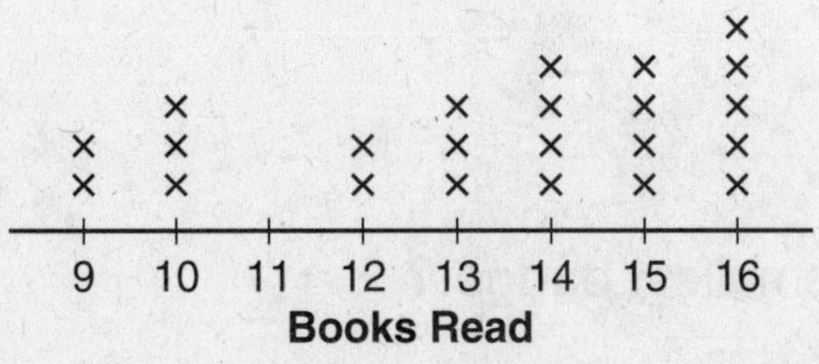

Mr. Parker's Class

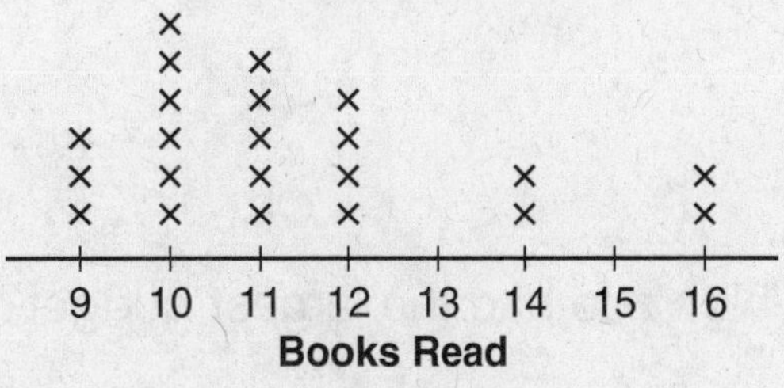

Answer: Mrs. Blane's class was more successful. More Xs are at the right end of the plot.

Look Back and Check

Is your answer reasonable?

Yes, the numbers in the table show the same trend.

1. What type of graph could you make with the above data?

____

Name ____________________

Make a Graph

Zoos in the United States have different budgets. The table shows budgets for five U.S. zoos in 2001. The budgets are in millions of dollars.

Budgets of U.S. Zoos in 2001

Zoo	Budget
Albuquerque Biological Park	$9
Cleveland Metroparks Zoo	$12
Oregon Zoo	$15
Phoenix Zoo	$16
San Diego Zoo	$56

1. Make a bar graph using the data to the right.

2. Which zoo had the largest budget? The smallest budget?

____

____

3. What was the greatest difference between zoo budgets?

____

____

Name ____________________

Mean, Median, and Mode

How to find the mean, median, and mode of:
2, 3, 8, 5, 6, 3, 1

Mean

The mean is the average. To find the mean, add all the data and divide by the number of data.

2 + 3 + 8 + 5 + 6 + 3 + 1 = 28

28 ÷ 7 = 4

The mean is 4.

Median

The median is the middle number. To find the median, arrange the data in order from least to greatest.

1, 2, 3, 3, 5, 6, 8
↑
middle number in data

The median is 3.

Mode

The mode is the data value that occurs most often.

1, 2, 3, 3, 5, 6, 8

The number 3 occurs most often.

The mode is 3.

1. Find the mean of this data set: 241, 563, 829, 755. ________

2. Find the median of this data set: 12, 18, 25, 32, 67. ________

3. Find the mode of this data set: 123, 354, 654, 123, 452, 185. ________

4. **Writing in Math** Explain how you would find the mean of this data set: 4, 3, 5.

____

____

The chart to the right shows the number of silver medals won by American athletes in recent Summer Olympic games.

Year	Medals
2000	24
1996	32
1992	38
1988	31
1984	61
1976	35
1972	31

5. What is the mean of this data set? ________

6. What is the median of this data set? ________

7. What is the mode of this data set? ________

Name ______________________________

Mean, Median, and Mode

P 5-6

1. Find the mean of this data set: 225 342 288 552 263 ________

2. Find the median of this data set: 476 234 355 765 470 ________

3. Find the mode of this data set:
16 7 8 5 16 7 8 4 7 8 16 7 ________

4. Find the range of this data set:
64 76 46 88 88 43 99 50 55 ________

5. **Reasoning** Would the mode change if a 76 was added to the data in Exercise 4?

____

____

The table gives the math test scores for Mrs. Jung's fifth-grade class.

76	54	92	88	76	88
75	93	92	68	88	76
76	88	80	70	88	72

Test Scores

6. Find the mean of the data. ________

7. Find the mode of the data. ________

8. Find the median of the data. ________

9. What is the range of the data set? ________

Test Prep

10. Find the mean of this data set: 247, 366, 785, 998.

A. 599 **B.** 598 **C.** 589 **D.** 579

11. **Writing in Math** Will a set of data always have a mode? Explain your answer.

____

____

____

Name ______________________________

Circle Graphs

How to read a circle graph

A random group of 100 adults were asked about their favorite source for news. The graph shows how they responded. It shows that more than 50% first get their news from newspapers. The Internet is the second favorite source. Magazines are the least favorite source.

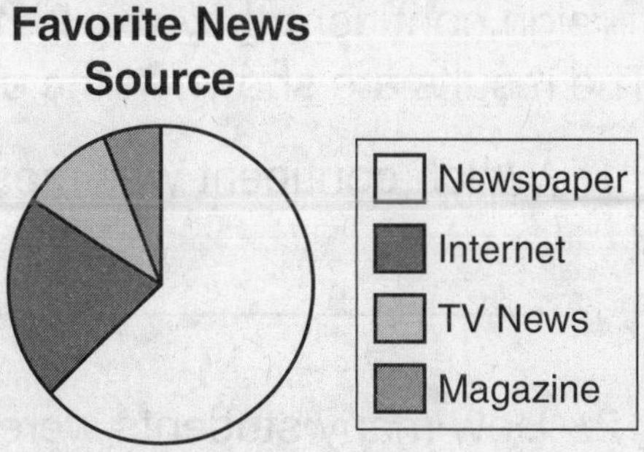

How to make a circle graph

Suppose that for the previous example you were given the following data for 100 adults who were randomly surveyed.

Newspaper: 63; Internet: 21; TV News: 10; Magazine: 6

To make a circle graph, you first draw a circle. Then you calculate how much 63% of the circle is. It is more than half but less than 3/4 of the circle. This section is labeled "newspapers." Then do the same for the other responses.

A group of 100 randomly selected people who attended a sports show were recorded for their ages and gender.

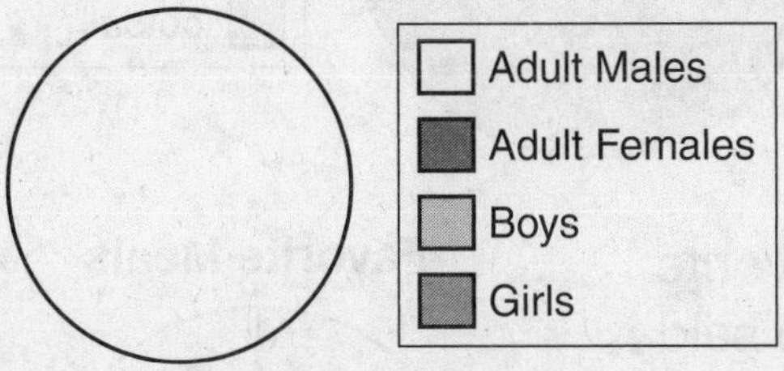

Data File

Adult Males	63
Adult Females	22
Boys	11
Girls	4

1. Use the information in the data file to complete the circle graph above. Be sure to label the graph.

2. Which group of people had the greatest attendance?

____

3. Which group of people had the least attendance?

____

4. About how many more adult males were there than girls?

____

Name ______________________________

Circle Graphs

Three thousand fifth graders were asked which foreign continent they would most like to visit. The results are shown in the circle graph.

Continent to Visit

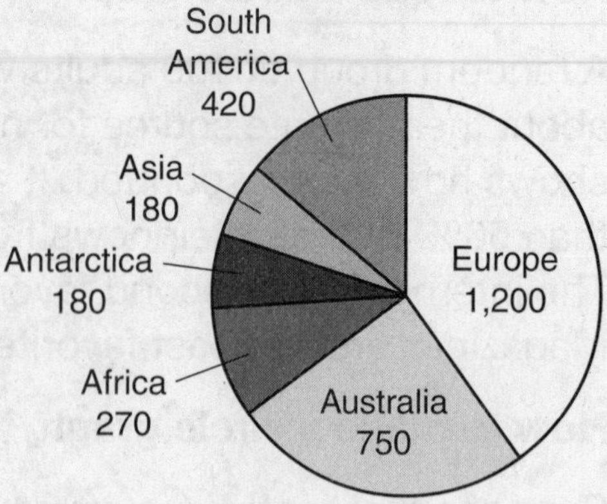

1. Which continent was most popular?

____

2. How many students were most interested in Africa?

____

3. **Estimation** About how many more students wanted to go to Europe than to Australia?

____

4. Bill surveyed the 100 students in fifth grade. Complete the graph to the right by labeling the missing categories. More students liked baseball than soccer.

Favorite Sports

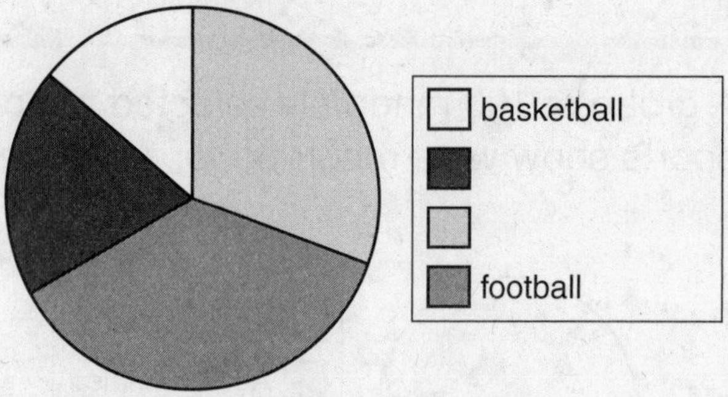

Test Prep

5. 40 people were asked to name their favorite meal. 5 said breakfast, 10 said lunch, 5 said snack, and 20 said dinner. Which meal selection will section 2 represent?

A. Breakfast **B.** Lunch

C. Snack **D.** Dinner

Favorite Meals

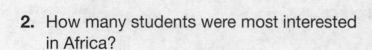

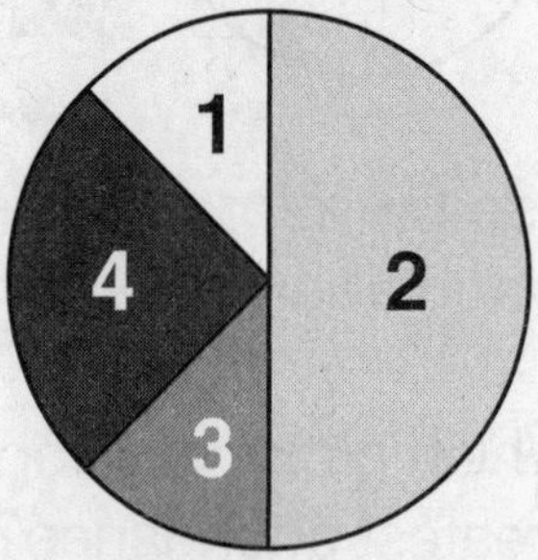

6. **Writing in Math** Explain how you would know which sections of the graph would represent the other meal situations.

____

____

Name ____________________

Choosing the Appropriate Graph

R 5-8

Barbara did a survey in her fifth-grade class about the students' favorite type of sandwich. Barbara made two graphs with the data.

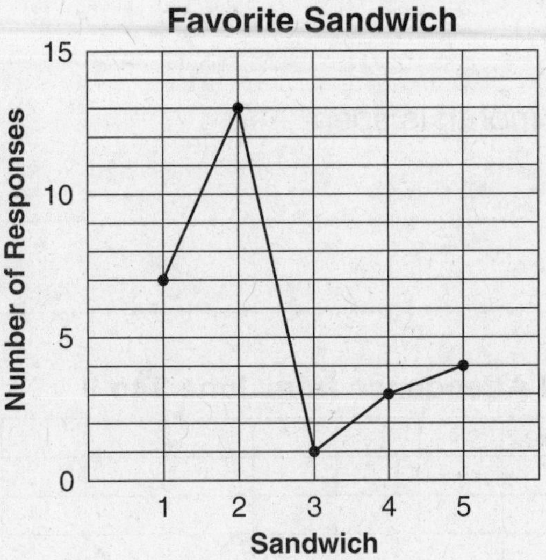

The line graph suggests that data exists between sandwiches. This graph is not appropriate for the data.

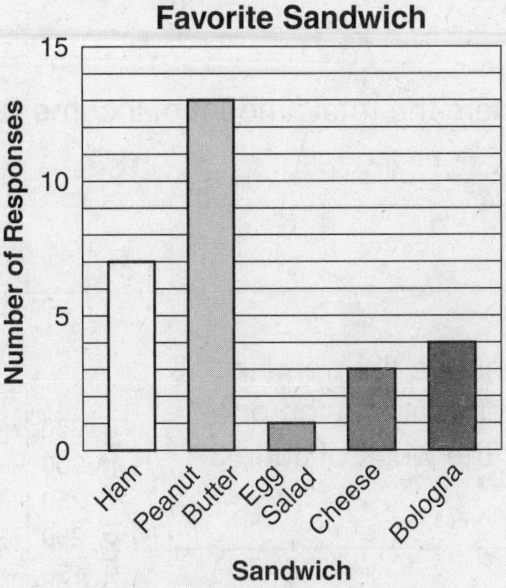

The bar represents the number of responses counted for each sandwich. This is an appropriate graph for the data.

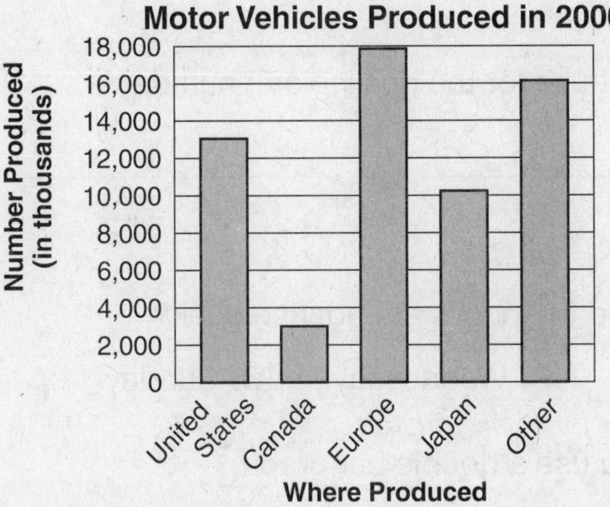

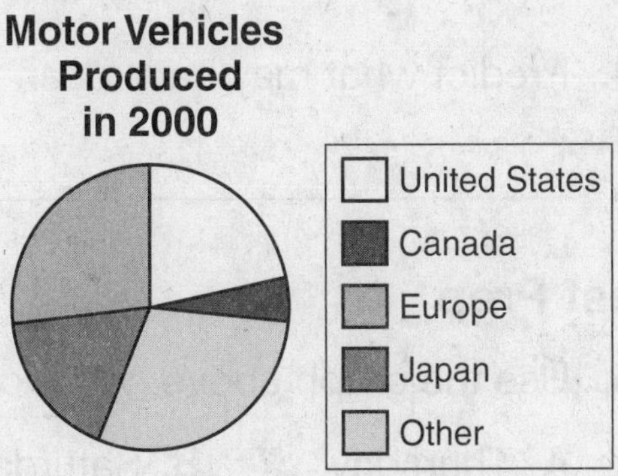

1. Which graph better represents the number of vehicles produced in each of the five locations in 2000? Explain.

____

Name ____________________

Choosing an Appropriate Graph

Tell what type of graph would be most appropriate to represent the data listed.

1. Flower sales over a week ____________________

2. Where the total amount of income for one month is spent

3. Describe the trend in attendance at the pool for the week of June 3.

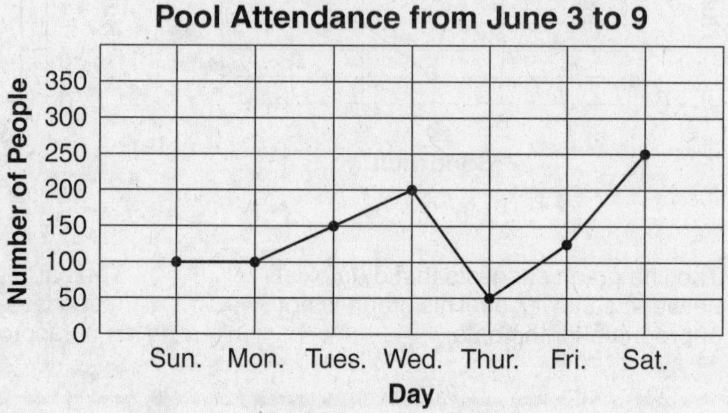

4. Predict what may have been the cause for the decline on Thursday.

Test Prep

5. Use the graph above. What day did the pool's attendance peak?

   A. Thursday **B.** Saturday **C.** Wednesday **D.** Sunday

6. **Writing in Math** When should you use a double bar graph or double line graph?

Name ____________________

PROBLEM-SOLVING SKILL **R 5-9**

Writing to Compare

The total points scored in the first five games for the Carlton Knights and Baxter Barons are shown in the line graphs.

Carlton Knights

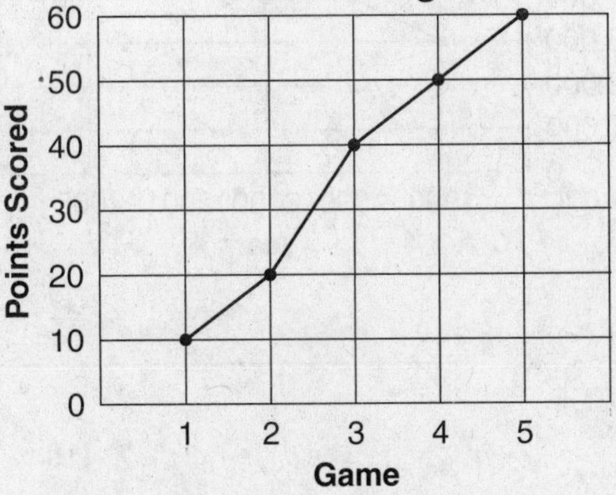

Baxter Barons

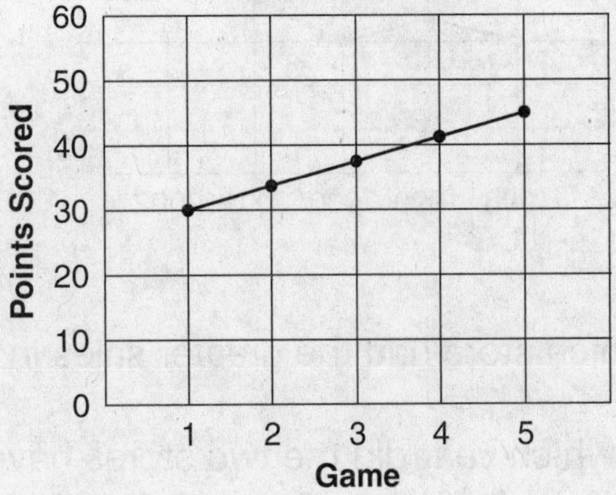

The number of points scored by both teams has been increasing for each game.

The scoring for the Knights has gone up faster because the line is steeper.

Corpus Christi, Texas Population

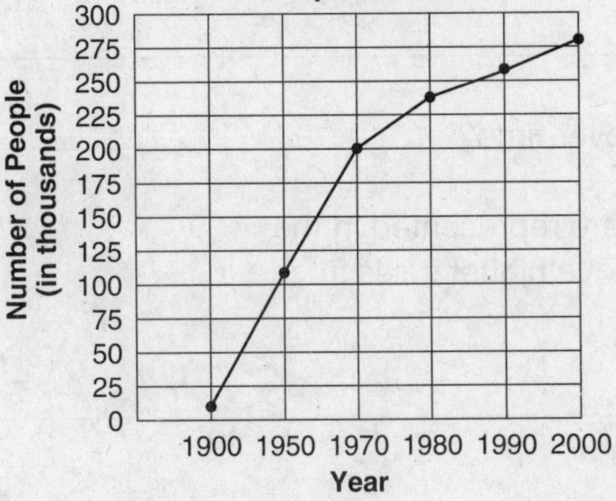

Aurora, Colorado Population

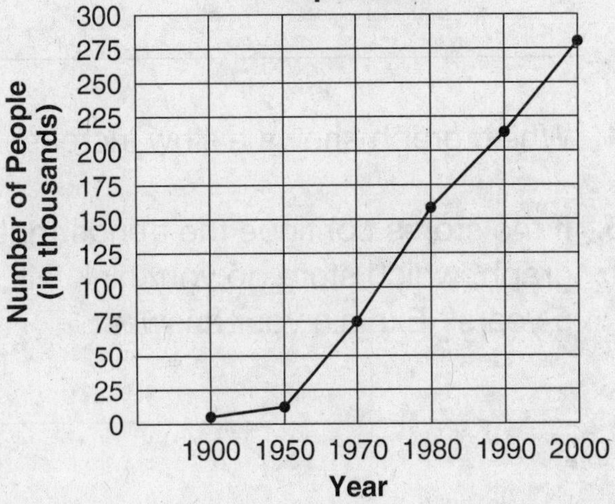

1. Which graph shows a faster increase in population between 1900 and 1950?

____

Name ______________________________

PROBLEM-SOLVING SKILL **P 5-9**

Writing to Compare

Analyze the graphs below. Then answer the questions.

Store A Jeans Sales

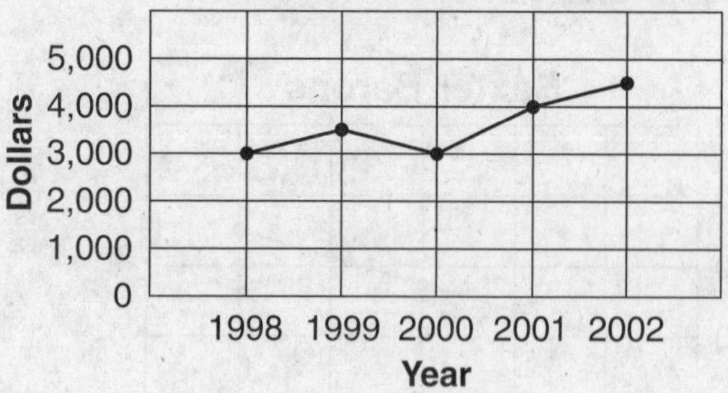

Store B Jeans Sales

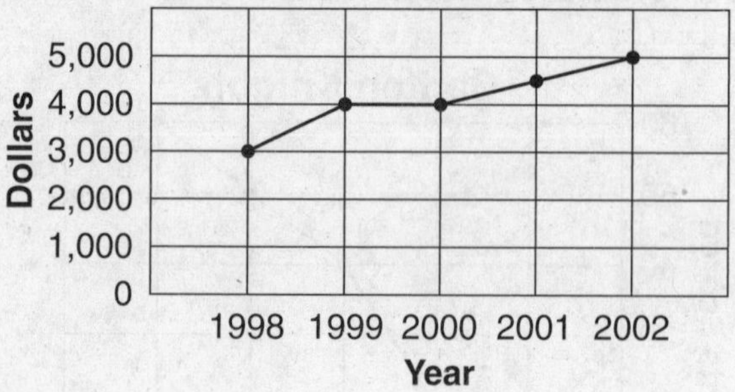

1. Which store had the greater sales in 2002? ______________

2. In which year did the two stores have the same sales? ______________

3. Is there a common trend between the two jeans stores? If so, explain.

____

____

____

4. Which graph shows a slow increase over time? ______________

5. If the stores continue the trends that are represented in the graph, which store do you think will have higher sales in 5 years? Explain your answer.

____

____

____

6. Which store has a greater range in sales? What is the range? ______________

Name ______________________________

Predicting Outcomes

R 5-10

You can use an experiment to predict outcomes.

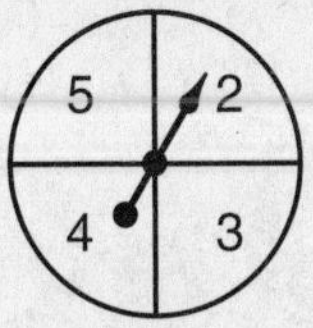 **Spinner A** Compare the chances of spinning an even number and spinning an odd number.	**Event:** Spinning an even number **Favorable outcomes:** 2, 4 2 out of 4 possible outcomes are favorable, so in 2 out of 4 spins, you can expect an even number.	**Event:** Spinning an odd number **Favorable outcomes:** 3, 5 2 out of 4 possible outcomes are favorable, so in 2 out of 4 spins, you can expect an odd number.	Spinning an even number and spinning an odd number are **equally likely** events.
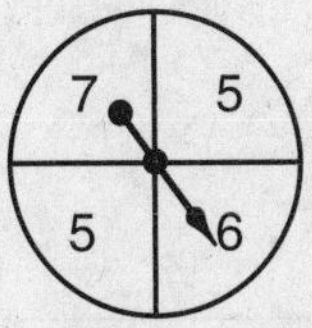 **Spinner B** Compare the chances of spinning an even number and spinning an odd number.	**Event:** Spinning an even number **Favorable outcomes:** 6 1 out of 4 possible outcomes are favorable, so in 1 out of 4 spins, you can expect an even number.	**Event:** Spinning an odd number **Favorable outcomes:** 5, 5, 7 3 out of 4 possible outcomes are favorable, so in 3 out of 4 spins, you can expect an odd number.	Spinning an even number is **less likely** than spinning an odd number. Spinning an odd number is **more likely** than spinning an even number.

Think about tossing a standard number cube.

1. What are the possible outcome numbers? Are the numbers equally likely? Explain.

____

____

____

____

2. In 6 tosses, how many times would you expect to toss the number 6?

____

Name ____________________

Predicting Outcomes

The nature club is planning a field trip. They have decided to write their destination choices on slips of paper and have their instructor select the destination by drawing a slip of paper out of a bag. The slips of paper shown below are the destination choices in the bag.

Nature museum	Beach	Forest preserve	Beach
Beach	Beach	Forest preserve	

1. Is it equally likely that the instructor will draw the nature museum or the forest preserve? Explain. ____________________

____

____

2. Which destination is the instructor least likely to draw? ____________________

3. Which destination is the instructor most likely to draw? ____________________

Test Prep

4. Use data from Exercises 1–3. What is the chance of the instructor drawing the nature museum?

A. 3 out of 7 **B.** 2 out of 7

C. 1 out of 7 **D.** Impossible event

5. **Writing in Math** Explain the difference between an outcome and a favorable outcome.

____

____

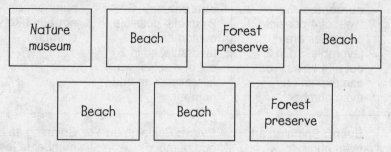

Name ____________________

Listing Outcomes

R 5-11

Almond, Keisha, and Mona are running for student council president. Barry, Andy, and Maurice are running for vice-president. Each student has an equal chance of being elected.

You can use a tree diagram to find all the possible outcomes. All of the possible outcomes is called the sample space.

President	Vice-President	Outcome
Almond	Barry	Almond, Barry
	Andy	Almond, Andy
	Maurice	Almond, Maurice
Keisha	Barry	Keisha, Barry
	Andy	Keisha, Andy
	Maurice	Keisha, Maurice
Mona	Barry	Mona, Barry
	Andy	Mona, Andy
	Maurice	Mona, Maurice

There are 9 possible outcomes in the sample space.

1. Complete the tree diagram to show the possible outcomes when Spinner A and Spinner B are spun.

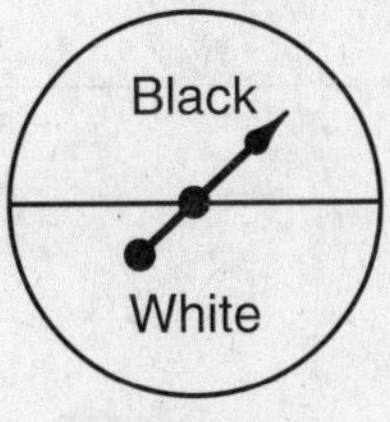

Spinner A

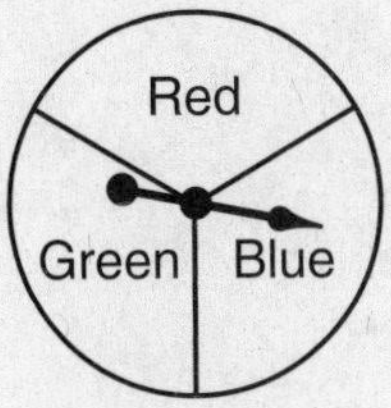

Spinner B

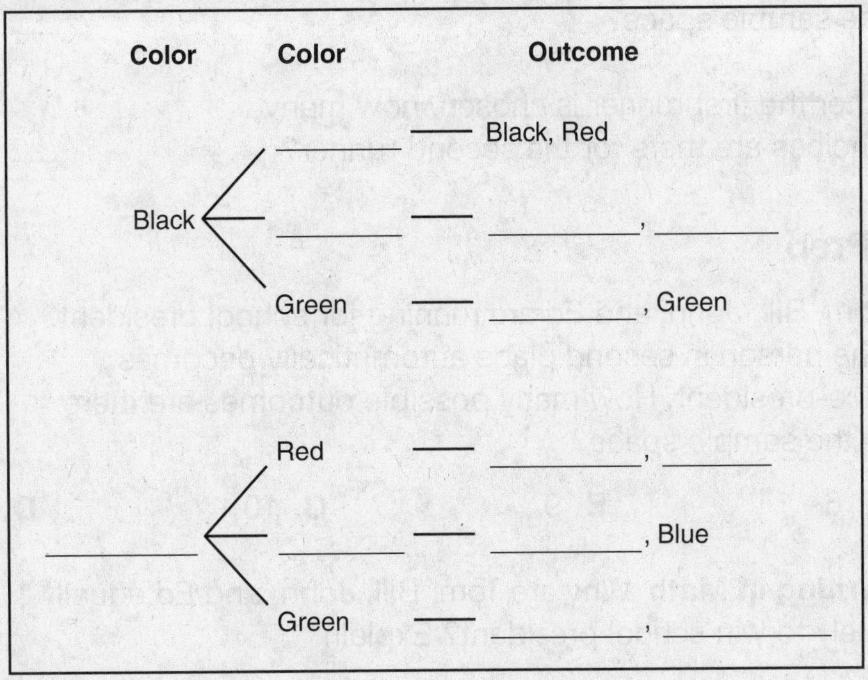

2. How many times does the outcome black/green occur in the tree diagram?

____

Name ______________________

Listing Outcomes

The coach is trying to decide in what order Jane, Pete, and Lou will run a relay race.

1. Complete the tree diagram below to show the sample space.

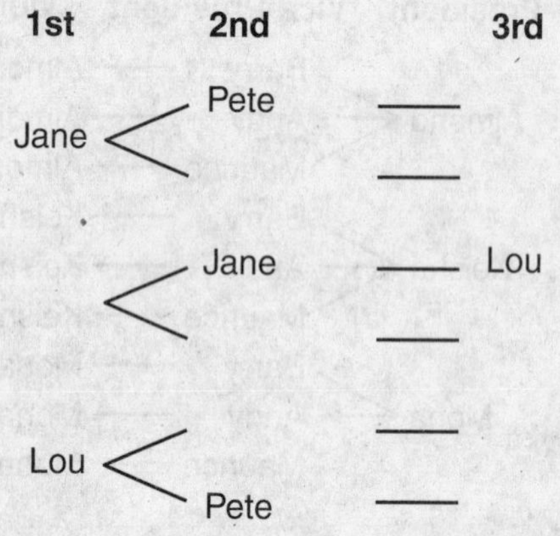

2. How many possible outcomes are there in the sample space? ______________

3. After the first runner is chosen, how many choices are there for the second runner? ______________

Test Prep

4. Tom, Bill, John, and Ed are running for school president. The person in second place automatically becomes vice-president. How many possible outcomes are there in the sample space?

A. 6 **B.** 9 **C.** 10 **D.** 12

5. Writing in Math Why are Tom, Bill, John, and Ed equally likely to win school president? Explain.

____

____

____

Name ______________________________

Expressing Probability as a Fraction

R 5-12

The probability of an event is a number that describes the chance that an event will occur. Probability can be expressed as a fraction.

$$\text{Probability of an event} = \frac{\text{number of favorable outcomes}}{\text{number of possible outcomes}}$$

If Felice spins the spinner, what is the probability of landing on Orange?

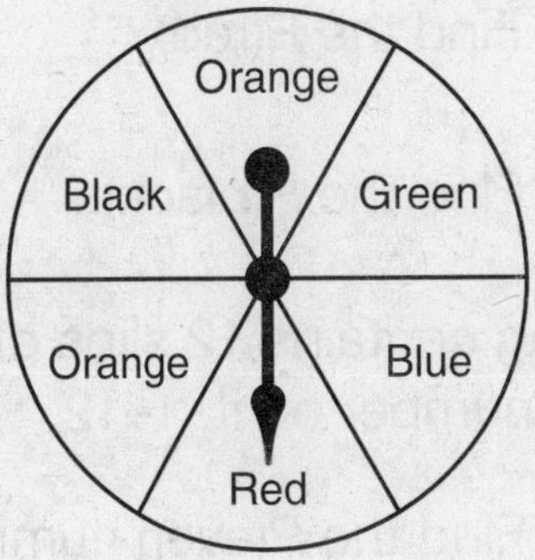

There are 6 possible outcomes (colors) and 2 favorable outcomes (Orange).

$$\text{Probability (landing on Orange)} = \frac{\text{number of Orange}}{\text{number of colors}} = \frac{2}{6}$$

The probability of landing on Orange is $\frac{2}{6}$ or $\frac{1}{3}$.

The probability of landing on Orange can be written as $P(\text{Orange}) = \frac{1}{3}$.

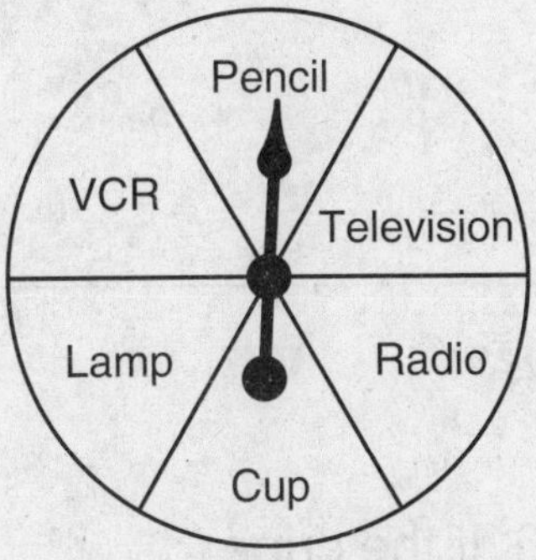

1. Find *P*(object that does not use electricity) ____________

2. Find *P*(object that uses electricity) ____________

3. Find *P*(object used for writing) ____________

Name ______________________________

Expressing Probability as a Fraction

P 5-12

Tom put 4 yellow marbles, 2 blue marbles, 6 red marbles, and 5 black marbles in a bag.

1. Find the *P*(yellow). ________

2. Find the *P*(blue). ________

3. Find the *P*(red). ________

4. Find the *P*(black). ________

A bag contains 12 slips of paper of the same size. Each slip has one number on it, 1–12.

5. Find the *P*(even number). ________

6. Find the *P*(a number less than 6). ________

7. Find the *P*(an odd number). ________

8. Find the *P*(a number greater than 8). ________

9. Describe an impossible event.

____

Test Prep

10. A cube has 6 sides and is numbered 1 through 6. If the cube is tossed, what is the probability that a 3 will be tossed?

A. $\frac{1}{6}$ **B.** $\frac{2}{6}$ **C.** $\frac{3}{6}$ **D.** $\frac{6}{6}$

11. Explain the probability of tossing a prime number when you toss the cube with numbers 1 through 6.

____

____

Name ____________________

PROBLEM-SOLVING APPLICATION **R 5-13**

Sports Data

Susan and Louise are the top scorers on their basketball teams. The graph to the right shows how many points each of them scored in their first three games of the season.

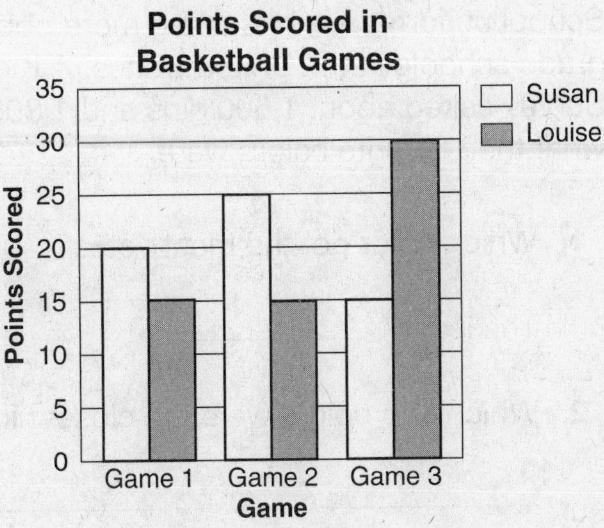

How many total points did Susan score in the first three games?

20 + 25 + 15 = 60

So, Susan scored 60 points total.

How many more points did Louise score than Susan in Game 3?
15 points

The line graph at the right shows how many games the Strikers won from 1999 to 2003. Use it for questions 1–3.

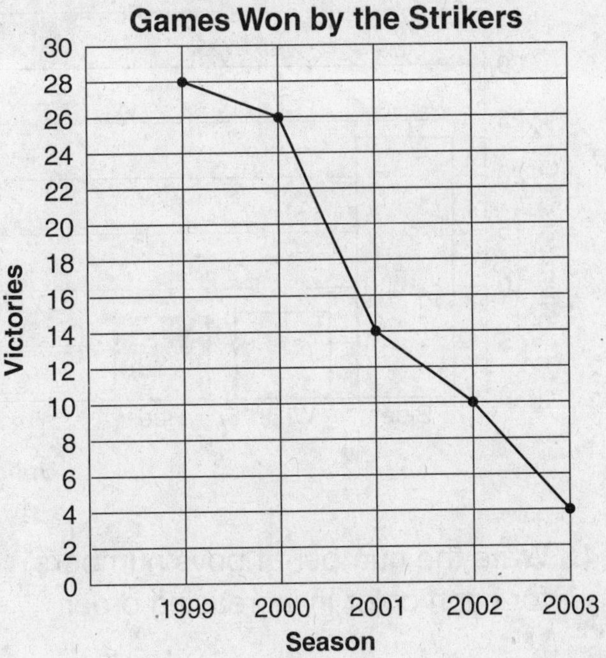

1. During which season did the Strikers win 26 games?

____

2. How many fewer games did the Strikers win between the 2000 and 2001 seasons?

____

____

3. Describe the trend that is shown in the graph.

____

____

____

Name ____

PROBLEM-SOLVING APPLICATION **P 5-13**

School Uniforms

School uniforms are becoming more popular at grade schools in the United States. A Kids USA Survey asked about 1,600 girls and 1,300 boys what their favorite colors were.

Favorite Uniform Colors for Girls (per 100 surveyed)

Color	Number of Girls
Blue	24
White	8
Red	7
Green	12
Yellow	3
Black	30
Other	16

1. Which color got the most votes? __________

The least? __________

2. Which two colors were the closest in votes?

____

3. Complete the bar graph for the data.

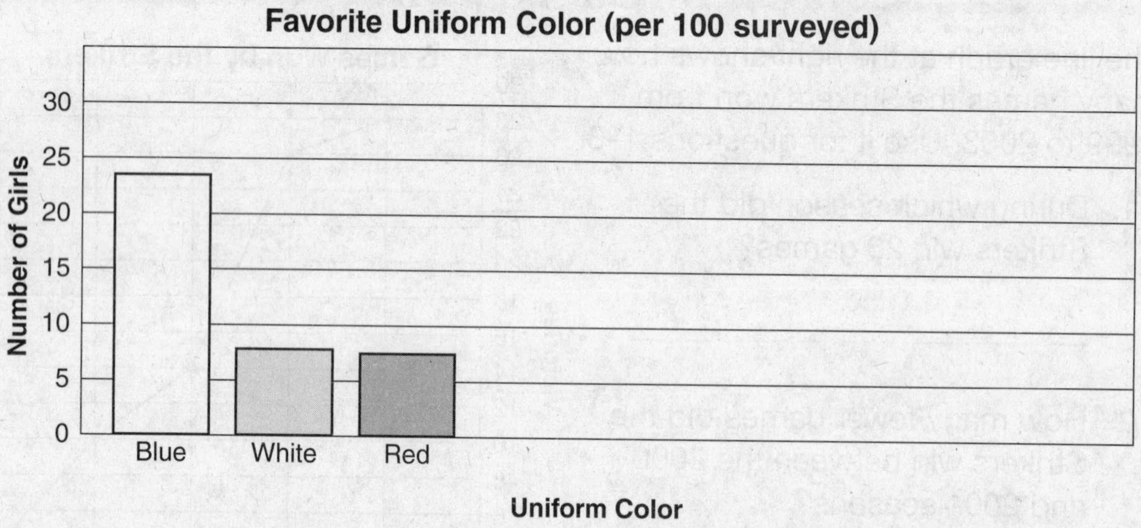

4. Write the number of boys numbers for each color in increasing order.

____

____

Favorite Uniform Colors for Boys (per 100 surveyed)

Color	Number of Boys
Blue	22
White	7
Red	7
Green	13
Yellow	3
Black	31
Other	17

5. What is the median? __________

6. What is the mode? __________

Name ____________________

Geometric Ideas

Lines, line segments, and rays are basic geometric ideas. They are sometimes described by the relationship they have to other lines, line segments, and rays.

Draw	Write	Say	Description
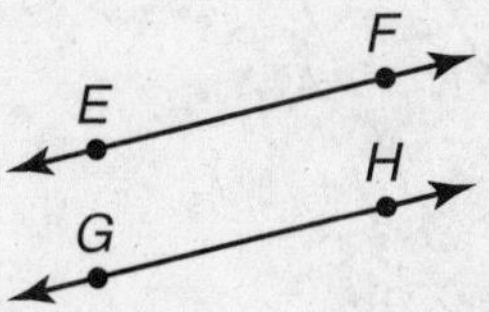	$\overleftrightarrow{EF} \parallel \overleftrightarrow{GH}$	Line *EF* is parallel to line *GH*.	$\overleftrightarrow{EF}$ and $\overleftrightarrow{GH}$ are parallel lines. They are the same distance apart and will not cross each other.
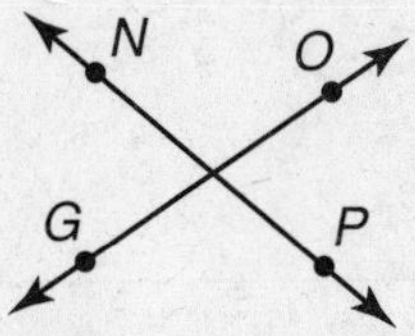	$\overleftrightarrow{NP}$ intersects $\overleftrightarrow{GO}$	Line *NP* intersects line *GO*.	$\overleftrightarrow{NP}$ and $\overleftrightarrow{GO}$ are intersecting lines. They pass through the same point.
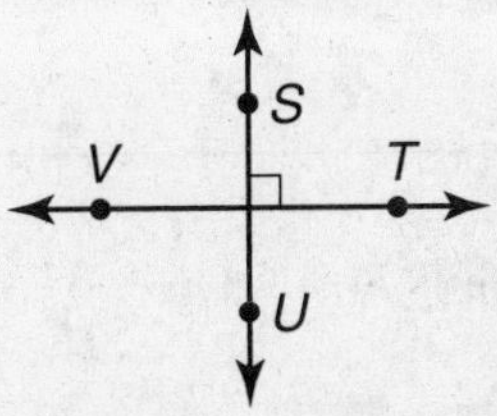	$\overleftrightarrow{SU} \perp \overleftrightarrow{VT}$	Line *SU* is perpendicular to line *VT*.	$\overleftrightarrow{SU}$ and $\overleftrightarrow{VT}$ are perpendicular lines. They intersect and form square corners.

Use the diagram at the right. Name the following.

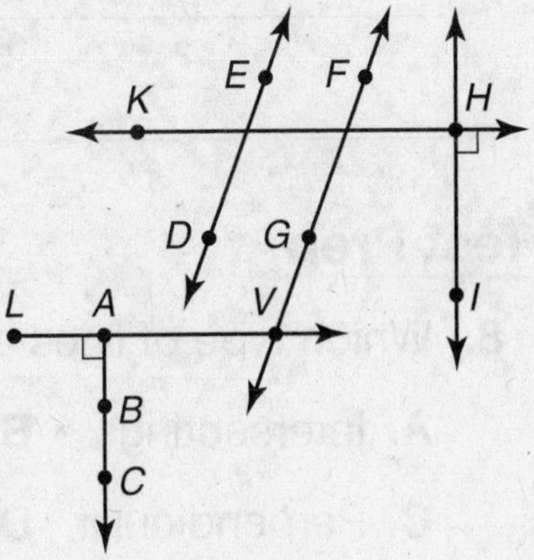

1. two parallel lines ____________________

2. a line segment ____________________

3. two perpendicular lines ____________________

4. two lines ____________________

5. a ray ____________________

6. two perpendicular rays ____________________

7. a point ____________________

Name ________________

Geometric Ideas

Use the diagram at the right. Name the following.

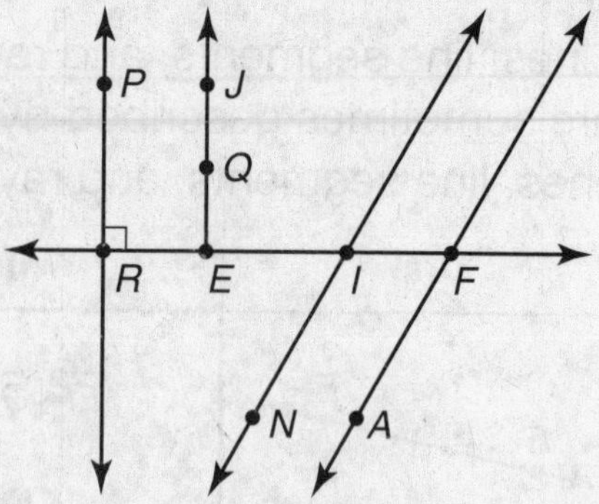

1. three points

2. a ray

3. two intersecting lines but not perpendicular

4. two parallel lines

5. a line segment

6. two perpendicular lines

7. **Reasoning** Can a line segment have two midpoints? Explain.

Test Prep

8. Which type of lines are shown by the figure?

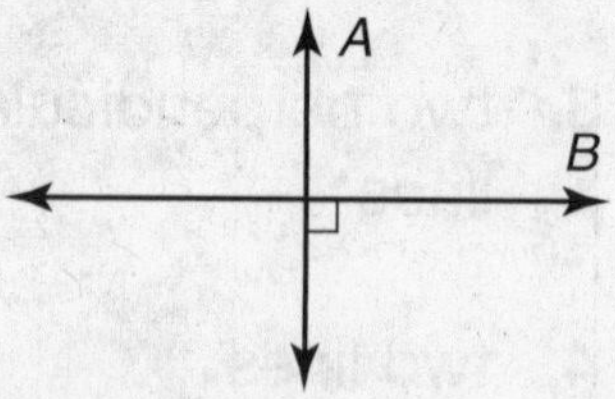

A. Intersecting **B.** Parallel

C. Perpendicular **D.** Curved

9. **Writing in Math** Draw and label two perpendicular line segments $\overline{KL}$ and $\overline{MN}$.

Name ______________________________

Measuring and Classifying Angles

R 6-2

The chart below can help you to describe and identify an angle.

Measure ∠*EFG*.

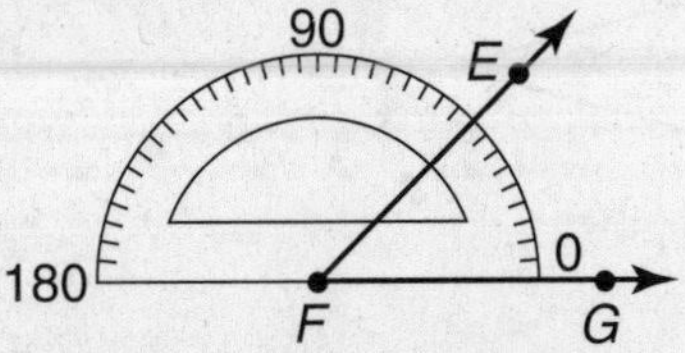

Remember to place the 0° mark on one side of the angle.

∠*EFG* measures 45°.

Draw an angle of 65°.

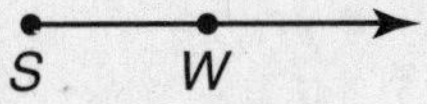

Place the center of the protractor on *S*. Line up $\overrightarrow{SW}$ with the 0° mark. Place a point at 65°. Label it *J*. Draw $\overrightarrow{SJ}$.

Classifying Angles

Acute — measures between 0° and 90°

Right — measures exactly 90°

Obtuse — measures between 90° and 180°

Straight — measures exactly 180°

Classify each angle as acute, right, obtuse, or straight. Then measure each angle.

1. 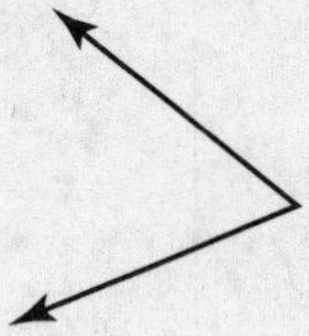

2. 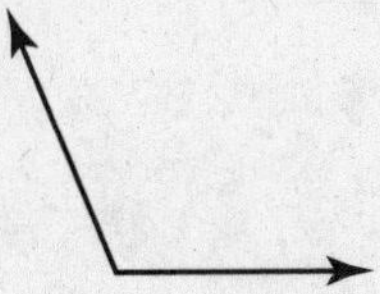

3. 

______________ ______________ ______________

Draw an angle with each measure.

4. 100°

5. 170°

6. 90°

7. Reasoning ∠*ABC* measures less than 180° but more than 90°. Is ∠*ABC* a right, an acute, an obtuse, or a straight angle?

____

Name ______________________________

Measuring and Classifying Angles

P 6-2

Classify each angle as *acute, right, obtuse,* or *straight.* Then measure each angle. (Hint: Draw longer sides if necessary.)

1.

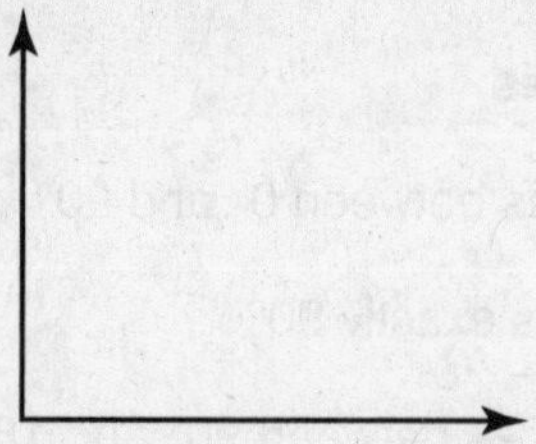

____

2.

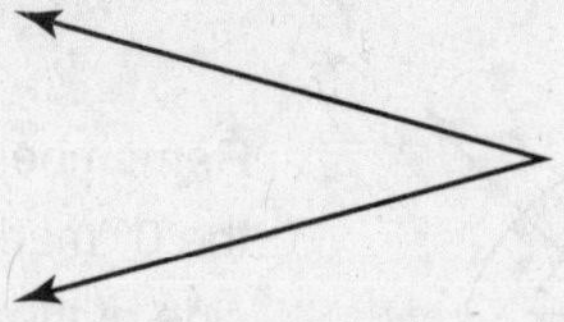

____

Draw an angle with each measure.

3. 120°

4. 180°

5. Draw an acute angle. Label it with the letters *A, B,* and *C.* What is the measure of the angle? ____________

Test Prep

6. Which kind of angle is shown in the figure below?

A. Acute **B.** Obtuse

C. Right **D.** Straight

7. Writing in Math Explain how to use a protractor to measure an angle.

____

____

____

____

Name ____________________

Segments and Angles Related to Circles

R 6-3

All the points on a **circle** are the same distance from the center. The center of circle *C* is at point *C*.

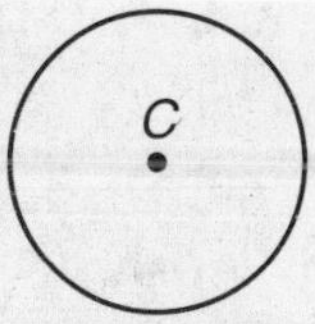

A **radius** goes from the center to any point on the circle. $\overline{RS}$ is a radius of circle *R*. (plural: radii)

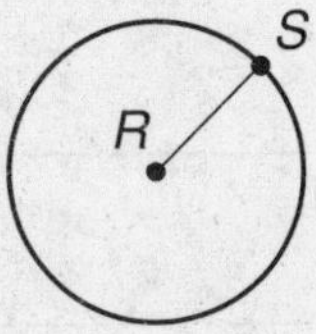

A **chord** has both endpoints on a circle. $\overline{HD}$ is a chord of circle *O*.

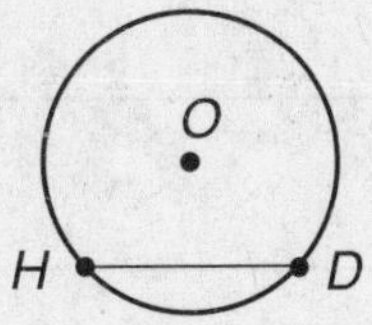

A **diameter** passes through the center of a circle. $\overline{DR}$ is a diameter of circle *M*. A diameter of a circle is also the longest chord of that circle. A circle's diameter is twice as long as its radius.

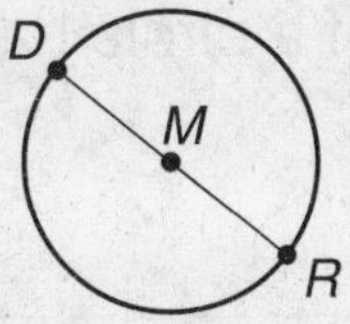

A **central angle** is an angle whose vertex is the center. $\angle ACB$ is a central angle.

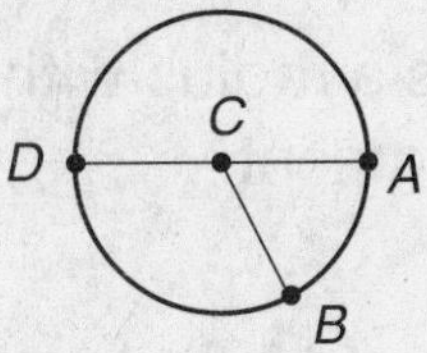

Use the terms at the top of this page to identify each figure in circle *F*.

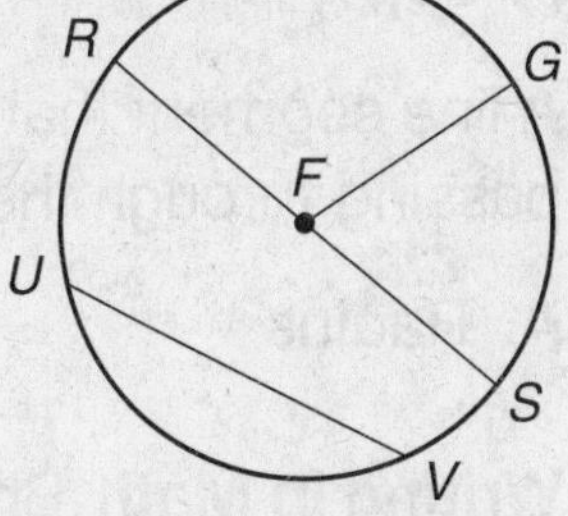

1. point *F* ____________________

2. $\angle GFS$ ____________________

3. $\overline{RS}$ ____________________

4. $\overline{UV}$ ____________________

5. $\overline{GF}$ ____________________

6. Reasoning If a circle has a radius of 12 in., what is the circle's diameter? ____________________

Name ______________________________

Segments and Angles Related to Circles

P 6-3

Identify each figure in circle D.

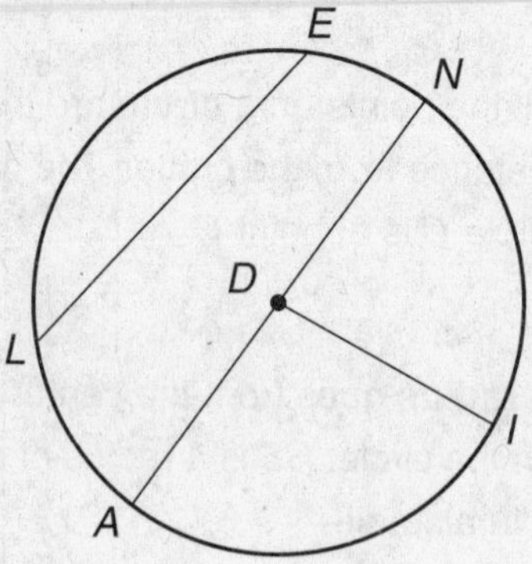

1. $\angle NDI$ ______________________

2. $\overline{LE}$ ______________________

3. $\overline{DI}$ ______________________

4. $\overline{AN}$ ______________________

5. point D ______________________

6. $\overline{DA}$ ______________________

7. **Reasoning** Is the radius of a circle half of the diameter? Explain.

____

8. Construct a circle that has a radius with an equal length to the given line segment.

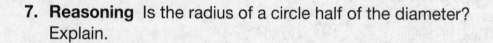

Test Prep

9. A line segment that connects two points on a circle passing through the center is called a

A. Radius **B.** Diameter **C.** Chord **D.** Central angle

10. **Writing in Math** Brenda thinks that a chord can be many different lengths on a given circle. Is she right? Explain your thinking.

____

____

Name ____________________

Polygons

R 6-4

A polygon is a closed plane figure made up of line segments. Common polygons have names that tell the number of sides the polygon has.

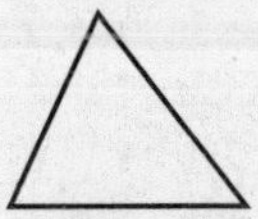
Triangle
3 sides

Pentagon
5 sides

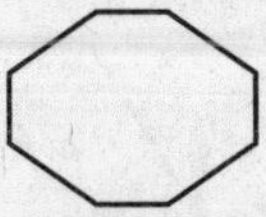
Octagon
8 sides

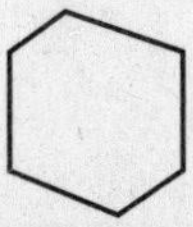
Hexagon
6 sides

Open Figure

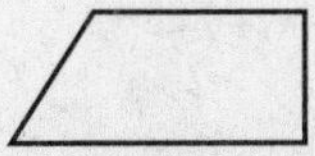
Quadrilateral
4 sides

A **regular polygon** has sides of equal length and angles of equal measure.

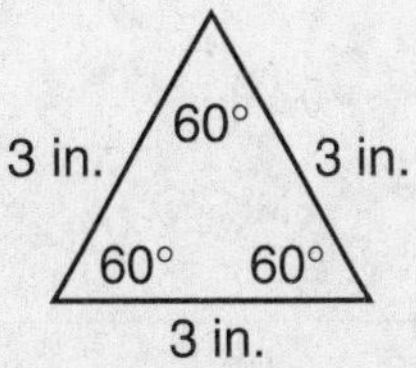

Each side is 3 in. long.
Each angle is 60°.

Name each polygon. Then tell if it appears to be a regular polygon.

1. 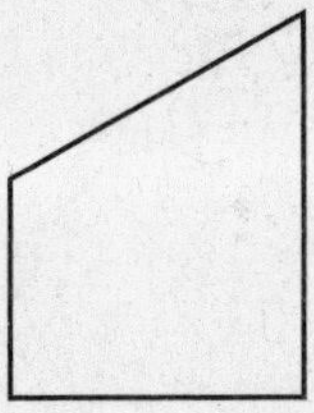

____

____

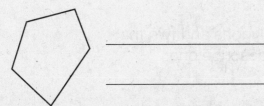

2. 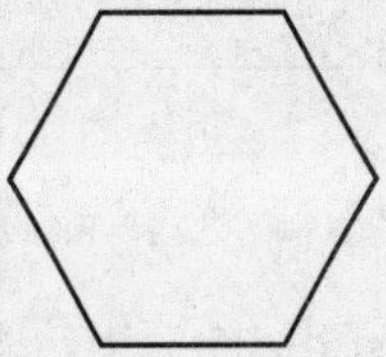

____

____

3. 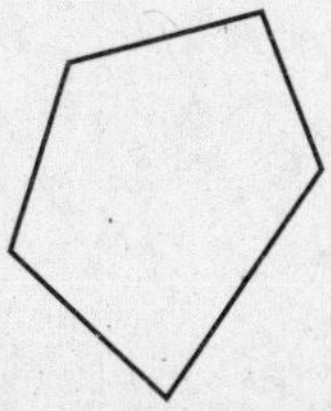

____

____

4. 

____

____

5. Reasoning Shakira sorted shapes into two different groups. Use geometric terms to describe how she sorted the shapes.

Group A	Group B
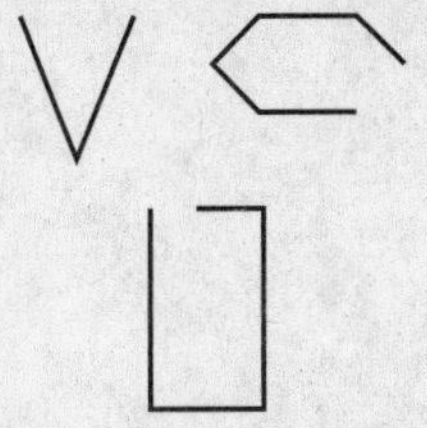	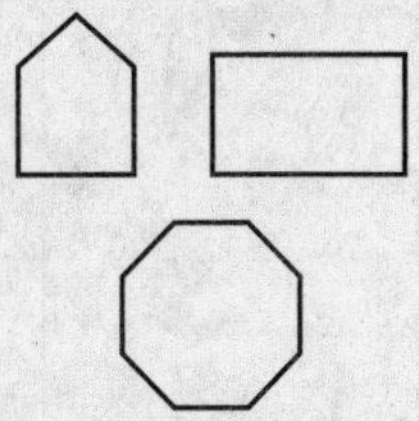

____

____

____

____

Name ____________________

Polygons

Name each polygon. Then tell if it appears to be a regular polygon.

1. 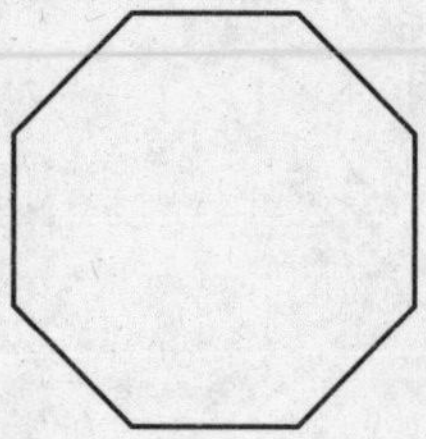

____

____

2. 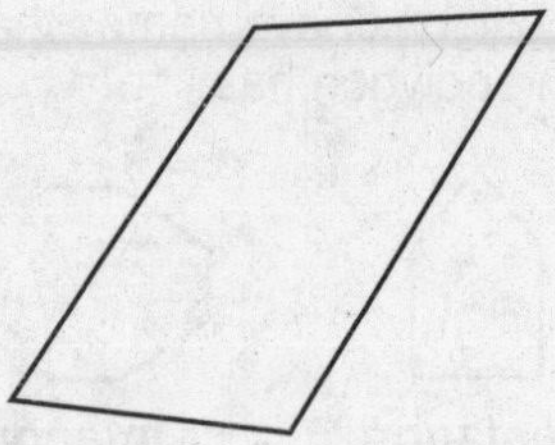

____

____

3. Name the polygon. Name the vertices.

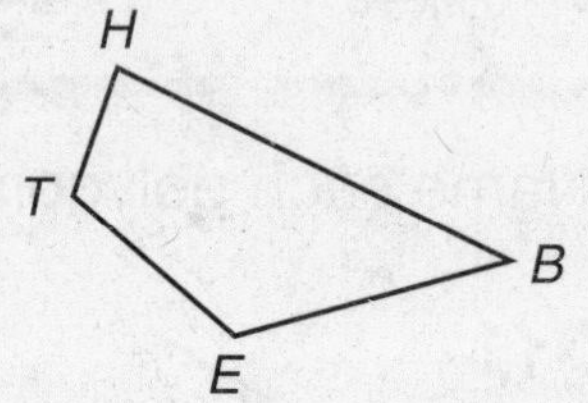

____

____

Test Prep

4. Which polygon has eight sides?

A. Quadrilateral **B.** Pentagon **C.** Hexagon **D.** Octagon

5. **Writing in Math** Draw two regular polygons and two that are irregular. Use geometric terms to describe one characteristic of each type.

____

____

____

Name ______________________________

Classifying Triangles

You can classify triangles by the lengths of their sides and the sizes of their angles.

acute
all angles less than 90°

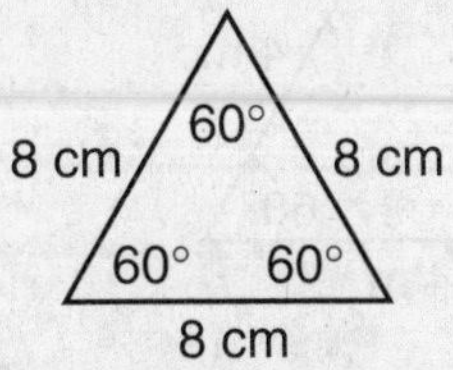

equilateral
all sides the same length

This triangle is both equilateral and acute.

Not all acute triangles are equilateral.

right
one right angle

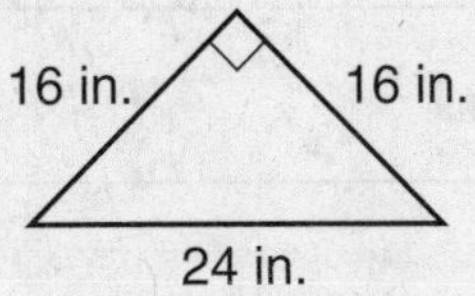

isosceles
two sides the same length

This triangle is both isosceles and right.

Not all right triangles are isosceles.

obtuse
one obtuse angle

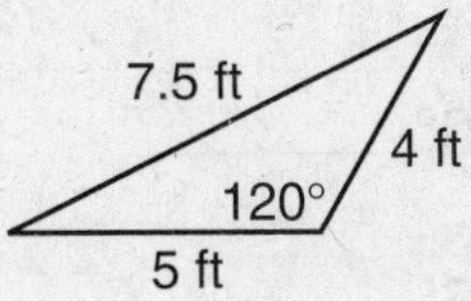

scalene
no sides the same length

This triangle is both scalene and obtuse.

Not all obtuse triangles are scalene.

Remember that the sum of the measures of the angles of a triangle is 180°.

Classify each triangle by its sides and then by its angles.

1.

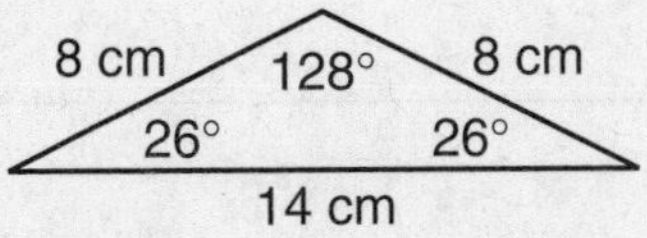

____

____

2.

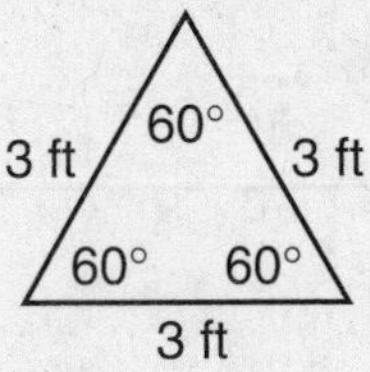

____

____

3.

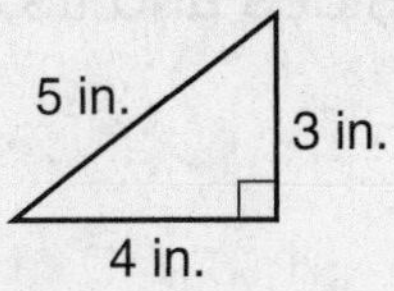

____

____

The measures of two angles of a triangle are given. Find the measure of the third angle.

4. 40°, 100°, ________ **5.** 14°, 98°, ________ **6.** 38°, 38°, ________

Name ____________________

Classifying Triangles

P 6-5

Classify each triangle by its sides and then by its angles.

1.

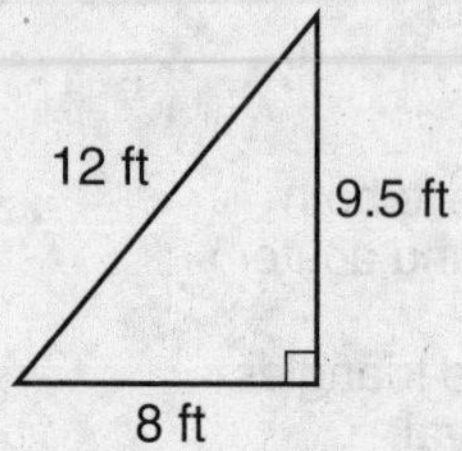

____

____

2.

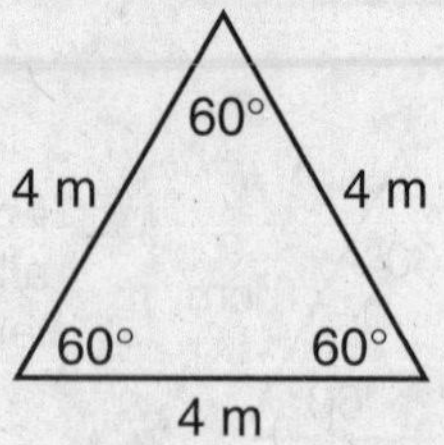

____

____

The measures of two angles of a triangle are given. Find the measure of the third angle.

3. 47°, 62°, ______

4. 29°, 90°, ______

5. 75°, 75°, ______

6. 54°, 36°, ______

7. Judy bought a new tent for a camping trip. Look at the side of the tent with the opening to classify the triangle by its sides and its angles.

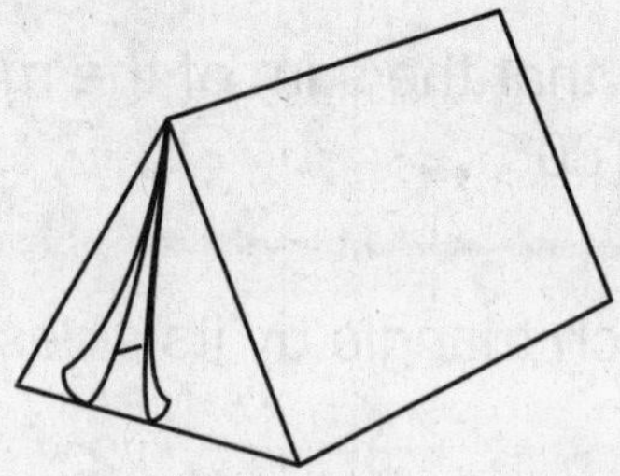

____

Test Prep

8. Which describes a scalene triangle?

A. 4 equal sides **B.** 3 equal sides **C.** 2 equal sides **D.** 0 equal sides

9. **Writing in Math** The lengths of two sides of a triangle are 15 in. each. The third side measures 10 in. What type of triangle is this? Explain your answer using geometric terms.

____

____

Name ____

Classifying Quadrilaterals

R 6-6

Quadrilateral	Definition	Example

Parallelogram A quadrilateral with both pairs of opposite sides parallel and equal in length

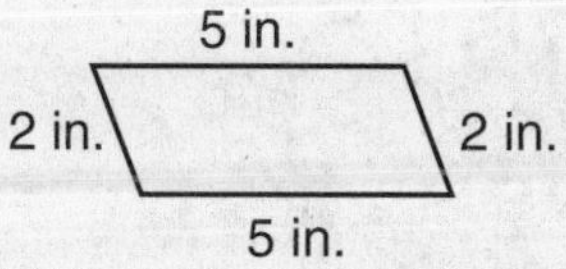

Rectangle A parallelogram with four right angles

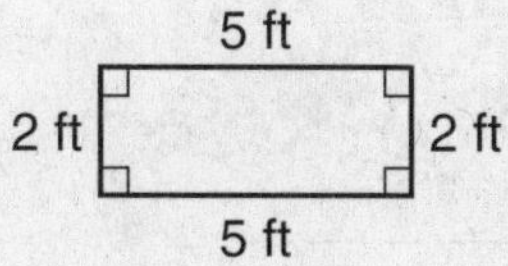

Rhombus A parallelogram with all sides the same length

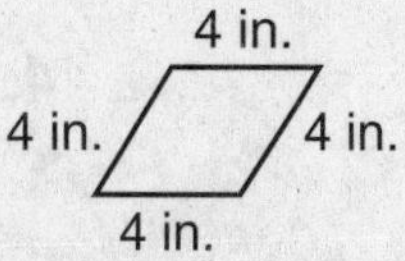

Square A rectangle with all sides the same length

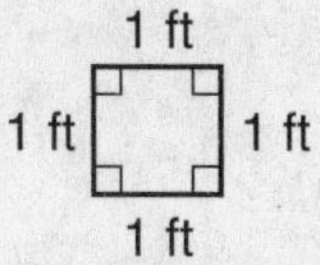

Trapezoid A quadrilateral with only one pair of parallel sides

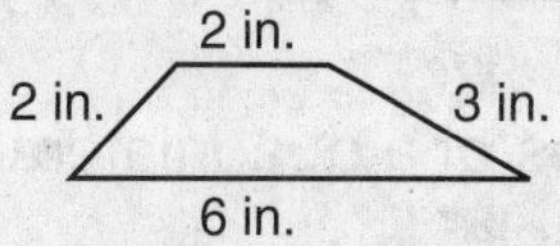

Remember that the sum of the measures of the angles of a quadrilateral is 360°.

Classify each quadrilateral. Be as specific as possible.

1.

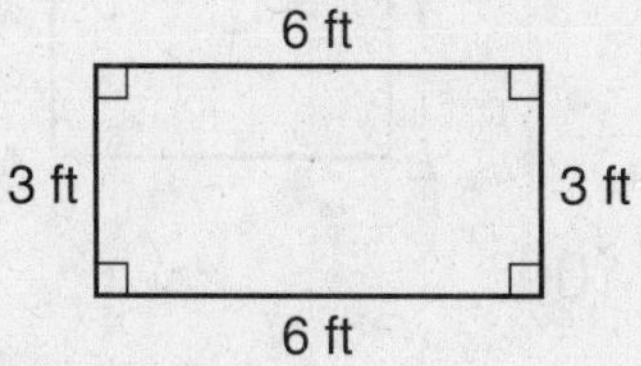

____

2.

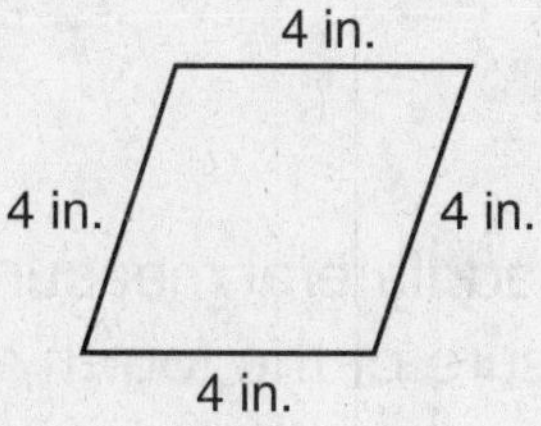

____

3.

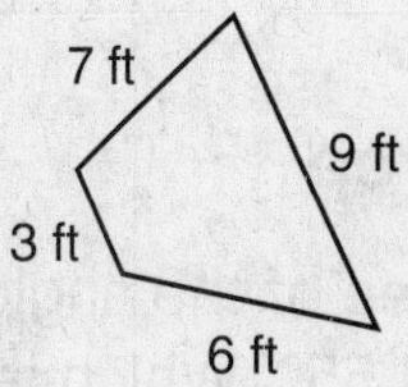

____

The measures of three angles of a quadrilateral are given. Find the measure of the fourth angle.

4. 65°, 150°, 89°, ________

5. 100°, 80°, 100°, ________

6. 82°, 78°, 90°, ________

Name ____________________

Classifying Quadrilaterals

P 6-6

Classify each quadrilateral. Be as specific as possible.

1.

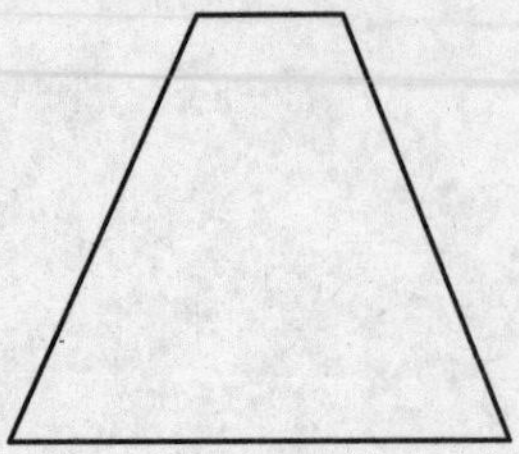

____

2.

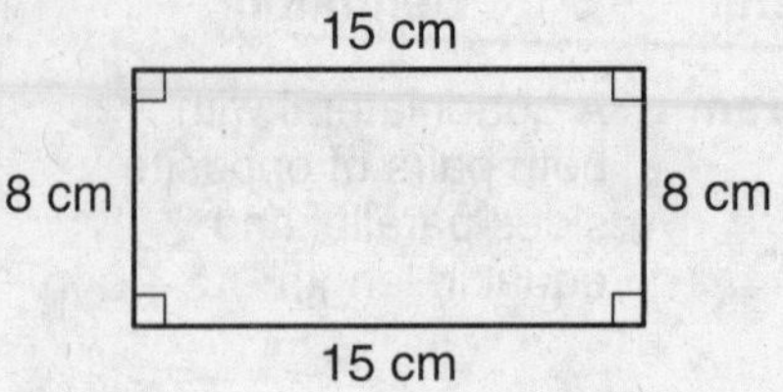

____

3.

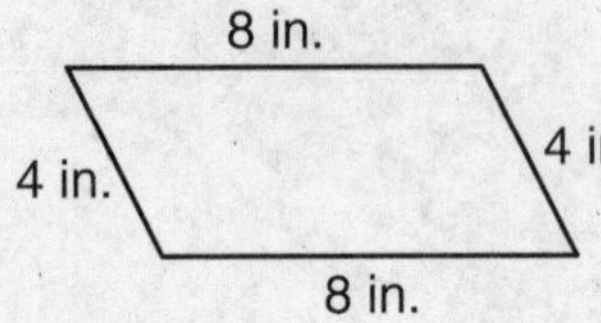

____

4.

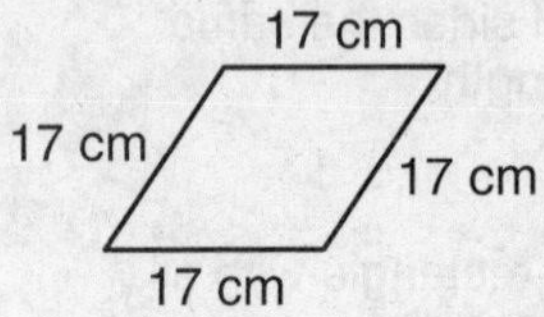

____

The measures of three angles of a quadrilateral are given. Find the measure of the fourth angle.

5. 90°, 145°, 78°, ________

6. 110°, 54°, 100°, ________

7. Name the vertices of the square.

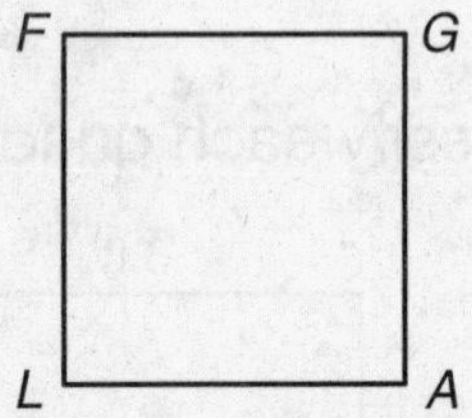

____

Test Prep

8. Three of the angles of a quadrilateral measure 80°, 100°, and 55°. Which is the measure of the fourth angle?

A. 115° **B.** 120° **C.** 125° **D.** 130°

9. Writing in Math Can a trapezoid have four obtuse angles? Explain.

____

____

____

Name ____________________

PROBLEM-SOLVING STRATEGY **R 6-7**

Solve a Simpler Problem

Give Away During a grand opening, a mall provides prizes for the first 70 customers. The 1st customer receives a coupon book, the 2nd customer, a travel mug, and the 3rd customer, a T-shirt. If the prizes continue to be given away in the same pattern, which prize would the 70th customer receive?

Read and Understand

Step 1: What do you know?

There are 3 different prizes given away in a pattern.

Step 2: What are you trying to find?

Which gift the 70th customer will receive

Plan and Solve

Step 3: What strategy will you use?

Strategy: Solve a simpler problem

I can divide 69 by 3. I know the 69th customer will receive the 3rd prize. The 70th customer will receive the coupon book.

Look Back and Check

Is your work correct?

Yes, 69 can be divided by 3 evenly to find the 3rd prize. The 70th customer would be next for the 1st prize.

Solve the simpler problem. Use the solution to help you solve the original problem.

1. Anna can choose from white or yellow paper. She can choose from thin or wide paintbrushes. She can choose from green, purple, or blue paint. How many different combinations of art supplies are possible?

___

___

___

Name ____________________

PROBLEM-SOLVING STRATEGY **P 6-7**

Solve a Simpler Problem

Solve the simpler problems. Use the solutions to help you solve the original problem.

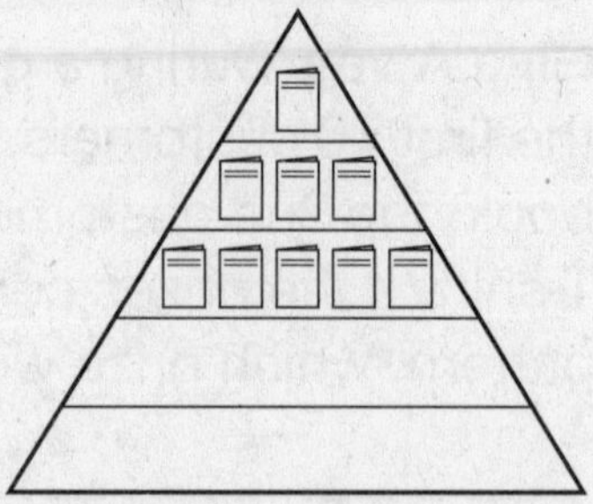

1. Reggie is designing a triangular magazine rack with 5 shelves. The top shelf will hold 1 magazine. The second shelf will hold 3 magazines, and the third shelf will hold 5 magazines. This pattern continues to the bottom shelf. How many magazines will the magazine rack hold altogether?

Simpler Problem What is the pattern?

____

____

How many magazines will the fourth shelf hold? ____________

How many magazines will the bottom shelf hold? ____________

Solution: ____________________

____

2. At the deli, you receive 1 free sub after you buy 8 subs. How many free subs will you receive from the deli if you buy 24 subs?

____

3. The chef has 5 different kinds of pasta and 3 different flavors of sauce. How many different meals is she able to make?

____

____

Name ______________________________

PROBLEM-SOLVING SKILL **R 6-8**

Writing to Describe

Use geometric terms to describe one characteristic of the lines in each group.

Group 1	Group 2
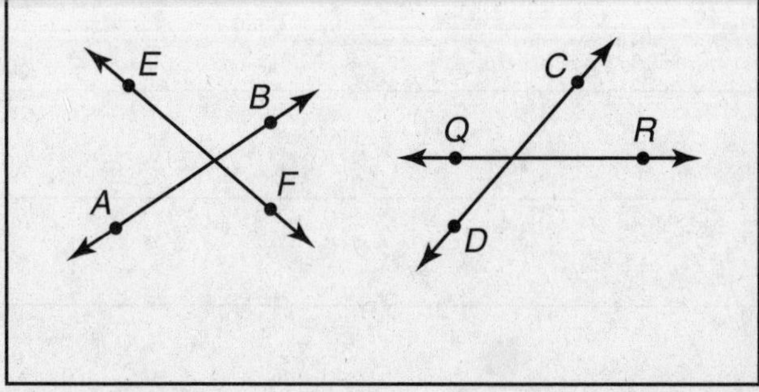	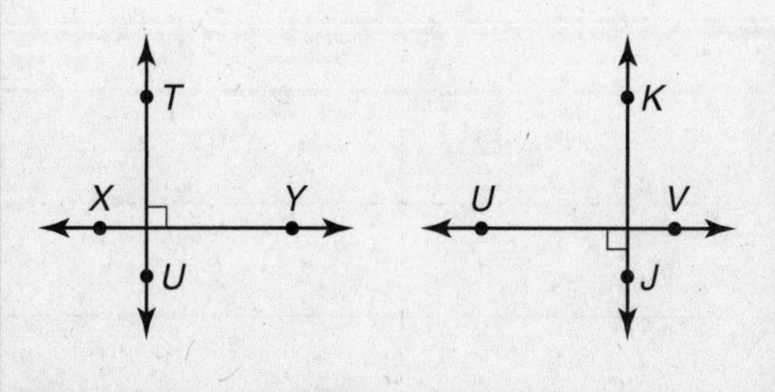

You can brainstorm to help you describe the characteristics.

Group 1	Group 2
no right angles	all right angles
not parallel	not parallel
all intersecting	all intersecting
no perpendicular lines	all perpendicular lines

When you write your description, use mathematical terms correctly and be brief.

All of the lines in Group 1 are intersecting and not perpendicular.

All of the lines in Group 2 are intersecting and are perpendicular.

1. Abdul sorted the polygons to the right into two groups. Use geometric terms to describe a characteristic in each group.

Group A	Group B
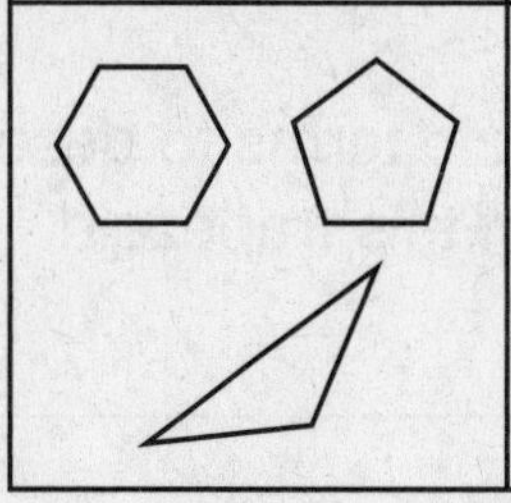	

Name ______________________________

PROBLEM-SOLVING SKILL

Writing to Describe

Solve each problem. You may use a brainstorming table to help plan your description.

1. Use geometric terms to describe three properties of a square.

____

____

____

2. Use mathematical terms to describe the numbers in each set.

____

____

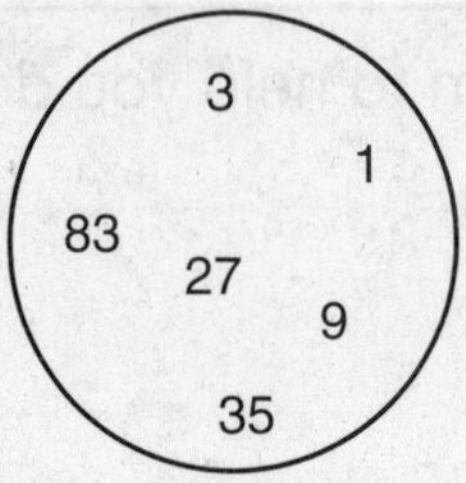

Set C

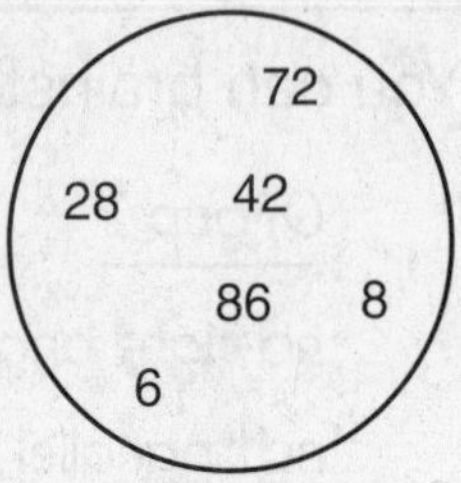

Set D

3. Mariam created two patterns. Use mathematical terms to describe the numbers in each pattern.

Pattern 1: 12, 16, 20, 24, 28, 32

Pattern 2: 1, 2, 4, 8, 16, 32, 64

____

____

4. Use geometric terms to describe three properties of this trapezoid.

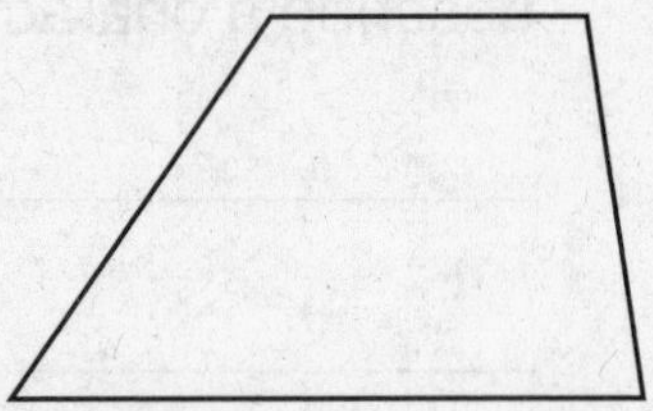

____

____

____

____

Name ____________________

Congruence and Similarity

R 6-9

Similar polygons have the same angle measures, but the lengths are different. Think: same shape, different size

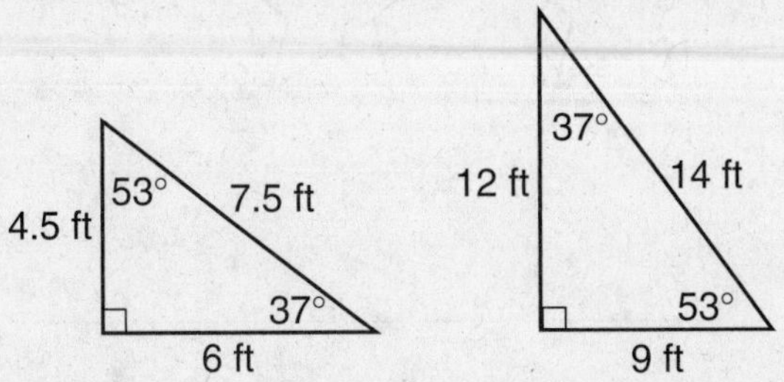

Congruent polygons have the same angle measures and the lengths of the sides are the same. Think: same shape, same size

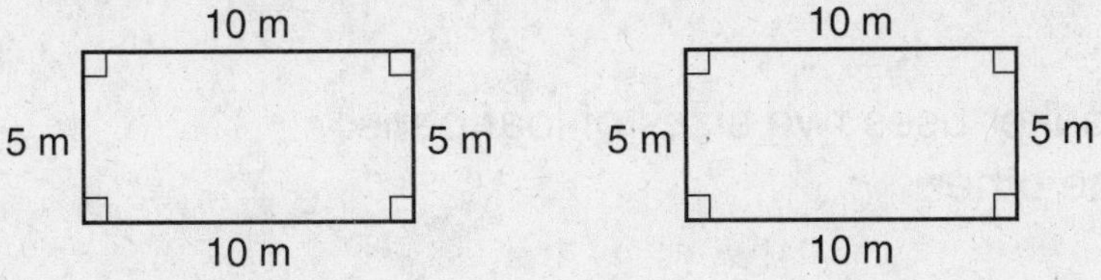

Do the figures in each pair appear to be similar? If so, are they also congruent?

1.

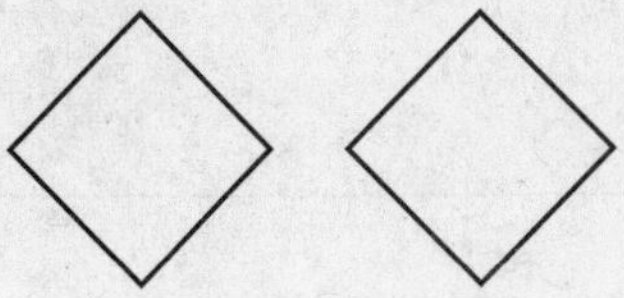

____

____

2.

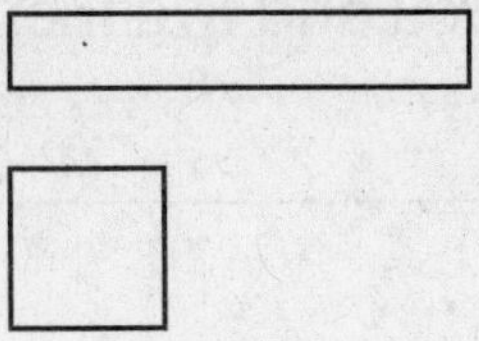

____

____

3.

____

____

4.

____

____

Name________________________________

Congruence and Similarity

P 6-9

Do the figures in each pair appear to be similar? If so, are they also congruent?

1.

2.

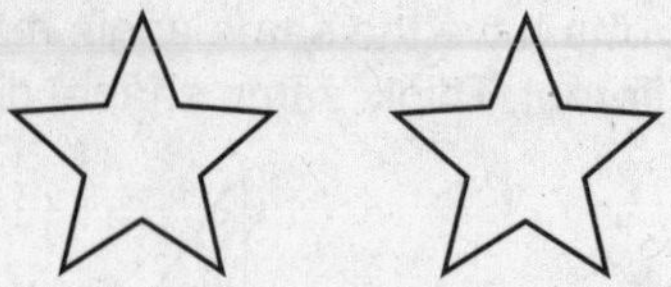

Is each situation an example of congruent or similar figures? Explain your reasoning.

3. When baking bread, the baker uses two sizes of loaf pans. One loaf pan fits inside the other.

4. A friend gave you and five friends each a quarter.

Test Prep

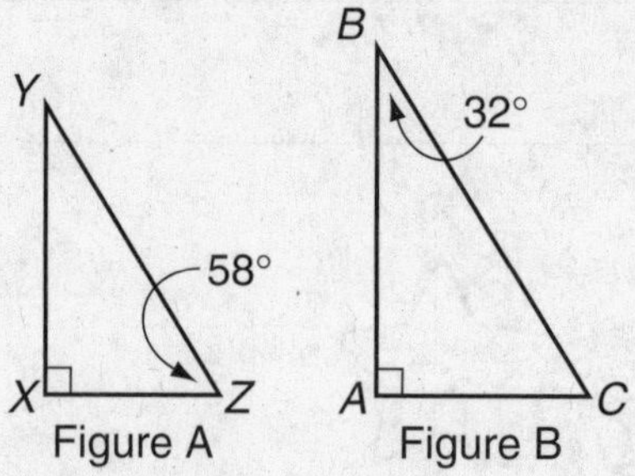

5. If Figure A is similar to Figure B, which is the measure of $\angle XYZ$ in Figure A?

A. 90° **B.** 58°

C. 45° **D.** 32°

6. Writing in Math If two circles are congruent, are the diameters the same length? Explain.

Name________________________________

Transformations

The size and shape of a figure do not change when it is slid, flipped, or turned.

1. A slide, or translation, moves a figure in a straight direction.

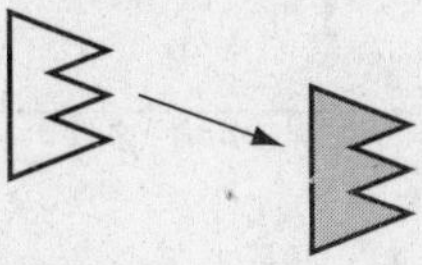

2. A flip, or reflection, of a figure gives its mirror image.

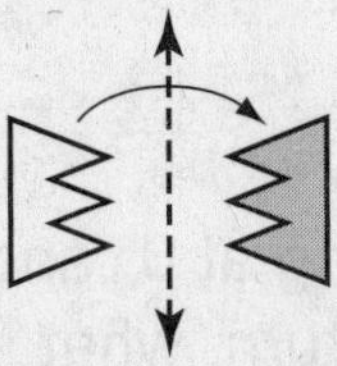

3. A turn, or rotation, moves a figure about a point.

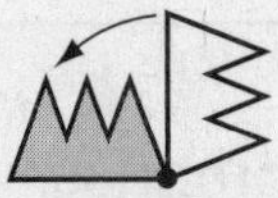

Turns can be measured in degrees. Here are some common turns.

90° or $\frac{1}{4}$ turn	180° or $\frac{1}{2}$ turn	270° or $\frac{3}{4}$ turn	360° or full turn
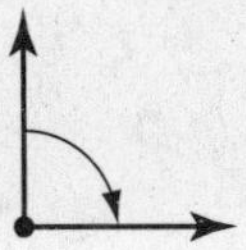		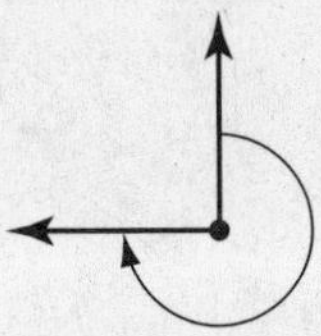	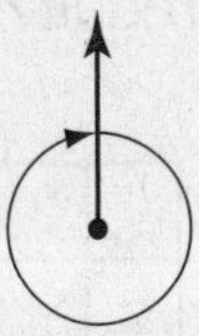

Tell whether the figures in each pair are related by a slide, a flip, or a turn. If a turn, tell what type of turn.

1. 

____

2. 

____

3. 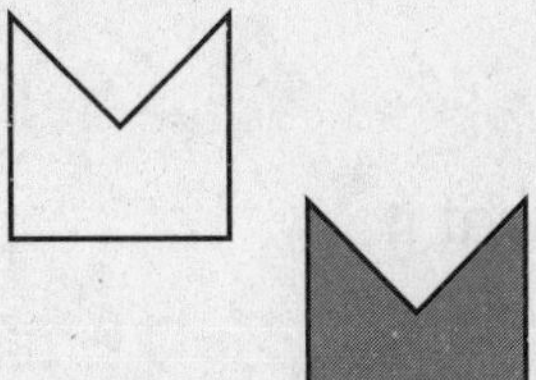

____

4. 

____

Name________________________________

Transformations

Tell whether the figures in each pair are related by a flip, slide, or turn. If a turn, describe it.

1. 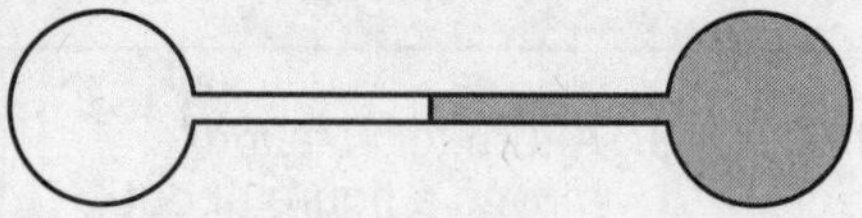

2. 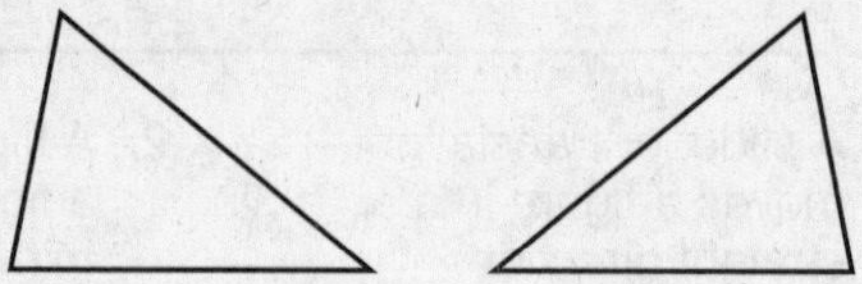

______________________ ______________________

3. On a compass, if you are standing at 0° and you turn to your right to make a 90° turn, what fraction of a turn is that? ______________

4. If a figure is flipped over the dashed line and then rotated a $\frac{1}{4}$ turn counterclockwise, which of the figures below shows the result?

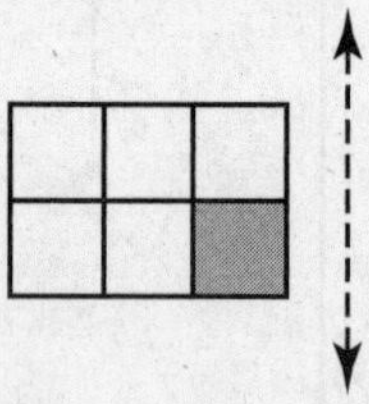

A. 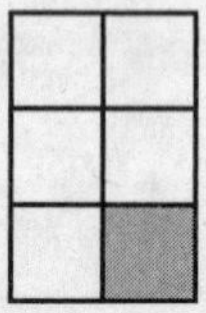 **B.** 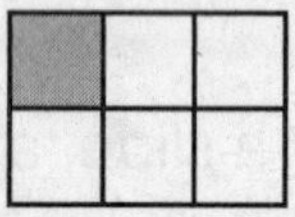 **C.** 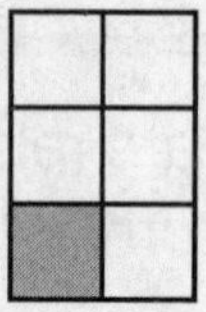 **D.** 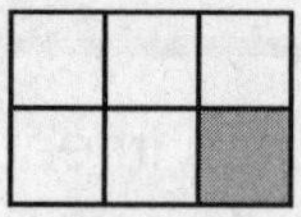

Test Prep

5. Which term describes the mirror image of a figure?

A. Slide **B.** Flip **C.** Turn **D.** Pattern

6. **Writing in Math** Mark says that the figure above was flipped. Faith says that it made a $\frac{3}{4}$ turn. Steven says that it made a 90° turn. Who is correct?

____

Name ______________________________

Symmetry

R 6-11

If a figure is symmetric, it can be split in half so that one side reflects onto the other side. The fold line is called the line of symmetry.

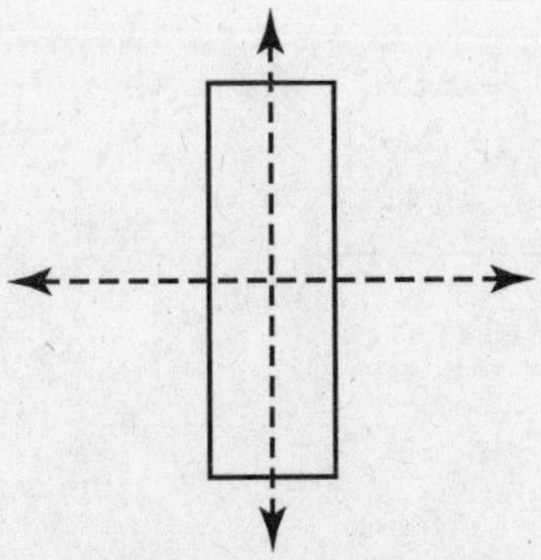

This figure has two lines of symmetry. If you folded along one of the lines, the two sides would fit on top of each other.

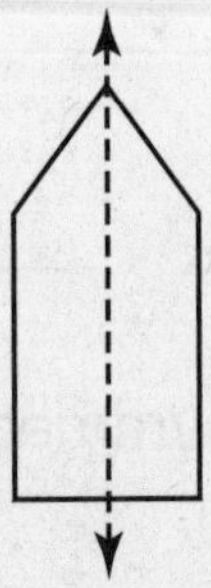

This figure has one line of symmetry. There is only one way to fold it exactly in half.

This figure has no lines of symmetry. It cannot be folded in half so that one side reflects onto the other side.

How many lines of symmetry does each figure have? You may trace the figure to check.

1. 

____

____

2. 

____

____

3. 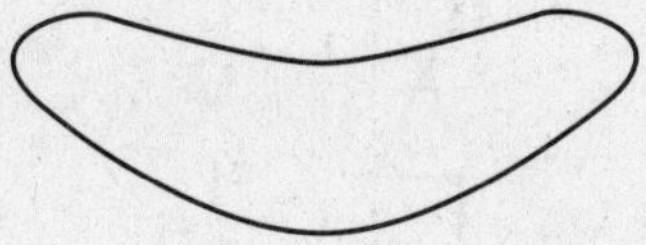

____

____

Part of a symmetric trademark is shown. Complete the drawing.

4. 

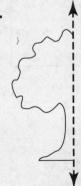

Name ____________________

Symmetry

How many lines of symmetry does each figure have? You may fold your paper to check.

1. 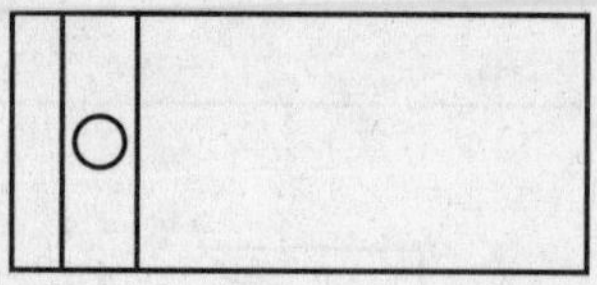

____

2. 

____

3. **Reasoning** How many lines of symmetry does an equilateral triangle have? Explain.

____

____

Part of a symmetric trademark is shown. Complete each drawing.

4. 

5. 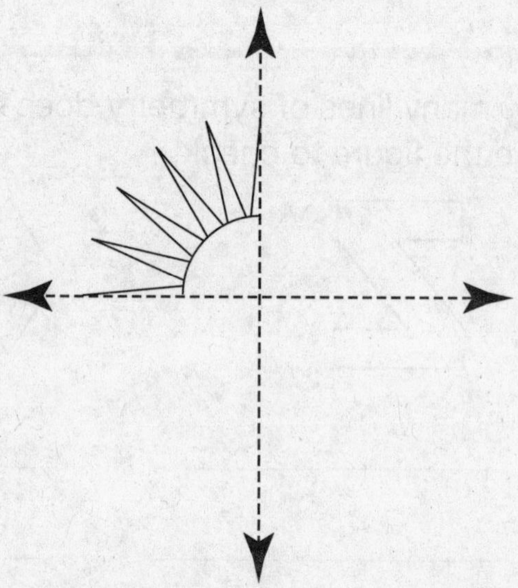

Test Prep

6. Which figure has more than two lines of symmetry?

A. 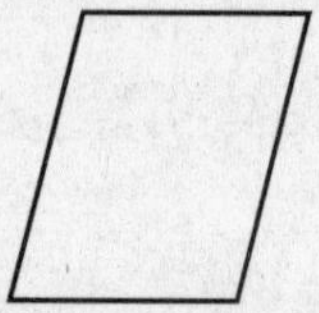

B. 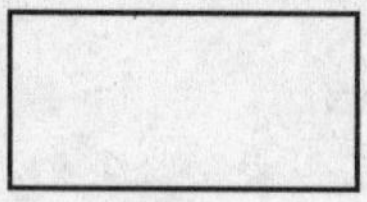

C. 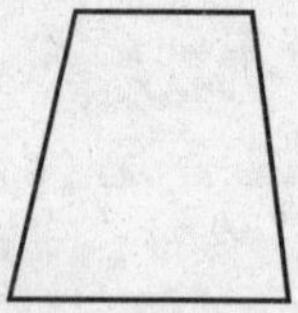

D. 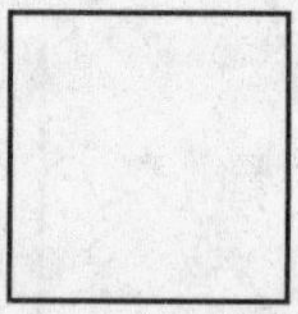

7. **Writing in Math** Draw a shape or figure that has more than 2 lines of symmetry. Put the lines of symmetry into your drawing.

Name

PROBLEM-SOLVING APPLICATIONS **R 6-12**

The Geometry of Life

Juanita and her friend Kim decided to meet at the park. Use geometric terms to describe the location of their houses and the park in relation to the line segment.

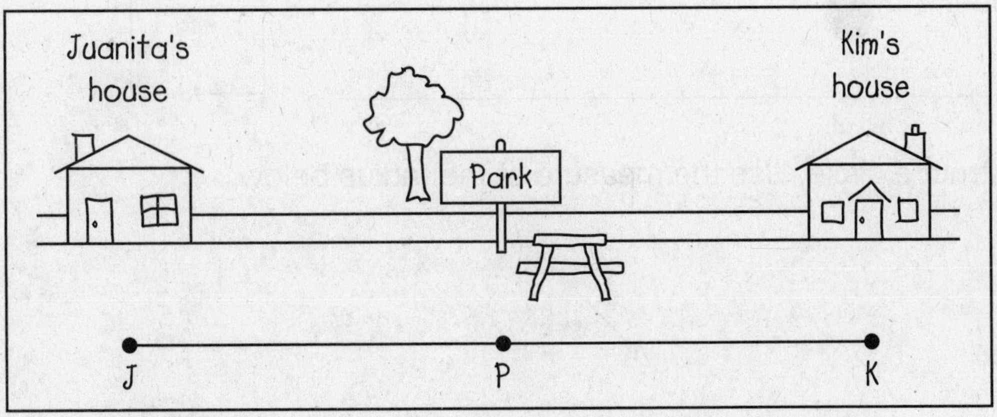

Juanita's house is located at point J on $\overline{JK}$. Kim's house is located at point K on $\overline{JK}$. The park is located at P, the midpoint of $\overline{JK}$.

Use the diagram above for question 1.

1. What is the shape of the chimney at Juanita's house?

____

2. Kenneth's mother ordered a pizza for his graduation party. The pizza has a diameter of 12 in. What is the measurement of the radius of the pizza? ______________

3. If it is 3:00 P.M., what is the measure of the angle that can be formed between the hour hand and the minute hand? ______________

4. Angelina saw the sign at the right. What is the name of this polygon?

____

Name ______________________________

PROBLEM-SOLVING APPLICATION **P 6-12**

The Shape We Are In

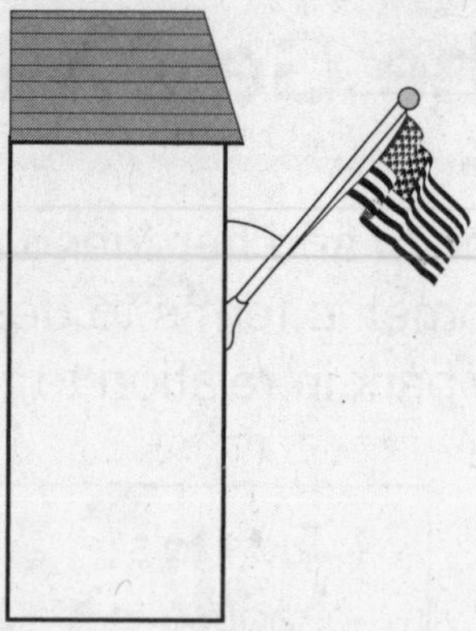

1. Tarah hung an American flag from the front porch of her house. She placed it in a flag stand on one of the posts of the porch. Measure the angle of the flagpole from the post.

____

2. Construct a circle. Use the measure of the radius below.

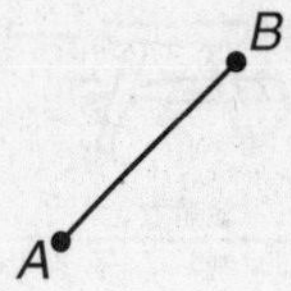

3. Karen and Willie took a walk on the streets near their home. The path of their walk is shown at the right. Classify the triangle formed by the path by its angles and its sides.

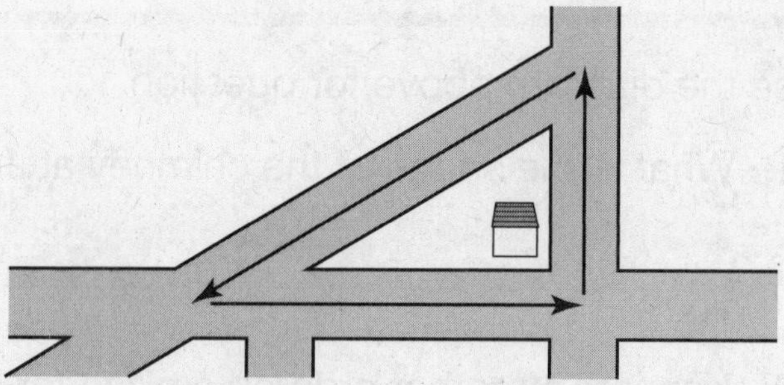

____

____

4. Part of a symmetric figure is shown. Complete the drawing.

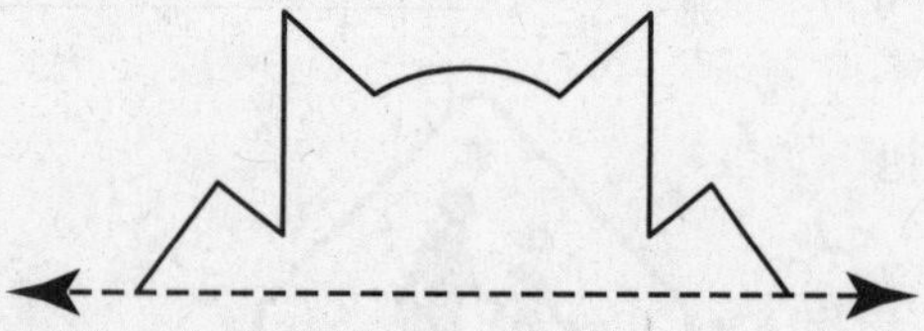

Name ____________________

Meanings of Fractions

R 7-1

What fraction of the set of shapes are squares?

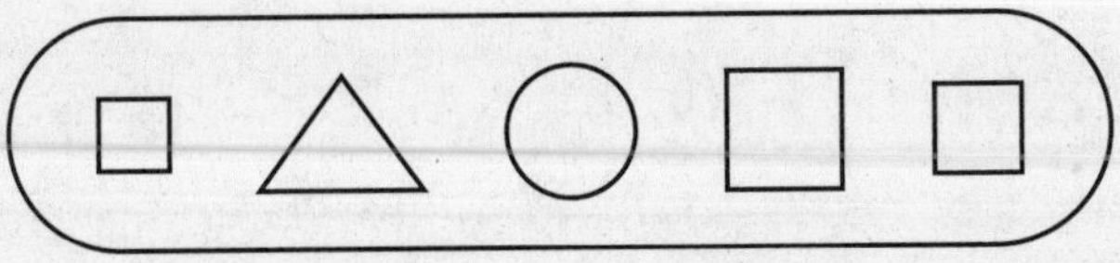

Step 1: Find the denominator.

How many shapes are there in the set?

There are 5 shapes in the set.

The denominator is the total number of shapes. So, the denominator is 5.

Step 2: Find the numerator.

How many squares are there in the set?

There are 3 squares in the set.

The numerator is the number of squares in the set. So, the numerator is 3.

Step 3: Write the fraction.

Write the numerator over the denominator.

$\frac{3}{5}$ 3 ⟵ Numerator, 5 ⟵ Denominator

$\frac{3}{5}$ of the set are squares.

Write the fraction that names the shaded part.

1. 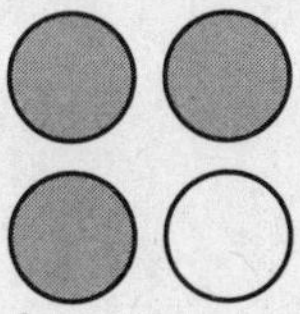

____

2. 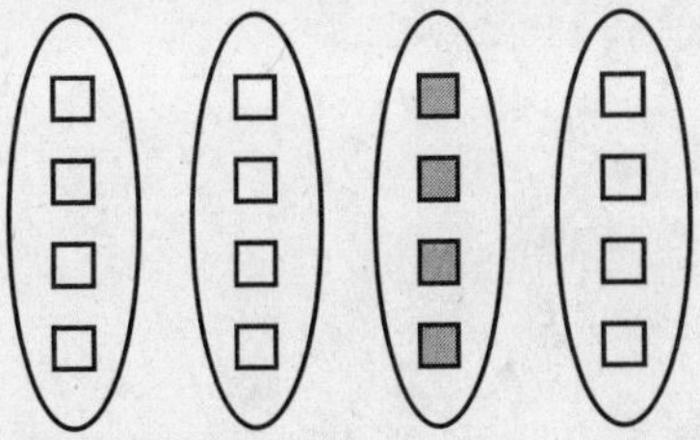

____

3. 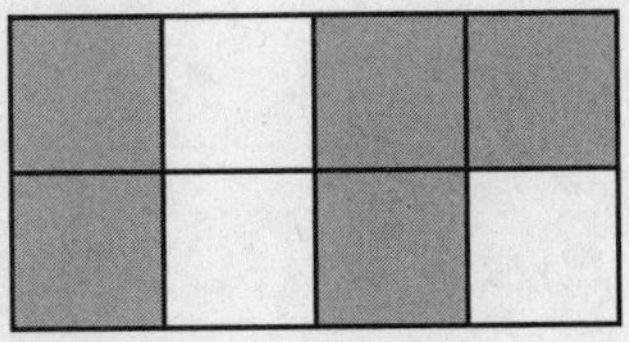

____

4. 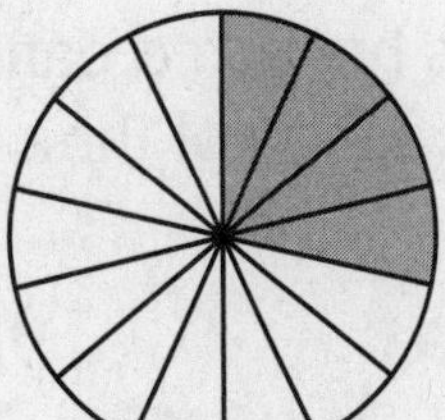

____

5. **Number Sense** If $\frac{1}{5}$ of a region is not shaded, what part is shaded? ________

6. Alex has 7 dimes and 3 nickels. What fraction of the coins are dimes? ________

Name ____________________

Meanings of Fractions

P 7-1

Write the fraction that names the shaded part or point on a number line.

1. 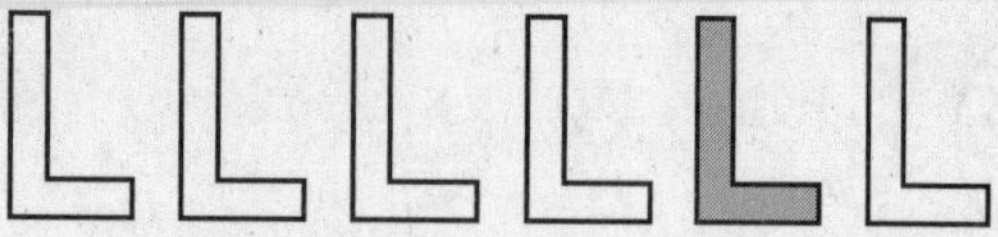

______

2. 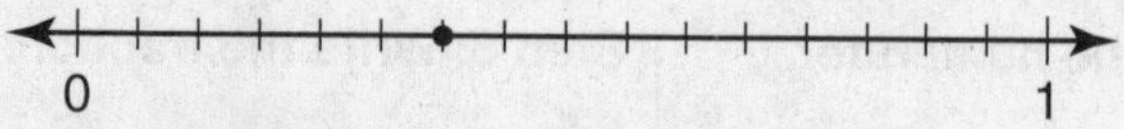

______

3. 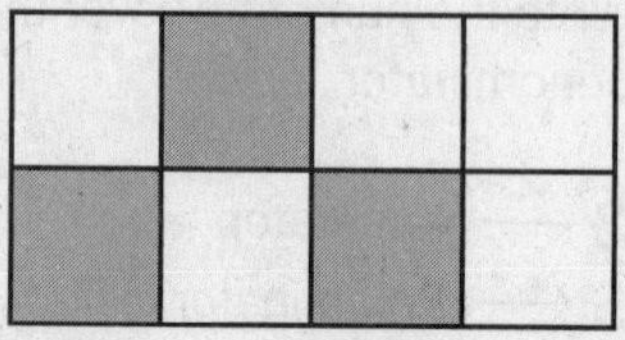

______

In 4 and 5, draw a model to show each fraction.

4. $\frac{4}{8}$ as part of a set

5. $\frac{5}{10}$ as part of a region

6. **Number Sense** If $\frac{5}{17}$ of a region is shaded, what part is not shaded?

______

7. Camp Big Trees has 3 red canoes and 4 blue canoes. What fraction of the canoes are red?

______

Test Prep

8. Which is the value of x, if $\frac{x}{9} = 1$?

A. 0 **B.** 1 **C.** 9 **D.** 19

9. **Writing in Math** Trisha says that if $\frac{5}{7}$ of her pencils are yellow, then $\frac{2}{7}$ are not yellow. Is she correct? Explain.

______

______

Name ___________________________________

Fractions and Division

R 7-2

Fractions can represent division. You can write a division expression as a fraction. For example:

Write a fraction for 5 ÷ 7.

The first number in the division expression is the numerator of the fraction. The second number in the division expression is the denominator of the fraction.

$5 \div 7 \rightarrow \frac{5}{7}$ — 5: Numerator; 7: Denominator

So, $5 \div 7 = \frac{5}{7}$.

Give each answer as a fraction.

1. 3 ÷ 10 ________ **2.** 7 ÷ 12 ________ **3.** 2 ÷ 3 ________

4. 8 ÷ 9 ________ **5.** 2 ÷ 5 ________ **6.** 1 ÷ 6 ________

7. 6 ÷ 10 ________ **8.** 9 ÷ 13 ________ **9.** 14 ÷ 16 ________

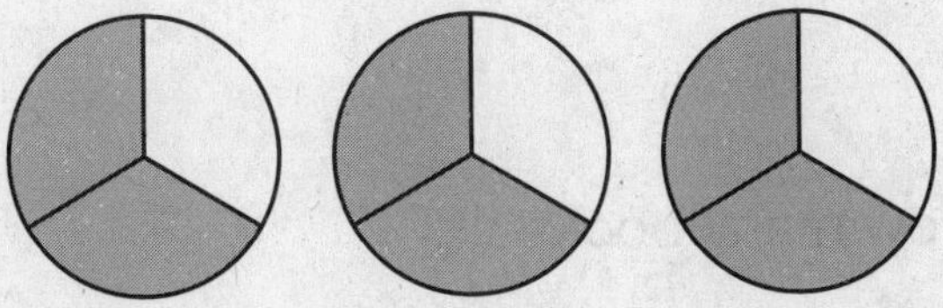

Reasoning Each of three congruent circles is divided into three equal parts. Use for 10–12.

10. What part of a whole circle is shown by the white, or unshaded, area of one circle? ________

11. What part of a whole circle is shown by the white, or unshaded, area of two circles? ________

12. What part of a whole circle is shown by the white, or unshaded, area of three circles? ________

Name ____________________

Fractions and Division

P 7-2

Give each answer as a fraction.

1. 3 ÷ 7 ______ **2.** 4 ÷ 9 ______ **3.** 1 ÷ 5 ______

4. 2 ÷ 11 ______ **5.** 3 ÷ 5 ______ **6.** 5 ÷ 8 ______

At a golf course, there are 18 holes. Of the 18 holes, 3 are par threes, 8 are par fours, and 7 are par fives. What fraction of the holes are

7. par fives? ______ **8.** par threes? ______ **9.** par fours? ______

10. Number Sense Explain how you know that 7 ÷ 9 is less than 1.

____

____

11. After school, Chase spends 20 min reading, 30 min practicing the piano, 15 min cleaning his room, and 40 min doing his homework. Chase is busy for 105 min. What fraction of the time does he spend cleaning his room? ______

Test Prep

12. Venietta read 4 books in 7 weeks. How many books did she read each week?

A. $\frac{6}{7}$ **B.** $\frac{4}{7}$ **C.** $\frac{3}{7}$ **D.** $\frac{2}{7}$

13. Writing in Math In 5 min, Peter completed 2 math problems. Yvonne says he did $\frac{3}{5}$ of a problem each minute. Is she correct? Explain.

____

____

____

Name ____________________

Mixed Numbers

A mixed number has a whole number and a fraction.

Whole number $\rightarrow 3\frac{5}{8} \leftarrow$ Fraction

An improper fraction has a numerator greater than or equal to its denominator.

$\frac{17}{9}$ ← Numerator is greater than denominator

How to write an improper fraction as a mixed number

$\frac{13}{4} = 13 \div 4$

- Divide the numerator by the denominator.
- Write the remainder as a fraction.

$$\begin{array}{r} 3 \\ 4\overline{)13} \\ -12 \\ \hline 1 \end{array}$$

$\frac{13}{4} = 3\frac{1}{4}$

How to write a mixed number as an improper fraction

$5\frac{1}{3}$ = what improper fraction?

- Multiply the denominator by the whole number: $3 \times 5 = 15$.
- Add the numerator: $15 + 1 = 16$.
- Use the same denominator.

$\frac{16}{3}$ ← $(3 \times 5) + 1$; 3 ← Same denominator from mixed number

$5\frac{1}{3} = \frac{16}{3}$

Write each improper fraction as a mixed number.

1. $\frac{8}{3}$ ______ **2.** $\frac{10}{7}$ ______ **3.** $\frac{5}{2}$ ______

4. $\frac{7}{4}$ ______ **5.** $\frac{13}{10}$ ______ **6.** $\frac{17}{15}$ ______

Write each mixed number as an improper fraction.

7. $1\frac{2}{5}$ ______ **8.** $4\frac{6}{7}$ ______ **9.** $2\frac{5}{8}$ ______

10. $3\frac{1}{2}$ ______ **11.** $5\frac{1}{6}$ ______ **12.** $3\frac{2}{9}$ ______

13. Algebra If $2\frac{n}{4} = \frac{9}{4}$, what is the value of n? ______

Name ____________________

Mixed Numbers

P 7-3

Write an improper fraction and a mixed number for each model.

1. 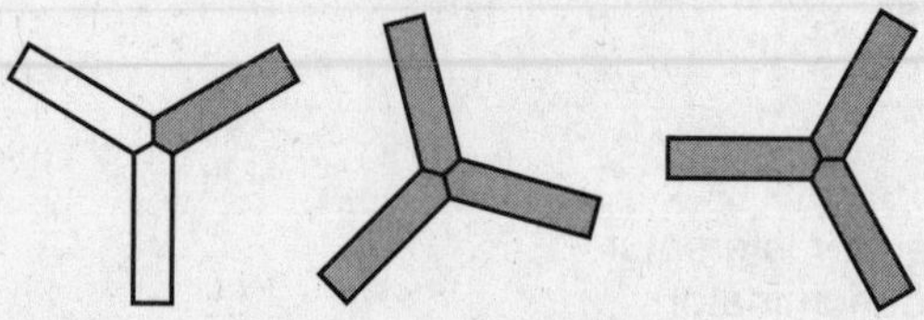 ____________

2. 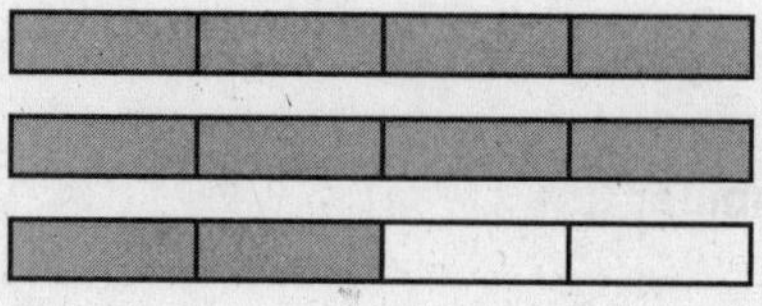 ____________

Write each improper fraction as a mixed number.

3. $\frac{12}{7}$ ________ **4.** $\frac{7}{3}$ ________ **5.** $\frac{5}{2}$ ________

6. $\frac{9}{4}$ ________ **7.** $\frac{29}{13}$ ________ **8.** $\frac{34}{8}$ ________

Write each mixed number as an improper fraction.

9. $2\frac{4}{5}$ ________ **10.** $8\frac{7}{9}$ ________ **11.** $3\frac{6}{7}$ ________

12. $7\frac{1}{8}$ ________ **13.** $4\frac{3}{7}$ ________ **14.** $5\frac{1}{4}$ ________

Test Prep

15. Jasmine has 41 lb of dog food to evenly pour into 5 dishes. How many pounds of dog food should she pour in each dish?

A. $4\frac{1}{5}$ lb **B.** $8\frac{1}{5}$ lb **C.** 10 lb **D.** $11\frac{1}{8}$ lb

16. Writing in Math Hank needs 3 quarters to play one video game each time. If he has 14 quarters, how many times can he play? Explain.

____

____

____

____

Name______________________________________

Estimating Fractional Amounts

Estimate the shaded part of the figure.

Think about benchmark fractions, which include $\frac{1}{4}$, $\frac{1}{3}$, $\frac{1}{2}$, $\frac{2}{3}$, and $\frac{3}{4}$. What benchmark fraction can you use to estimate the shaded region?

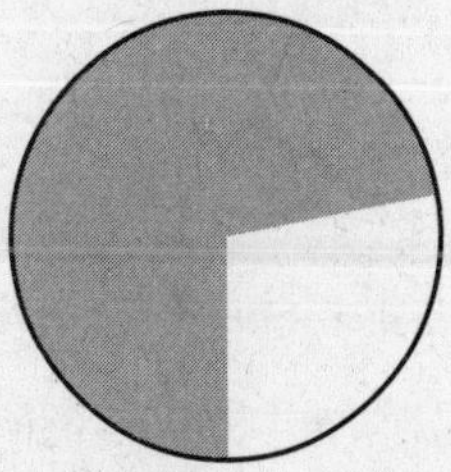

You can use $\frac{1}{4}$.

How many $\frac{1}{4}$ regions of the circle are shaded? 3

About $\frac{3}{4}$ of the circle is shaded.

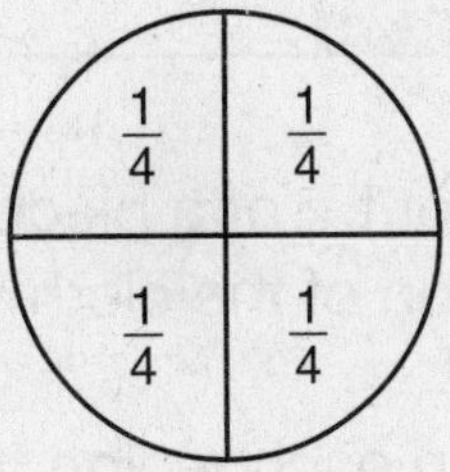

Estimate the shaded part of each.

1.

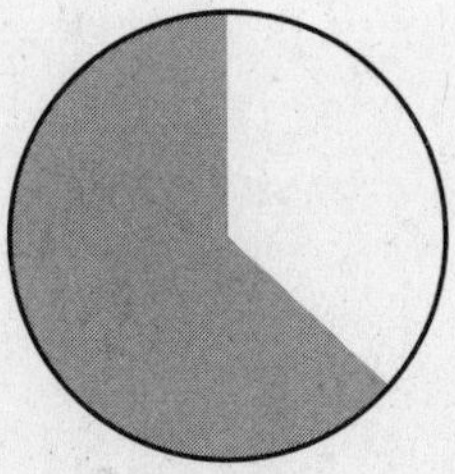

____

2.

____

3.

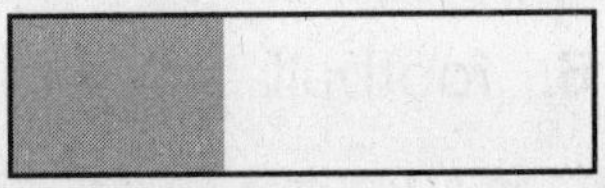

____

4. Reasoning Estimate the fraction of the clock that is between the minute and hour hand when it is almost 6:00.

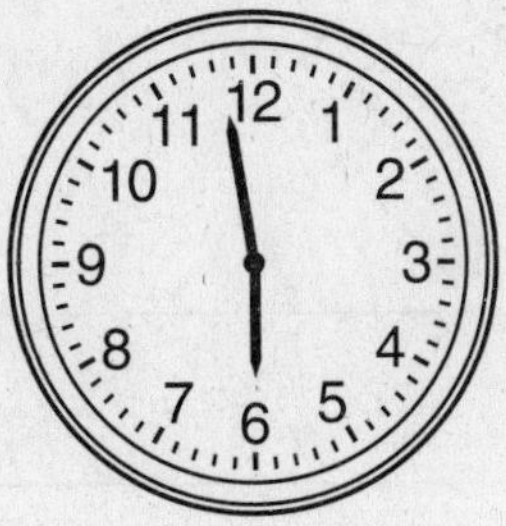

____

Name________________________________

Estimating Fractional Amounts

P 7-4

Estimate the shaded part of each.

1. 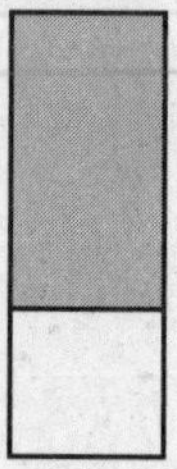 ________

2. 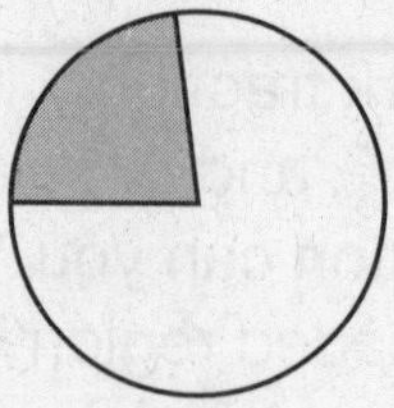 ________

3. 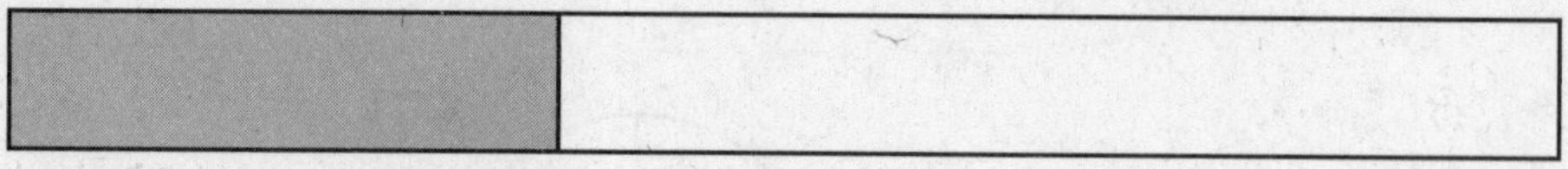 ________

4. Reasoning If about $\frac{2}{3}$ of a piece of cloth is used, about what fraction of the cloth was not used? ________

Estimate the fraction in each region for the most popular sports.

5. basketball ________

6. football ________

7. baseball ________

Favorite Sports

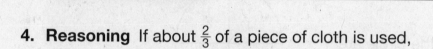

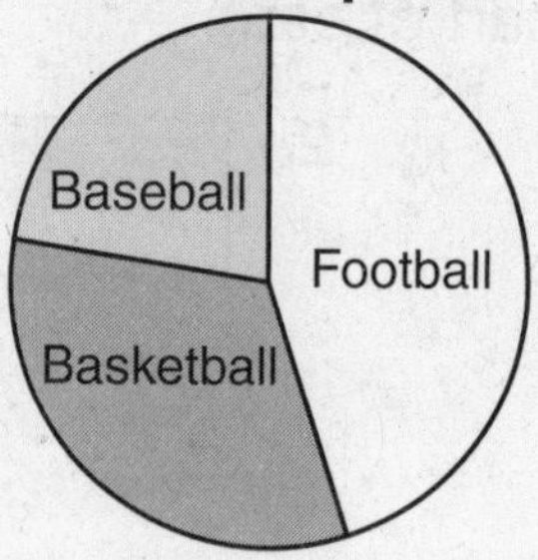

Test Prep

8. Jim ate about $\frac{1}{4}$ of the pizza, and Jane ate about $\frac{1}{4}$ of the pizza. About how much of the pizza is left?

A. $\frac{1}{4}$ **B.** $\frac{2}{5}$ **C.** $\frac{2}{8}$ **D.** $\frac{2}{4}$

9. Writing in Math Explain how you know that $\frac{1}{2}$ of a grapefruit is larger than $\frac{1}{2}$ of a grape.

____

____

____

Name ____

Fractions and Mixed Numbers on the Number Line

R 7-5

Locate points for $2\frac{1}{4}$, $\frac{3}{4}$, and $2\frac{2}{4}$ on a number line.
Then order them from least to greatest.

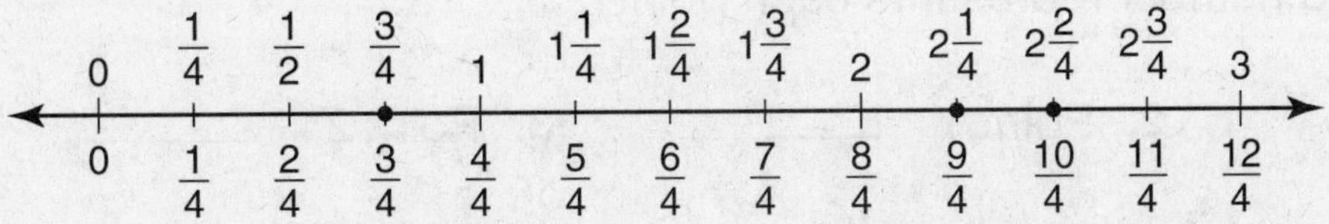

Since $2\frac{2}{4}$ is the number farthest to the right, it is the greatest.
Since $\frac{3}{4}$ is the farthest left, it is the least. Therefore,
$\frac{3}{4} < 2\frac{1}{4} < 2\frac{2}{4}$.

Which fraction or mixed number represents each point?

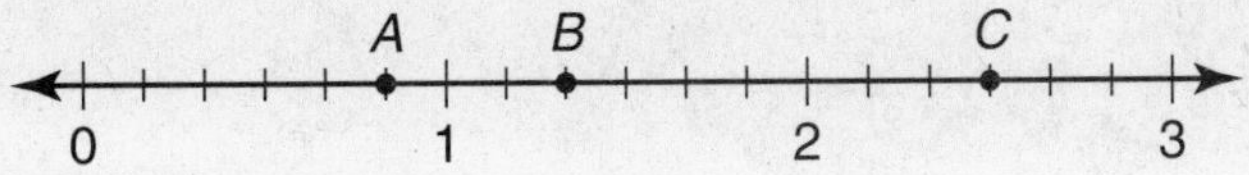

1. Point *A* ____________

2. Point *B* ____________

3. Point *C* ____________

Draw a number line to show each set of numbers.
Then order the numbers from least to greatest.

4. $\frac{13}{5}$, $2\frac{1}{5}$, $\frac{7}{5}$ ____________________

5. $1\frac{2}{4}$, $\frac{10}{4}$, $2\frac{3}{4}$ ____________________

Name ____________________

Fractions and Mixed Numbers on the Number Line

P 7-5

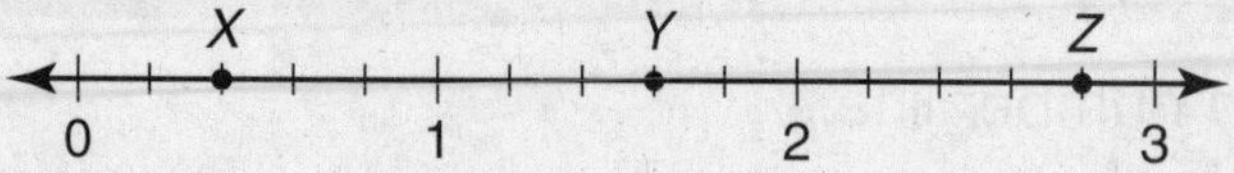

What fraction or mixed number represents each point?

1. Point *X* ________ **2.** Point *Y* ________ **3.** Point *Z* ________

Draw a number line to show each set of numbers. Then order the numbers from least to greatest.

4. $\frac{2}{3}, \frac{5}{6}, \frac{1}{6}$ ________

5. $1\frac{3}{4}, 1\frac{9}{10}, 1\frac{1}{2}$ ________

Test Prep

6. Which number would be to the right of $7\frac{9}{10}$ on a number line?

A. $7\frac{10}{12}$ **B.** $7\frac{7}{8}$ **C.** $7\frac{25}{30}$ **D.** $7\frac{10}{11}$

7. Writing in Math If, on a number line, point *R* is $3\frac{3}{8}$ and point *T* is $3\frac{7}{8}$, where could point *S* be if it is between points *R* and *T*? Explain.

____

____

____

Name ____________________

PROBLEM-SOLVING SKILL **R 7-6**

Extra or Missing Information

Casseroles Jackie is making casseroles. She has 4 blocks of cheese. Does she have enough cheese to make 6 casseroles?

Read and Understand

Step 1: What do you know? Jackie has 4 blocks of cheese. She wants to make 6 casseroles.

Step 2: What are you trying to find? You want to know if Jackie can make 6 casseroles with 4 blocks of cheese.

Plan and Solve

There is not enough information to solve the problem. To solve the problem, you need to know how much cheese Jackie uses in each casserole.

Decide if each problem has extra or missing information. Solve if you have enough information.

1. Donna bought one pair of shoes for $29.50 and another for half that price. She paid with a $50 bill. How much did the other pair of shoes cost?

____

2. Jorge is saving money from mowing lawns. He makes $5.00 for each lawn he mows. Jorge wants to buy a gift for his mother that costs $23.69. Does he have enough money?

____

3. Alexis runs $2\frac{1}{2}$ mi per day. She likes to run through the park near the river. Her friend Tony runs 4 mi per day. How far does Alexis run in 5 days?

____

Name ______________________

PROBLEM-SOLVING SKILL **P 7-6**

Extra or Missing Information

Decide if each problem has extra or missing information. Solve if you have enough information.

1. Jared and Cody went on a backpacking trip for 3 days. They brought 2 boxes of spaghetti. Each box weighed 16 oz. They also brought 4 cans of sauce. Each can weighed 8 oz. How many ounces did each person carry if each carried the same amount?

____

2. Each backpack weighed 25 lb and each tent weighed 3 lb. If there are 30 backpackers, how much did their backpacks weigh altogether?

____

For 3–5, use the table at the right.

Trail Name	Length
Hiawatha	6 mi
Pontiac	2 mi
Black Hawk	10 mi
Keokuk	7 mi

3. The backpackers hiked the Black Hawk trail on Monday. They planned to hike on Tuesday. What is the total number of trails they hiked on Monday and Tuesday?

____

4. How much longer is twice around the Black Hawk trail than twice around the Hiawatha trail?

____

5. Mariah hiked the Pontiac trail 5 days in 1 week. She did not hike on Wednesday and Friday. How many miles did she hike throughout 1 week?

____

Name ____________________

Understanding Equivalent Fractions

R 7-7

Find equivalent fractions for the shaded part of the set shown.

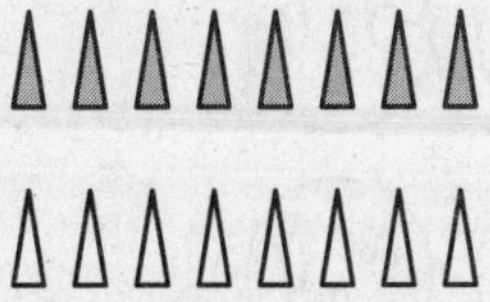

The fraction shown is $\frac{8}{16}$.

Divide the triangles into groups of 2.

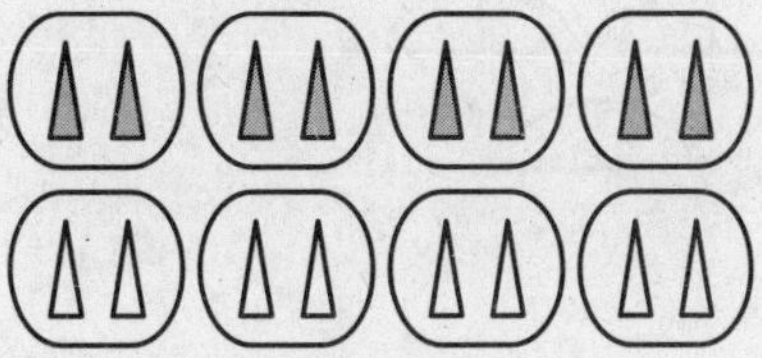

$\frac{4}{8}$ is equivalent to $\frac{8}{16}$.

Divide the triangles into groups of 4.

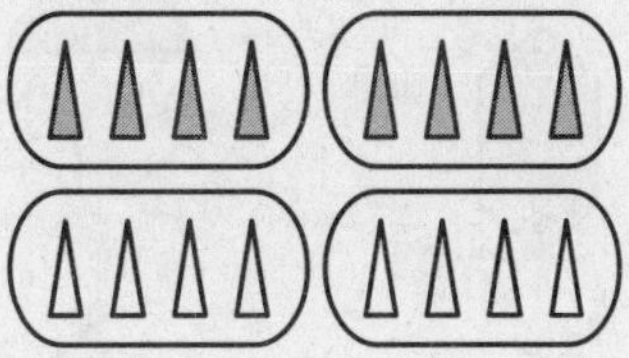

$\frac{2}{4}$ is equivalent to $\frac{8}{16}$.

Divide the triangles into groups of 8.

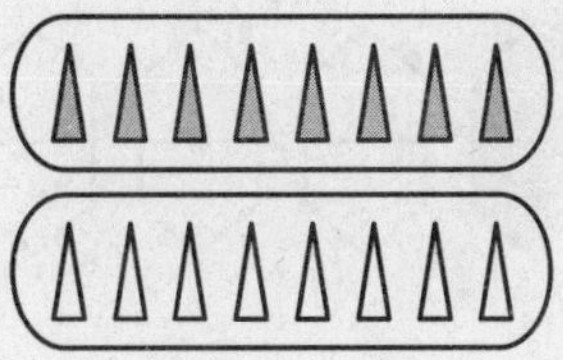

$\frac{1}{2}$ is equivalent to $\frac{8}{16}$.

Write two fractions that name each shaded part.

1.

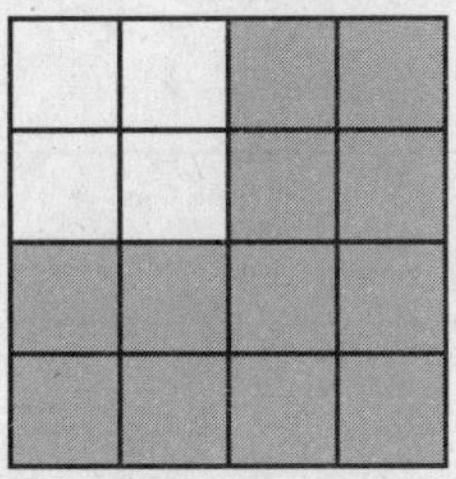

____

2.

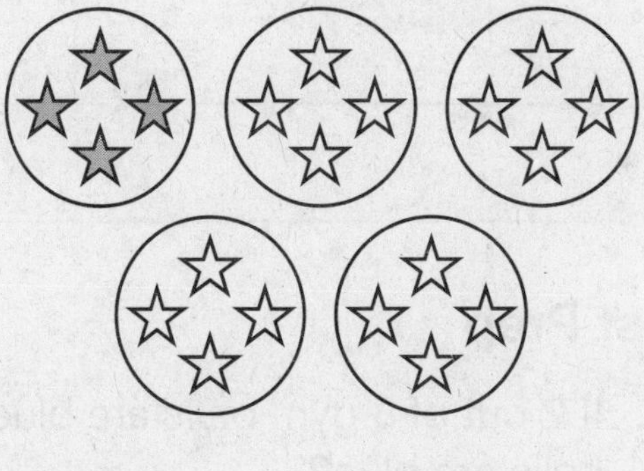

____

3. Writing in Math Explain how you could draw a picture to show $\frac{4}{5} = \frac{8}{10}$.

____

____

____

Name ____________________

Understanding Equivalent Fractions

P 7-7

Write two fractions that name each shaded part.

1.  ________

2. 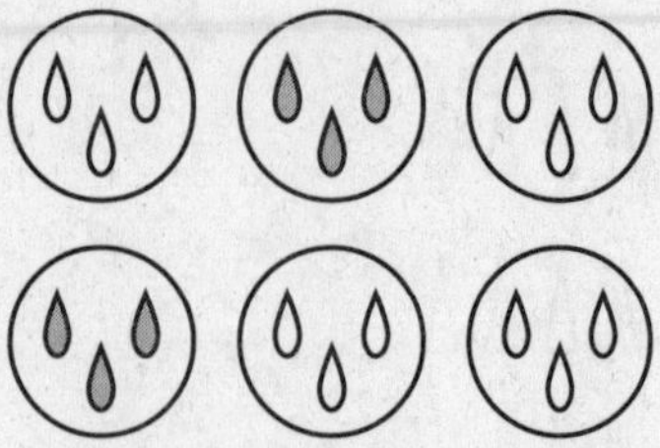 ________

3. 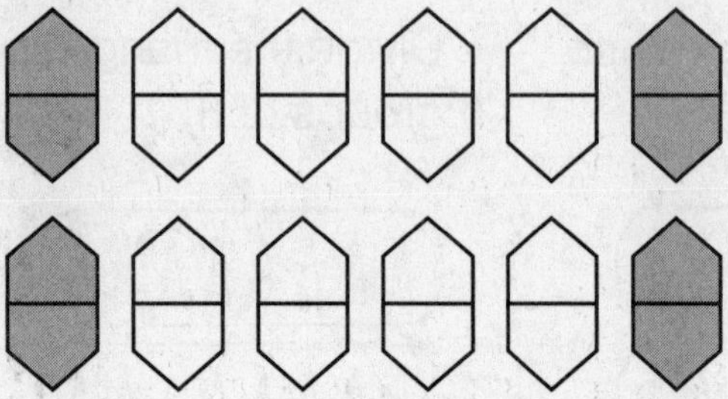 ________

4.  ________

5. Trinity attends 6 classes. Each class lasts 1 hr. Her younger sister attends 10 classes that last 30 min each. Who is in class longer? How much longer?

____

____

Test Prep

6. If 2 out of 3 gym balls are blue, how many out of 6 gym balls are blue?

A. 2 **B.** 3 **C.** 4 **D.** 5

7. **Writing in Math** Explain how you know that $\frac{4}{5} = \frac{8}{10}$.

____

____

____

Name ____

To find an equivalent fraction, multiply or divide the numerator and denominator of a fraction by the same nonzero number. For example:

Name a fraction equivalent to $\frac{3}{5}$.

$$\frac{3 \times 7}{5 \times 7} = \frac{21}{35} \qquad \frac{3}{5} = \frac{21}{35}$$

Both numerator and denominator were multiplied by 7.

Sometimes you must find a missing numerator or a denominator.

Find the missing denominator.

$\frac{3}{7} = \frac{6}{■}$

Think: What number times 3 equals 6?

Multiply 3 and 7 by 2.

$$\frac{3 \times 2}{7 \times 2} = \frac{\rightarrow 6}{\rightarrow 14}$$

So, $\frac{3}{7} = \frac{6}{14}$.

Find the missing numerator.

$\frac{6}{9} = \frac{■}{3}$

Think: What number can 9 be divided by to get 3?

Divide 6 and 9 by 3.

$$\frac{6 \div 3}{9 \div 3} = \frac{\rightarrow 2}{\rightarrow 3}$$

So, $\frac{6}{9} = \frac{2}{3}$.

Name two equivalent fractions for each fraction.

1. $\frac{1}{3}$ ________, ________

2. $\frac{2}{12}$ ________, ________

3. $\frac{4}{20}$ ________, ________

4. $\frac{2}{16}$ ________, ________

Find the missing number to make the fractions equivalent.

5. $\frac{4}{7} = \frac{8}{■}$ ________

6. $\frac{■}{18} = \frac{4}{6}$ ________

7. $\frac{3}{4} = \frac{■}{12}$ ________

8. $\frac{15}{■} = \frac{3}{4}$ ________

9. Number Sense Are $\frac{3}{4}$ and $\frac{12}{16}$ equivalent fractions? Explain.

____

Name ______________________________

Equivalent Fractions

Name two equivalent fractions for each fraction.

1. $\frac{5}{15}$ ____________ **2.** $\frac{6}{36}$ ____________ **3.** $\frac{2}{12}$ ____________

4. $\frac{4}{28}$ ____________ **5.** $\frac{3}{21}$ ____________ **6.** $\frac{2}{11}$ ____________

Find the missing number to make the fractions equivalent.

7. $\frac{9}{13} = \frac{18}{x}$ ____________ **8.** $\frac{12}{30} = \frac{n}{90}$ ____________

9. $\frac{q}{54} = \frac{2}{9}$ ____________ **10.** $\frac{14}{h} = \frac{7}{20}$ ____________

11. Renie gave each of six people $\frac{1}{10}$ of a veggie pizza. Renie has $\frac{2}{5}$ of the pizza left. Explain how this is true.

____

____

____

Test Prep

12. Which fraction is equivalent to $\frac{3}{7}$?

A. $\frac{3}{6}$ **B.** $\frac{6}{14}$ **C.** $\frac{3}{17}$ **D.** $\frac{7}{7}$

13. Writing in Math Jacqueline has four \$5 bills. She bought a shirt for \$10. She has spent half of her money. Explain how much money Jacqueline spent. Use equivalent fractions.

____

____

____

____

____

Name____

Greatest Common Factor

The greatest common factor (GCF) of two numbers is the greatest number that is a factor of both.

Find the greatest common factor of 12 and 18.

Step 1: List the factors of 12 and 18. Think of all the numbers that can be divided into 12 and 18 evenly.

12: 1, 2, 3, 4, 6, 12

18: 1, 2, 3, 6, 9, 18

Step 2: Circle the common factors.

12: (1), (2), (3), 4 , (6), 12

18: (1), (2), (3), (6), 9 , 18

Step 3: Find the greatest common factor.

The greatest common factor of 12 and 18 is 6.

Find the GCF of each pair of numbers.

1. 9, 27 ______ **2.** 25, 40 ______

3. 7, 36 ______ **4.** 40, 48 ______

5. 16, 28 ______ **6.** 24, 42 ______

7. 21, 35 ______ **8.** 30, 70 ______

9. Number Sense Can the GCF of 18 and 36 be greater than 18? Explain.

____

____

____

____

Name ______________________

Greatest Common Factor

P 7-9

Find the GCF of each pair of numbers.

1. 15, 50 ________ **2.** 6, 27 ________ **3.** 10, 25 ________

4. 18, 32 ________ **5.** 7, 28 ________ **6.** 54, 108 ________

7. 25, 55 ________ **8.** 14, 48 ________ **9.** 81, 135 ________

10. Number Sense Can the GCF of 16 and 42 be less than 16? Explain.

____

____

____

11. A restaurant received a shipment of 42 gal of orange juice and 18 gal of cranberry juice. The juice needs to be equally poured into containers. What is the largest amount of juice that each container can hold of each kind of juice? ________

12. At a day camp, there are 56 girls and 42 boys. The campers need to be split into equal groups. Each has either all girls or all boys. What is the greatest number of campers each group can have? ________

Test Prep

13. Which is the GCF of 24 and 64?

A. 4 **B.** 8 **C.** 14 **D.** 12

14. Writing in Math Do all even numbers have 2 as a factor? Explain.

____

____

____

Name ______________________

Fractions in Simplest Form

R 7-10

There are two different ways to write a fraction in simplest form.

Write $\frac{20}{24}$ in simplest form.

Divide by Common Factors

- Divide by common factors until the only common factor is 1.
- You can start by dividing by 2, since both numbers are even.

$$\frac{20 \div 2}{24 \div 2} = \frac{10}{12}$$

But both 10 and 12 can be divided by 2.

$$\frac{10 \div 2}{12 \div 2} = \frac{5}{6}$$

Divide by the GCF

- First find the GCF of 20 and 24.

20: 1, 2, 4, 5, 10, 20

24: 1, 2, 3, 4, 6, 8, 12, 24

The GCF of 20 and 24 is 4.

- Divide both numerator and denominator by 4.

$$\frac{20 \div 4}{24 \div 4} = \frac{5}{6}$$

Write each fraction in simplest form.

1. $\frac{16}{20}$ ______
2. $\frac{8}{16}$ ______
3. $\frac{5}{10}$ ______
4. $\frac{8}{32}$ ______
5. $\frac{18}{42}$ ______
6. $\frac{15}{100}$ ______
7. $\frac{18}{21}$ ______
8. $\frac{24}{40}$ ______
9. $\frac{55}{75}$ ______

10. **Number Sense** Explain how you can tell that $\frac{31}{33}$ is in simplest form.

____

____

____

____

____

____

Name ______________________

Fractions in Simplest Form

Write each fraction in simplest form.

1. $\frac{5}{10}$ ________ **2.** $\frac{6}{24}$ ________ **3.** $\frac{9}{27}$ ________

4. $\frac{3}{15}$ ________ **5.** $\frac{10}{12}$ ________ **6.** $\frac{9}{15}$ ________

7. $\frac{2}{18}$ ________ **8.** $\frac{25}{60}$ ________ **9.** $\frac{12}{72}$ ________

10. $\frac{30}{70}$ ________ **11.** $\frac{22}{48}$ ________ **12.** $\frac{16}{56}$ ________

13. $\frac{9}{90}$ ________ **14.** $\frac{72}{81}$ ________ **15.** $\frac{7}{28}$ ________

16. Number Sense Explain how you can tell $\frac{4}{5}$ is in simplest form.

____

____

____

Write in simplest form.

Math Test

⇒ 20 Multiple-choice problems
⇒ 10 Fill in the blanks
⇒ 5 Word problems

17. What fraction of the problems on the math test will be word problems?

____

18. What fraction of the problems on the math test will be multiple-choice problems? ________________

Test Prep

19. Which is the simplest form of $\frac{10}{82}$?

A. $\frac{1}{8}$ **B.** $\frac{1}{22}$ **C.** $\frac{10}{82}$ **D.** $\frac{5}{41}$

20. Writing in Math Explain how you can find the simplest form of $\frac{100}{1,000}$.

____

____

Name ____________________

Understanding Comparing Fractions R 7-11

You can use fraction strips to compare fractions.

Compare $\frac{3}{4}$ and $\frac{7}{10}$.

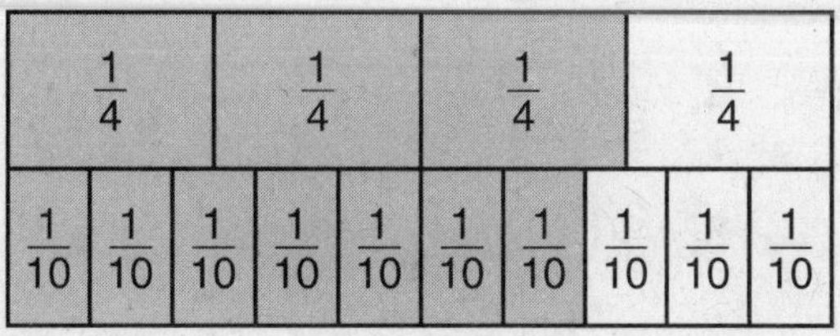

So, $\frac{3}{4} > \frac{7}{10}$.

Write >, <, or = for each ◯.

You may use fraction strips or drawings to help.

1. $\frac{1}{8}$ ◯ $\frac{3}{10}$ **2.** $\frac{3}{4}$ ◯ $\frac{4}{10}$ **3.** $\frac{4}{8}$ ◯ $\frac{2}{4}$ **4.** $\frac{2}{3}$ ◯ $\frac{3}{4}$

5. Number Sense Explain how you can tell $\frac{26}{100}$ is greater than $\frac{1}{4}$.

____

____

____

Dish	Flour Needed
Casserole	$\frac{9}{10}$ c
Breaded beef	$\frac{3}{4}$ c
Enchiladas	$\frac{5}{8}$ c
Waffles	$\frac{1}{2}$ c

6. Which dish needs the most flour?

____

7. Which needs more flour, breaded beef or enchiladas?

____

Name ____________________

Understanding Comparing Fractions P 7-11

Write >, <, or = for each ◯. You may use fraction strips or drawings to help.

1. $\frac{4}{12}$ ◯ $\frac{4}{16}$

2. $\frac{7}{14}$ ◯ $\frac{3}{5}$

3. $\frac{5}{10}$ ◯ $\frac{1}{2}$

4. $\frac{1}{9}$ ◯ $\frac{1}{6}$

5. $\frac{2}{6}$ ◯ $\frac{2}{7}$

6. $\frac{3}{9}$ ◯ $\frac{1}{3}$

7. $\frac{4}{5}$ ◯ $\frac{5}{10}$

8. $\frac{6}{10}$ ◯ $\frac{7}{8}$

9. **Number Sense** Kelvin says that $\frac{22}{30}$ is greater than $\frac{22}{32}$. Do you agree? Explain.

____

____

____

____

10. Jane bought $\frac{3}{5}$ lb of apples. Jack bought $\frac{2}{7}$ lb of apples. Who bought more pounds of apples? ____________

11. Lyman and Amalia each painted part of the garage and their dad painted the rest. Lyman painted $\frac{2}{6}$ of the garage. Amalia painted $\frac{2}{8}$ of the garage. Who painted more? ____________

Test Prep

12. Which of the fractions is less than $\frac{1}{3}$?

A. $\frac{2}{7}$ **B.** $\frac{2}{6}$ **C.** $\frac{2}{3}$ **D.** $\frac{3}{4}$

13. **Writing in Math** How do you know $\frac{72}{80}$ is greater than $\frac{7}{8}$? Explain.

____

____

Name ______________________________

Comparing and Ordering Fractions and Mixed Numbers

R 7-12

Compare $\frac{4}{10}$ and $\frac{5}{12}$.

One way to compare fractions is to find a common denominator.

10: 10, 20, 30, 40, 50, 60

12: 12, 24, 36, 48, 60, 72

Use 60 as the common denominator.

$\frac{4}{10} = \frac{24}{60}$ (× 6) $\frac{5}{12} = \frac{25}{60}$ (× 5)

Then compare:

$\frac{25}{60} > \frac{24}{60}$, so $\frac{5}{12} > \frac{4}{10}$.

How to order fractions.

Write $\frac{2}{3}$, $\frac{1}{6}$, and $\frac{1}{3}$ in order from least to greatest.

$\frac{2}{3} > \frac{1}{3}$ because the denominators are the same and $2 > 1$.

$\frac{1}{3} > \frac{1}{6}$ because $\frac{1}{3} = \frac{2}{6}$ (× 2) and $\frac{2}{6} > \frac{1}{6}$.

So $\frac{1}{6} < \frac{1}{3} < \frac{2}{3}$.

Compare. Write >, <, or = for each ◯.

1. $\frac{2}{3}$ ◯ $\frac{1}{6}$ **2.** $\frac{3}{4}$ ◯ $\frac{1}{2}$ **3.** $\frac{6}{8}$ ◯ $\frac{9}{12}$ **4.** $\frac{5}{6}$ ◯ $\frac{21}{24}$

Order the numbers from least to greatest.

5. $\frac{4}{5}, \frac{3}{5}, \frac{3}{4}$ ______, ______, ______

6. $\frac{6}{12}, \frac{3}{12}, \frac{1}{3}$ ______, ______, ______

7. $2\frac{1}{4}, 1\frac{3}{8}, 2\frac{2}{4}$ ______, ______, ______

8. $1\frac{5}{6}, 1\frac{3}{6}, 1\frac{2}{12}$ ______, ______, ______

9. Number Sense Explain why $\frac{5}{6} < \frac{13}{15}$.

____

____

____

____

Name ______________________________

Comparing and Ordering Fractions and Mixed Numbers

Compare. Write >, <, or = for each ◯.

1. $\frac{6}{7}$ ◯ $\frac{6}{8}$
2. $\frac{4}{9}$ ◯ $\frac{2}{3}$
3. $1\frac{1}{10}$ ◯ $1\frac{1}{12}$
4. $2\frac{4}{5}$ ◯ $2\frac{5}{6}$
5. $3\frac{6}{9}$ ◯ $3\frac{2}{3}$
6. $\frac{2}{5}$ ◯ $\frac{2}{8}$

Order the numbers from least to greatest.

7. $\frac{4}{5}, \frac{4}{8}, \frac{3}{4}, \frac{5}{8}$ ______________________

8. $4\frac{1}{4}, 4\frac{1}{8}, 4\frac{10}{11}, 4\frac{2}{15}$ ______________________

9. $1\frac{3}{7}, 1\frac{3}{4}, 1\frac{2}{4}, 1\frac{8}{13}$ ______________________

10. **Number Sense** How do you know that $5\frac{1}{4}$ is less than $5\frac{4}{10}$?

____

____

11. A mechanic uses four wrenches to fix Mrs. Aaron's car. The wrenches are different sizes: $\frac{5}{16}$ in., $\frac{1}{2}$ in., $\frac{1}{4}$ in., and $\frac{7}{16}$ in. Order the sizes of the wrenches from greatest to least.

____

Test Prep

12. Which is greater than $6\frac{1}{3}$?

A. $6\frac{1}{6}$ **B.** $6\frac{1}{5}$ **C.** $6\frac{1}{4}$ **D.** $6\frac{1}{2}$

13. **Writing in Math** Compare $3\frac{3}{22}$ and $3\frac{2}{33}$. Which is greater? How do you know?

____

____

____

Name ____________________

Fractions and Decimals

R 7-13

Fractions can also be named using decimals.

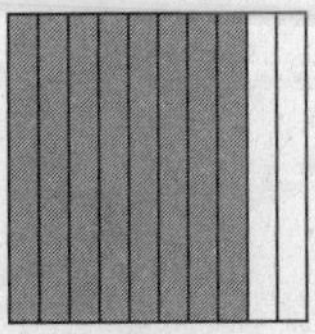

8 out of 10 sections are shaded.

The fraction is $\frac{8}{10}$.

The word name is eight tenths.

The decimal is 0.8.

Write $\frac{2}{5}$ as a decimal.

Sometimes a fraction can be rewritten as an equivalent fraction that has a denominator of 10 or 100.

$\frac{2}{5} = \frac{2 \times 2}{5 \times 2} = \frac{4}{10}$

$\frac{4}{10} = 0.4$

So, $\frac{2}{5} = 0.4$.

Write $3\frac{3}{5}$ as a decimal.

First write the whole number.

3

Change the fraction to a decimal.

$\frac{3}{5} = \frac{3 \times 2}{5 \times 2} = \frac{6}{10} = 0.6$

Write the decimal next to the whole number.

3.6

So, $3\frac{3}{5} = 3.6$.

Write 0.07 as a fraction.

The word name for 0.07 is seven hundredths.

"Seven" is the numerator, and "hundredths" is the denominator.

So, $0.07 = \frac{7}{100}$.

Write each fraction or mixed number as a decimal.

1. $\frac{1}{5}$ ________ **2.** $\frac{6}{25}$ ________ **3.** $2\frac{3}{4}$ ________ **4.** $3\frac{9}{10}$ ________

Write each decimal as a fraction or mixed number in simplest form.

5. 1.25 ____________ **6.** 3.29 ____________

7. 0.65 ____________ **8.** 5.6 ____________

9. **Number Sense** Dan says $\frac{3}{5}$ is the same as 3.5. Is he correct? Explain.

____

____

____

____

Name ______________________________

Fractions and Decimals

P 7-13

Write a decimal and a fraction in simplest form for the shaded portion of each model.

1. 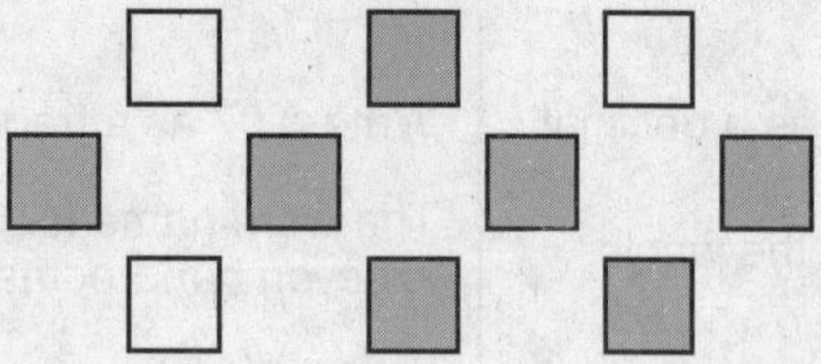

____

2. 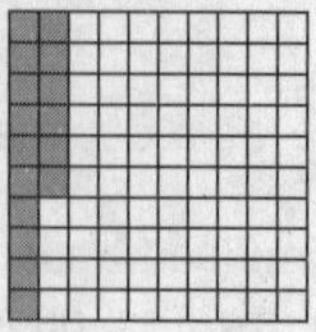

____

Write each decimal as a fraction or mixed number in simplest form.

3. 2.25 ______________

4. 3.74 ______________

5. 0.08 ______________

6. 0.375 ______________

Write each fraction or mixed number as a decimal.

7. $\frac{2}{16}$ ______________

8. $10\frac{3}{4}$ ______________

9. $7\frac{2}{5}$ ______________

10. $\frac{8}{40}$ ______________

11. In Ron's school, 12 out of 30 students wear brown shoes. Write the decimal that shows the portion of students who wear brown shoes. ______________

Test Prep

12. Which is the decimal equivalent of the mixed number $3\frac{3}{6}$?

A. 3.36 **B.** 3.5 **C.** 3.56 **D.** 3.63

13. Writing in Math Explain how knowing that $5 \div 8 = 0.625$ helps you find the decimal for $4\frac{5}{8}$.

____

____

____

Name ____________________

Fractions and Decimals on the Number Line

R 7-14

Show $\frac{2}{5}$, 1.2, and $1\frac{3}{5}$ on the same number line.

Step 1: Write each fraction or mixed number as a decimal.

$$\frac{2}{5} = \frac{2 \times 2}{5 \times 2} = \frac{4}{10} = 0.4$$

$$1.2 = 1.2$$

$$1\frac{3}{5} = 1\frac{6}{10} = 1.6$$

Step 2: Place the numbers on the number line.

The point for $\frac{2}{5}$ or 0.4 is between 0 and 1.

The point for $1\frac{3}{5}$ or 1.6 is between 1 and 2.

The point for 1.2 is between 1 and 2.

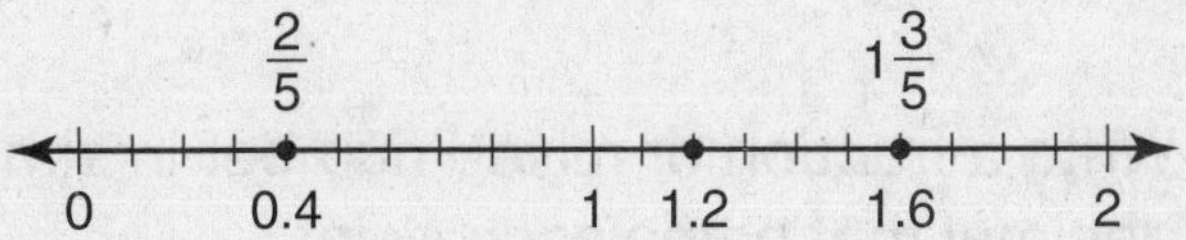

Write a fraction or a mixed number in simplest form and a decimal that name point *A*.

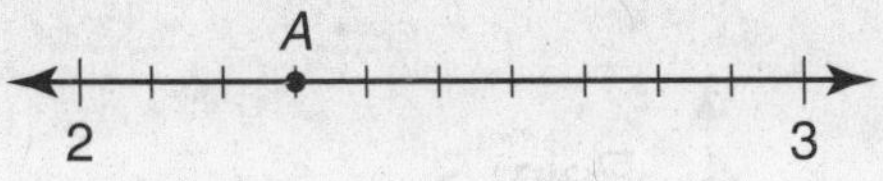

Step 1: Determine how the number line is separated.

The number line is separated into tenths.

Step 2: Write a fraction for point *A*.

Point *A* is at $2\frac{3}{10}$.

Step 3: Change $2\frac{3}{10}$ to a decimal.

$2\frac{3}{10} = 2.3$

Show each set of numbers on the same number line. Then order the numbers from least to greatest.

1. 1.2, 1.9, $1\frac{3}{5}$, ________, ________, ________

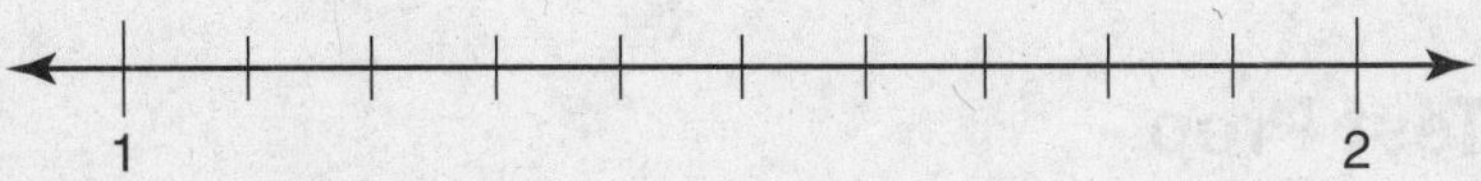

Write a fraction or mixed number in simplest form and a decimal that name each point.

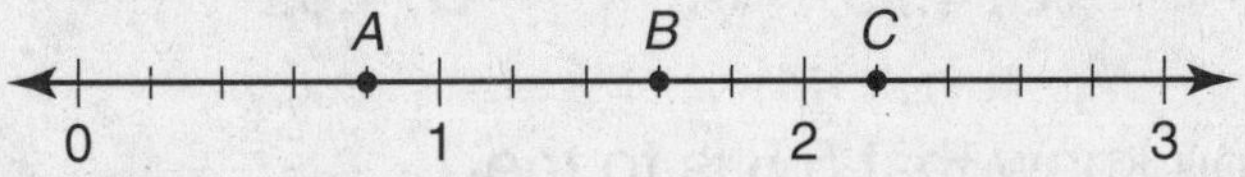

2. Point *A* ________

3. Point *B* ________

4. Point *C* ________

Name ______________________________

Fractions and Decimals on the Number Line

P 7-14

Show the set of numbers on the same number line. Then order the numbers from least to greatest.

1. 0.75, $\frac{8}{10}$, 0.2, $\frac{2}{5}$ ______________________

Write a fraction or mixed number in simplest form and a decimal that name each point.

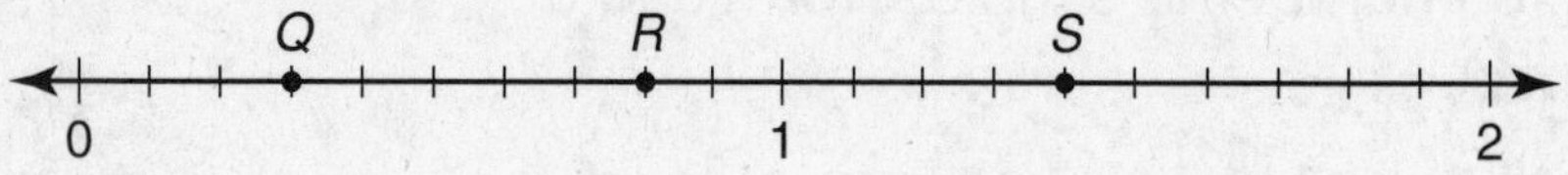

2. Point Q __________ **3.** Point R __________ **4.** Point S __________

5. Uma recorded the distances that volunteers walked in the charity event. Grace walked $1\frac{3}{5}$ mi, Wendell walked 1.3 mi, and Simon walked $1\frac{1}{10}$ mi. Show these amounts on a number line. Who walked the farthest?

____

Test Prep

6. Which is a decimal that could go between the mixed numbers $4\frac{3}{5}$ and $4\frac{9}{10}$ on a number line?

A. 4.45 **B.** 4.5 **C.** 4.75 **D.** 4.92

7. Writing in Math Explain how you know that 5.5 is to the right of $5\frac{1}{4}$ on the number line.

____

Name____

PROBLEM-SOLVING STRATEGY **R 7-15**

Use Logical Reasoning

The Travelers Justin, Aubrey, Greg, and Savannah have each visited between one to four of the same four states. Justin has visited all four states. Aubrey has not visited Ohio or Arizona. Greg has not visited Ohio. Savannah has visited only one state. The other two states are New York and Georgia. Which two people have visited Ohio?

Read and Understand

Step 1: What do you know?

Four people have traveled to four different states.

Step 2: What are you trying to find?

Which two people have visited Ohio.

Plan and Solve

Step 3: What strategy will you use? Strategy: Use logical reasoning

Use the information you are given and reasoning to make conclusions.

	Arizona	New York	Ohio	Georgia
Aubrey	No	Yes	No	Yes
Greg	Yes	Yes	No	Yes
Savannah	No	No	Yes	No
Justin	Yes	Yes	Yes	Yes

You know Justin has visited Ohio. You know Greg and Aubrey have not, so Savannah must be the second person.

	Orange	Green	Red
Sam			
Joan			
Becky	No	No	

1. Sam, Joan, and Becky each like either orange, green, or red best. Sam dislikes orange. Becky knows the people who like green and orange best. Complete the chart.

Name ____________________

PROBLEM-SOLVING STRATEGY **P 7-15**

Use Logical Reasoning

Use the chart and logical reasoning to finish solving each problem.

1. Jenna, Mason, and Sean split the household tasks they had to do on Saturday. Their parents gave them a list of jobs: mow the lawn, wash the car, and do the laundry. Sean and Jenna do not want to mow the lawn. Mason helped Jenna fold the laundry when he was done with his job. Who did which task?

	Mow Lawn	Wash Car	Laundry
Jenna			
Mason			
Sean			

____

____

____

2. Parker, Jaime, and Quincy need to choose a book to read for a school project. There are 3 kinds of books left and each student must choose a different kind of book. Jaime does not like science fiction. There are 4 consonants in the name of the student who chose mystery. Who chose which book?

	Mystery	Western	Science Fiction
Parker			
Jaime			
Quincy			

____

____

____

Name ______________________________

PROBLEM-SOLVING APPLICATIONS **R 7-16**

Logic, Fractions, and Decimals

The Walkers Jeff walked $1\frac{4}{10}$ mi. Kirsten walked $2\frac{1}{5}$ mi. Sally walked $1\frac{3}{5}$ mi. Which person walked the farthest? Which person walked the least?

Compare the whole number parts first.
Since $2 > 1$, $2\frac{1}{5} > 1\frac{3}{5}$ and $1\frac{4}{10}$. So Kirsten walked farther than Jeff and Sally.

Then compare the fractions.

Since $\frac{6}{10} > \frac{4}{10}$, $1\frac{3}{5} > 1\frac{4}{10}$. So Sally walked farther than Jeff.

Therefore, Kirsten walked the farthest, Sally walked the second farthest, and Jeff walked the least.

Find a common denominator.

5: 5, 10, 15

10: 10, 20, 30

$$\frac{3}{5} \xrightarrow{\times 2} = \frac{6}{10}$$

Order the numbers from least to greatest.

1. $\frac{3}{4}$, $1\frac{1}{4}$, $\frac{2}{8}$ ________, ________, ________

2. $3\frac{3}{10}$, $3\frac{1}{5}$, $3\frac{5}{10}$ ________, ________, ________

Estimate the shaded part of each.

3. 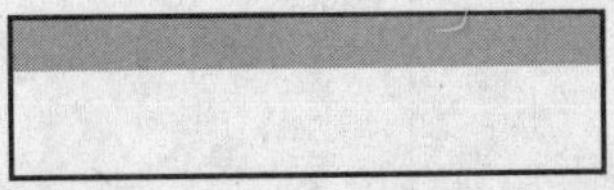 ________

4. 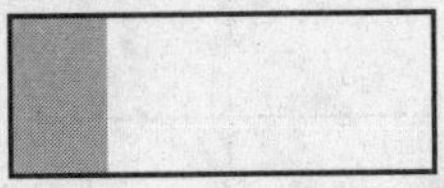 ________

Use the chart to finish solving the problem.

	Paints	Sculpts	Draws
Nicole			
Ali			
Mark			

5. Nicole, Ali, and Mark are artists. Each either paints, sculpts, or draws. Nicole does not draw. Mark knows the people who paint and draw. What is each person's art?

____

Name ______________________________

PROBLEM-SOLVING APPLICATIONS **P 7-16**

Helping the Birds

Simone's parents are bird-lovers. There is a birdhouse, some bird feeders, and a birdbath in their backyard. The family likes to watch the birds who come to enjoy the shelter, food, and water.

1. Simone's brother, Randy, says that he saw 12 birds today, and 6 of the birds were blue jays. Write the portion of the birds that were blue jays as a fraction and a decimal.

____

2. Simone and her mother went to the store to buy food for the bird feeders. They bought three different kinds of food. They bought $9\frac{3}{4}$ lb of one kind of food, 9.52 lb of another kind of food, and $9\frac{5}{12}$ lb of a third kind of food. Order the weights of the food from least to greatest.

____

3. Simone, Randy, and Kylie needed to clean and prepare the birdhouse, birdbath, and bird feeders for the winter. Randy does not like to clean the birdbath. Simone does the same job every year. Kylie cleaned the birdhouse. Who cleaned what?

	Birdhouse	Birdbath	Bird Feeders
Simone			
Randy			
Kylie			

____

____

____

____

____

Name ____________________

Adding and Subtracting Fractions with Like Denominators

R 8-1

When two fractions have the same denominator, their sum or difference also has the same denominator.

Find $\frac{7}{8} - \frac{5}{8}$.

Step 1: Subtract the numerators.

$7 - 5 = 2$

Step 2: Write the difference over the denominator.

$\frac{7}{8} - \frac{5}{8} = \frac{2}{8}$

Step 3: Simplify the difference.

$\frac{2}{8} = \frac{1}{4}$

So, $\frac{7}{8} - \frac{5}{8} = \frac{1}{4}$.

Add or subtract. Simplify, if possible.

1. $\frac{3}{8} + \frac{3}{8}$

2. $\frac{11}{12} - \frac{5}{12}$

3. $\frac{9}{10} + \frac{3}{10}$

4. $\frac{7}{9} - \frac{2}{9}$

5. $\frac{6}{9} + \frac{3}{9}$

6. $\frac{9}{10} - \frac{3}{10} =$ ______

7. $\frac{7}{8} + \frac{1}{8} + \frac{2}{8} =$ ______

8. $\frac{17}{18} - \frac{9}{18} =$ ______

9. $\frac{5}{6} + \frac{2}{6} + \frac{1}{6} =$ ______

10. $\frac{1}{14} + \frac{5}{14} + \frac{2}{14} =$ ______

11. Reasoning Is $\frac{15}{17} + \frac{4}{17}$ greater than or less than 1? Explain.

____

____

____

Name ______________________________

Adding and Subtracting Fractions with Like Denominators

Add or subtract. Simplify if possible.

1. $\frac{10}{12} + \frac{8}{12}$

2. $\frac{8}{9} - \frac{5}{9}$

3. $\frac{7}{10} + \frac{2}{10}$

4. $\frac{2}{3} - \frac{1}{3}$

5. $\frac{6}{8} + \frac{5}{8} + \frac{3}{8} =$ ________

6. $\frac{8}{10} - \frac{3}{10} =$ ________

7. $\frac{1}{4} + \frac{2}{4} + \frac{3}{4} =$ ________

8. $\frac{9}{11} - \frac{1}{11} =$ ________

9. $\frac{2}{5} + \frac{2}{5} + \frac{3}{5} =$ ________

10. $\frac{7}{8} - \frac{3}{8} =$ ________

11. **Number Sense** What fraction could you add to $\frac{4}{7}$ to get a sum greater than 1?

____

12. **Reasoning** Write three fractions, using 10 as the denominator, whose sum is 1.

____

Test Prep

13. Which of the following represents the difference between two equal fractions?

A. 1 **B.** $\frac{1}{2}$ **C.** $\frac{1}{4}$ **D.** 0

14. **Writing in Math** In one night, George reads 3 chapters of a book with 27 chapters. After the second night, he has read a total of $\frac{8}{27}$ of the book. Explain how you would determine the number of chapters George read the second night. Solve the problem.

____

____

Name ______________________________

Understanding Adding and Subtracting with Unlike Denominators

R 8-2

You can use fraction strips to add and subtract fractions with unlike denominators.

Find $\frac{1}{2} + \frac{1}{8}$.

Step 1: Use fraction strips to show $\frac{1}{2} + \frac{1}{8}$.

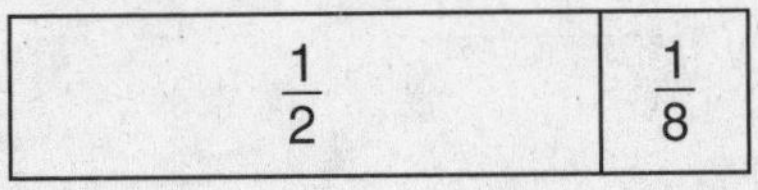

Step 2: Exchange the $\frac{1}{2}$ strip with $\frac{1}{8}$ strips to find a fraction for $\frac{1}{2}$ with a denominator of 8.

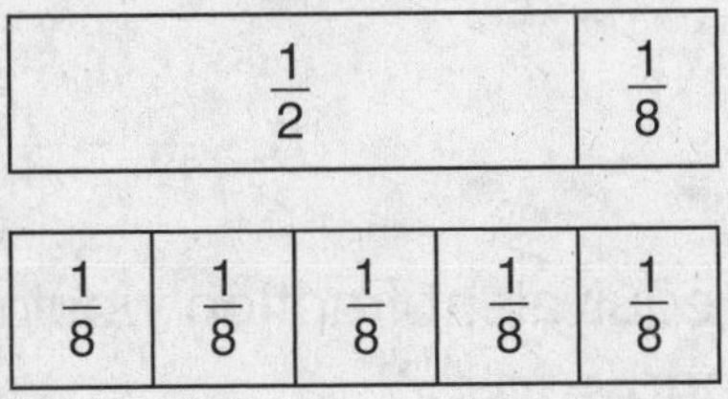

Step 3: Count to see how many $\frac{1}{8}$ strips there are. There are 5, or $\frac{5}{8}$.

So, $\frac{1}{2} + \frac{1}{8} = \frac{5}{8}$.

Find each sum or difference. Simplify the answer, if possible. You may use fraction strips or draw pictures to help.

1. $\frac{1}{2} + \frac{3}{8} =$ ______

2. $\frac{2}{5} - \frac{1}{10} =$ ______

3. $\frac{4}{5} + \frac{1}{10} =$ ______

4. $\frac{3}{4} - \frac{1}{2} =$ ______

5. $\frac{1}{3} + \frac{1}{12} =$ ______

6. $\frac{11}{12} - \frac{5}{6} =$ ______

7. $\frac{1}{6} + \frac{3}{4} =$ ______

8. $\frac{3}{4} - \frac{3}{8} =$ ______

9. Number Sense Which equivalent fraction would you use to subtract $\frac{1}{3}$ from $\frac{5}{9}$? ______

Leftover Fabric

Type	Amount
Silk	$\frac{3}{4}$ yd
Polyester	$\frac{3}{8}$ yd
Cotton	$\frac{5}{8}$ yd
Burlap	$\frac{1}{2}$ yd

10. How much polyester and cotton is there combined?

____

11. How much more silk is there than polyester?

____

Name ______________________

Understanding Adding and Subtracting with Unlike Denominators

P 8-2

Find each sum or difference. Simplify the answer, if possible. You may use fraction strips or draw pictures to help.

1. $\frac{10}{12} - \frac{1}{4} =$ ______

2. $\frac{9}{10} - \frac{3}{5} =$ ______

3. $\frac{2}{9} + \frac{1}{3} =$ ______

4. $\frac{3}{4} + \frac{4}{5} =$ ______

5. $\frac{5}{6} + \frac{4}{9} =$ ______

6. $\frac{7}{8} - \frac{2}{6} =$ ______

7. $\frac{1}{6} + \frac{5}{12} =$ ______

8. $\frac{7}{12} - \frac{1}{4} =$ ______

9. **Number Sense** Which equivalent fraction would you have to use in order to add $\frac{3}{5}$ to $\frac{21}{25}$? ______

Jeremy collected nickels for one week. He is making stacks of his nickels to determine how many he has. The thickness of one nickel is $\frac{1}{4}$ in.

10. How tall is a stack of 4 nickels? ______

11. What is the combined height of 3 nickels, 2 nickels, and 1 nickel? ______

12. How much taller is a stack of 3 nickels than 1 nickel? ______

Test Prep

13. Which fraction is greatest?

A. $\frac{5}{6}$ **B.** $\frac{7}{9}$ **C.** $\frac{2}{3}$ **D.** $\frac{9}{12}$

14. **Writing in Math** Explain why you cannot add fractions with unlike denominators.

____

____

____

Name ________________________________

Least Common Denominator

R 8-3

To find the least common denominator (LCD) of two or more fractions, you need to find the least common multiple (LCM) of the denominators.

How to find the least common multiple:

Find the least common multiple of 6 and 9.

Step 1: List the multiples of each number.

Multiples of 6: 6, 12, **18**, 24, 30, **36**, 42, 48, **54**

Multiples of 9: 9, **18**, 27, **36**, 45, **54**, 63

Step 2: Find the multiples the numbers have in common: 18, 36, 54.

Step 3: Find the least multiple the numbers have in common: 18.

So, 18 is the least common multiple of 6 and 9.

How to find the least common denominator:

Find the least common denominator of $\frac{5}{6}$ and $\frac{3}{4}$.

Step 1: List the multiples of each denominator.

Multiples of 6: 6, **12**, 18, **24**, 30, . . .

Multiples of 4: 4, 8, **12**, 16, 20, **24**, . . .

Step 2: Look for the smallest multiple that 6 and 4 have in common. Both numbers have 12 and 24 in common. 12 is the least number that they have in common.

So, 12 is the least common denominator of $\frac{5}{6}$ and $\frac{3}{4}$.

Find the LCM of each pair of numbers.

1. 4 and 3 ________

2. 8 and 12 ________

3. 5 and 6 ________

4. 10 and 2 ________

Find the LCD for each pair of fractions.

5. $\frac{4}{9}$ and $\frac{1}{6}$ ________

6. $\frac{2}{3}$ and $\frac{3}{4}$ ________

7. $\frac{5}{6}$ and $\frac{7}{12}$ ________

8. $\frac{7}{10}$ and $\frac{3}{5}$ ________

9. $\frac{3}{8}$ and $\frac{5}{12}$ ________

10. $\frac{3}{7}$ and $\frac{2}{3}$ ________

11. $\frac{3}{4}$ and $\frac{1}{2}$ ________

12. $\frac{9}{10}$ and $\frac{1}{3}$ ________

13. Mental Math Can the LCD of $\frac{4}{9}$ and $\frac{13}{17}$ be less than 17? Explain.

____

____

Name ______________________

Least Common Denominator

P 8-3

Find the LCD for each pair of fractions.

1. $\frac{2}{7}$ and $\frac{4}{5}$ ______

2. $\frac{5}{6}$ and $\frac{4}{9}$ ______

3. $\frac{7}{9}$ and $\frac{11}{15}$ ______

4. $\frac{1}{12}$ and $\frac{3}{9}$ ______

5. $\frac{12}{15}$ and $\frac{8}{10}$ ______

6. $\frac{5}{8}$ and $\frac{3}{4}$ ______

7. $\frac{1}{4}$ and $\frac{4}{5}$ ______

8. $\frac{3}{11}$ and $\frac{7}{8}$ ______

Two of the shortest fish in the world are the dwarf goby and the dwarf pygmy goby. Both fish are found in Southeast Asia. The table shows the lengths for each of these fish.

Fish	Length (inches)
Male dwarf pygmy goby	$\frac{1}{2}$
Female dwarf pygmy goby	$\frac{3}{4}$
Dwarf goby	$\frac{1}{3}$

9. What would the LCD be for the length of the male and the female dwarf pygmy goby? ______

10. What is the combined length of the male and female dwarf pygmy goby? ______

11. What would the LCD be for the length of all 3 fish? ______

12. What is the combined length of the 3 fish? ______

Test Prep

13. Which is the LCD for $\frac{1}{4}$, $\frac{1}{5}$, and $\frac{1}{6}$?

A. 20 **B.** 30 **C.** 60 **D.** 80

14. **Writing in Math** Explain the difference between the LCM and the LCD.

____

____

____

Name______________________________

Adding and Subtracting Fractions with Unlike Denominators

R 8-4

Moira's bread recipe calls for $\frac{3}{4}$ c of white flour and $\frac{1}{8}$ c of wheat flour. What is the total amount of flour needed for the recipe?

Step 1: Find the LCM of the denominators.

Multiples of 4: 4, **8**, 12, 16, 20, . . .

Multiples of 8: **8**, 16, 24, 32, 40, . . .

The LCD is 8.

Step 2: Write equivalent fractions with a denominator of 8.

$$\frac{3 \times 2}{4 \times 2} = \frac{6}{8}$$

Step 3: Add the fractions. Write the sum in simplest form.

$\frac{6}{8} + \frac{1}{8} = \frac{7}{8}$

So, the recipe calls for $\frac{7}{8}$ cups of flour.

Add or subtract. Simplify, if possible.

1. $\frac{3}{4} - \frac{2}{5}$

2. $\frac{4}{5} + \frac{1}{2}$

3. $\frac{7}{10} - \frac{1}{5}$

4. $\frac{8}{9} + \frac{5}{6}$

5. $\frac{7}{12} - \frac{1}{4} =$ ______

6. $\frac{4}{9} + \frac{3}{4} =$ ______

7. $\frac{5}{6} - \frac{3}{8} =$ ______

8. $\frac{1}{2} + \frac{1}{6} + \frac{3}{4} =$ ______

9. $\frac{23}{24} - \frac{7}{8} =$ ______

10. $\frac{2}{3} + \frac{1}{9} + \frac{5}{6} =$ ______

11. Reasoning Is the sum of $\frac{9}{12}$ and $\frac{1}{6}$ greater than or less than 1?

____

Name

Adding and Subtracting Fractions with Unlike Denominators

Add or subtract. Simplify, if possible.

1. $\frac{3}{8} + \frac{4}{5}$

2. $\frac{5}{12} - \frac{1}{3}$

3. $\frac{9}{10} + \frac{2}{5}$

4. $\frac{11}{12} - \frac{1}{4}$

5. $\frac{4}{9} + \frac{1}{3} + \frac{5}{6} =$ ______

6. $\frac{1}{2} + \frac{7}{8} + \frac{3}{10} =$ ______

7. $\frac{7}{8} - \frac{2}{3} =$ ______

8. $\frac{7}{10} - \frac{1}{4} =$ ______

9. $\frac{3}{4} + \frac{1}{2} + \frac{1}{12} =$ ______

10. $\frac{6}{7} - \frac{1}{3} =$ ______

11. Number Sense Write three fractions with different denominators that are equal to $\frac{1}{2}$.

______

The vervain hummingbird and the ruby-throated hummingbird lay the world's smallest bird eggs.

Egg Sizes

Bird	Length	Weight
Vervain hummingbird	$\frac{4}{10}$ in.	$\frac{13}{1{,}000}$ oz
Ruby-throated hummingbird	$\frac{5}{8}$ in.	$\frac{1}{50}$ oz

12. What is the difference in length between the ruby-throated hummingbird egg and the vervain hummingbird egg? ______

13. What is the difference in weight between the ruby-throated hummingbird egg and the vervain hummingbird egg? ______

Test Prep

14. Which is the sum of $\frac{8}{9} + \frac{4}{15} + \frac{3}{5}$ in simplest form?

A. $1\frac{34}{45}$ **B.** $\frac{79}{45}$ **C.** $\frac{15}{29}$ **D.** $1\frac{27}{45}$

15. Writing in Math Explain why $\frac{21}{14}$ is equal to $1\frac{1}{2}$.

______

Name

Understanding Adding and Subtracting Mixed Numbers

Homework Jerome worked on his English homework for $1\frac{1}{6}$ hr and his science homework for $1\frac{3}{6}$ hr. How much time did Jerome spend on homework?

You can use fraction strips to help you add the mixed numbers.

Step 1: Use fraction strips to show $1\frac{1}{6} + 1\frac{3}{6}$.

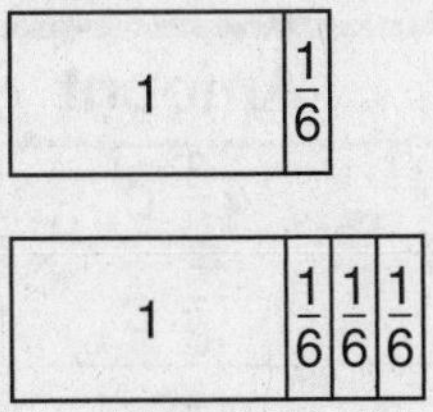

Step 2: Combine the $\frac{1}{6}$ strips. Then combine the 1 strips.

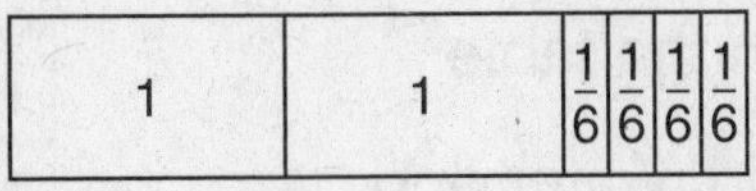

Step 3: Count the strips.

$1 + 1 + \frac{1}{6} + \frac{1}{6} + \frac{1}{6} + \frac{1}{6} = 2\frac{4}{6}$

So, $1\frac{1}{6} + 1\frac{3}{6} = 2\frac{4}{6}$.

$2\frac{4}{6}$ in simplest form is $2\frac{2}{3}$.

Jerome will spend $2\frac{2}{3}$ hr on homework.

Find each sum or difference. Simplify the answer, if necessary. You may use fraction strips or draw pictures to help.

1. $1\frac{5}{8} + 2\frac{2}{8}$

2. $5\frac{3}{4} - 2\frac{1}{4}$

3. $6 + 3\frac{7}{12}$

4. $5\frac{6}{7} - 3\frac{2}{7}$

5. $2\frac{9}{16} + 7\frac{5}{16} =$ ________

6. $5 - 3\frac{1}{2} =$ ________

7. $3\frac{1}{10} + \frac{4}{10} =$ ________

8. $4\frac{9}{16} - \frac{5}{16} =$ ________

9. $4\frac{3}{11} + 12\frac{5}{11} =$ ________

10. $8\frac{4}{9} - 8\frac{1}{9} =$ ________

11. Number Sense If you want to subtract $\frac{3}{7}$ from 12, how should you rename 12? ________

Name ____________________

Understanding Adding and Subtracting Mixed Numbers

Find each sum or difference. Simplify the answer, if necessary. You may use fraction strips or draw pictures to help.

1. $4\frac{1}{5} + 2\frac{2}{5} =$ ______ **2.** $8\frac{3}{7} + 5\frac{1}{7} =$ ______ **3.** $6\frac{7}{8} - 2\frac{5}{8} =$ ______

4. $5\frac{8}{11} - 5\frac{3}{11} =$ ______ **5.** $7\frac{2}{5} + 6\frac{3}{5} =$ ______ **6.** $10 - 3\frac{7}{8} =$ ______

Kevin is making lemonade for his family. The ingredients are shown in the table.

One Batch of Lemonade

Ingredient	Amount
Water	$4\frac{3}{8}$ c
Lemon juice	$\frac{5}{8}$ c
Sugar	$2\frac{1}{4}$ c

7. How many cups of liquid (water and lemon juice) will Kevin use?

____

8. How much water should Kevin use if he wants to decrease the amount of water by $\frac{5}{8}$ c? ______

9. How much lemon juice should Kevin use if he wants to increase the amount used by $\frac{3}{8}$ c? ______

10. Number Sense Explain why $8\frac{3}{5}$ is the same as $7\frac{8}{5}$.

____

____

Test Prep

11. In order to subtract $6\frac{7}{16}$ from $7\frac{1}{16}$, what must you do?

A. Rename $6\frac{7}{16}$ **B.** Rename $7\frac{1}{16}$

C. Rename both $6\frac{7}{16}$ and $7\frac{1}{16}$ **D.** You cannot subtract $6\frac{7}{16}$ from $7\frac{1}{16}$

12. Writing in Math Explain what happens when you add $\frac{1}{8}$ to $3\frac{7}{8}$.

____

____

Name ______________________________

Estimating Sums and Differences of Mixed Numbers

R 8-6

Orange Juice Veronica squeezed $3\frac{7}{8}$ c of orange juice. She drank $2\frac{1}{4}$ c. About how much orange juice was left?

Step 1: Round each mixed number to the nearest whole number.

Round $3\frac{7}{8}$ to 4.

Round $2\frac{1}{4}$ to 2.

Step 2: Subtract.

$4 - 2 = 2$

So, there were about 2 c of orange juice left.

Estimate each sum or difference. Round to the nearest whole number.

1. $5\frac{8}{9} + 2\frac{3}{4}$ ______

2. $10\frac{1}{8} - 6\frac{5}{6}$ ______

3. $2\frac{13}{16} - \frac{7}{8}$ ______

4. $4\frac{6}{7} - 2\frac{1}{5}$ ______

5. $6 + 2\frac{1}{3} + 4\frac{11}{12}$ ______

6. $9 - 6\frac{9}{10}$ ______

7. $5\frac{3}{4} + 2\frac{10}{11} + 3\frac{7}{8}$ ______

8. $\frac{15}{16} + 3\frac{7}{9} + 2\frac{13}{14}$ ______

9. **Number Sense** Is the difference between $2\frac{3}{4}$ and $1\frac{1}{8}$ greater than or less than 1? Explain.

____

____

____

10. About how much taller is Angela than Austin?

____

Height Chart

Martina	$48\frac{1}{4}$ in.
Zachary	$50\frac{7}{8}$ in.
Angela	$52\frac{1}{16}$ in.
Austin	$49\frac{9}{10}$ in.

Name ______________________

Estimating Sums and Differences of Mixed Numbers

P 8-6

Estimate. First round to the nearest whole number.

1. $\frac{2}{3} + 4\frac{1}{4}$ ______
2. $7\frac{2}{5} + 8\frac{7}{8}$ ______
3. $5\frac{6}{7} - 3\frac{1}{3}$ ______
4. $8\frac{3}{4} - 8\frac{1}{8}$ ______
5. $1\frac{8}{9} + 1\frac{1}{5} + 1\frac{3}{7}$ ______
6. $9\frac{1}{8} + 4\frac{3}{4} + 6\frac{2}{3}$ ______

Distances in miles and time are shown for the Seattle region in Washington.

Travel in Washington

Destinations	Hours	Miles
Seattle → Ellensburg	$1\frac{7}{12}$	104
Ellensburg → Wenatchee	$1\frac{1}{2}$	70
Wenatchee → Everett	$2\frac{3}{4}$	124
Everett → Port Angeles	$1\frac{5}{6}$	84

7. Estimate the driving time between Seattle and Wenatchee.

____

8. Estimate the difference in driving time between the distance from Wenatchee to Everett and the distance from Everett to Port Angeles. ______________________

9. **Number Sense** The difference between two mixed numbers is about 3. One of the numbers is $4\frac{4}{5}$. What could the other number be? ______________________

Test Prep

10. Which is a good estimate for the sum of $45\frac{16}{25} + 32\frac{13}{18} + 51\frac{3}{20}$?

A. 128 **B.** 129 **C.** 130 **D.** 131

11. **Writing in Math** Describe a situation in which estimating mixed numbers would not be a good idea.

____

____

____

Name ______________________________

Adding Mixed Numbers

Find $4\frac{5}{6} + 2\frac{1}{12}$.

Step 1	Step 2	Step 3
Write equivalent fractions with the LCD.	Add the fractions.	Add the whole numbers. Simplify the sum, if necessary.
$4\frac{5}{6} = 4\frac{10}{12}$	$4\frac{5}{6} = 4\frac{10}{12}$	$4\frac{5}{6} = 4\frac{10}{12}$
$+\ 2\frac{1}{12} = 2\frac{1}{12}$	$+\ 2\frac{1}{12} = 2\frac{1}{12}$	$+\ 2\frac{1}{12} = 2\frac{1}{12}$
	$\frac{11}{12}$	$6\frac{11}{12}$

So, $4\frac{5}{6} + 2\frac{1}{12} = 6\frac{11}{12}$.

Estimate the sum first. Then add. Simplify, if necessary.

1. $2\frac{5}{6} + 3\frac{1}{4}$

2. $1\frac{3}{8} + 6\frac{3}{4}$

3. $5\frac{2}{5} + 4\frac{1}{2}$

4. $10\frac{1}{3} + \frac{7}{9}$

5. $6 + 3\frac{1}{3}$

6. $3\frac{1}{4} + 6\frac{2}{3}$

7. $2\frac{1}{7} + 4\frac{2}{6}$

8. $3\frac{2}{5} + 9\frac{1}{15}$

9. $1\frac{5}{7} + 3\frac{1}{2} =$ ____________

10. $4 + 5\frac{15}{16} =$ ____________

11. $7\frac{3}{10} + 5\frac{2}{5} =$ ____________

12. $9\frac{1}{3} + 3\frac{2}{5} =$ ____________

13. Mental Math What is the sum of $2\frac{1}{5}$ and $3\frac{4}{5}$? ____________

Name ______________________

Adding Mixed Numbers

Estimate the sum first. Then add. Simplify, if necessary.

1. $7\frac{2}{3} + 8\frac{5}{6}$ ____________ **2.** $4\frac{3}{4} + 2\frac{2}{5}$ ____________

3. $11\frac{9}{10} + 3\frac{1}{20}$ ____________ **4.** $7\frac{6}{7} + 5\frac{2}{7}$ ____________

5. $5\frac{8}{9} + 3\frac{1}{2}$ ____________ **6.** $21\frac{11}{12} + 17\frac{2}{3}$ ____________

7. **Number Sense** Write two mixed numbers with a sum of 3.

____

8. What is the total measure of an average man's brain and heart in kilograms?

____

Vital Organ Measures

Average woman's brain	$1\frac{3}{10}$ kg	$2\frac{4}{5}$ lb
Average man's brain	$1\frac{2}{5}$ kg	3 lb
Average human heart	$\frac{3}{10}$ kg	$\frac{7}{10}$ lb

9. What is the total weight of an average woman's brain and heart in pounds? ____________

10. What is the sum of the measures of an average man's brain and an average woman's brain in kilograms? ____________

Test Prep

11. Which is a good comparison of the estimated sum and the actual sum of $7\frac{7}{8} + 2\frac{11}{12}$?

A. Estimated $<$ actual **B.** Actual $>$ estimated

C. Actual $=$ estimated **D.** Estimated $>$ actual

12. **Writing in Math** Can the sum of two mixed numbers be equal to 2? Explain why or why not.

____

____

____

Name____________________

Subtracting Mixed Numbers

R 8-8

Find $4\frac{1}{2} - 1\frac{5}{8}$.

Step 1

Write equivalent fractions with the LCD.

$$\begin{array}{rcl} 4\frac{1}{2} & = & 4\frac{4}{8} \\ -\ 1\frac{5}{8} & = & 1\frac{5}{8} \\ \hline \end{array}$$

Step 2

Rename $4\frac{4}{8}$ to show more eighths.

$$\begin{array}{rcccl} 4\frac{1}{2} & = & 4\frac{4}{8} & = & 3\frac{12}{8} \\ -\ 1\frac{5}{8} & = & 1\frac{5}{8} & = & 1\frac{5}{8} \\ \hline \end{array}$$

Step 3

Subtract the fractions. Then subtract the whole numbers. Simplify the difference.

$$\begin{array}{rcccl} 4\frac{1}{2} & = & 4\frac{4}{8} & = & 3\frac{12}{8} \\ -\ 1\frac{5}{8} & = & 1\frac{5}{8} & = & 1\frac{5}{8} \\ \hline & & & & 2\frac{7}{8} \end{array}$$

So, $4\frac{1}{2} - 1\frac{5}{8} = 2\frac{7}{8}$.

Find $9 - 3\frac{1}{6}$.

Step 1

Rename 9 to show sixths.

$$\begin{array}{rcl} 9 & = & 8\frac{6}{6} \\ -\ 3\frac{1}{6} & = & 3\frac{1}{6} \\ \hline \end{array}$$

Step 2

Subtract the fractions. Then subtract the whole numbers.

$$\begin{array}{rcl} 9 & = & 8\frac{6}{6} \\ -\ 3\frac{1}{6} & = & 3\frac{1}{6} \\ \hline & & 5\frac{5}{6} \end{array}$$

So, $9 - 3\frac{1}{6} = 5\frac{5}{6}$.

Estimate the difference first. Then subtract. Simplify, if necessary.

1. $\begin{array}{r} 4\frac{3}{5} \\ -\ 2\frac{1}{3} \\ \hline \end{array}$

2. $\begin{array}{r} 5\frac{6}{7} \\ -\ 1\frac{1}{2} \\ \hline \end{array}$

3. $\begin{array}{r} 3 \\ -\ 1\frac{3}{4} \\ \hline \end{array}$

4. $\begin{array}{r} 6\frac{5}{6} \\ -\ 5\frac{1}{2} \\ \hline \end{array}$

Name ____________________

Subtracting Mixed Numbers

Estimate the difference first. Then subtract.
Simplify, if necessary.

1. $10\frac{3}{4} - 7\frac{1}{4}$

2. $7\frac{3}{7} - 2\frac{8}{21}$

3. $3 - 2\frac{2}{3}$

4. $17\frac{7}{8} - 12\frac{3}{12}$

5. $9\frac{5}{9} - 6\frac{5}{6}$ ____________

6. $4\frac{3}{4} - 2\frac{2}{3}$ ____________

7. $6\frac{1}{4} - 3\frac{1}{3}$ ____________

8. $5\frac{1}{5} - 3\frac{7}{8}$ ____________

9. $8\frac{2}{7} - 7\frac{1}{3}$ ____________

10. $2\frac{9}{10} - 2\frac{1}{3}$ ____________

The table shows the length and width of several kinds of bird eggs.

Egg Sizes

Bird	Length	Width
Canada goose	$3\frac{2}{5}$ in.	$2\frac{3}{10}$ in.
Robin	$\frac{3}{4}$ in.	$\frac{3}{5}$ in.
Turtledove	$1\frac{1}{5}$ in.	$\frac{9}{10}$ in.
Raven	$1\frac{9}{10}$ in.	$1\frac{3}{10}$ in.

11. How much longer is the Canada goose egg than the raven egg?

____

12. How much wider is the turtledove egg than the robin egg? ____________

Test Prep

13. Which is the difference of $21\frac{5}{16} - 18\frac{3}{4}$?

A. $2\frac{7}{16}$ **B.** $2\frac{9}{16}$ **C.** $3\frac{7}{16}$ **D.** $3\frac{9}{16}$

14. Writing in Math Explain why it is necessary to rename $4\frac{1}{4}$ if you subtract $\frac{3}{4}$ from it.

____

____

____

Name

PROBLEM-SOLVING STRATEGY **R 8-9**

Work Backward

Car Wash Jake's neighborhood had a car wash to raise money for improvements to a nearby park. They earned twice as much money on Saturday as they did on Sunday. On Friday they earned $50 less than the amount earned on Saturday. On Thursday the car wash took in $422 which was $38 more than on Friday. What did they earn on Friday, Saturday, and Sunday?

Read and Understand

Step 1: What do you know?

The car wash took in twice as much money on Saturday as on Sunday.

The money raised on Friday was $50 less than the amount earned on Saturday.

Thursday's amount was $422 which was $38 more than was earned on Friday.

Step 2: What are you trying to find?

How much money was earned on Friday, Saturday, and Sunday?

Plan and Solve

Step 3: What strategy will you use?

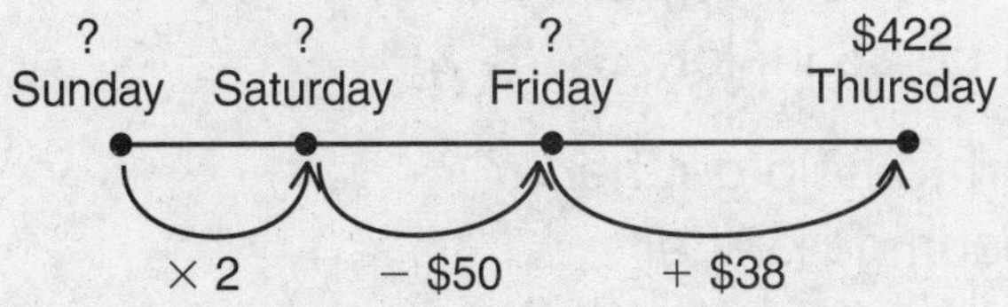

Strategy: Work backward

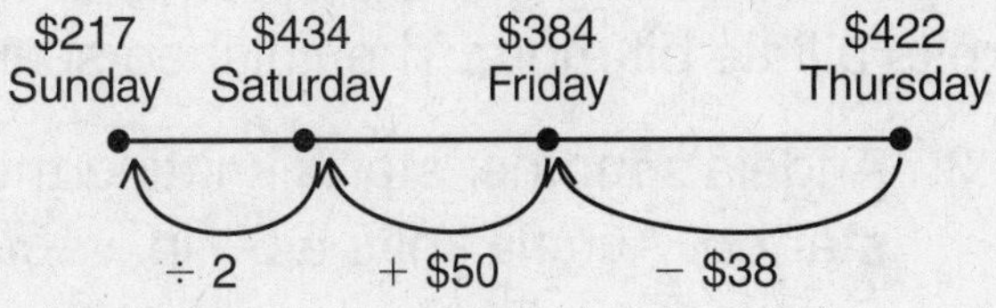

The car wash brought in $384 on Friday, $434 on Saturday, and $217 on Sunday.

Look Back and Check

Step 4: Is your answer reasonable?

Yes, because when I work forward from the initial amount, I get the end result.

Solve the problem by working backward. Write the answer in a complete sentence.

1. Brett has promised he would be back home by 5:30 P.M. It takes him 20 min to skate over to his friend's house. He will stay there for 2 hr. On the way home, he always stops for a snack, so the return trip takes 30 min. If Brett is to keep his promise, by what time must he leave home?

Name ______________________________

PROBLEM-SOLVING STRATEGY **P 8-9**

Work Backward

Solve each problem by working backward. Write the answers in complete sentences.

Barbara is refilling her bird feeders and squirrel feeders in her yard.

1. After filling her bird feeders, Barbara has $3\frac{1}{2}$ c of mixed birdseed left. The two feeders in the front yard took $4\frac{1}{2}$ c each. The two feeders in the backyard each took $2\frac{3}{4}$ c. The two feeders next to the living room window each took $3\frac{1}{4}$ c. How much mixed birdseed did Barbara have before filling the feeders?

____

2. After Barbara fills each of her 4 squirrel feeders with $2\frac{2}{3}$ c of peanuts, she has $1\frac{3}{4}$ c of peanuts left. How many cups of peanuts did Barbara start with?

____

Angela is knitting a scarf for her grandmother. Every day she knits a little bit more. The finished scarf will be 36 in. long.

3. Angela's mother starts knitting the scarf to help get her started. Angela knits a $6\frac{1}{2}$ in. section each day. After 5 days, the scarf is done. How many inches did Angela's mother knit?

____

4. How many more days would Angela have to knit to make the scarf 48 in. long?

____

Clint spends $\frac{1}{2}$ hr practicing trumpet, $\frac{3}{4}$ hr doing tasks around the house, $1\frac{1}{2}$ hr doing homework, and $\frac{1}{4}$ hr cleaning his room. He is finished at 7:30 P.M.

5. When did Clint start?

____

Name ____________________

Multiplying Fractions by Whole Numbers

R 8-10

You can use multiplication to find a fraction of a whole number.

Example A

Find $\frac{1}{3}$ of 30. Use mental math.

$\frac{1}{3}$ of 30 gives the same result as dividing 30 by 3.

$30 \div 3 = 10$

So, $\frac{1}{3}$ of 30 = 10.

Example B

Find $8 \times \frac{3}{4}$. Use mental math.

Think: $\frac{3}{4}$ is 3 times as much as $\frac{1}{4}$.

$\frac{1}{4}$ of 8 = 2.

Multiply 2 by 3.

$2 \times 3 = 6$

So, $8 \times \frac{3}{4} = 6$.

Find each product.

1. $20 \times \frac{2}{5} =$ ________

2. $\frac{1}{6}$ of 18 = ________

3. $50 \times \frac{3}{10} =$ ________

4. $\frac{7}{8}$ of 64 = ________

5. Reasoning How could you use the product of $\frac{1}{5} \times 40$ to find the product of $\frac{4}{5} \times 40$?

____

The chart shows the maximum speed for different animals.

Speeds of Animals

Animal	Speed (in mph)
Cat	30
Cheetah	70
Jackal	35

6. What is $\frac{1}{7}$ the speed of a cheetah?

____

7. What is $\frac{1}{5}$ the speed of a cat? ________

8. What is $\frac{1}{5}$ the speed of a jackal? ________

Name ______________________________

Multiplying Fractions by Whole Numbers

P 8-10

Find each product.

1. $\frac{1}{4}$ of 96 = ______
2. $\frac{4}{7}$ of 28 = ______
3. $\frac{3}{4} \times 72$ = ______
4. $45 \times \frac{3}{9}$ = ______
5. $56 \times \frac{7}{8}$ = ______
6. $42 \times \frac{3}{7}$ = ______
7. $\frac{1}{2}$ of 118 = ______
8. $\frac{3}{8}$ of 56 = ______
9. $\frac{1}{10} \times 400$ = ______
10. $84 \times \frac{1}{6}$ = ______
11. $64 \times \frac{5}{16}$ = ______
12. $40 \times \frac{11}{20}$ = ______
13. $\frac{5}{8}$ of 48 = ______
14. $\frac{1}{7}$ of 77 = ______
15. $\frac{4}{5} \times 90$ = ______
16. $42 \times \frac{3}{14}$ = ______
17. $72 \times \frac{5}{8}$ = ______
18. $18 \times \frac{2}{3}$ = ______
19. $\frac{5}{6} \times 84$ = ______
20. $\frac{11}{12} \times 144$ = ______
21. $\frac{6}{7} \times 42$ = ______

22. **Patterns** Complete the table by writing the product of each expression in the box below it. Use a pattern to find each product. Explain the pattern.

$\frac{1}{2} \times 32$	$\frac{1}{4} \times 32$	$\frac{1}{8} \times 32$	$\frac{1}{16} \times 32$

____

23. **Reasoning** If $\frac{1}{2}$ of 1 is $\frac{1}{2}$, what is $\frac{1}{2}$ of 2, 3, and 4? ______

Test Prep

24. Which is $\frac{2}{3}$ of 225?

A. 75 **B.** 113 **C.** 150 **D.** 450

25. **Writing in Math** Explain why $\frac{1}{2}$ of 2 equals one whole.

____

____

Name ____________________

Estimating Products of Fractions

R 8-11

You can use compatible numbers and benchmark fractions to estimate products of fractions.

One Way

Find $\frac{2}{3} \times 92$.

Think: 92 is close to 90.

$\frac{1}{3} \times 90 = 30$, and $\frac{2}{3} \times 90 = 60$.

So, $\frac{2}{3} \times 92$ is about 60.

Another Way

Find $\frac{3}{7} \times 40$.

Change the fraction to the closest benchmark fraction. Remember that benchmarks are numbers like $\frac{1}{2}$ and 1.

Think: $\frac{3}{7}$ is close to $\frac{1}{2}$.

$\frac{1}{2} \times 40 = 20$

So, $\frac{3}{7} \times 40$ is about 20.

Estimate each product.

1. $\frac{1}{4} \times 17$ ________ **2.** $\frac{2}{3} \times 10$ ________ **3.** $\frac{1}{5} \times 21$ ________

4. $\frac{5}{6} \times 37$ ________ **5.** $\frac{3}{12} \times 25$ ________ **6.** $\frac{4}{5} \times 42$ ________

7. Number Sense Do you think the actual product of $\frac{1}{8} \times 55$ is greater than or less than 7? Explain.

____

____

____

8. Estimate the amount of orange juice it takes to make 8 pitchers of punch.

____

9. About how much pineapple juice is needed for 25 pitchers of punch?

____

Recipe for Pitcher of Tropical Punch

$\frac{3}{4}$ c	pineapple juice
$\frac{2}{3}$ c	orange juice
$\frac{4}{5}$ c	cranberry juice
$\frac{1}{2}$ c	soda water

Name ____________________

Estimating Products of Fractions

P 8-11

Estimate each product.

1. $\frac{7}{8} \times 57$ ______ **2.** $\frac{3}{8} \times 28$ ______ **3.** $\frac{8}{9} \times 27$ ______

4. $24 \times \frac{2}{7}$ ______ **5.** $80 \times \frac{4}{7}$ ______ **6.** $\frac{5}{7} \times 50$ ______

7. $\frac{1}{8} \times 46$ ______ **8.** $\frac{2}{7} \times 58$ ______ **9.** $\frac{4}{9} \times 70$ ______

10. $18 \times \frac{3}{5}$ ______ **11.** $91 \times \frac{1}{10}$ ______ **12.** $\frac{3}{4} \times 39$ ______

Distance Measurements

40 rods	=	1 furlong
8 furlongs	=	1 mi
3 mi	=	1 league
5,280 ft	=	1 mi

13. About how many furlongs is $\frac{2}{3}$ of 1 mi?

____

14. About how many rods is $\frac{4}{7}$ of 1 furlong?

____

15. About how many miles is $\frac{7}{9}$ of 1 league?

____

16. About how many feet is $\frac{23}{48}$ of 1 mi?

____

17. **Number Sense** Is the product of $\frac{3}{9} \times 100$ greater than or less than 30? Explain.

____

____

Test Prep

18. Which is the most reasonable estimate for $55 \times \frac{5}{7}$?

A. 30 **B.** 35 **C.** 55 **D.** 60

19. **Writing in Math** Which is easier, finding $\frac{2}{7}$ of 65 or $\frac{2}{7}$ of 63? Explain your answer.

____

____

Name ______________________________

Multiplying Fractions

R 8-12

	How to multiply two fractions	How to multiply three or more fractions
	Find $\frac{3}{4} \times \frac{2}{5}$.	Find $\frac{1}{4} \times \frac{2}{5} \times \frac{2}{3}$.
Step 1	Multiply the numerators. $\frac{3}{4} \times \frac{2}{5} = \frac{3 \times 2}{} = \frac{6}{}$	Multiply the numerators. $\frac{1}{4} \times \frac{2}{5} \times \frac{2}{3} = \frac{1 \times 2 \times 2}{} = \frac{4}{}$
Step 2	Multiply the denominators. $\frac{3}{4} \times \frac{2}{5} = \frac{3 \times 2}{4 \times 5} = \frac{6}{20}$	Multiply the denominators. $\frac{1}{4} \times \frac{2}{5} \times \frac{2}{3} = \frac{1 \times 2 \times 2}{4 \times 5 \times 3} = \frac{4}{60}$
Step 3	Simplify the product. $\frac{3}{4} \times \frac{2}{5} = \frac{3 \times 2}{4 \times 5} = \frac{6}{20} = \frac{3}{10}$ So, $\frac{3}{4} \times \frac{2}{5} = \frac{3}{10}$.	Simplify the product. $\frac{1}{4} \times \frac{2}{5} \times \frac{2}{3} = \frac{1 \times 2 \times 2}{4 \times 5 \times 3} = \frac{4}{60} = \frac{1}{15}$ So, $\frac{1}{4} \times \frac{2}{5} \times \frac{2}{3} = \frac{1}{15}$.

Find each product. Simplify, if necessary.

1. $\frac{5}{7} \times \frac{1}{2} =$ __________

2. $\frac{4}{5} \times \frac{2}{3} =$ __________

3. $\frac{3}{4} \times \frac{2}{5} =$ __________

4. $\frac{1}{2} \times \frac{3}{8} =$ __________

5. $\frac{1}{5} \times \frac{6}{7} =$ __________

6. $\frac{2}{3} \times \frac{1}{4} =$ __________

7. $\frac{7}{8} \times \frac{1}{2} \times \frac{2}{3} =$ __________

8. $\frac{2}{4} \times \frac{4}{5} \times \frac{3}{5} =$ __________

9. Number Sense Mark missed $\frac{1}{5}$ of the questions on his test. He corrected $\frac{3}{4}$ of the questions he missed. What fraction of the questions on the test did he correct? __________

Name ______________________________

Multiplying Fractions

P 8-12

Write the multiplication problem that each model represents.

1. 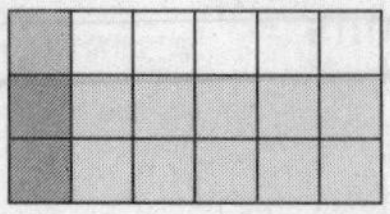

2. 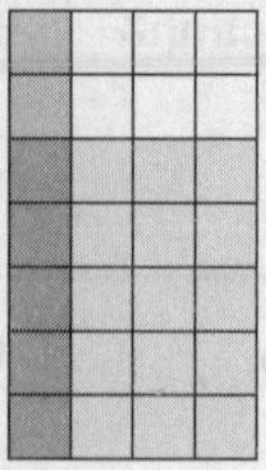

______________________________ ______________________________

Find each product. Simplify, if necessary.

3. $\frac{7}{8} \times \frac{4}{5} =$ ________

4. $\frac{3}{7} \times \frac{2}{3} =$ ________

5. $\frac{1}{6} \times \frac{2}{5} =$ ________

6. $\frac{2}{7} \times \frac{1}{4} =$ ________

7. $\frac{2}{9} \times \frac{1}{2} =$ ________

8. $\frac{3}{4} \times \frac{1}{3} =$ ________

9. $\frac{3}{8} \times \frac{4}{9} =$ ________

10. $\frac{1}{5} \times \frac{5}{6} =$ ________

11. $\frac{2}{3} \times \frac{5}{6} \times \frac{1}{4} =$ ________

12. $\frac{1}{2} \times \frac{1}{3} \times \frac{1}{4} =$ ________

13. Algebra If $\frac{4}{5} \times \blacksquare = \frac{2}{5}$, what is $\blacksquare$? ______________________________

14. Ms. Shoemaker's classroom has 35 desks arranged in 5 by 7 rows. How many students does Ms. Shoemaker have in her class if there are $\frac{6}{7} \times \frac{4}{5}$ desks occupied? ______________

Test Prep

15. Which does the model represent?

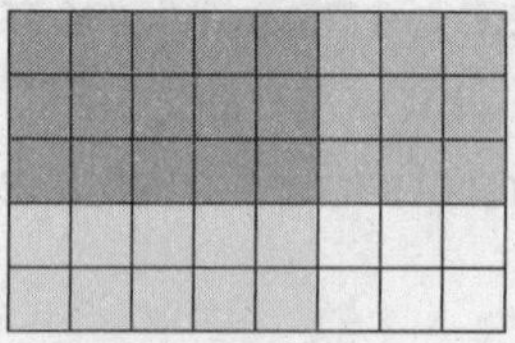

A. $\frac{3}{8} \times \frac{3}{5}$ **B.** $\frac{3}{5} \times \frac{5}{8}$

C. $\frac{7}{8} \times \frac{2}{5}$ **D.** $\frac{4}{8} \times \frac{3}{5}$

16. Writing in Math Describe a model that represents $\frac{3}{3} \times \frac{4}{4}$.

____

____

Name ____________________

Multiplying Mixed Numbers

R 8-13

Estimate $3\frac{3}{4} \times 2\frac{1}{8}$.

$3\frac{3}{4} \times 2\frac{1}{8}$ Round each mixed number to the nearest whole number.

$\downarrow \quad \downarrow$

$4 \times 2 = 8$ So, $3\frac{3}{4} \times 2\frac{1}{8}$ is about 8.

	How to multiply a mixed number by a mixed number	How to multiply a mixed number by a fraction	How to multiply a mixed number by a whole number
	Find $1\frac{1}{4} \times 2\frac{1}{2}$.	Find $3\frac{1}{2} \times \frac{1}{3}$.	Find $6 \times 3\frac{1}{3}$.
Step 1	Write the mixed numbers as improper fractions. $1\frac{1}{4} = \frac{5}{4}$ $\quad 2\frac{1}{2} = \frac{5}{2}$	Write the mixed number as an improper fraction. $3\frac{1}{2} = \frac{7}{2}$	Write both numbers as improper fractions. $6 = \frac{6}{1}$ $\quad 3\frac{1}{3} = \frac{10}{3}$
Step 2	Multiply as you would multiply fractions. $\frac{5}{4} \times \frac{5}{2} = \frac{25}{8}$	Multiply as you would multiply fractions. $\frac{7}{2} \times \frac{1}{3} = \frac{7}{6}$	Multiply as you would multiply fractions. $\frac{6}{1} \times \frac{10}{3} = \frac{60}{3}$
Step 3	Simplify the product. $\frac{25}{8} = 3\frac{1}{8}$ So, $1\frac{1}{4} \times 2\frac{1}{2} = 3\frac{1}{8}$.	Simplify the product. $\frac{7}{6} = 1\frac{1}{6}$ So, $3\frac{1}{2} \times \frac{1}{3} = 1\frac{1}{6}$.	Simplify the product. $\frac{60}{3} = 20$ So, $6 \times 3\frac{1}{3} = 20$.

Estimate. Then find each product. Simplify.

1. $1\frac{3}{4} \times 2\frac{1}{2} =$ ____________

2. $1\frac{1}{5} \times 1\frac{2}{3} =$ ____________

3. $2 \times 2\frac{1}{4} =$ ____________

4. $1\frac{2}{5} \times 2\frac{1}{4} =$ ____________

5. $2\frac{1}{2} \times 10 =$ ____________

6. $1\frac{2}{3} \times \frac{1}{5} =$ ____________

7. **Number Sense** Write a multiplication sentence for $4\frac{4}{5} + 4\frac{4}{5} + 4\frac{4}{5}$.

____

Name ______________________________

Multiplying Mixed Numbers

Estimate the product. Then complete the multiplication.

1. $5\frac{4}{5} \times 7 = \frac{\square}{5} \times \frac{7}{1} = \square$

____

2. $3\frac{2}{3} \times 5\frac{1}{7} = \frac{\square}{3} \times \frac{\square}{7} = \square$

____

Estimate. Then find each product. Simplify.

3. $4\frac{3}{5} \times \frac{2}{3}$ ______________

4. $6 \times 2\frac{2}{7}$ ______________

5. $7\frac{4}{5} \times 2\frac{1}{3}$ ______________

6. $3\frac{3}{4} \times 2\frac{4}{5}$ ______________

7. $2\frac{1}{5} \times \frac{7}{8}$ ______________

8. $6\frac{1}{3} \times 1\frac{5}{6}$ ______________

9. $1\frac{4}{5} \times 1\frac{1}{3} \times 1\frac{3}{4}$ ______________

10. $\frac{3}{4} \times 2\frac{2}{3} \times 5\frac{1}{5}$ ______________

11. Algebra Write a mixed number for *p* so that $3\frac{1}{4} \times p$ is more than $3\frac{1}{4}$. ______________

12. A model house is built on a base that measures $9\frac{1}{4}$ in. wide and $8\frac{4}{5}$ in. long. What is the total area of the model house's base? ______________

Test Prep

13. Which is $1\frac{3}{4}$ of $150\frac{1}{2}$?

A. 263 **B.** $263\frac{1}{8}$ **C.** $263\frac{3}{8}$ **D.** $264\frac{3}{8}$

14. Writing in Math Megan's dog Sparky eats $4\frac{1}{4}$ c of food each day. Explain how Megan can determine how much food to give Sparky if she needs to feed him only $\frac{2}{3}$ as much. Solve the problem.

____

____

____

Name ____________________

Understanding Division with Fractions

R 8-14

Find $3 \div \frac{1}{6}$.

Think: How many $\frac{1}{6}$s are in 3?

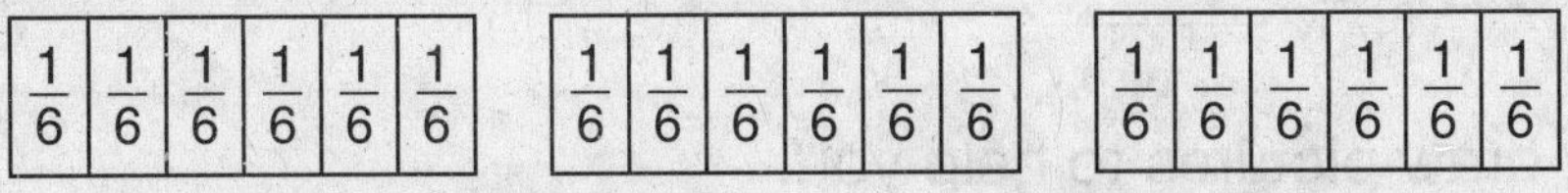

There are 3 wholes. Each whole is divided into sixths.

By counting, you can see that there are 18 $\frac{1}{6}$s in 3.

Use the picture to find each quotient.

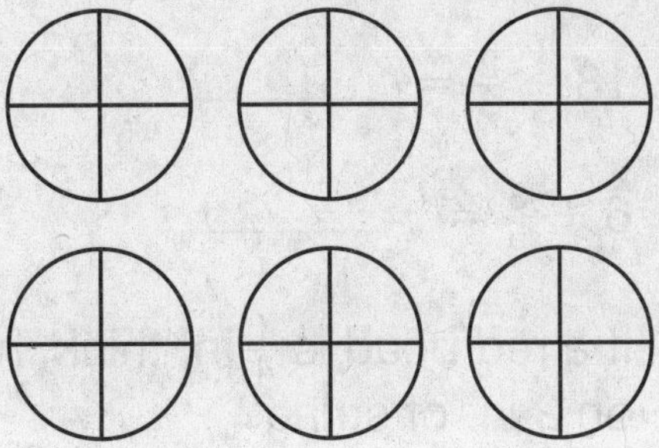

1. How many $\frac{1}{4}$s are in 2? ________

2. How many $\frac{2}{4}$s are in 5? ________

3. How many $\frac{3}{4}$s are in 6? ________

Find each quotient. You can draw pictures to help you.

4. $5 \div \frac{1}{3} =$ ________

5. $4 \div \frac{1}{5} =$ ________

6. $1 \div \frac{1}{9} =$ ________

7. $8 \div \frac{2}{5} =$ ________

8. $6 \div \frac{3}{8} =$ ________

9. $9 \div \frac{3}{5} =$ ________

10. **Number Sense** Brandy has 8 yd of fabric. She is cutting it into $\frac{8}{9}$ yd strips. How many strips can she cut?

____

Name________________________________

Understanding Division with Fractions **P 8-14**

Use the pictures to find each quotient.

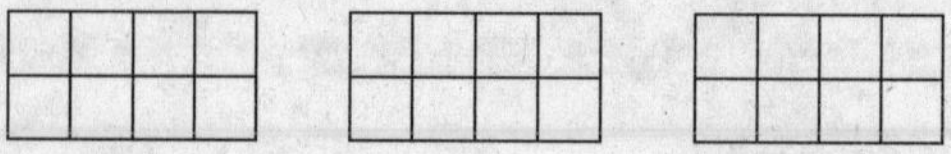

1. How many $\frac{1}{8}$s are in 1? $1 \div \frac{1}{8} =$ ______

2. How many $\frac{3}{8}$s are in 3? $3 \div \frac{3}{8} =$ ______

Find each quotient. You can draw pictures to help you.

3. $9 \div \frac{1}{3} =$ ______

4. $8 \div \frac{2}{5} =$ ______

5. $4 \div \frac{4}{5} =$ ______

6. $12 \div \frac{4}{7} =$ ______

7. $18 \div \frac{2}{3} =$ ______

8. $10 \div \frac{1}{8} =$ ______

9. $6 \div \frac{3}{5} =$ ______

10. $16 \div \frac{4}{9} =$ ______

11. If a red bead is $\frac{1}{4}$ in. thick, how many can you fit on 2 in. of string? ______

12. If a blue bead is $\frac{3}{4}$ in. thick, how many can you fit on 3 in. of string? ______

13. If you alternate red beads and blue beads, how many red beads and blue beads can you fit on 4 in. of string?

______

Test Prep

14. Which number is the quotient of $36 \div \frac{6}{7}$?

A. 40 **B.** 41 **C.** 42 **D.** 43

15. **Writing in Math** Explain why dividing any fraction by 1 equals the fraction.

______

______

______

Name

PROBLEM-SOLVING SKILL

Choose an Operation

Bow	Ribbon Needed
Small	$\frac{1}{2}$ yd
Medium	$\frac{2}{3}$ yd
Large	$\frac{3}{4}$ yd

Bows Hector's store gift wraps customers' purchases at the counter. He is making bows for the packages. The chart shows how much ribbon is needed for each size bow. How much ribbon is needed to make 9 medium bows?

Read and Understand

Show the main idea.

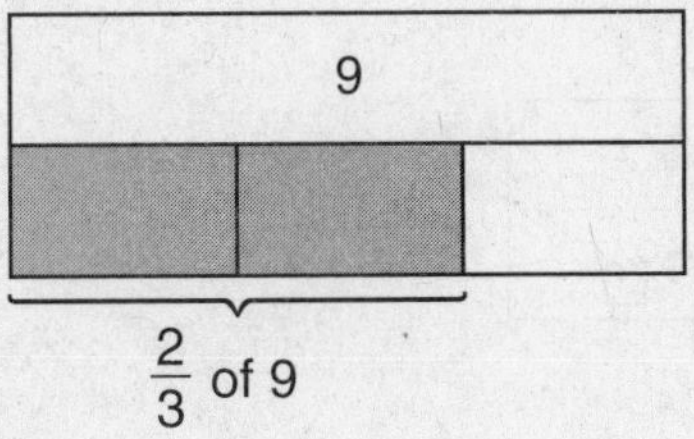

Plan and Solve

Choose an operation. Multiply to find out how much ribbon is needed.

$\frac{9}{1} \times \frac{2}{3} = \frac{18}{3} = 6$

It takes 6 yd to make 9 medium bows.

Draw a picture to show the main idea. Then choose an operation to solve the problem. Use the chart above for 1 and 2.

1. How much ribbon is needed to make 16 large bows?

____

2. How much ribbon is needed to make 12 small bows?

____

Name____

PROBLEM-SOLVING SKILL **P 8-15**

Choose an Operation

Draw a picture to show the main idea.
Then choose an operation to solve the problem.

About one-third of all solid waste in the United States comes from packaging materials.

Material Components of Packaging Waste

Material	Percentage
Paper	$47\frac{7}{10}\%$
Glass	$24\frac{1}{2}\%$
Plastic	■%
Steel	$6\frac{1}{2}\%$
Wood	■%
Aluminum	$2\frac{1}{3}\%$

1. The total percentage of packaging waste from plastic and paper is $62\frac{1}{5}\%$. What is the percentage of plastic?

$62\frac{1}{5}\%$	
$47\frac{7}{10}\%$	$n\%$

____

2. What is the combined total percentage of paper and glass in packaging waste?

$n\%$	
$47\frac{7}{10}\%$	$24\frac{1}{2}\%$

____

3. The sum of the percentage from steel, aluminum, and wood is $13\frac{1}{3}\%$. What is the percentage from wood?

$13\frac{1}{3}\%$		
$6\frac{1}{2}\%$	$2\frac{1}{3}\%$	$n\%$

____

4. If $27\frac{5}{6}$ tons of paper waste were produced in 1 year, how many tons of paper waste would be produced in 5 years?

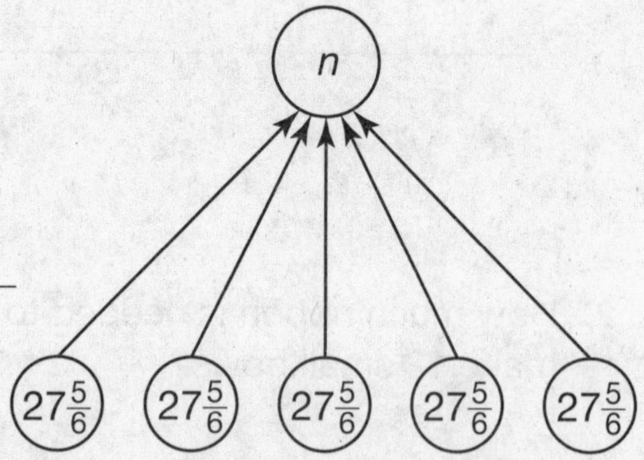

____

Name____

PROBLEM-SOLVING APPLICATIONS **R 8-16**

Mountain Biking

Anna, Gustavo, and Emily went mountain biking. Each person rode a different trail. Anna rode $7\frac{3}{10}$ mi. Gustavo biked $8\frac{9}{10}$ mi. Emily rode $10\frac{5}{10}$ mi. How many miles combined did the bikers ride?

First add the fractions.	Then add the whole numbers.	Simplify the sum, if necessary.
$7\frac{3}{10} + 8\frac{9}{10} + 10\frac{5}{10} \rightarrow \frac{17}{10}$	$7\frac{3}{10} + 8\frac{9}{10} + 10\frac{5}{10} = 25\frac{17}{10}$	$25\frac{17}{10} = 26\frac{7}{10}$

So, they rode a total of $26\frac{7}{10}$ mi.

1. How much farther did Emily bike than Gustavo? How much more than Anna? ________

2. On the second day, Terry joined the group. If you add the distance Terry biked, the group total increases to $35\frac{3}{10}$ mi. How far did Terry bike? ________

3. One trail is $\frac{3}{5}$ mi long. Gustavo wants to ride only $\frac{1}{3}$ of the trail, then stop for lunch. How long would the bikers ride? ________

4. Emily wants to ride the Mountain Trail. The trail is $7\frac{2}{3}$ mi long. If she rides the trail three times, how many miles total will she ride? ________

5. Each of the bikers is carrying a small bag of trail mix. Anna's bag has $\frac{2}{3}$ oz, Gustavo's has $\frac{5}{6}$ oz, and Emily's has $\frac{1}{5}$ oz. How many ounces of trail mix do they have altogether? ________

Name ____

PROBLEM-SOLVING APPLICATIONS **P 8-16**

Natural Facts

Solve. Write your answers in complete sentences.

The skin is considered the heaviest and largest organ of the human body. The table lists some interesting facts about the thickness of the skin.

Skin Facts

Average thickness	$\frac{2}{25}$ in.
Thickest (upper back)	$\frac{1}{5}$ in.
Thinnest (eyelids)	$\frac{1}{50}$ in.

1. How many eyelids have an equal thickness to the skin on the upper back?

____

2. What is the difference in thickness between the average thickness of the skin and the thickness of the skin on the eyelid?

____

3. How much thicker is the skin on the upper back than the skin of the eyelid?

____

The table at the right shows the percentage of some elements in the human body.

The Human Body

Element	Percentage
Carbon	$18\frac{1}{2}\%$
Hydrogen	$9\frac{1}{2}\%$
Nitrogen	$3\frac{1}{3}\%$
Calcium	$1\frac{1}{2}\%$
Phosphorous	1%

4. What percentage of the human body do carbon and hydrogen make up?

____

____

5. How much greater is the percentage of calcium and nitrogen combined than the percentage of phosphorus?

____

____

Name ____________________

Customary Units of Length

R 9-1

Customary Units of Length

12 inches (in.) = 1 foot (ft)

36 in. = 3 ft = 1 yard (yd)

5,280 ft = 1,760 yd = 1 mile (mi)

How to change between one customary unit of length and another:

A blue whale can measure up to 110 ft long. How long is that in inches?

Remember, 12 in. = 1 ft.

Multiply to find the length in inches.

110 × 12 = 1,320

110 ft is equal to 1,320 in.

So, a blue whale can be up to 1,320 in. long.

How to add and subtract measurements:

```
   3 ft 8 in.
+  2 ft 9 in.
-------------
   5 ft 17 in.
```

17 in. is greater than 1 ft, so you need to rename the answer.

17 in. = 1 ft 5 in.

5 ft + 1 ft + 5 in. = 6 ft 5 in.

So, 3 ft 8 in. + 2 ft 9 in. = 6 ft 5 in.

Complete.

1. 5 ft = ________ in.

2. 3 mi = ________ ft

3. 24 ft = ________ yd

4. 108 in. = ________ ft

5. 70 in. = ________ ft ________ in.

6. 13 yd = ________ ft

7.
```
      6 in.
+ 12 ft 2 in.
-------------
```

8.
```
   7 yd 8 ft
−  2 yd 5 ft
-------------
```

9.
```
   5 yd 2 ft
−       4 ft
-------------
```

10.
```
   5 ft 8 in.
−  1 ft 2 in.
-------------
```

11. Estimation What unit of length would you use to measure the length of a river? ________

Name____

Customary Units of Length

P 9-1

Complete.

1. 12 yd = __________ in.
2. 30 ft = __________ yd
3. 75 ft = __________ in.
4. 10 ft 7 in = __________ in.
5. 6 mi = __________ ft
6. 2 mi = __________ yd
7. 32 yd 2 ft + 4 yd 3 ft
8. 6 mi 10 yd − 4 mi 9 yd
9. 18 ft 4 in. + 22 ft 9 in.

The Statue of Liberty was a gift to the United States from the people of France. Some of the dimensions of the statue are shown here.

Measurements of the Statue of Liberty

Height from base of statue to the torch	151 ft 1 in.
Length of hand	16 ft 5 in.
Length of index finger	8 ft
Length of nose	4 ft 6 in.
Thickness of right arm	12 ft

10. What is the height, from the base of the statue to the torch, in inches? __________
11. What is the thickness of the statue's right arm in yards? __________

Test Prep

12. Which is equal to 435 in.?

A. 37 ft **B.** 36 ft **C.** 12 yd 3 in. **D.** 12 ft 3 in.

13. **Writing in Math** Explain how you can find the number of feet in 40 yd.

____

____

Name______________________________

Measuring with Fractions of an Inch

R 9-2

Measure the length of the pen to the nearest inch, nearest $\frac{1}{2}$ inch, nearest $\frac{1}{4}$ inch, and nearest $\frac{1}{8}$ inch.

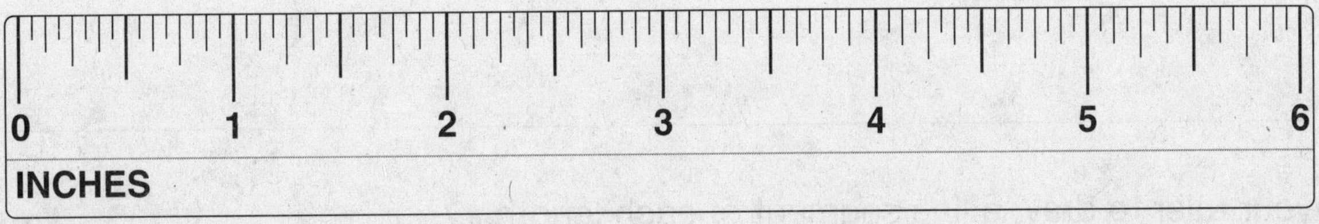

Step 1: Measure to the nearest inch.

The length is closest to 5 in.

Step 2: Measure to the nearest $\frac{1}{2}$ inch.

The length of the pen is closest to $4\frac{1}{2}$ in.

Step 3: Measure to the nearest $\frac{1}{4}$ inch.

The length is closest to $4\frac{3}{4}$ in.

Step 4: Measure to the nearest $\frac{1}{8}$ inch.

The length is closest to $4\frac{5}{8}$ in.

Measure each object to the nearest inch, $\frac{1}{2}$ inch, $\frac{1}{4}$ inch, and $\frac{1}{8}$ inch.

1.

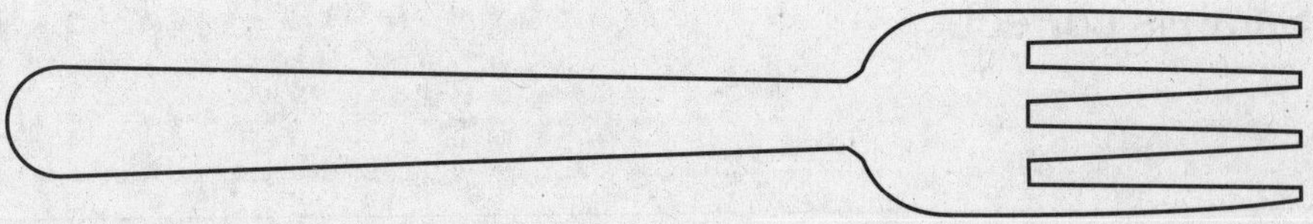

____

2.

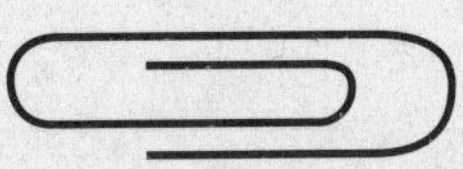

____

Use your ruler to draw a line segment of each length.

3. $\frac{7}{8}$ in.

4. $2\frac{1}{4}$ in.

5. $3\frac{1}{2}$ in.

Name ______________________________

Measuring with Fractions of an Inch

P 9-2

Measure each segment to the nearest inch, $\frac{1}{2}$ inch, $\frac{1}{4}$ inch, and $\frac{1}{8}$ inch.

1. ├──────────────┤

____

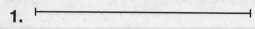

2. ├──────────┤

____

Use your ruler to draw a line segment of each length.

3. $\frac{3}{4}$ in.

4. $2\frac{1}{8}$ in.

5. Reasoning Sarah gave the same answer when asked to round $4\frac{7}{8}$ in. to the nearest $\frac{1}{2}$ inch and the nearest inch. Explain why Sarah is correct.

____

____

6. A real car is 18 times larger than a model car. If the model car is $5\frac{1}{4}$ in. long, how long is the real car? ________

Test Prep

7. What is the length of the segment? ├───────────┤

A. $1\frac{7}{8}$ in. **B.** $1\frac{3}{4}$ in. **C.** $1\frac{1}{2}$ in. **D.** 1 in.

8. Writing in Math If a line is measured as $1\frac{4}{8}$ in. long, explain how you could simplify the measurement.

____

____

Name ____________________

Metric Units of Length

R 9-3

Measurements in the metric system are based on the meter.

Example A

Which metric unit of length would be most appropriate to measure the length of a bumblebee?

A bumblebee is very small, so the millimeter is the most appropriate unit of length.

Example B

Write mm, cm, m, or km to complete the following sentence.

A chair is about 1 ______ tall; and a child's hand is about 8 ______ wide.

A chair is about 1 m tall, and a child's hand is about 8 cm wide.

Example C

What is the length to the nearest centimeter and to the nearest millimeter?

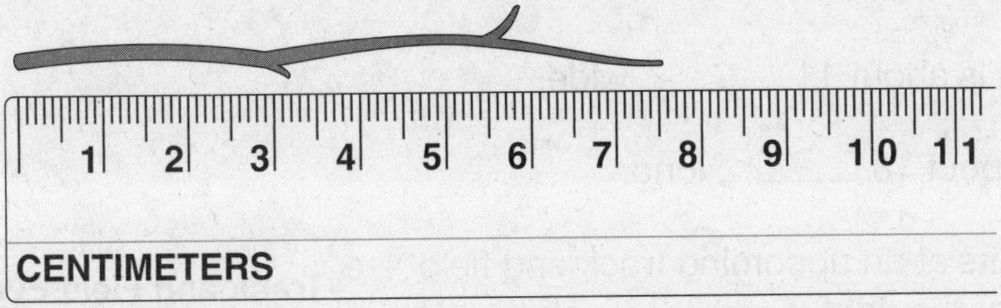

The twig is between 7 cm and 8 cm long, but it is closer to 8 cm long. There are 10 mm in every centimeter. The twig is 76 mm long.

Nearest cm: 8 cm

Nearest mm: 76 mm

Which unit would be most appropriate for each measurement? Write mm, cm, m, or km.

1. distance between two cities ______

2. length of a marker ______

3. width of a room ______

Measure each segment to the nearest centimeter and to the nearest millimeter.

4.

______; ______

5.

______; ______

Name ____________________

Metric Units of Length

P 9-3

Which unit would be most appropriate for each measurement? Write mm, cm, m, or km.

1. height of a basketball hoop ________
2. distance from Chicago to Miami ________

Measure each segment to the nearest centimeter and to the nearest millimeter.

3. ├───────────────┤ ________

4. ├───────────┤ ________

Complete each sentence with mm, cm, m, or km.

5. A classroom is about 11 ______ wide.
6. A pencil is about 18 ______ long.

Some of the events at an upcoming track and field meet are shown at the right.

Track and Field Events

50 m dash
1,500 m dash
400 m dash
100 m dash

7. In which event or events do athletes travel more than a kilometer?

____

8. In which event or events do athletes travel less than a kilometer?

____

Test Prep

9. Which is the correct measurement of the line segment? ├───────────┤

A. 410 mm **B.** 4.1 cm **C.** 44 mm **D.** 4 km

10. **Writing in Math** List one item in your classroom you would measure using centimeters and one item in the classroom you would measure using meters.

____

Name ____________________

Converting Metric Units Using Decimals

How to change from one metric unit to another:

In the metric system, every unit is 10 times more or less than the units next to it. This makes it easy to change from one unit to another.

For example:

The Olympic record in the women's high jump is 2.05 m. How many centimeters is that?

Remember, 1 m = 100 cm.

To change meters to centimeters, multiply.

$2.05 \times 100 = 205$

2.05 m = 205 cm

So, the record high jump is 205 cm.

How to change from one metric unit to another when decimals are involved:

To change large units to small units, multiply.

52.07 cm = ______ mm

Remember, 1 cm = 10 mm.

$52.07 \times 10 = 520.7$

So, 52.07 cm = 520.7 mm.

To change small units to large units, divide.

672 mm = ______ cm

Remember, 10 mm = 1 cm.

$672 \div 10 = 67.2$

So, 672 mm = 67.2 cm.

Find each equal measure.

1. 2.4 km = __________ m

2. 83 m = __________ dm

3. 0.9 dm = __________ mm

4. 2.4 m = __________ cm

5. 3 m = __________ cm

6. 52 km = __________ m

7. 204 cm = __________ m

8. 355 mm = __________ cm

9. 36 m = __________ cm

10. Number Sense Is 3.2 m the same as 320 mm? Explain.

____

Name ____________________

Converting Metric Units Using Decimals

P 9-4

Find each equal measure.

1. 25 m = __________ dam
2. 4.5 m = __________ cm
3. 200 hm = __________ m
4. 987 mm = __________ cm
5. 4.2 km = __________ m
6. 0.35 dm = __________ mm
7. 345 cm = __________ m
8. 10 m = __________ mm
9. **Number Sense** List three measurements with different units equal to 5 m.

____

Mount St. Helens, a volcano in the state of Washington, erupted on May 18, 1980. Before the eruption, Mount St. Helens was 2,950 m high. After the eruption, it was 2,550 m high.

10. What is the difference in height of Mount St. Helens before and after the eruption expressed in meters? __________
11. Before the eruption, how many kilometers high was Mount St. Helens? __________
12. After the eruption, how many hectometers high was Mount St. Helens? __________

Test Prep

13. Which measurement is equal to 10 dam?

A. 100 hm **B.** 1 m **C.** 0.1 hm **D.** 100 m

14. **Writing in Math** Explain how you would convert 4 m to millimeters.

____

____

Name ______________________________

Finding Perimeter

Perimeter is the distance around the outside of a polygon. You can find perimeter in two different ways.

Add the lengths of the sides:

Find the perimeter of the figure.

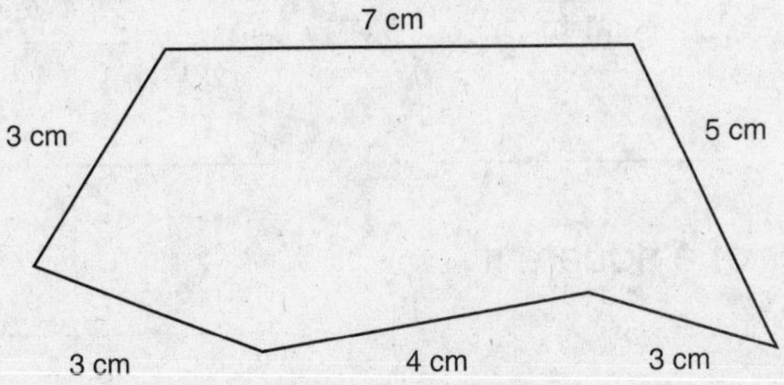

To find the perimeter, add up the sides.

$3 + 3 + 7 + 5 + 3 + 4 = 25$

So, the perimeter of the figure is 25 cm.

Use a formula:

Find the perimeter of the rectangle.

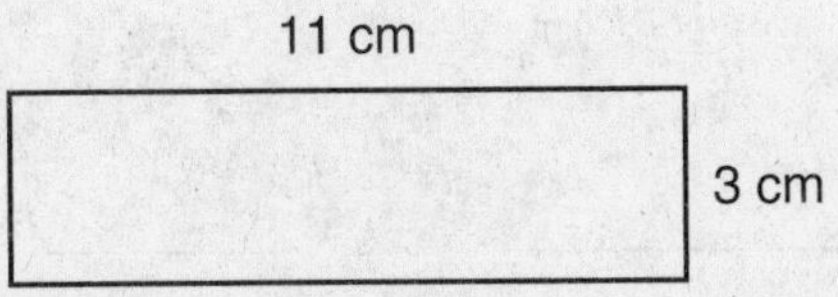

Perimeter = $(2 \times \text{length}) + (2 \times \text{width})$
$P = (2 \times l) + (2 \times w)$
$P = (2 \times 11) + (2 \times 3)$
$P = 22 + 6 = 28$ cm

So, the perimeter of the rectangle is 28 cm.

Find the perimeter of each figure.

1.

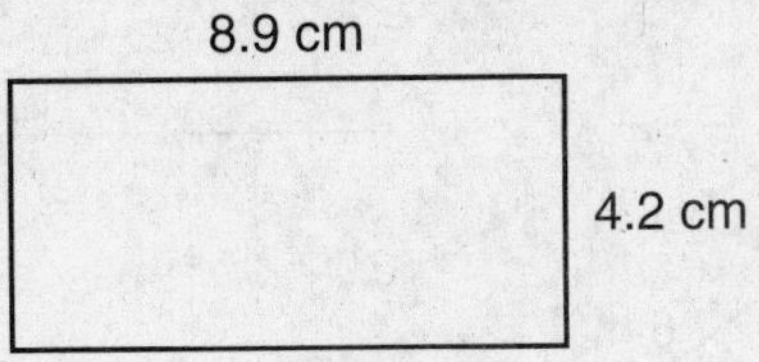

____

2.

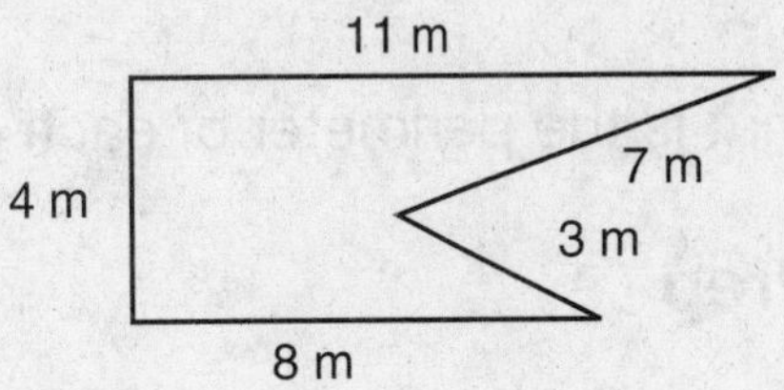

____

3.

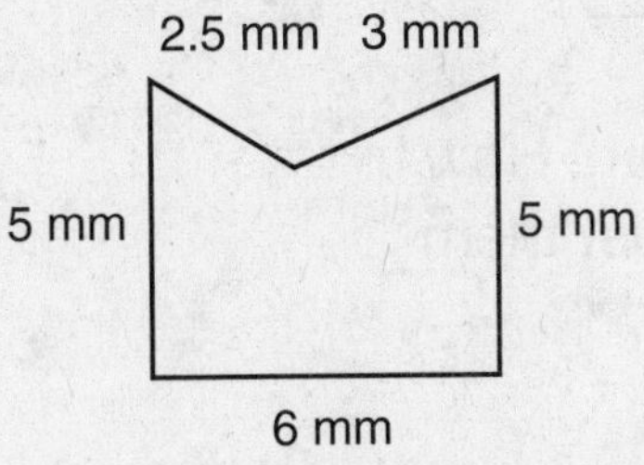

____

4.

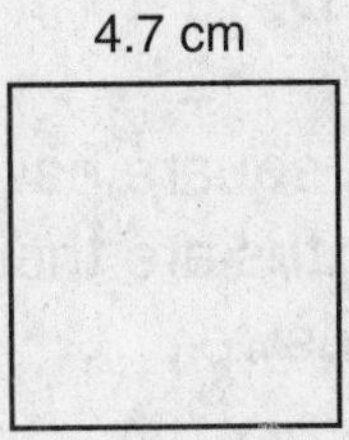

____

5. Number Sense The perimeter of a square is 24 in. What is the length of each side? ____________

Name

Finding Perimeter

Find the perimeter of each figure.

1. 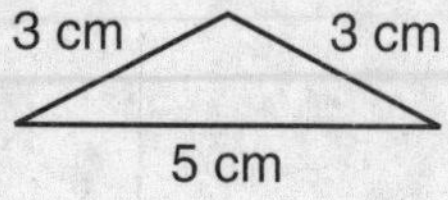

2. 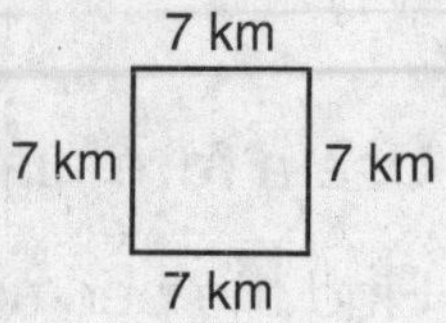

3. 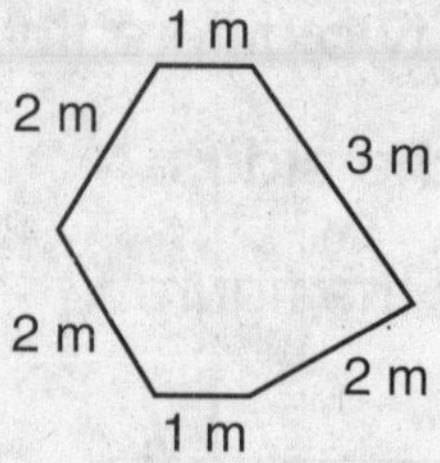

4. 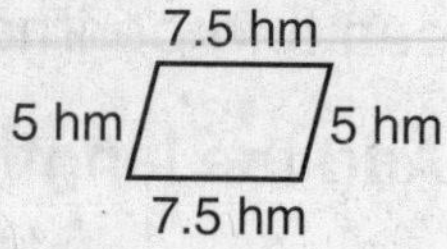

5. **Number Sense** What is the perimeter of a square if one of the sides is 3 mi?

The dimensions of a football field are shown at the right.

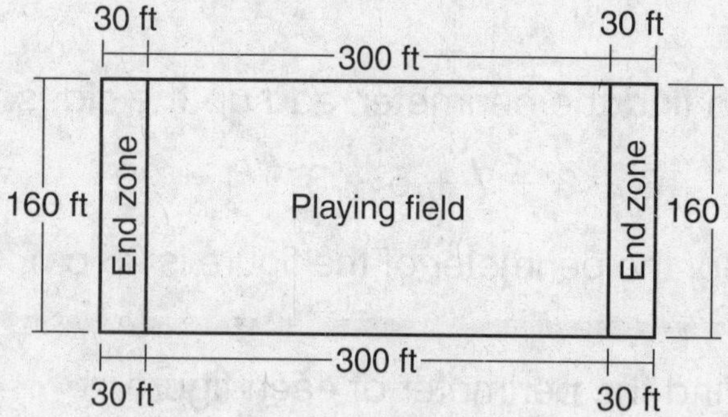

6. What is the perimeter of the entire football field including the end zones?

7. What is the perimeter of each end zone?

Test Prep

8. What is the perimeter of this figure?

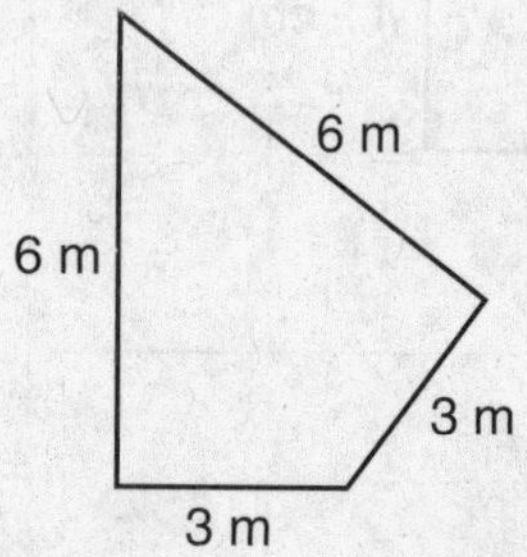

A. 18 m **B.** 15 m

C. 12 ft **D.** 10 ft

9. **Writing in Math** A square has a perimeter of 12 m. How many possible lengths are there for each side? List them and explain your answer.

Name ____________________

Finding Circumference

R 9-6

The circumference is the distance around a circle. You can use either of the formulas illustrated below to find the circumference of a circle.

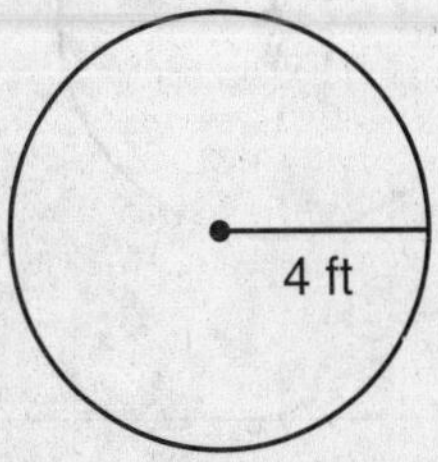

$C = \pi \times 2 \times r$

$C = 3.14 \times 2 \times 4$

$C = 25.12$

So, the circumference of the circle is 25.12 ft.

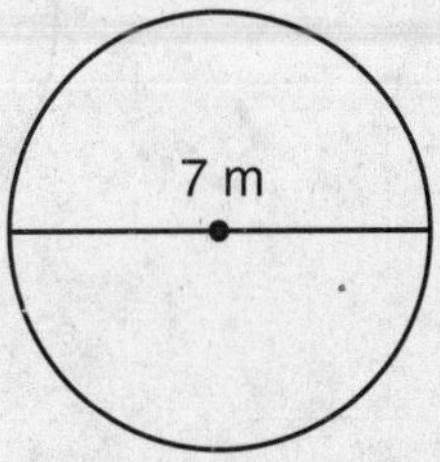

$C = \pi \times d$

$C = 3.14 \times 7$

$C = 21.98$

So, the circumference of the circle is 21.98 m.

Find each circumference. Use 3.14 for π.

1.

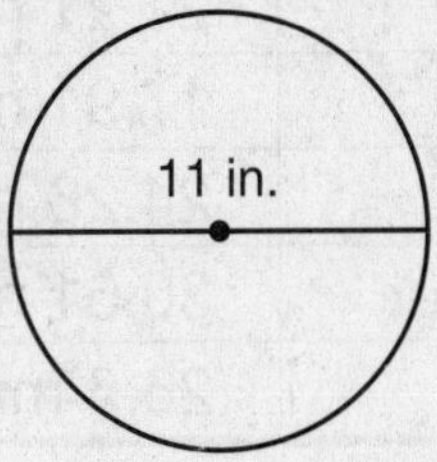

____

2.

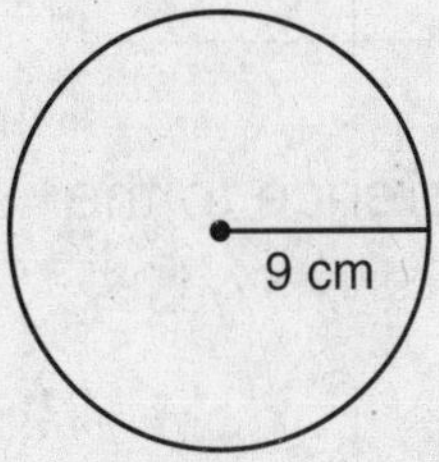

____

3.

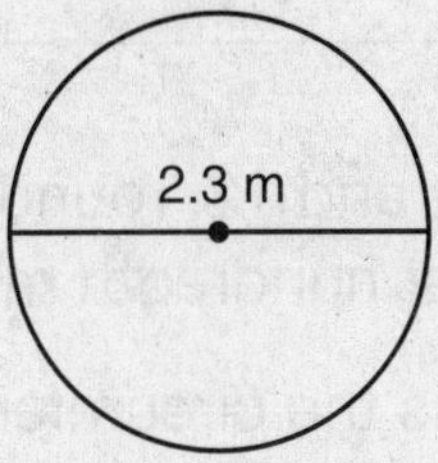

____

4.

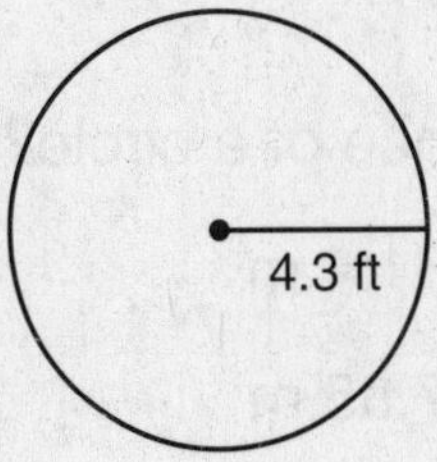

____

5.

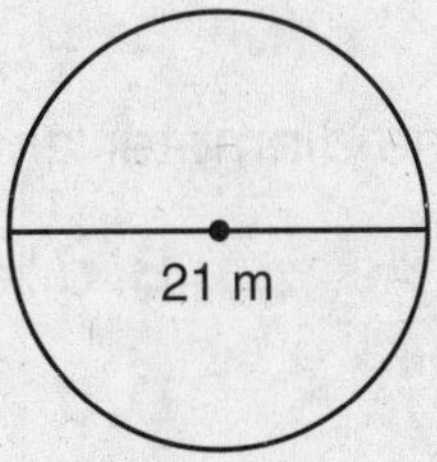

____

6.

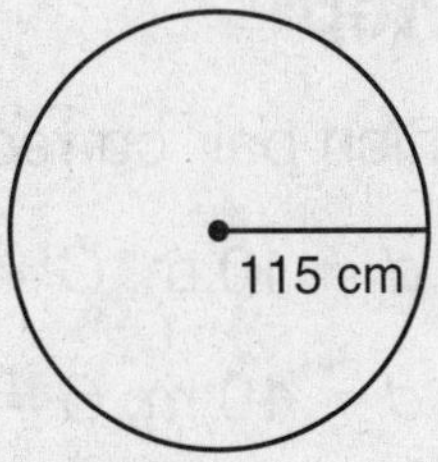

____

Name ____________________

Finding Circumference

P 9-6

Find each circumference. Use 3.14 for π.

1.

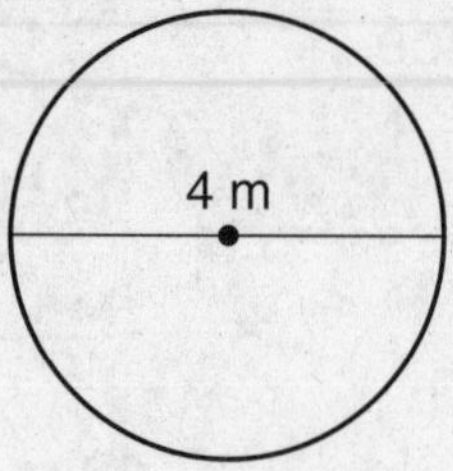

2.

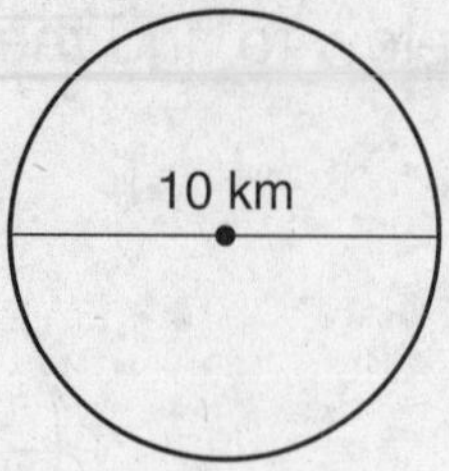

3.

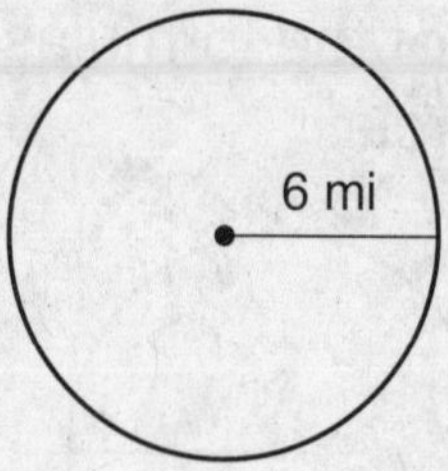

4. $d = 7$ hm

5. $r = 7$ in.

6. $r = 9$ km

7. $d = 2$ in.

8. $d = 8$ cm

9. $d = 6$ yd

10. Which of the U.S. coins listed in the table have circumferences greater than 68 mm?

Coin	Diameter
Penny	19.05 mm
Nickel	21.21 mm
Dime	17.91 mm
Quarter	24.26 mm
Half-dollar	30.61 mm
Dollar	26.5 mm

For 11 and 12, round the circumference to the nearest hundredth millimeter.

What is the circumference of a

11. penny? ____________

12. dime? ____________

Test Prep

13. Which pair correctly shows the diameter and circumference of a circle?

A. $d = 10$ m, $C = 15.7$ m

B. $d = 10$ m, $C = 31.4$ m

C. $d = 10$ m, $C = 50$ m

D. $d = 10$ m, $C = 7.85$ m

14. Writing in Math Could you find the circumference of a circle using the exact value for π? Why or why not?

Name ____________________

Finding Area

R 9-7

Area is the number of squares needed to cover a surface or figure. You can count square units to find the area of a figure.

What is the area of the figure?

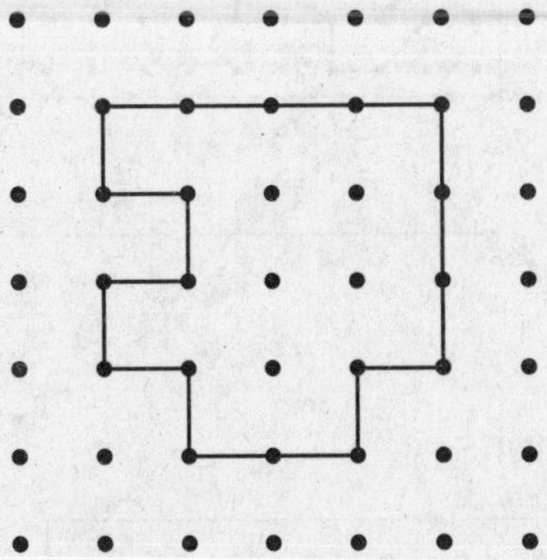

Count the number of square units.

There are 13 square units.

So, the area is 13 square units.

Draw a figure with an area of $8\frac{1}{2}$ square units.

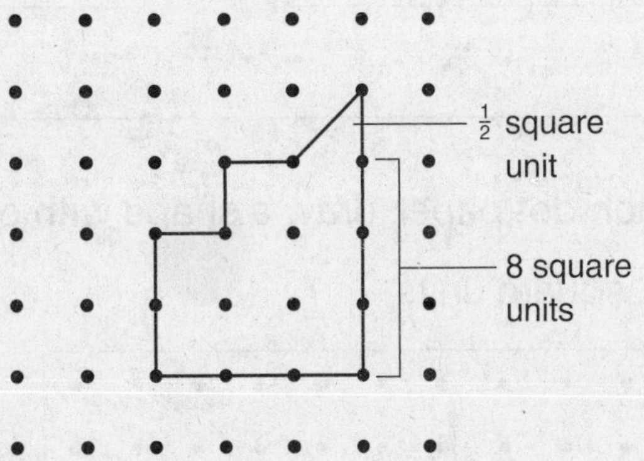

Find the area of each figure.

1.

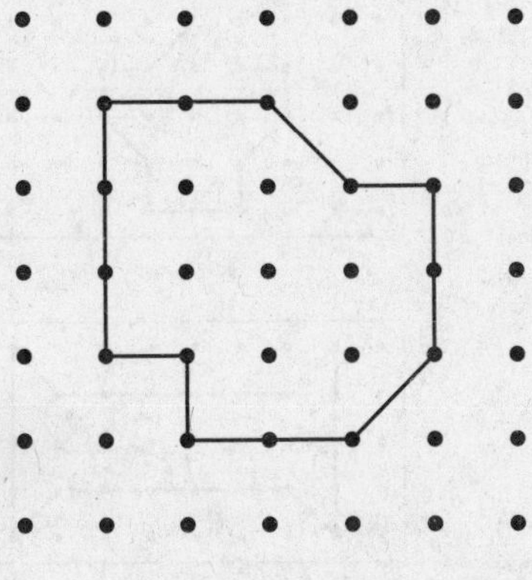

2.

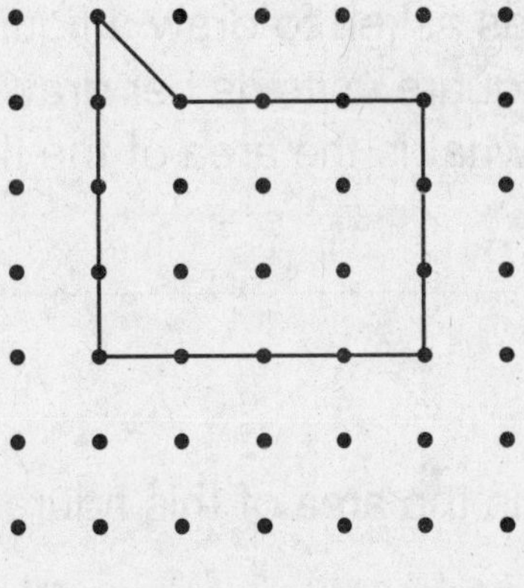

____________________ ____________________

On dot paper, draw a shape with each given area.

3. $8\frac{1}{2}$ square units

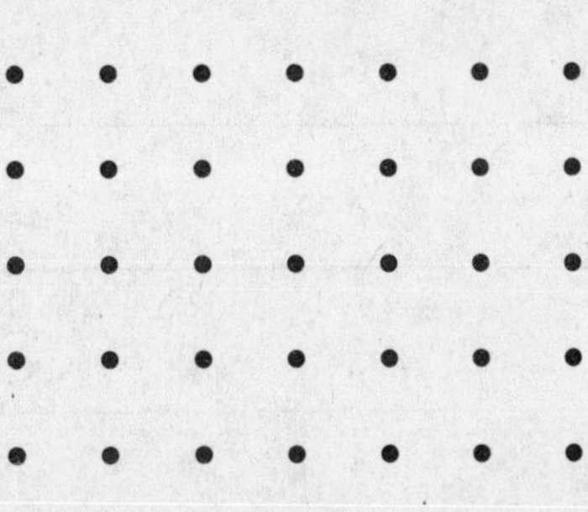

4. 18 square units

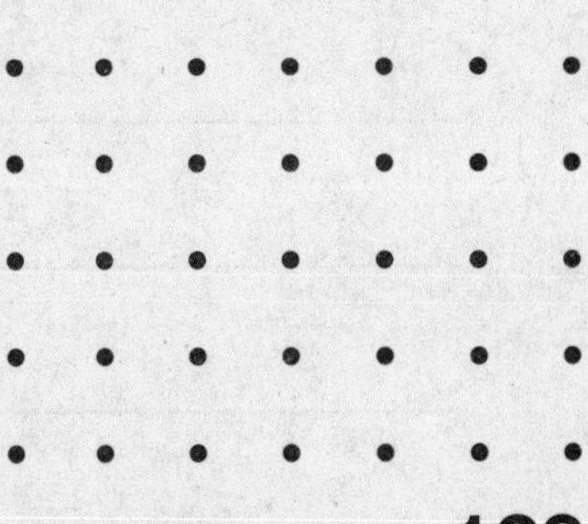

Name ____________________

Finding Area

P 9-7

Find the area of each figure.

1. 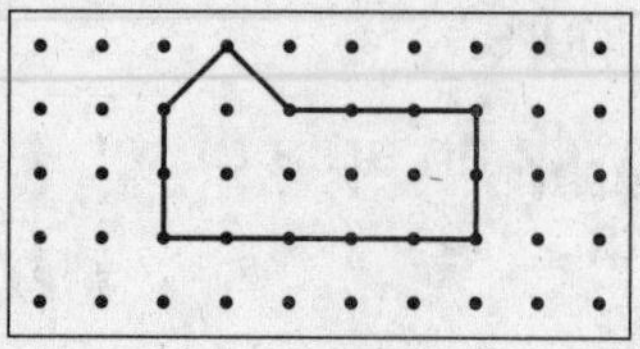

2. 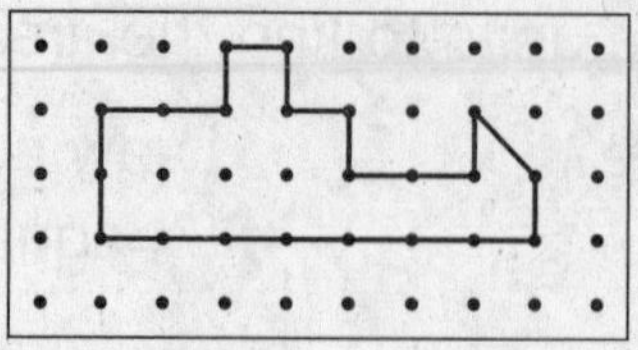

3. 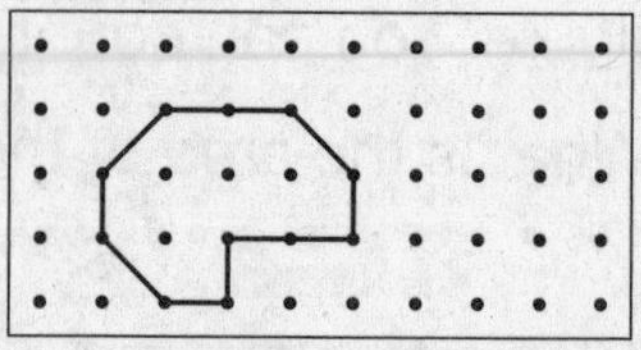

On each dot paper, draw a shape with each given area.

4. 7 square units

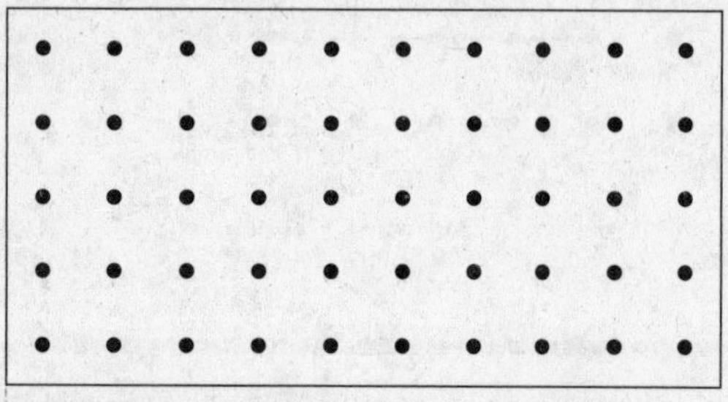

5. $5\frac{1}{2}$ square units

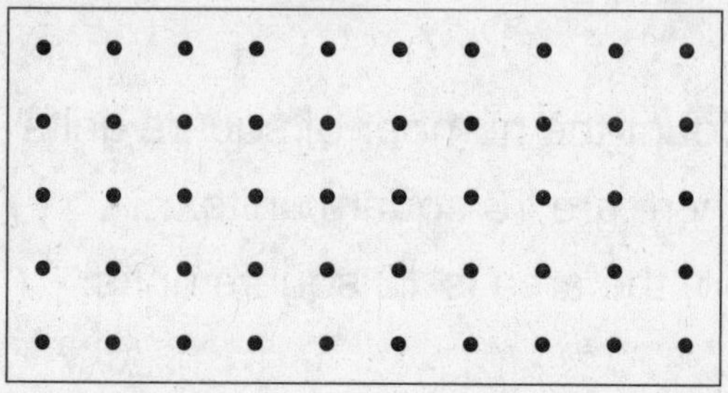

6. Tara was asked to draw a figure with an area of 11 square units. Is her drawing correct? If not, what is the area of the figure she drew?

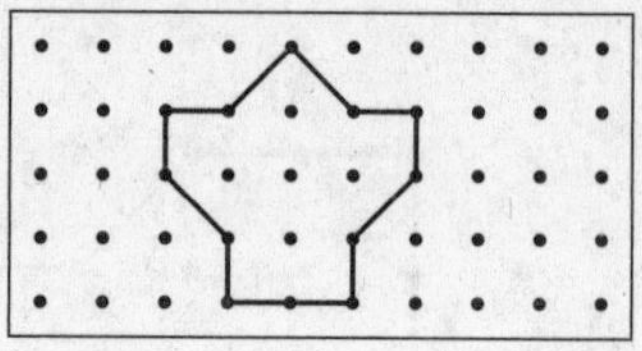

Test Prep

7. Which is the area of this figure?

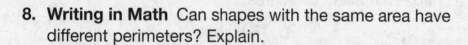

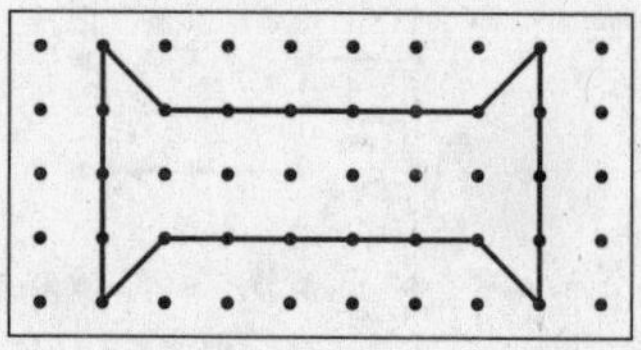

A. 17 square units

B. 16 square units

C. 15 square units

D. 14 square units

8. **Writing in Math** Can shapes with the same area have different perimeters? Explain.

Name ____________________

Areas of Squares and Rectangles

You can use formulas to find the areas of rectangles and squares.

Find the area of the rectangle.

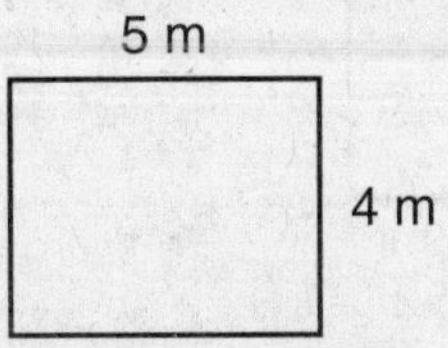

Use this formula for rectangles:

Area = length × width

$A = l \times w$

$A = 5 \text{ m} \times 4 \text{ m}$

$A = 20$ square meters $= 20 \text{ m}^2$

Find the area of the square.

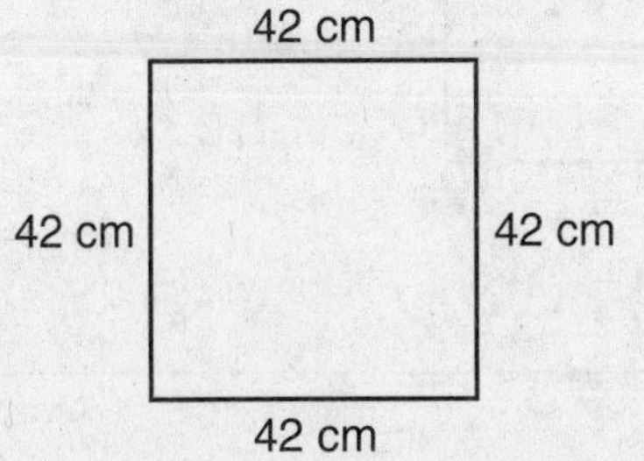

Use this formula for squares:

Area = side × side

$A = 42 \text{ cm} \times 42 \text{ cm}$

$A = 1{,}764$ square centimeters $=$ $1{,}764 \text{ cm}^2$

Find the area of each figure.

1.

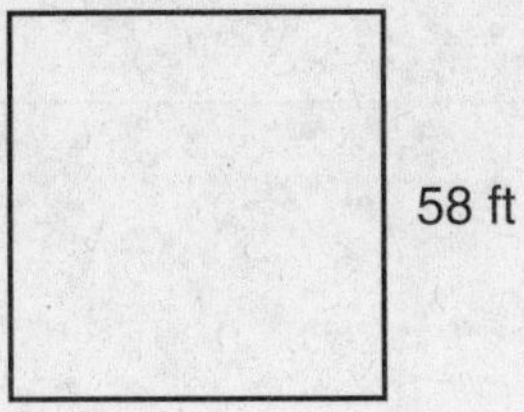

____

2.

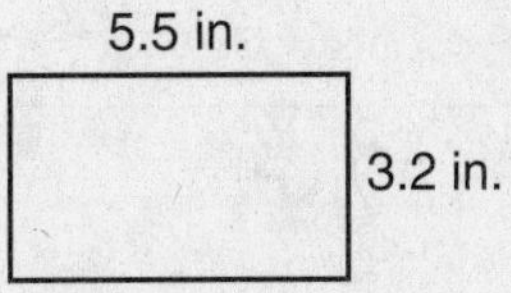

____

3. a square with a side of 12.4 m ____________________

4. a rectangle with a length of 9.7 cm and a width of 7.3 cm ____________________

5. **Number Sense** If the area of a square is 81 in^2, what is the length of one side? ____________________

6. What is the area of the tennis court?

____

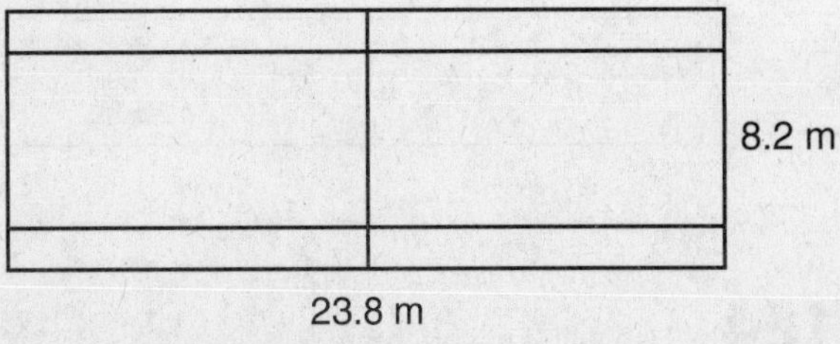

Name

Areas of Squares and Rectangles

P 9-8

Find the area of each figure.

1.

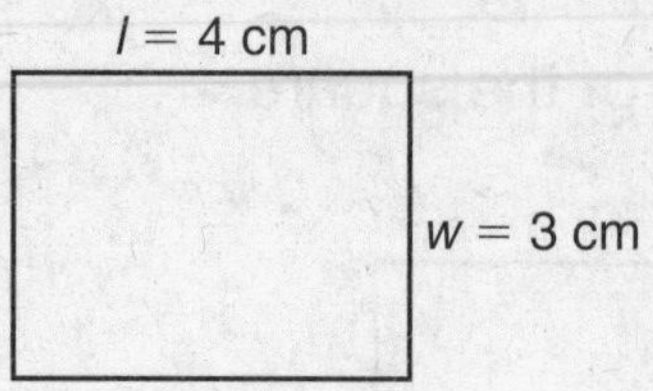

2.

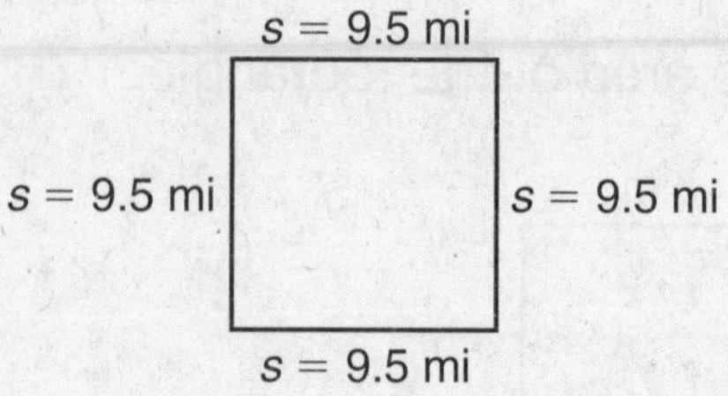

3. a rectangle with sides 6.5 km and 3.4 km

4. a square with a side of 10.2 ft

5. a rectangle with sides 9 m and 9.2 m

6. **Number Sense** Which units would you use to measure the area of a rectangle with $l = 1$ m and $w = 34$ cm? Explain.

Test Prep

7. Which of the following shapes has an area of 34 ft^2?

A. A square with $s = 8.5$ m

B. A rectangle with $l = 15$ ft, $w = 2$ ft

C. A square with $s = 16$ ft

D. A rectangle with $l = 17$ ft, $w = 2$ ft

8. **Writing in Math** The area of a square is 49 m^2. What is the length of one of its sides? Explain how you solved this problem.

Name ______________________________

Areas of Parallelograms

R 9-9

The formula used to find the area of a parallelogram is similar to the one you used to find the area of a rectangle. Instead of using length × width, use base × height.

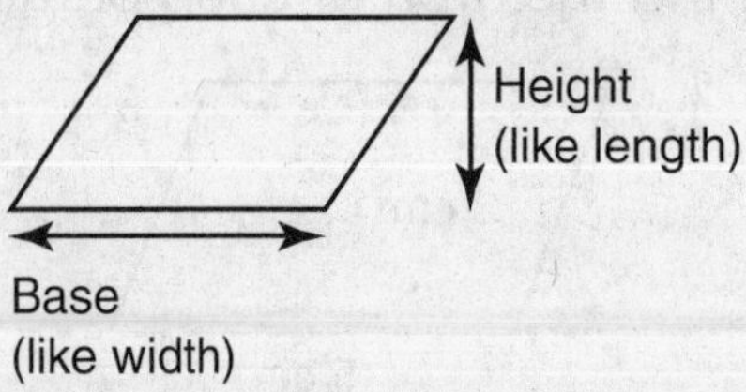

How to find the area of a parallelogram:

Find the area of the parallelogram.

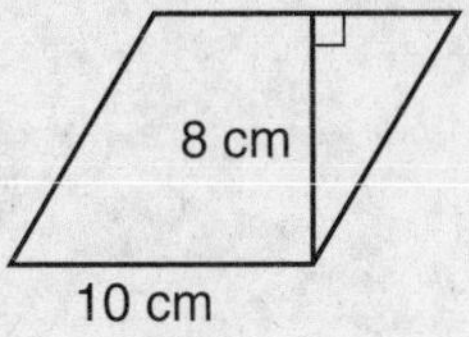

Area = base × height

$A = b \times h$

$A = 10\text{ cm} \times 8\text{ cm}$

$A = 80\text{ cm}^2$

How to find the missing measurement of a parallelogram:

Area = 55 cm^2 base = 11 cm
height = ? cm

Remember, area = base × height.

$55\text{ cm}^2 = 11\text{ cm} \times ?\text{ cm}$

$55\text{ cm}^2 = 11\text{ cm} \times 5\text{ cm}$

So, the height of the parallelogram is 5 cm.

Find the area of each parallelogram.

1.

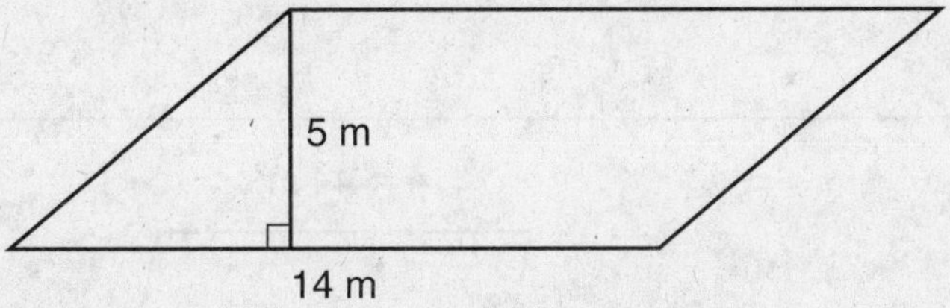

____

2.

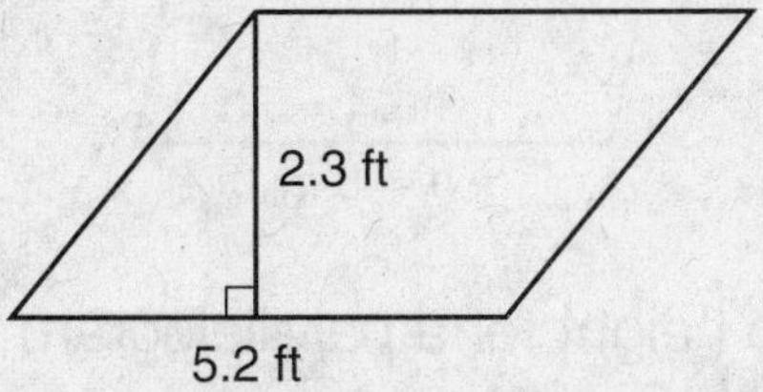

____

Find the missing measurement for each parallelogram.

3. $A = 72\text{ in}^2$, $b = 9$ in, $h =$ ______________

4. $A = 238\text{ ft}^2$, $b =$ ______________, $h = 14$ ft

Name ______________________________

Areas of Parallelograms

Find the area of each parallelogram.

1.

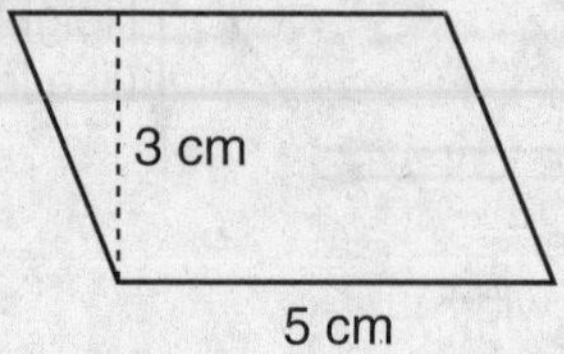

____

2.

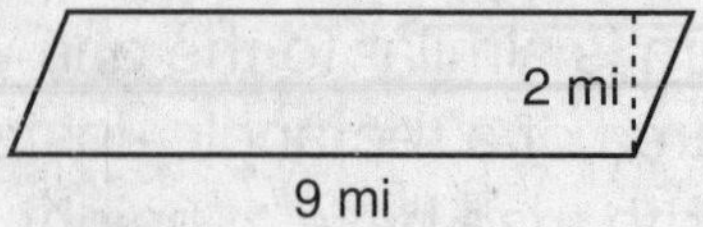

____

3.

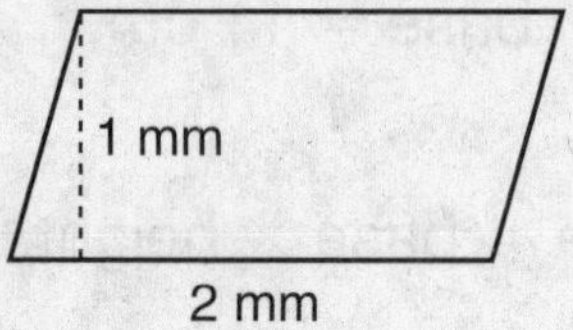

____

4.

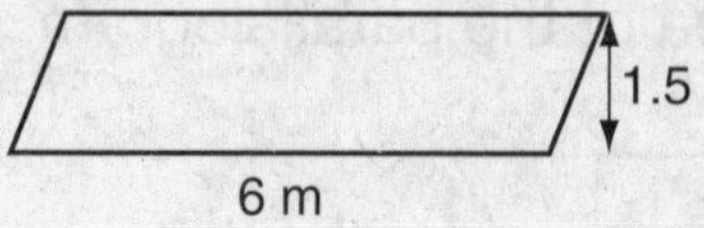

____

Algebra Find the missing measurement for the parallelogram.

5. $A = 34 \text{ in}^2$, $b = 17$ in., $h =$ ______________

6. List three sets of base and height measurements for parallelograms with areas of 40 square units.

____

____

Test Prep

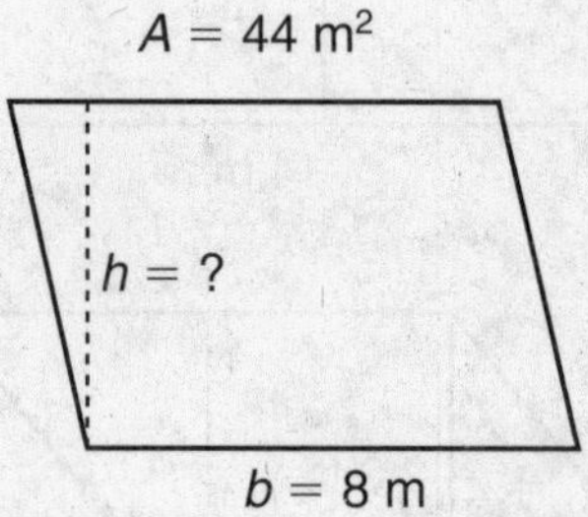

7. Which is the height of the parallelogram?

A. 55 m **B.** 55.5 m

C. 5 m **D.** 5.5 m

8. Writing in Math What are a possible base and height for a parallelogram with an area of 45 ft^2? Explain how you solved this problem.

____

____

Name ____________________

Areas of Triangles

Area of a triangle $= \frac{1}{2} \times$ base $\times$ height

How to find the area of a triangle:

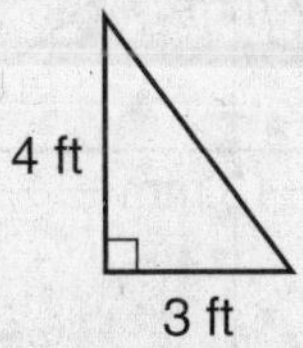

$A = \frac{1}{2} \times b \times h$

$A = \frac{1}{2} \times 3 \text{ ft} \times 4 \text{ ft}$

$A = \frac{1}{2} \times 12 \text{ ft}$

$A = 6 \text{ ft}^2$

How to find the missing measurement of a triangle:

Area $= 100 \text{ cm}^2$ base $= 40$ cm
height $=$? cm

Remember, Area $= \frac{1}{2} \times$ base $\times$ height.

$100 \text{ cm}^2 = \frac{1}{2} \times 40 \text{ cm} \times ? \text{ cm}$

$100 \text{ cm}^2 = 20 \text{ cm} \times ? \text{ cm}$

$100 \text{ cm}^2 = 20 \text{ cm} \times 5 \text{ cm}$

So, the height of the triangle is 5 cm.

Find the area of each triangle.

1.

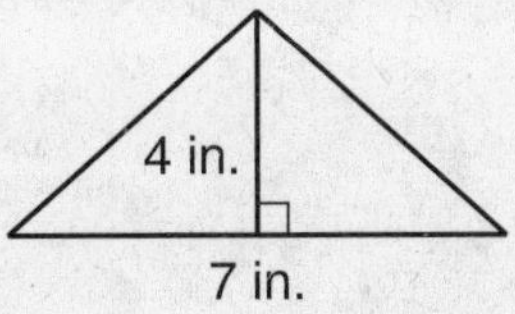

____

2.

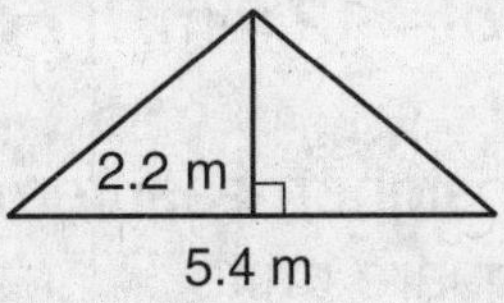

____

3.

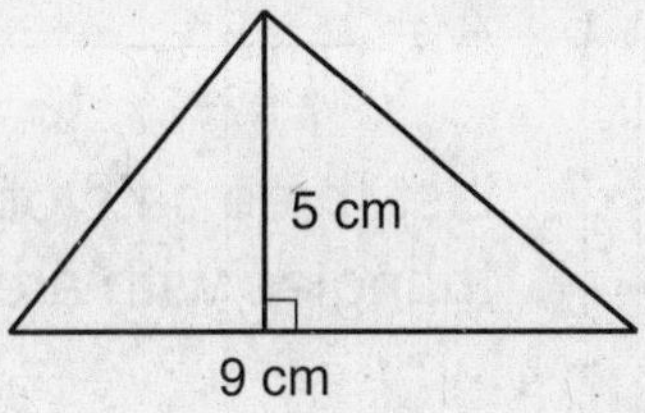

____

Find the missing measurement for each triangle.

4. $A = 16 \text{ in}^2$, $b = 8$ in., $h =$ ____________

5. $A = 20 \text{ m}^2$, $b =$ ____________, $h = 4$ m

6. $A =$ ____________, $b = 6.4$ ft, $h = 7.6$ ft

7. $A = 14 \text{ cm}^2$, $b = 2$ cm, $h =$ ____________

Name ______________________________

Areas of Triangles

Find the area of each triangle.

1.

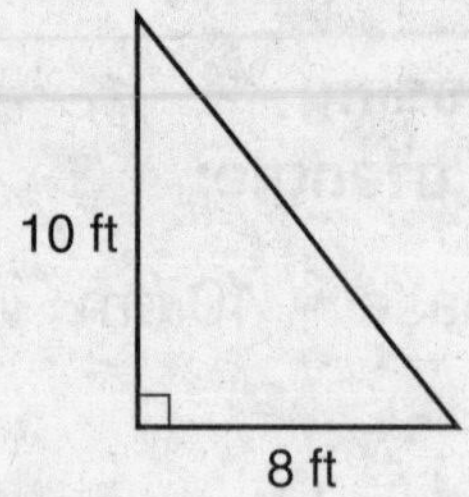

____

2.

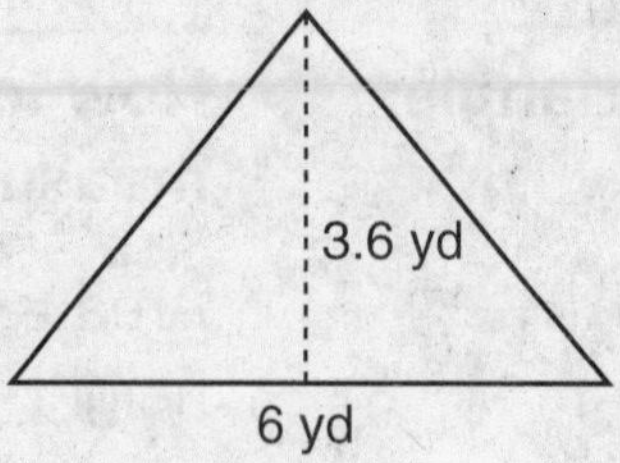

____

3.

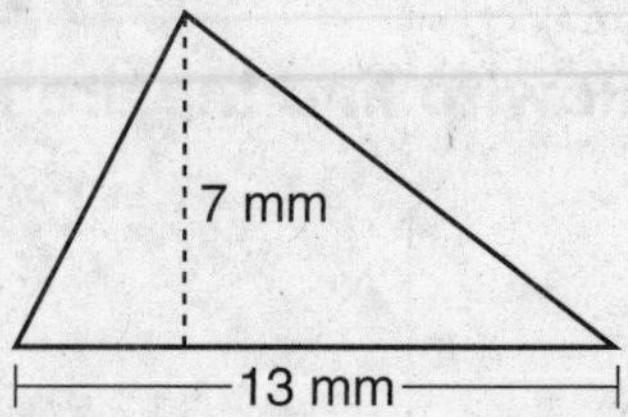

____

4. **Number Sense** What is the base measurement of a triangle with an area of 30 m^2 and a height of 10 m? ________

Algebra Find the missing measurement for each triangle.

5. $A = 36\text{ mi}^2$, $b =$ ______________, $h = 12$ mi

6. $A =$ ______________, $b = 12$ mm, $h = 7.5$ mm

7. List three sets of base and height measurements for triangles with areas of 30 square units.

____

____

Test Prep

8. Which is the height of the triangle?

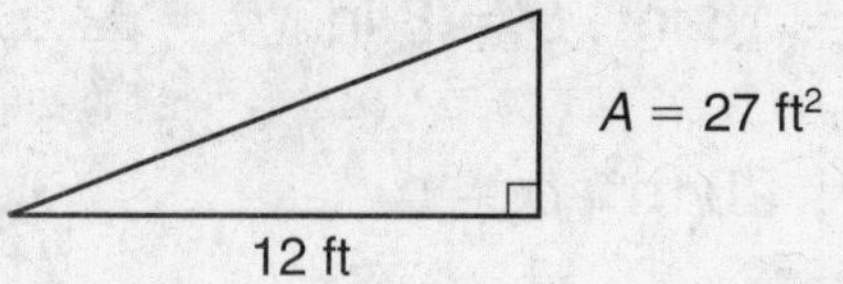

A. 4.5 ft　　**B.** 6 ft

C. 8 ft　　**D.** 9 ft

9. **Writing in Math** Can you find the base and height measurements for a triangle if you know that the area is 22 square units? Explain why or why not.

____

____

Name ____________________

PROBLEM-SOLVING STRATEGY **R 9-11**

Draw a Picture

Tiles Paula's new room is shaped like a rectangle and has an area of 12 square feet. She has purchased 12 square tiles to place on the floor. Each tile is 1 ft long on each side. Will all 12 of the tiles fit if the room has a perimeter of 16 ft?

Read and Understand

Step 1: What do you know?

The room is shaped like a rectangle and has an area of 12 square feet. Paula has 12 tiles that are 1 ft long on each side.

Step 2: What are you trying to find?

If all the tiles will fit on the floor if the room has a perimeter of 16

Plan and Solve

Step 3: What strategy will you use?

Strategy: Draw a picture

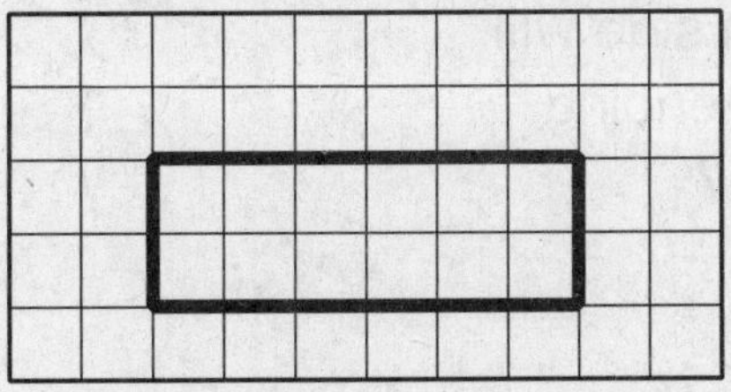

The rectangle has an area of 12 square feet and a perimeter of 16 ft.
So Paula's 12 tiles will fit.

Look Back and Check

Step 4: Is your answer reasonable?

Yes, I found the area of the rectangle by counting squares, and the perimeter by counting the units on each side. The work is correct.

Solve.

1. Elise wants to plant a garden with an area of 35 ft^2. What could the length and width of the garden be?

____

____

Name ______________________________

PROBLEM-SOLVING STRATEGY **P 9-11**

Draw a Picture

Solve. Write the answer in a complete sentence.

1. Erica painted a picture of her dog. The picture has an area of 3,600 cm^2 and is a square. She has placed the picture in a frame that is 5 cm wide. What is the perimeter of the picture frame?

____

____

2. The new playground at Middledale School will be enclosed by a fence. The playground will be a square and will have an area of 225 yd^2. The number of yards on each side will be a whole number. What is the least amount of fencing that could be required to enclose the playground?

____

____

3. The floor in the back of Karl's truck is 6 ft long and has an area of 24 ft^2. Karl wants to haul as many boxes on the floor as possible. He cannot stack the boxes or they will fall out as he drives. If each square box is 2 ft long, how many boxes can Karl fit in the back of his truck?

____

____

Name ______________________________

Time

How to convert from one unit of time to another:

How many days have passed if 96 hr have gone by?

To change from smaller units to larger units, divide.

96 hours = _____ days

Remember, there are 24 hr in one day. So divide 96 by 24.

$96 \div 24 = 4$

So, 4 days passed if 96 hr went by.

Units of Time

60 seconds (sec) = 1 minute (min)

60 minutes = 1 hour (hr)

24 hours = 1 day (d)

7 days = 1 week (wk)

12 months (mo) = 1 year (yr)

52 weeks = 1 year

365 days = 1 year

366 days = 1 leap year

100 years = 1 century

Find each equal measure.

1. 7 min = ____________ sec

2. 3 yr = ____________ wk

3. 1 century = ____________ d

4. 4 yr, 15 wk = ____________ d

5. 216 hr = ____________ d

6. 91 d = ____________ wk

7. 8 hr = ____________ sec

8. 6 hr 20 min = ____________ sec

9. 68 min = ____________ sec

10. 154 d = ____________ wk

11. 336 hr = ____________ d

12. 7 yr, 22 wk = ____________ d

13. **Reasoning** Is 500,000 sec more or less than 1 wk?

____

14. The men's Olympic record for running 800 m is 1 min, 43 sec. How many seconds is that?

____

Name ______________________

Time

P 9-12

Find each equal measure.

1. 96 hr = __________ d

2. 343 d = __________ wk

3. 6 yr 9 d = __________ d

4. 1,416 hr = __________ d

5. 12 h 9 min = __________ sec

6. 3 yr 5 d = __________ hr

7. **Reasoning** Are there more days or weeks in a century? How do you know?

____

____

Information about the International Space Station is in the table.

Expedition Number	Time from Launching to Landing
Expedition One	138 d, 18 hr, 39 min
Expedition Two	167 d, 6 hr, 4 min

8. Express the length of Expedition One in hours and minutes.

____

9. Express the length of Expedition Two in weeks, days, hours, and minutes.

____

Test Prep

10. Which length of time is equivalent to 92 hr?

A. 4 d **B.** 331,200 min **C.** 5,520 min **D.** 3,200 sec

11. **Writing in Math** How many hours are in 43,200 sec? Explain how you solved this problem.

____

____

Name ______________________________

Elapsed Time

How to find elapsed time:

Iris left her house at 11:15 A.M. and arrived at her grandparents' house at 1:30 P.M. How long did the trip take?

Use a number line to count up.

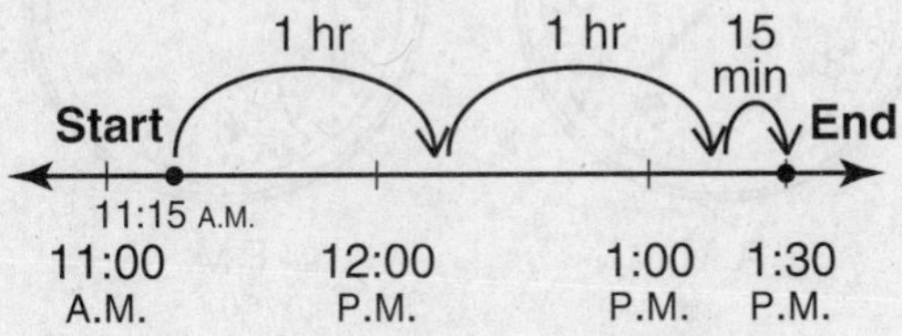

The trip took 2 hr, 15 min.

How to use elapsed time to find when an event began or ended:

Omar and his brothers played floor hockey for 1 hr, 9 min. They finished playing at 6:30 P.M. At what time did they begin playing?

You can subtract to find the start time.

End Time − Elapsed Time = Start Time

   6 hr 30 min
− 1 hr   9 min
____
   5 hr 21 min

So, they began playing at 5:21 P.M.

Find each elapsed time.

1. 8:13 P.M. to 10:00 P.M. ______________

2. 11:24 A.M. to 2:47 P.M. ______________

3. 3:35 P.M. to 6:09 P.M. ______________

4. 9:55 P.M. to 11:42 P.M. ______________

Find each start time or end time using the given elapsed time.

5. Start: 8:49 A.M.
Elapsed: 5 hr, 20 min
____

6. End: 8:27 P.M.
Elapsed: 4 hr, 13 min
____

Add or subtract.

7.   6 hr 31 min
\+ 7 hr 16 min
____

8.   7 hr 12 min
− 3 hr 30 min
____

9.   3 hr 5 min
\+ 8 hr 55 min
____

10.   9 hr 5 min
− 8 hr 22 min
____

Name ____________________

Elapsed Time

Find each elapsed time.

1. 9:59 P.M. to 10:45 P.M. ____________

2. 11:45 A.M. to 3:38 P.M. ____________

3. 

A.M. A.M.

____

4. 

A.M. P.M.

____

Find the start time using the given elapsed time.

5. Start: 3:46 P.M Elapsed: 2 hr 20 min ____________

6. Add.

$$\begin{array}{r} 2 \text{ hr } 45 \text{ min} \\ + \ 3 \text{ hr } 58 \text{ min} \\ \hline \end{array}$$

7. Add.

$$\begin{array}{r} 6 \text{ hr } 47 \text{ min} \\ + \ 5 \text{ hr } 28 \text{ min} \\ \hline \end{array}$$

The White House Visitor Center is open from 7:30 A.M. until 4:00 P.M.

8. Tara and Miguel got to the Visitor Center when it opened, and spent 1 hr 20 min there. At what time did they leave?

____

9. Jennifer left the Visitor Center at 3:30 P.M. after spending 40 min there. At what time did she arrive?

____

Test Prep

10. A football game lasted 2 hr 37 min. It finished at 4:22 P.M. When did it start?

A. 1:45 P.M. **B.** 1:55 P.M. **C.** 2:45 P.M. **D.** 2:50 P.M.

11. **Writing in Math** What is 1 hour and 35 minutes before 4:05 P.M.? Explain how you solved this problem.

____

Name ____________________

Temperature

How to read temperature:

Miami's average high temperature in June is 87°F. What is the average high temperature in degrees Celsius?

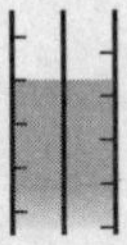

Step 1: Find 87° on the Fahrenheit scale.

Step 2: Read across to find the temperature on the Celsius scale.

31°C is the same as 87°F.

How to find changes in temperatures:

Find the change in temperature from 57°F to 18°F.

Step 1: Find the difference between 57°F and 18°F by subtracting. 57°F − 18°F = 39°F

Step 2: Tell if the difference is an increase or decrease. Since the second temperature is less than the first temperature, there was a decrease.

So, the change is a decrease of 39°F.

Write each temperature in Celsius and Fahrenheit.

1.

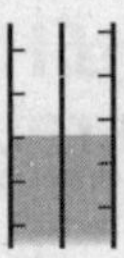

________ ; ________

2.

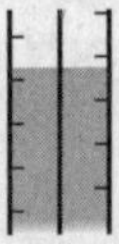

________ ; ________

Find each change in temperature.

3. 34°F to 89°F ________

4. 11°C to 26°C ________

5. 86°F to 54°F ________

6. 30°C to 8°C ________

7. 3°F to 81°F ________

8. 12°C to 5°C ________

9. **Number Sense** Yesterday's high temperature was 76°F. The difference between the high and low temperature was 33°F. What was yesterday's low temperature? ________

Name ______________________________

Temperature

Write each temperature in Celsius and Fahrenheit.

1. °F 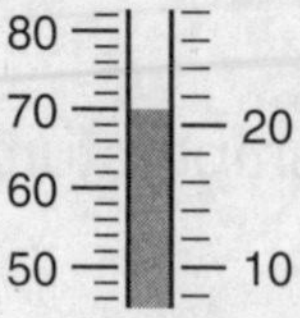

°C

2. °F 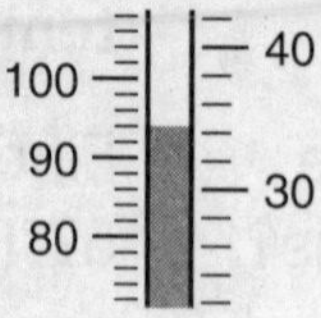

°C

3. °F 

°C

_______, _______ _______, _______ _______, _______

Find each change in temperature.

4. 34°F to 67°F _______ **5.** 12°C to 7°C _______

6. Number Sense Which is a smaller increase in temperature: a 5°F increase or a 5°C increase?

____

Information about the record highest temperatures in four states is shown.

Record High Temperature

State	°F	°C
Alaska	100	38
Florida	109	43
Michigan	112	44
Hawaii	100	38

7. What is the difference between the record high temperature in Florida and the record high temperature in Alaska in °C?

____

8. What is the difference between the record high temperature in Michigan and the record high temperature in Florida in °F? _______

Test Prep

9. What is the difference between −6°C and 12°C?

A. 6°C **B.** 12°C **C.** 18°C **D.** 19°C

10. Writing in Math Which is warmer, 1°F or 1°C? Explain how you found this answer.

____

____

Name ______________________

PROBLEM-SOLVING SKILL **R 9-15**

Writing to Explain

Write and explain how you would find the area of the triangle.

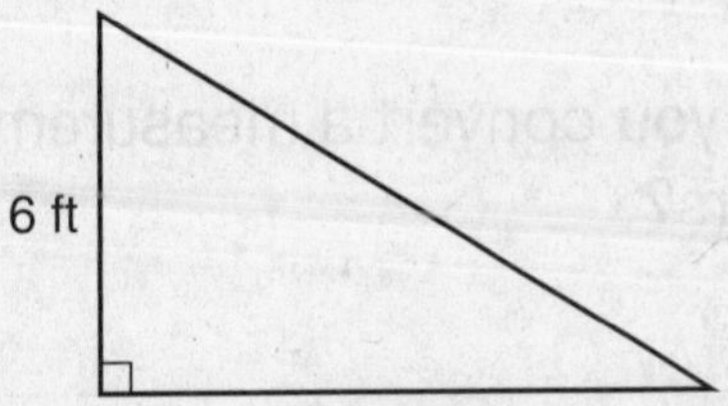

- Break the process into steps.
- Use pictures and words to explain.
- Tell about things to watch out for and be careful about.
- Use words like *find* and *put* when explaining a process.

1. First, write the formula for finding the area of a triangle. Make sure you have the correct formula.

$A = \frac{1}{2} \times b \times h$

2. Next, put the numbers for the base and height into the formula.

$A = \frac{1}{2} \times 10 \text{ ft} \times 6 \text{ ft}$

3. Multiply. It is usually easier to multiply the base and height first.

$10 \times 6 = 60$

Then multiply this amount by $\frac{1}{2}$.

$\frac{1}{2} \times 60 = 30$ So, the area = 30 ft^2.

1. Explain how you would find the perimeter of the figure to the right.

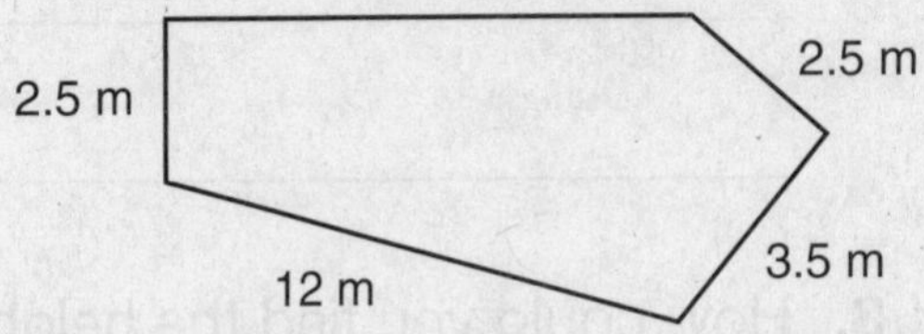

____

____

____

____

____

Name ____________________

PROBLEM-SOLVING SKILL **P 9-15**

Writing to Explain

Write to explain.

1. How could you convert a measurement given in millimeters to kilometers?

____

____

____

____

____

2. How could you find the perimeter of a brick in this wall?

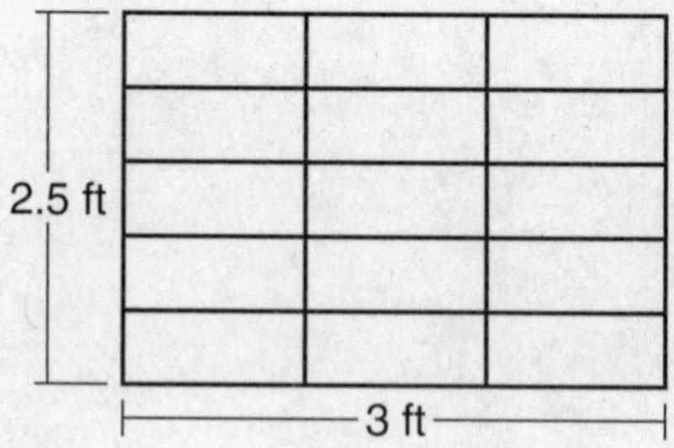

____

____

____

____

____

____

____

3. How could you find the height of this triangle?

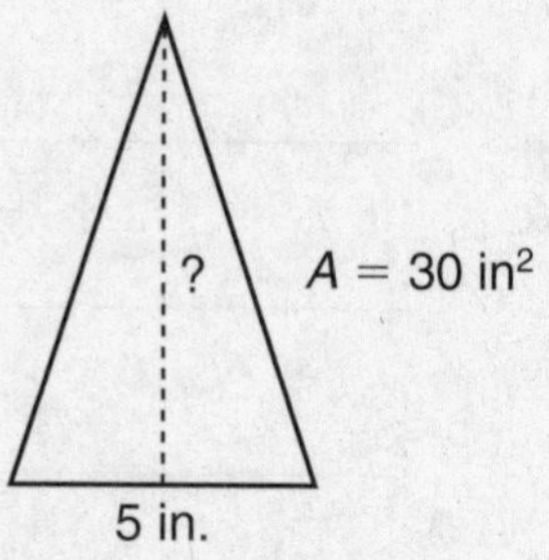

____

____

Name ____________________

PROBLEM-SOLVING APPLICATIONS **R 9-16**

The Clubhouse

Andrew wants to build a clubhouse in the backyard for his children. He has drawn several different plans for the clubhouse. Which clubhouse will have the greatest perimeter?

Clubhouse A

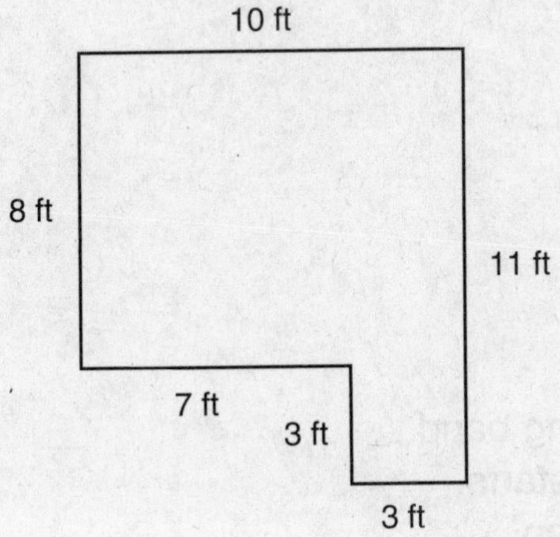

Clubhouse B

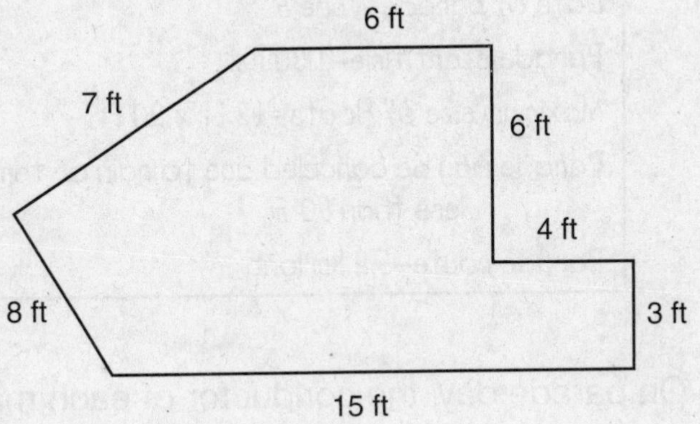

Add up the sides of each clubhouse.

Clubhouse A

$10 + 11 + 3 + 3 + 7 + 8 = 42$ ft

Clubhouse B

$6 + 6 + 4 + 3 + 15 + 8 + 7 = 49$ ft

So, Clubhouse B would have the greater perimeter.

1. Andrew is considering building a clubhouse in the shape of a rectangle. His sketch of the clubhouse is to the right. What would the area of this clubhouse be?

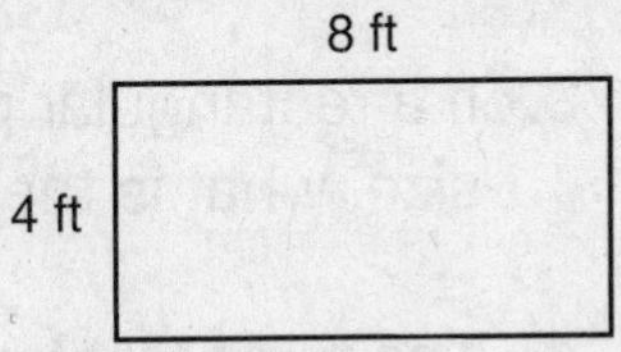

____

2. On one wall of the clubhouse, Andrew wants to cut a large circular opening to be a window. The circle's radius is 2 ft. What will the circle's circumference be? ____________________

3. Andrew started to build the clubhouse at 6:15 A.M. He completed the job at 4:30 P.M. He took a $\frac{1}{2}$ hr break for lunch. How long did it take him to build the clubhouse? ____________________

Name ______________________________

Summer Parade

The parade-planning committee met to organize the summer parade. Here are some notes from the meeting.

Springdale Summer Parade

Planning Information:

Date of parade–June 5

Parade start time–1:30 P.M.

Maximum size of floats–12 ft x 20 ft

Parade may be canceled due to rain or temp less than 50°F

Parade route–5.2 km long

1. On parade day, the conductor of each marching band must check in at least 2 hr before the parade starts. What is the latest time the band conductors can check in? ____________

2. The floats and marching groups will be judged, and prizes will be awarded. The judge's stand is exactly halfway through the parade route. How many meters from the beginning of the parade is the judge's stand? ____________

3. If a rectangular parade float is the maximum allowed size, what is the area of the parade float? ____________

4. The temperature on June 5 is 85°F. How many degrees greater than the minimum temperature for the parade is this? ____________

5. The parade-planning committee met 6 weeks before the parade. How many days before the parade was this? ____________

Name ________________________________

Solid Figures

R 10-1

The solid's vertices are: *A*, *B*, *C*, *D*, *E*, *F*, *G*, and *H*.

The solid's edges are: $\overline{AC}$, $\overline{AB}$, $\overline{CD}$, $\overline{DB}$, $\overline{AH}$, $\overline{BG}$, $\overline{HG}$, $\overline{HE}$, $\overline{GF}$, $\overline{EF}$, $\overline{CE}$, and $\overline{DF}$.

The solid's faces are: *ACEH*, *BDFG*, *ABCD*, *EFGH*, *CDEF*, and *ABHG*.

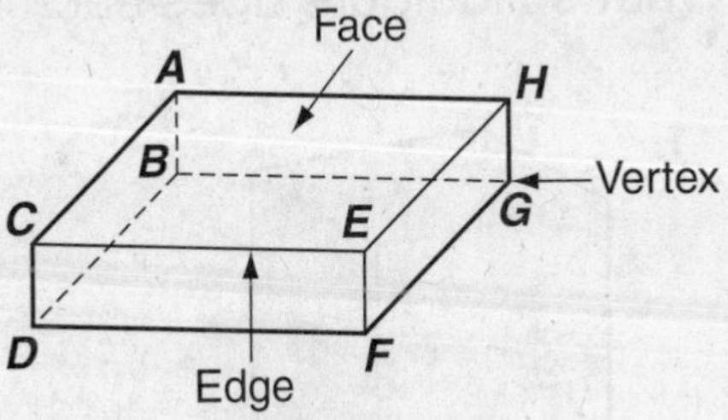

Here are some common solid figures:

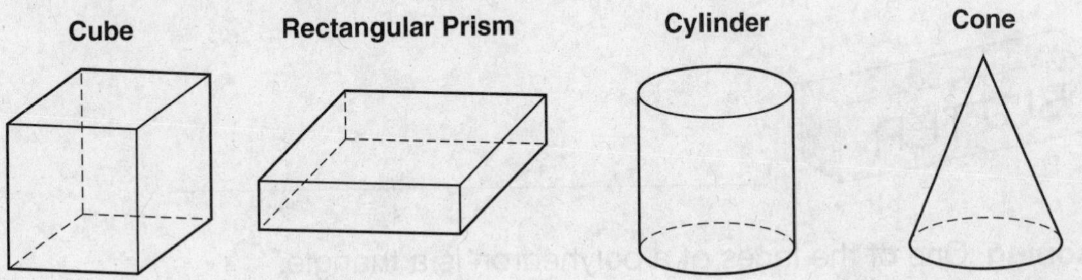

Use the solid at the right for 1–3.

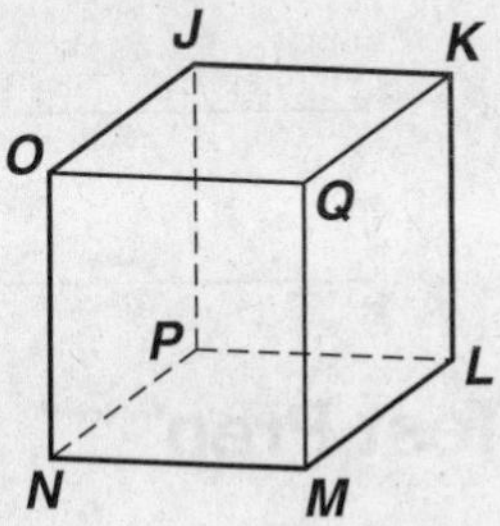

1. Name the edges.

____

____

2. Name the faces.

____

3. Name the vertices. ________________________________

What solid figure does each object resemble?

4.

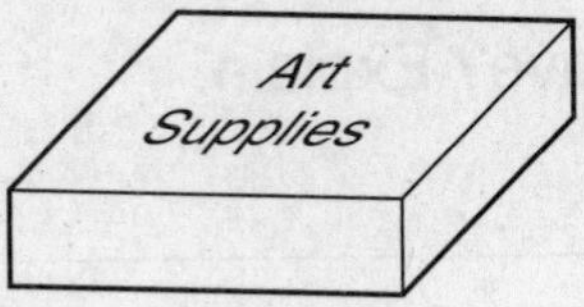

5.

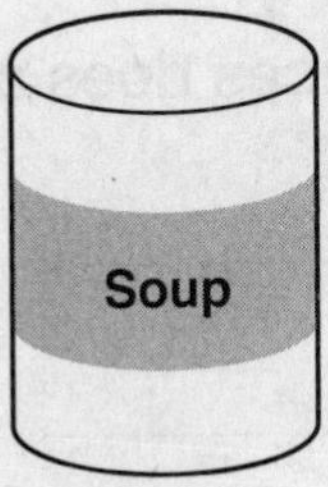

6.

________________ ________________ ________________

Name

Solid Figures

P 10-1

What solid figure does each object resemble?

1. 

2. 

3. 

4. Reasoning One of the faces of a polyhedron is a triangle. What are two possible types of polyhedrons this might be?

Test Prep

5. Which term best describes the figure?

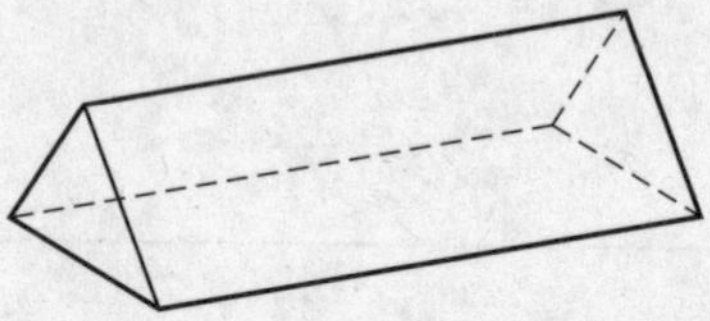

A. Cone

B. Triangular prism

C. Pyramid

D. Rectangular prism

6. Writing in Math How many vertices does a cone have? Explain.

Name____

Views of Solid Figures

R 10-2

If the net on the left was folded, it would form the figure on the right.

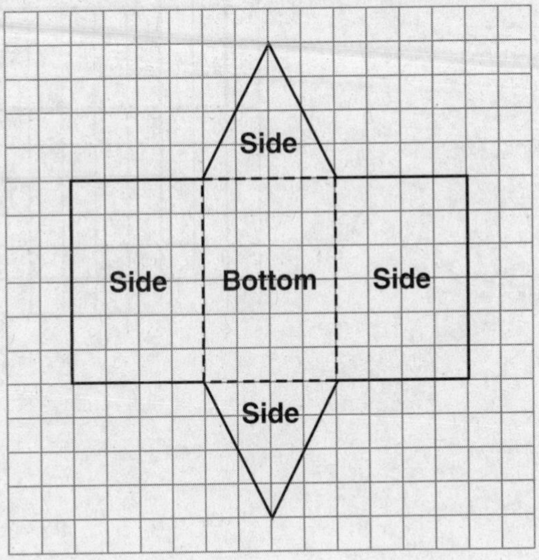

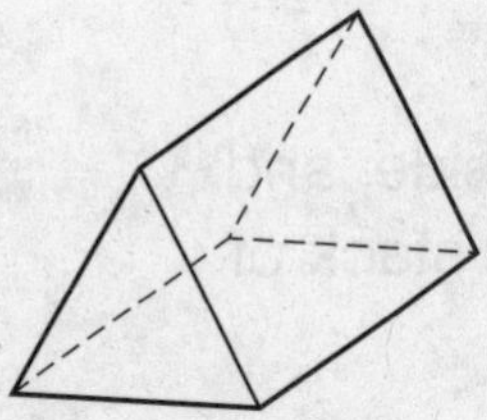

Here is how the figure below would look from the front, side, and top.

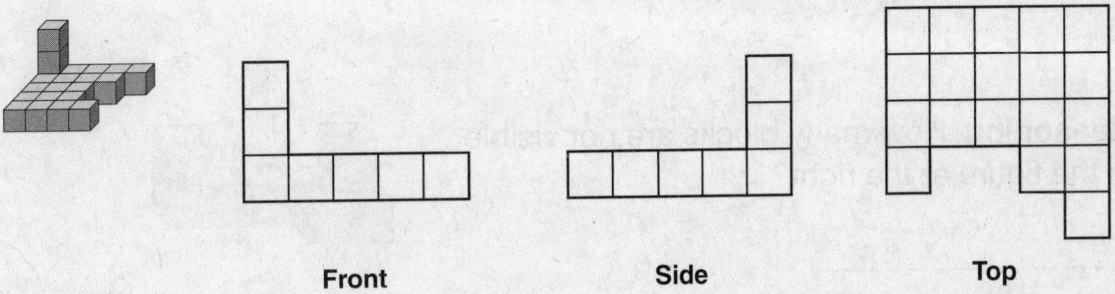

What solid does each net represent?

1.

2.

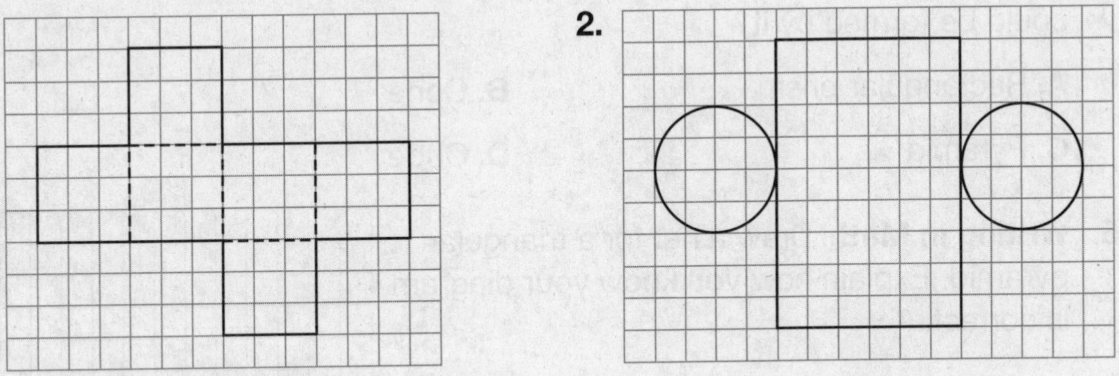

1. ____________________

2. ____________________

Name

Views of Solid Figures

1. What solid does the net represent?

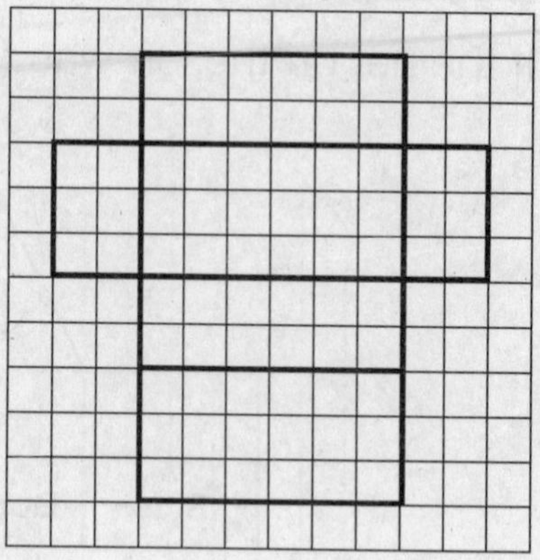

Draw the front, side, and top views of the stack of unit blocks.

2.

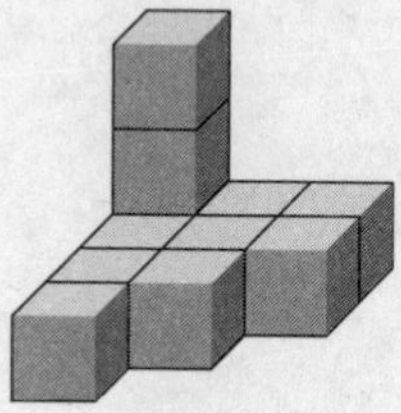

3. **Reasoning** How many blocks are not visible in the figure at the right?

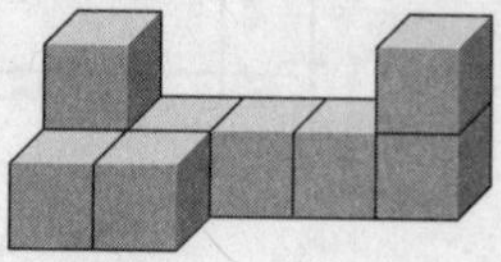

Test Prep

4. If a net consists of 6 squares, what is a solid figure that could be formed by it?

A. Rectangular prism

B. Cone

C. Pyramid

D. Cube

5. **Writing in Math** Draw a net for a triangular pyramid. Explain how you know your diagram is correct.

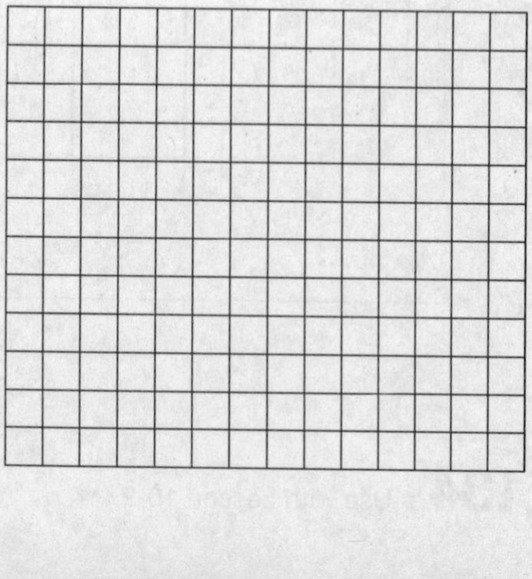

Name ____________________

Surface Area

R 10-3

How to find the surface area of a rectangular prism:

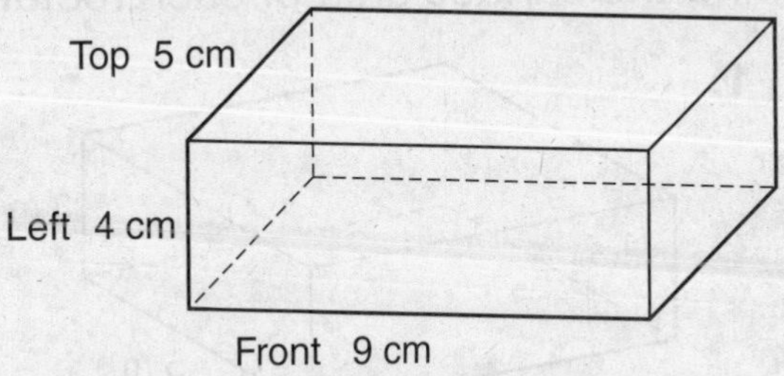

The formula for finding the surface area of a rectangular prism is:

$2(l \times w) + 2(l \times h) + 2(w \times h)$

Remember, l = length, w = width, and h = height.

To find the surface area for the prism above, plug the numbers into the formula.

Surface area $= 2(l \times w) + 2(l \times h) + 2(w \times h)$

Surface area $= 2(4 \times 9) + 2(5 \times 9) + 2(4 \times 5)$

Surface area $= 2(36) + 2(45) + 2(20)$

Surface area $= 72 + 90 + 40$

Surface area $= 202 \text{ cm}^2$

So, the surface area of the prism is 202 cm^2.

Find the surface area of each rectangular prism.

1. 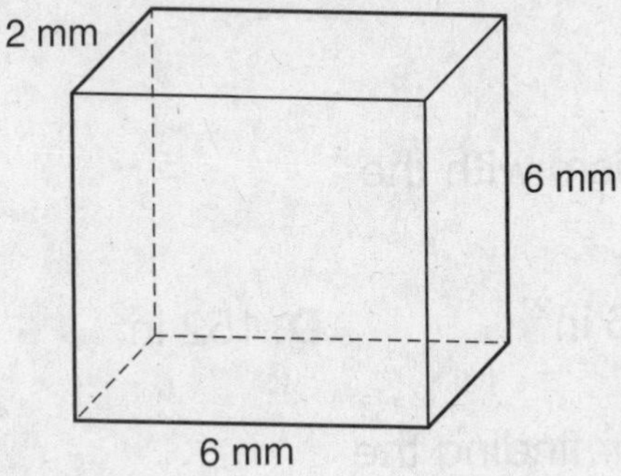

____

2. 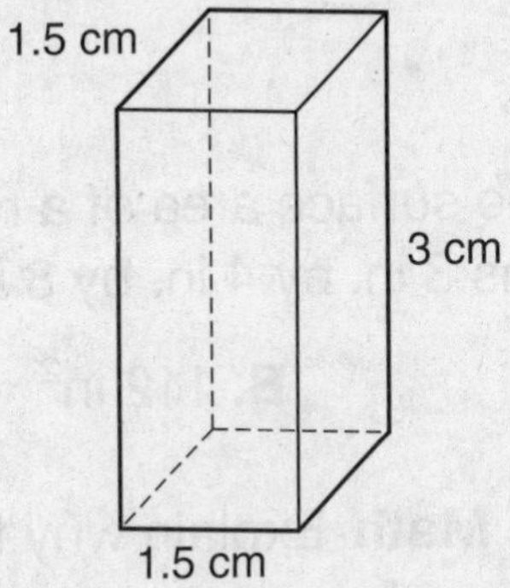

____

3. 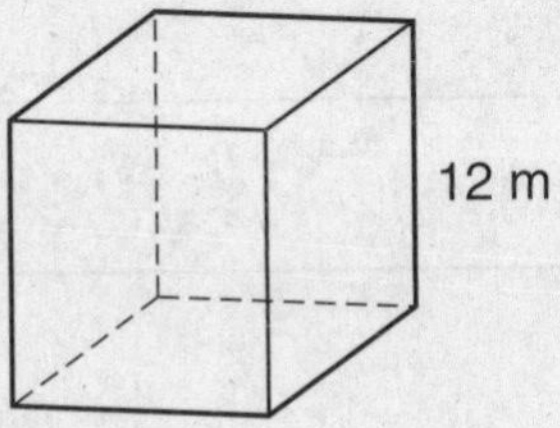

____

4. 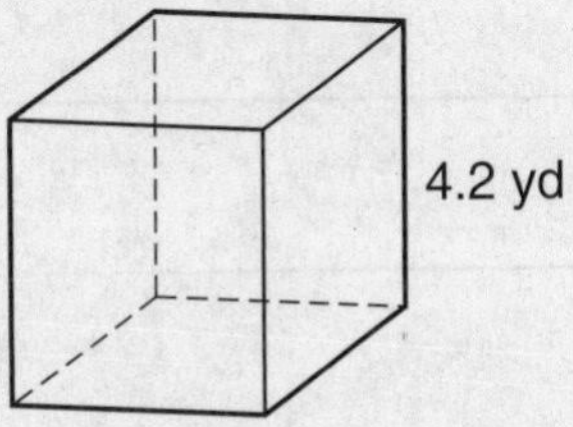

____

Name ______________________________

Surface Area

Find the surface area of each rectangular prism.

1.

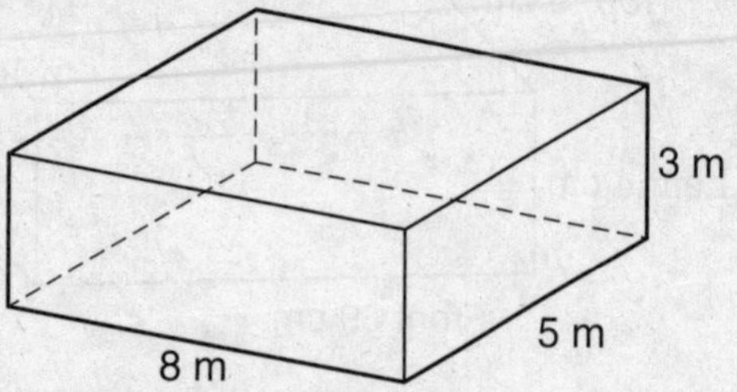

2.

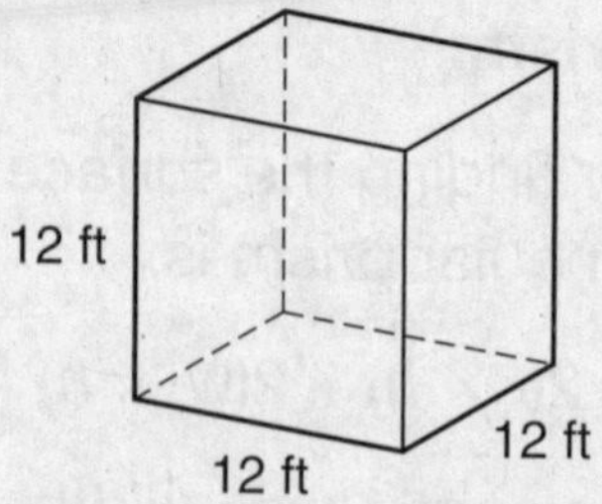

______________________ ______________________

Music and computer CDs are often stored in plastic cases called jewel cases.

3. One size of jewel case is 140 mm × 120 mm × 4 mm. What is the surface area of this jewel case?

____

4. A jewel case that holds 2 CDs is 140 mm × 120 mm × 9 mm. What is the surface area of this jewel case?

____

Test Prep

5. What is the surface area of a rectangular prism with the dimensions 3 in. by 4 in. by 8 in.?

A. 96 in^2 **B.** 112 in^2 **C.** 136 in^2 **D.** 152 in^2

6. **Writing in Math** Explain why the formula for finding the surface area of a rectangular prism is helpful.

____

____

____

____

Name ______________________

PROBLEM-SOLVING STRATEGY **R 10-4**

Use Objects

The Students Six students sit in one row in Mrs. Ussery's class. Vicky sits in the last desk. Tim sits between Pete and Vicky. Frank sits in the second desk, behind Barb and in front of Carrie. What is their order from front to back?

Read and Understand

Step 1: What do you know?

Vicky sits in the last desk. Tim sits between Pete and Vicky.
Frank sits in the second desk, behind Barb and in front of Carrie.

Step 2: What are you trying to find?

The order of six students from front to back

Plan and Solve

Step 3: What strategy will you use?

Use note cards with one name on each. Put the cards in the correct order to solve the problem.

Barb	Frank	Carrie	Pete	Tim	Vicky

Look Back and Check

Step 4: Is your answer reasonable?

Yes, the order matches the description in the problem.

Write each name on a slip of paper: Greg, Ali, Ruth, Stacy, and Pedro. Put the name cards in the correct order to solve the problem.

1. Five friends are sitting on a park bench. Stacy is sitting on the far right. Ruth is sitting between Pedro and Stacy. Ali is sitting to the left of Greg. Use the clues to determine in what order the friends are seated.

____

____

Name ____________________

PROBLEM-SOLVING STRATEGY **P 10-4**

Use Objects

Use Centimeter Cubes to Solve a Problem Use centimeter cubes to find the surface area.

1. Make a model of a cube that has a surface area of 54 cm^2. What are the measurements of the model?

____

2. Make a model of a rectangular prism that is not a cube and has a surface area of 62 cm^2. What are the measurements of this rectangular prism?

____

____

____

____

Use Cards to Solve a Problem Write the information on slips of paper to help solve the problem.

3. Yu-Li takes six classes each day. The classes are math, science, language arts, social studies, music, and physical education. Use the clues to figure out the order of the classes.
   - There is a class before and after social studies.
   - There is no class after music.
   - There is one class before math.
   - There are two classes between social studies and music.
   - Physical education is right after science.

____

____

____

Name ____________________

Volume

R 10-5

Find the volume of the rectangular prism.

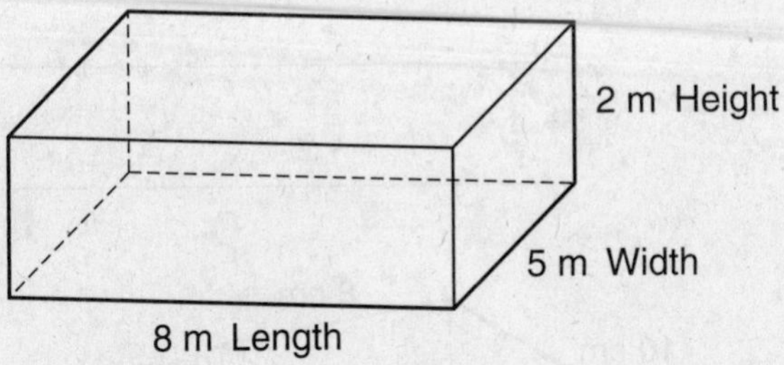

$V = (l \times w) \times h$

$V = (8 \times 5) \times 2$

$V = 40 \times 2$

$V = 80\ m^3$

So, the volume is 80 m^3.

Find the volume of the rectangular prism.

base area: 75 ft^2

height: 9 ft

$V = Bh$

$V = 75 \times 9$

$V = 675\ ft^3$

Use unit cubes, make a drawing, or use the formula to find the volume of each rectangular prism.

1. base area: 32 cm^2
height: 4 cm

____

2. base area: 52.4 in^2
height: 5 in.

____

3. base area: 81 ft^2
height: 6 ft

____

4.

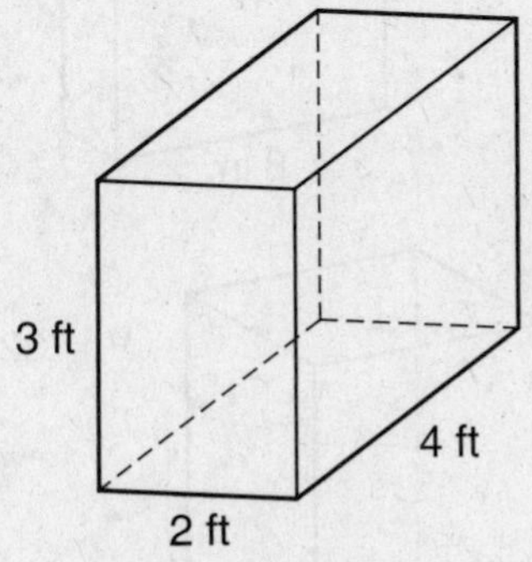

____

5.

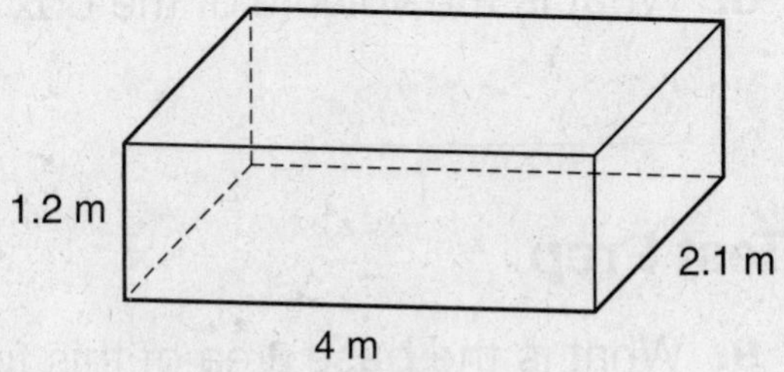

____

Name ______________________________

Volume

P 10-5

Find the volume of each rectangular prism.

1. base area 56 in^2, height 6 in. ____________

2. base area 32 cm^2, height 12 cm ____________

3. base area 42 m^2, height 8 m ____________

4.

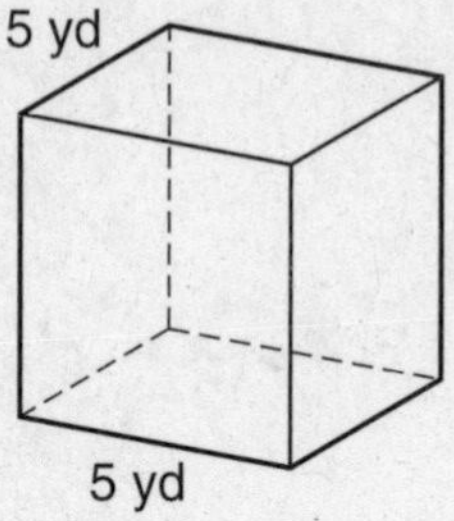

____

5.

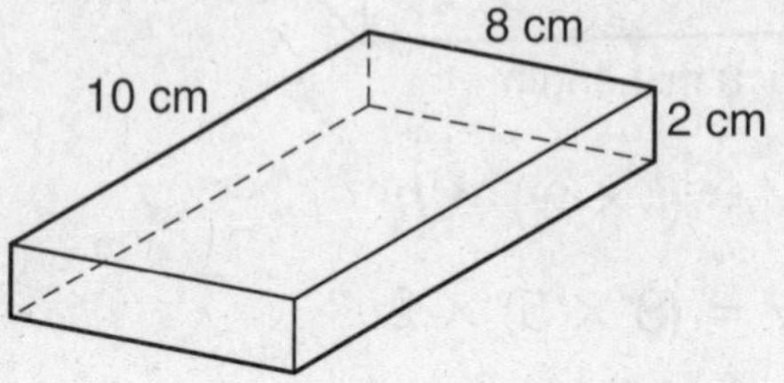

____

6. Algebra What is the height of a solid with a volume of 120 m^3 and base area of 30 m^2? ____________

Michael bought some cereal at the grocery store.

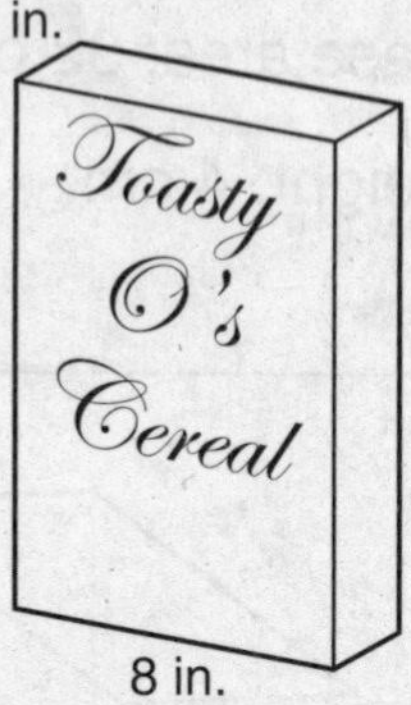

7. What is the base area of the box?

____

8. What is the volume of the box?

____

Test Prep

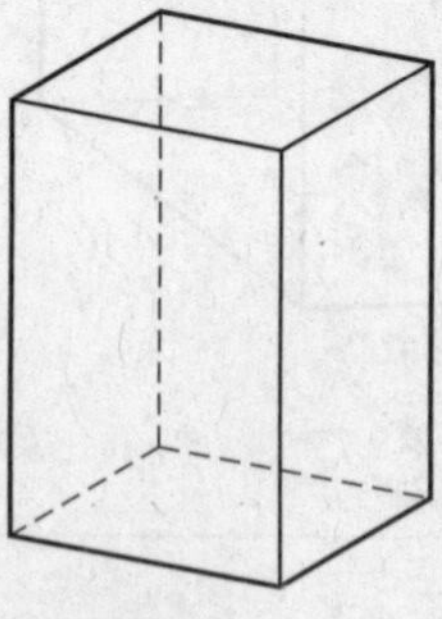

9. What is the base area of this figure?

A. 3.2 m^2 **B.** 32 m^2

C. 320 m^2 **D.** 3,200 m^2

10. Writing in Math Explain how you would find the base area of a rectangular prism if you know the volume and the height.

____

Name ______________________

Customary Units of Capacity

R 10-6

Capacity is a measure of an amount of liquid. Many different units can be used to measure capacity.

1 teaspoon (tsp) = $\frac{1}{3}$ tbsp

1 tablespoon (tbsp) = 3 tsp

1 fluid ounce (fl oz) = 2 tbsp

1 cup (c) = 8 fl oz

1 pint (pt) = 2 c

1 quart (qt) = 2 pt

1 gallon (gal) = 4 qt

Changing one unit of capacity to another:

8 pt = ________ c

Think: 1 pt = 2 c

$8 \times 2 = 16$

So, 8 pt = 16 c.

Adding and subtracting units of capacity:

7 qt 2 pt	=	6 qt 4 pt
− 3 qt 3 pt	=	− 3 qt 3 pt
		3 qt 1 pt

Because there are 2 pt in 1 qt, you can rename 7 qt 2 pt to 6 qt 4 pt.

So, 7 qt 2 pt − 3 qt 3 pt = 3 qt 1 pt.

Complete.

1. 16 fl oz = ________ c

2. 8 gal = ________ qt

3. 6 tbsp = ________ tsp

4. 10 c = ________ pt

Write each answer in simplest form.

5. 5 qt 1 pt
+ 1 pt

6. 4 gal 3 qt
− 2 gal 1 qt

7. 6 c 7 fl oz
− 4 c 5 fl oz

8. Estimation Estimate the number of cups in 642 fl oz.

____

Name ____________________

Customary Units of Capacity

P 10-6

Complete.

1. 2 qt = ______ pt
2. 5 c = ______ pt ______ c
3. 3 gal = ______ pt
4. 2 fl oz = ______ tsp
5. 4 qt = ______ c
6. 9 pt = ______ c

Write each answer in simplest form.

7. 5 c 4 fl oz − 4 c 3 fl oz
8. 7 gal 2 qt + 3 gal 1 qt
9. 6 qt 1 pt + 2 qt 1 pt

10. **Estimation** Estimate the number of tablespoons in 445 teaspoons.

____

11. **Reasoning** If you needed only 1 c of milk, what is your best choice at the grocery store—a quart container, a pint container, or a $\frac{1}{2}$ gal container?

____

Test Prep

12. Which of the following is equivalent to 1 c?

A. 4 fl oz **B.** 2 pt **C.** 48 tsp **D.** 32 tbsp

13. **Writing in Math** Explain how you would convert a measurement given in tablespoons into pints.

____

____

____

____

Name ____________________

Metric Units of Capacity

R 10-7

Milliliters (mL) are used to measure very small amounts of liquid. One milliliter is about 20 drops of water.

Liters (L) are used to measure larger amounts of liquid. You may have seen soda sold in 1 L or 2 L bottles. One liter is a little more than a quart: 1 L = 1,000 mL.

To change from milliliters to liters, divide by 1,000.

780 mL = ________ L

Think: 1,000 mL = 1 L

780 ÷ 1,000 = 0.78

So, 780 mL = 0.78 L.

To change from liters to milliliters, multiply by 1,000.

0.007 L = ________ mL

Think: 1 L = 1,000 mL

0.007 × 1,000 = 7

So, 0.007 L = 7 mL.

Complete.

1. 2,400 mL = ____________ L

2. 0.9 L = ____________ mL

3. 334 mL = ____________ L

4. 293 L = ____________ mL

5. 42,000 mL = ____________ L

6. 2.118 L = ____________ mL

7. 3,500 mL = ____________ L

8. 3.75 L = ____________ mL

9. 82.4 L = ____________ mL

10. 93,000 mL = ____________ L

11. **Estimation** Which metric unit of capacity is most reasonable for each object?

a. glass of water

150 mL or 1 L

____

b. bucket of water

12 L or 3,500 mL

____

Name ____________________

Metric Units of Capacity

Complete.

1. 5 L = __________ mL

2. 1,298 mL = __________ L

3. 3.4 L = __________ mL

4. 956 mL = __________ L

5. 82 mL = __________ L

6. 98 L = __________ mL

7. **Estimation** Which capacity is most reasonable for each object?

a. drinking glass
50 mL or 50 L
____

b. swimming pool
80,000 mL or 80,000 L
____

c. bottle cap
20 mL or 20 L
____

8. Latoya's science fair experiment measured the rate at which the temperature of water changed. She tested four different-sized containers of water: 1 L, 2 L, 4 L, and 5 L. Express these capacities in milliliters.

____

Test Prep

9. Which of the following is equivalent to 2 mL?

A. 20 L **B.** 0.2 L **C.** 0.02 L **D.** 0.002 L

10. **Writing in Math** Tell whether you would use multiplication or division to convert milliliters to liters. Explain your answer.

____

____

____

____

Name ____________________

Customary Units of Weight

Changing from one unit of weight to another:

A blue whale can weigh up to 209 tons (T). How many pounds is that?

209 T = ________ lb

Think: 1 T = 2,000 lb

Multiply to find the weight in pounds.

$209 \times 2{,}000 = 418{,}000$

So, 209 T = 418,000 lb.

36 oz = ________ lb

Think: 16 oz = 1 lb

Divide to find the weight in pounds.

$36 \div 16 = 2 \text{ R}4$

So, 36 oz = 2 lb 4 oz.

Adding and subtracting units of weight:

	5 T 1,750 lb
+	2 T 1,000 lb
	7 T 2,750 lb

Think: 2,000 lb = 1 T. So, add 1 T to 1 T. 750 are left.

7 T 2,750 lb = 8 T 750 lb

	9 lb 3 oz	=		8 lb 19 oz
−	5 lb 8 oz	=	−	5 lb 8 oz
				3 lb 11 oz

To subtract 8 oz from 3 oz, rename 9 lb 3 oz to 8 lb 19 oz.

Complete.

1. 0.3 T = ________ lb

2. 272 oz = ________ lb

3. 3,200 lb = ________ T

4. 0.8 lb = ________ oz

Write each answer in simplest form.

5.

	4 lb 5 oz
+	6 lb 12 oz

6.

	1 T 300 lb
+	2,500 lb

7. Estimation Estimate the number of pounds in 162 oz.

____

Name ____________________

Customary Units of Weight

Complete.

1. 200 lb = ________ T
2. 56 oz = ________ lb ________ oz
3. 2.5 lb = ________ oz
4. 4,000 lb = ________ T
5. 40 oz = ________ lb ________ oz
6. 90 lb = ________ oz

Write each answer in simplest form.

7. 5 lb 12 oz − 4 lb 13 oz
8. 7 T 200 lb + 1,900 lb
9. 29 lb 4 oz + 11 lb 13 oz

10. **Estimation** Estimate the number of ounces of potatoes in a 5 lb bag of potatoes. ________

11. Did you know that there is litter in outer space? Humans exploring space have left behind bags of trash, bolts, gloves, and pieces of satellites. There are currently about 4,000,000 lb of litter in orbit around Earth. About how many tons of space litter is this? ________

12. Karla bought 2 lb of red beads, $1\frac{3}{4}$ lb of green beads, and 10 oz of string at the craft store. How much did Karla's supplies weigh altogether? ________

Test Prep

13. Which of the following is equivalent to 92.5 lb?

A. 1,472 oz **B.** 1,480 oz **C.** 1,479 oz **D.** 1,488 oz

14. **Writing in Math** Explain the difference between 1 fl oz and 1 oz.

____

____

Name ____________________

Metric Units of Mass

To change a measurement from one unit to another, multiply or divide by a power of 10.

2.79 kg = ________ g

Think: 1 kg = 1,000 g

Multiply to find the number of grams.

2.79 × 1,000 = 2,790

So, 2.79 kg = 2,790 g.

935 mg = ________ g

Think: 1,000 mg = 1 g

Divide to find the number of grams.

935 ÷ 1,000 = 0.935

So, 935 mg = 0.935 g.

Complete.

1. 25 kg = ____________ g

2. 0.009 kg = ____________ g

3. 425 g = ____________ kg

4. 2.4 kg = ____________ g

5. 32.6 mg = ____________ g

6. 526 mg = ____________ g

7. **Number Sense** Which is greater, 5,200 g or 5.6 kg? ____________

8. What is the mass of a penny in milligrams?

____

U.S. Coins

Coin	Mass
Penny	2.5 g
Quarter	5.67 g
Half-dollar	11.34 g

9. What is the mass of a half-dollar in kilograms?

____

10. What is the mass of a quarter in milligrams? ____________

11. Peter's father has 867 mg of silver. How many grams is that? ____________

Name ______________________________

Metric Units of Mass

Complete.

1. 20 kg = ____________ g

2. 520 g = ____________ kg

3. 0.189 kg = ____________ g

4. 45 g = ____________ mg

5. 1.45 kg = ____________ g

6. 1,200 mg = ____________ g

7. **Number Sense** Which has less mass, 800 g or 8 kg? ____________

The list shows Jeffrey's grocery list.

1 box of pasta	454 g
1 can of soup	298 g
1 jar of peanut butter	1,130 g
1 box of cereal	432 g

8. Do any items on the list have a mass greater than 400,000 mg? If so, which ones?

____

9. Do any items on the list have a mass less than 0.3 kg? If so, which ones?

____

Test Prep

10. Which of the following is equivalent to 80 mg?

A. 8 g **B.** 0.8 g **C.** 0.08 g **D.** 0.008 g

11. **Writing in Math** Which do you think is easier to convert, units of customary measurement or units of metric measurement? Explain your answer.

____

____

Name

PROBLEM-SOLVING SKILL **R 10-10**

Exact Answer or Estimate

The Sandbox Erik built a sandbox. He wants to fill the sandbox with as much sand as it can hold. How much sand does he need?

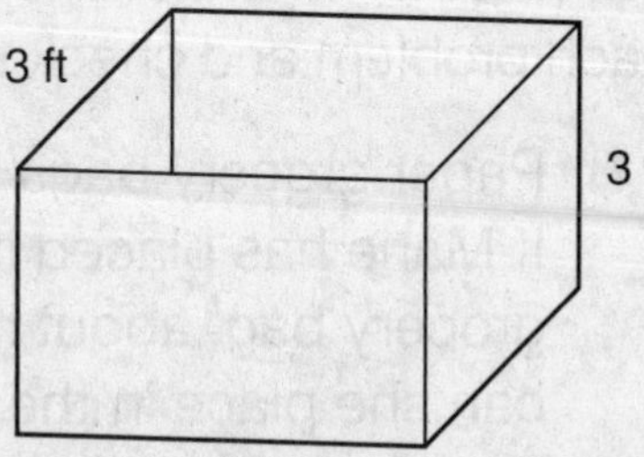

Read and Understand

Step 1: What do you know?

The sandbox is 3 ft by 4 ft by 3 ft.

Step 2: What are you trying to find?

The amount of sand needed

Plan and Solve

Do you need an exact answer or an estimate?

An exact answer

Find the volume of the sandbox.

$V = l \times w \times h$

$V = 3 \text{ ft} \times 4 \text{ ft} \times 3 \text{ ft}$

$V = 36 \text{ ft}^3$

So, Erik needs 36 ft^3 of sand.

Tell whether an exact answer or an estimate is needed. Then solve each problem and check to see if your answer is reasonable.

1. James is wrapping a box. How many square feet of wrapping paper will he need?

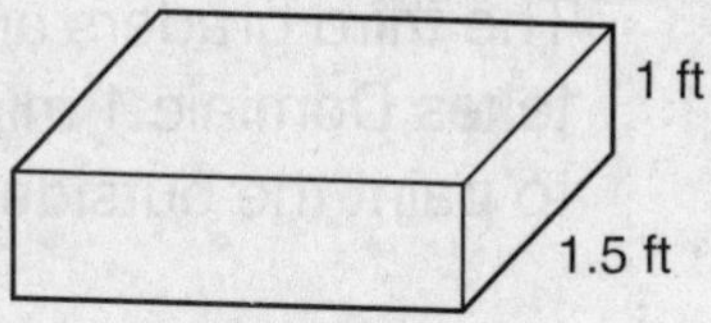

____

2. Hannah is buying mulch for her flower bed. The dimensions of her flower bed are 6 ft by 4 ft by 2 ft. How much mulch does she need to fill the flower bed?

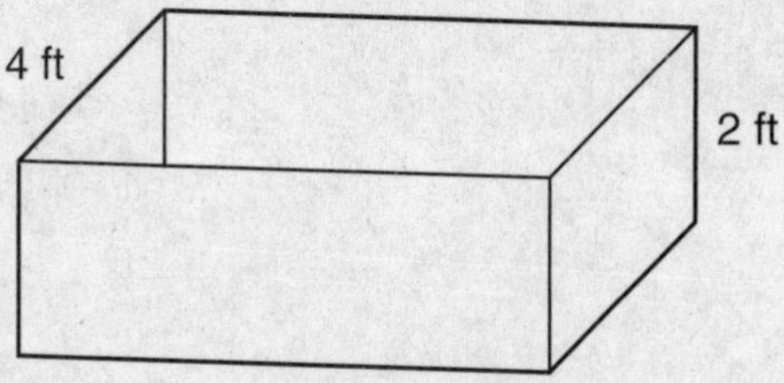

____

Name ____________________

PROBLEM-SOLVING SKILL **P 10-10**

Exact Answer or Estimate

Tell whether an exact answer or an estimate is needed. Then solve each problem and check to see if your answer is reasonable.

1. Paper grocery bags hold between 9 and 10 kg of groceries. If Marie has placed items with a mass of 5.3 kg in a paper grocery bag, about how many more kilograms of groceries can she place in the bag?

____

2. The water cooler for the cross-country team holds 20 L of water. If each of the 25 runners has had 500 mL of water to drink from the cooler, exactly how much water is left in the cooler?

____

3. A recipe for lemonade calls for about 2 qt of ice water. How many pints of ice water are needed?

____

4.

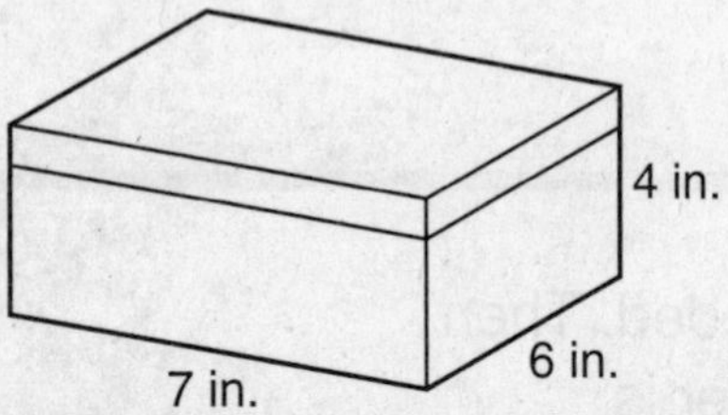

The third graders are painting shoe boxes in art class. If it takes Dominic 1 min to paint 4 in^2, how long will it take him to paint the outside of this box?

____

Name ______________________________

PROBLEM-SOLVING APPLICATION **R 10-11**

The Trucker

Karen owns 5 trucks, and people pay her to transport things. A local artist has produced a block-shaped sculpture that he needs to have transported to another city. Will the sculpture fit in Karen's truck? Find the volume of the back of the truck as well as the sculpture in order to solve the problem.

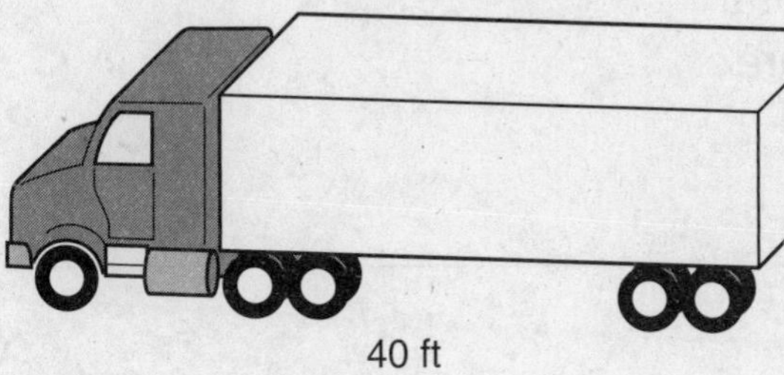

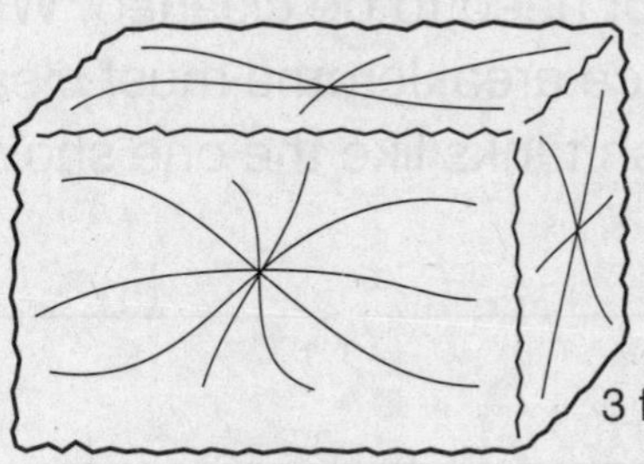

Truck:

$V = l \times w \times h$

$V = 40 \times 6 \times 5$

$V = 240 \times 5$

$V = 1{,}200 \text{ ft}^3$

Sculpture:

$V = l \times w \times h$

$V = 8 \times 3 \times 4$

$V = 24 \times 4$

$V = 96 \text{ ft}^3$

So, the sculpture would fit into the truck.

1. Karen is considering buying a larger truck that can carry larger loads. The new truck would have a base area of 450 ft^2 and a height of 9 ft. What would be the volume of the new truck? ______

2. Karen's smallest truck can carry up to 500 kg. How many grams is that? ______

3. A construction company needs Karen's truck to deliver 8,000 lb of sand to a work site. How many tons is that? ______

4. On Friday, one truck carried 3 T 650 lb of crates. On Saturday the same truck carried 5 T 1,600 lb of crates. How much weight in total did the truck carry? ______

Name ____________________

PROBLEM-SOLVING APPLICATION **P 10-11**

Tropical Fish

Solve. Write your answer in a complete sentence.

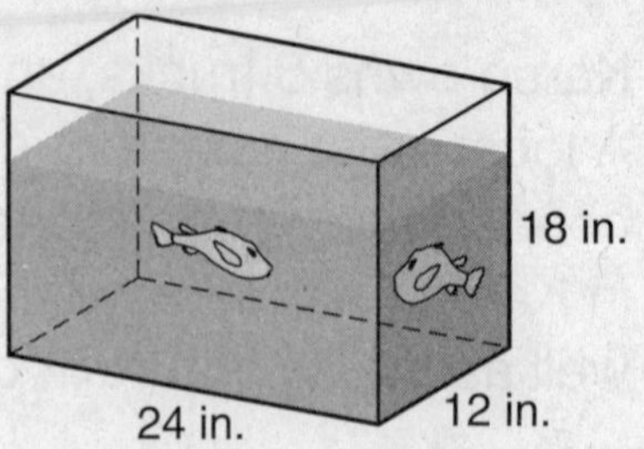

1. Jerome works in a tropical fish store. Every day, he cleans the outside of the fish tanks with glass cleaner. The fish tanks do not have lids, and the bottoms of the fish tanks do not need to be cleaned. What is the total surface area Jerome must clean if there are 50 fish tanks like the one shown here?

____

____

2. The fish tanks at the tropical fish store hold 20 gal of water each. How many quarts of water are in the 50 fish tanks at the store?

____

____

3. Jerome's job duties include feeding the fish. There are 5 kinds of fish that he feeds: guppies, zebra danios, betas, platys, and neon tetras. Use the following clues to find the order in which Jerome feeds them.

- Jerome feeds the guppies third.
- Jerome does not feed the betas right before or right after the guppies.
- Jerome feeds the zebra danios last.
- Jerome feeds the platys after the betas.

____

____

____

Name ____________________

Understanding Ratios

Ratios are written to compare two quantities.

There are 25 students in the class; 13 are boys and 12 are girls.

Write a ratio for the number of boys in the class to the whole class.	Write a ratio for the number of girls in the class to the whole class.	Write a ratio for the number of boys to girls in the class.
13 to 25, 13:25, $\frac{13}{25}$	12 to 25, 12:25, $\frac{12}{25}$	13 to 12, 13:12, $\frac{13}{12}$

Write a ratio for each comparison in three ways.

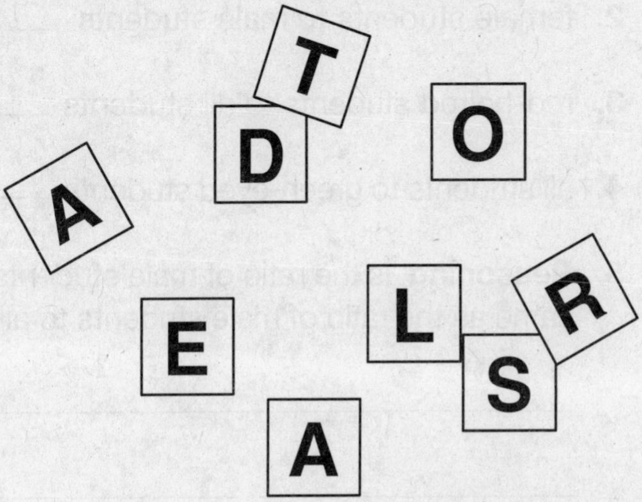

1. vowel tiles to non-vowel tiles ____________

2. vowel tiles to letter tiles ____________

3. letter A tiles to vowel tiles ____________

4. non-vowel tiles to letter tiles ____________

5. letter tiles to letter T tiles ____________

6. **Reasoning** Is the ratio of letter A tiles to letter tiles the same as the ratio of letter A tiles to vowel tiles? Explain.

____

____

____

Name ______________________________

Understanding Ratios

P 11-1

Use the chart below in 1–5 to write each ratio three ways.

Mr. White's 3rd Grade Class (24 Students)

Gender:	Male	8	Female	16				
Eye Color:	Blue	6	Brown	4	Hazel	12	Green	2
Hair Color:	Blond	5	Red	1	Brown	15	Black	3

1. male students to female students ______________________

2. female students to male students ______________________

3. red-haired students to all students ______________________

4. all students to green-eyed students ______________________

5. **Reasoning** Is the ratio of male students to female students the same as the ratio of male students to all students? Explain.

____

____

Test Prep

6. George has 2 sons and 1 daughter. What is the ratio of daughters to sons?

A. 2 to 1 **B.** 1 to 2 **C.** 3:1 **D.** $\frac{2}{1}$

7. **Writing in Math** The ratio of blue beads to white beads in a necklace is 3:8. Nancy says that for every 11 beads, 3 are blue. Do you agree? Explain.

____

____

____

Name ____________________

Equal Ratios

R 11-2

How to write ratios in simplest form:

Write 24:30 in simplest form.

First, write the ratio as a fraction. $\frac{24}{30}$

Think: What is the GCF of each number? 6

Divide numerator and denominator by 6.

$\frac{24}{30} = \frac{24 \div 6}{30 \div 6} = \frac{4}{5}$

So, 24:30 in simplest form is $\frac{4}{5}$.

Are the ratios equal?

$\frac{5}{20}$ and $\frac{2}{4}$

First, change each fraction to simplest form. If they are the same, then the ratios are equal.

$\frac{5}{20} = \frac{1}{4}$ and $\frac{2}{4} = \frac{1}{2}$

$\frac{1}{4}$ is not the same as $\frac{1}{2}$, so $\frac{5}{20}$ and $\frac{2}{4}$ are not equal.

How to write equal ratios:

Write two other ratios equal to $\frac{30}{40}$.

You can use multiplication.

$\frac{30 \times 2}{40 \times 2} = \frac{60}{80}$

So, $\frac{30}{40} = \frac{60}{80}$.

You can use division.

$\frac{30 \div 2}{40 \div 2} = \frac{15}{20}$

So, $\frac{30}{40} = \frac{15}{20}$.

Write each ratio in simplest form.

1. 5 to 30 ________

2. 60 to 24 ________

Give 2 other ratios that are equal to each.

3. 6 to 2 ________

4. 14:20 ________

Are the ratios in each pair equal?

5. $\frac{4}{5}$ and $\frac{80}{100}$ ________

6. $\frac{16}{4}$ and $\frac{60}{20}$ ________

7. Number Sense The ratio of cats to dogs at a pet shelter is 3 to 2. What equal ratio has the number of dogs as 12? ________

Name ________________________________

Equal Ratios

Write each ratio in simplest form.

1. 9 to 3 ________ **2.** 2:12 ________

3. 20 to 45 ________ **4.** 16:80 ________

Give two other ratios that are equal to each.

5. 1 to 7 ________ **6.** $\frac{3}{9}$ ________

7. 4:3 ________ **8.** 9:24 ________

Are the ratios in each pair equal?

9. $\frac{1}{2}$ and $\frac{4}{8}$ ________ **10.** $\frac{16}{18}$ and $\frac{4}{6}$ ________

11. $\frac{1}{5}$ and $\frac{5}{30}$ ________ **12.** $\frac{10}{34}$ and $\frac{15}{51}$ ________

A cereal company has packaged a movie ticket in some of its cereal boxes. In other boxes, there is either a plastic ring or a puzzle. Out of 50 cereal boxes, there are 21 plastic rings, 28 puzzles, and 1 movie ticket.

13. If 200 boxes of cereal are produced, how many have movie tickets in them? ________

14. What is the ratio of puzzles to total boxes when there are 56 puzzles? ________

Test Prep

15. Which ratio is equal to 13:26?

A. 2:1 **B.** 1:3 **C.** 1:2 **D.** 1:7

16. Writing in Math Use the information from Exercises 13 and 14. Explain how you could find the total number of plastic rings in cereal boxes if there are a total of 3 movie tickets.

____

____

Name____

Graphs of Equal Ratios

R 11-3

Number of birds	1	2	3	4	5
Number of wings	2	4	6	8	10

Plot each ordered pair from the table on the graph. Then connect each of the points using a straight line.

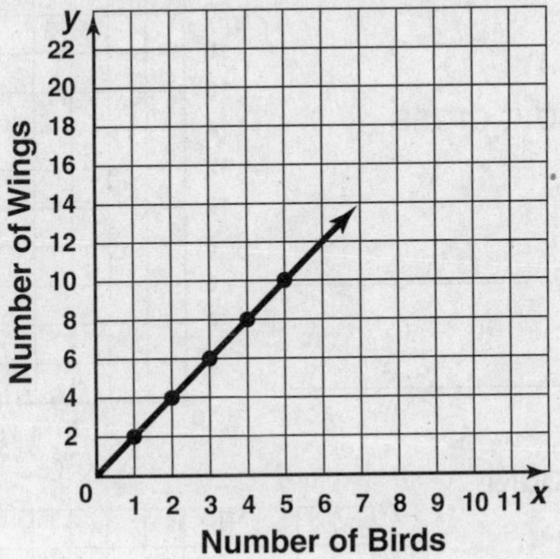

Notice that when the line is extended, it will give you values for other ratios that are equal to the ones that you found.

The line crosses the point (6, 12). The ratio $\frac{6}{12} = \frac{1}{2}$.

1. A block weighs 20 lb. Complete the table of equal ratios.

Number of blocks	1	2	3	4	5
Weight in pounds	20				

2. On the grid, graph the ordered pairs from the table. Connect the ordered pairs with a straight line.

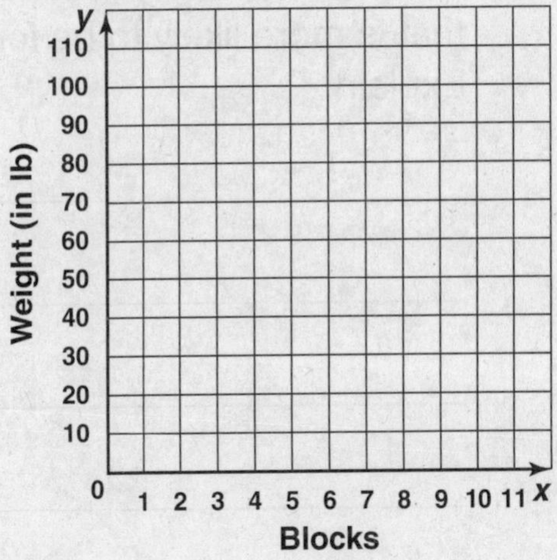

Name____

Graphs of Equal Ratios

P 11-3

1. A square has four angles. Complete this table of equal ratios.

Squares	1	2	3	4	5	6
Angles	4	8				

2. On the grid, graph the ordered pairs from the table. Connect them with a line.

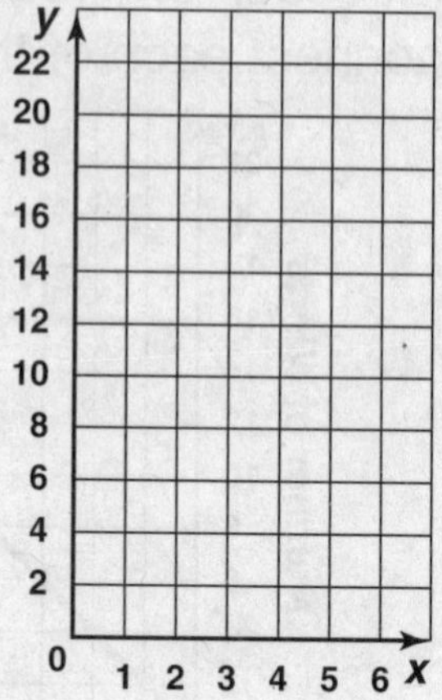

3. If the line in Exercise 2 is extended, would it cross the point (10, 36)? Explain.

____

____

4. Give three equal ratios not shown that would be found on the line of the given graph.

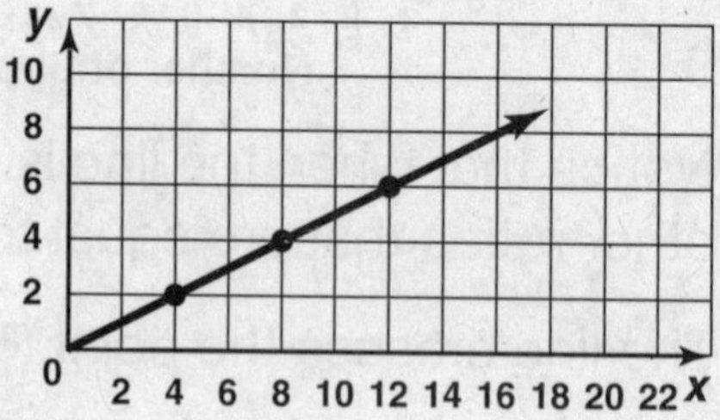

____

____

Test Prep

5. Which ordered pair will be found on the graph for the ratio 2:3?

A. (3, 6) **B.** (6, 4) **C.** (4, 6) **D.** (12, 16)

6. **Writing in Math** Does the given graph show a line that is more likely to be for ratios equal to 1:3 or 3:1? Explain.

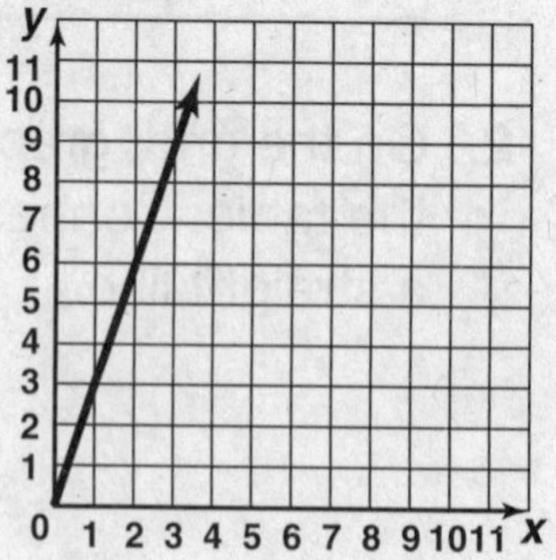

____

____

____

____

Name ______________________________

Rates

R 11-4

A rate is a ratio that compares unlike quantities, like feet per second, miles per hour, dollars per hour, or miles per gallon.

56 ft in 6 sec

In the ratio above, feet and seconds are compared.

When a rate is written to compare one unit, the rate is called the unit rate.

If you are paid \$27 for 3 hr, the rate is written as $\frac{\$27}{3\text{ hr}}$. The unit rate is found by finding an equal ratio with a unit of 1 in the hour's place.

$27 \div \frac{3}{3} \div 3 = \frac{9}{1}$

The unit rate is $\frac{\$9}{\text{h}}$.

Tell the two quantities that are being compared in each rate.

1. \$3.29 per gallon ______________

2. 42 ft in 6 min ______________

3. 3 cans per lb ______________

Write each rate as a unit rate.

4. \$25 for 2 hr work ______________

5. 195 mi in 3 hr ______________

6. \$1.20 for 4 bags of lima beans ______________

7. 96 m in 10 sec ______________

8. 54 words in 3 lines ______________

9. 160 pencils for 40 students ______________

10. A normal housefly can fly at a rate of $\frac{8\text{ km}}{\text{hr}}$. How many kilometers can a housefly travel in 5 hr? ______________

Name ____________________

Rates

Tell the two quantities being compared in each.

1. 32 mi per hour ____________

2. $16.00 each hour ____________

3. 32 cents per mile ____________

Write each rate as a unit rate.

4. 18 mi in 2 hr ____________

5. $60.00 for 5 blankets ____________

6. 300 beats in 2 min ____________

7. At a carnival for the school, you can purchase booth tickets in groups of 4 or 25. Four tickets cost $1, and 25 tickets cost $5. Which is a better buy? Use the unit rate to explain.

____

____

____

Test Prep

8. Which rate is the best buy?

A. $19 for 3 lb **B.** $12 for 2 lb **C.** $55 for 10 lb **D.** $350 for 50 lb

9. **Writing in Math** Sharon says that she changed jobs because she gets paid a better rate now. Her old job paid her $8 per hour. Her new job pays her $300 per week. Sharon has worked 40 hr per week in each job. Does Sharon get paid a better rate for her new job? Explain.

____

____

Name____

PROBLEM-SOLVING STRATEGY **R 11-5**

Make a Table

Cleaners A cleaning company divides into groups of 7 cleaners, 2 dusters for every 5 sweepers. There are 45 sweepers. How many dusters are needed?

Read and Understand

Step 1: What do you know?

For every 5 sweepers, 2 dusters are needed in a group.

Step 2: What are you trying to find?

The number of dusters needed when there are 45 sweepers.

Plan and Solve

Step 3: What strategy will you use?

Strategy: Make a table

First, set up a table with correct labels, and enter the known data in the table. Then find a pattern and extend the table.

Number of Groups	1	2	3	4	5	6	7	8	9	10
Number of Dusters	2	4	6	8	10	12	14	16	18	20
Number of Sweepers	5	10	15	20	25	30	35	40	45	50

Answer: When there are 45 sweepers, there are 18 dusters. 18 dusters are needed.

Look Back and Check

Step 4: Is your work correct?

Yes, each group has 2 more dusters and 5 more sweepers.

1. Every week Catherine receives $4.50 in allowance. If she saves the entire amount, how many weeks will it take her to save $22.50?

Number of Weeks	1				
Total Dollars Saved	4.50				

____

Name ______________________________

PROBLEM-SOLVING STRATEGY

Make a Table

Solve. Write the answer in a complete sentence.

1. Brenda is making bracelets that each use three 6 in. strips of leather. She wants to make 6 bracelets. How many strips of leather does Brenda need?

2. Charles can type 72 words per minute. He needs to type a paper with 432 words. How many minutes will it take Charles to type the paper?

3. Samuel is building a brick wall. Each row has 15 bricks. Samuel has 75 bricks. How many rows of bricks can he build?

4. Maggie is taking her cats into the vet for their shots. The vet charges $18 for one shot and $16 for each shot after that. How much will it cost Maggie to get shots for all of her 6 cats?

5. A baseball team is ordering equipment for their practice sessions. For every 2 bats they order, they also order 9 balls. The coach decides to order 12 new baseball bats. How many balls did he order?

Name ____________________

Scale Drawings

R 11-6

Ralph made a scale drawing of his living room and the furniture in it. The scale he has chosen is 1 cm:2 ft, or 1 cm = 2 ft.

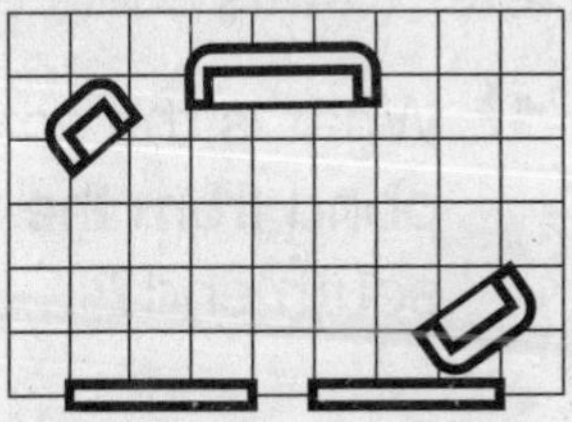

What is the actual length of the living room? Remember, each square centimeter in the drawing is equal to 2 ft. By counting the squares, you can see that the room is 9 cm long.

Multiply: $9 \times 2 = 18$

So, the living room is 18 ft long.

What is the actual width of the living room?

The room is 6 cm wide.

Multiply: $6 \times 2 = 12$

So, the living room is 12 ft wide.

Refer to the scale drawing of the garden.

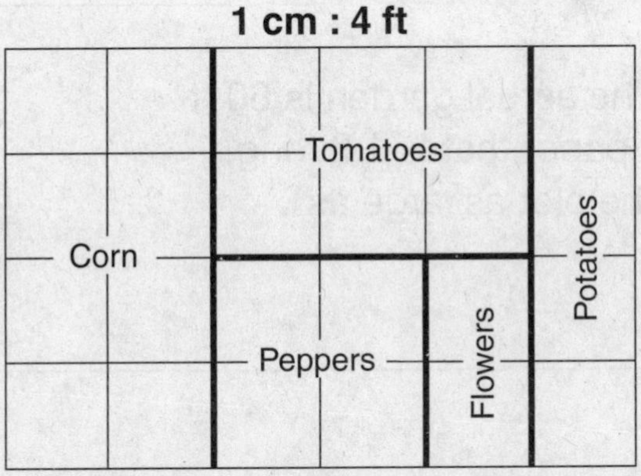

1. What is the actual length of the garden? ____________

2. What is the actual width of the garden? ____________

3. **Number Sense** Darrel says the actual length of the potato section of the garden is 20 ft. Is he correct? How do you know?

____

____

____

Name ______________________________

Scale Drawings

Refer to this scale drawing of a park.

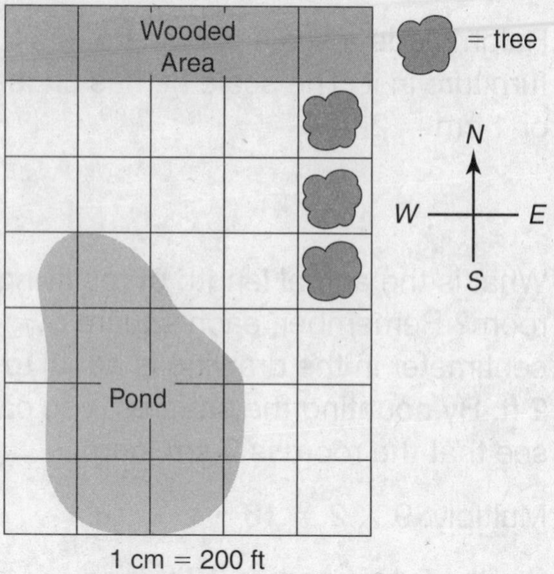

1. What is the actual length of the pond from the north end to the south end?

____

2. What is the actual width, from west to east, of the wooded area?

____

3. A common highway map scale is 1 cm = 5 mi. If you were going to make a map that covered a distance of 900 mi wide, how wide would your map need to be?

____

4. A garden plot is drawn to scale. The actual garden is 60 ft long and 20 ft wide. If you have a paper that is 1 ft long, what scale can you use to draw the plot as large as possible on the paper?

____

Test Prep

5. In a scale drawing of a house that uses a scale of 5 mm = 3 ft, how tall will a house that is 27 ft tall appear on the drawing?

A. 9 mm **B.** 27 mm **C.** 30 mm **D.** 45 mm

6. Writing in Math David drew a scale drawing of an airplane. The actual airplane was 32 ft long and David's drawing was 8 in. long. Find the scale and explain.

____

____

____

Name ______________________________

PROBLEM-SOLVING SKILL **R 11-7**

Writing to Explain

Times Brendan ran 4 laps around the track on Tuesday. It took him 16 min. On Wednesday he ran 6 laps around the track and it took him 24 min. If he runs 8 laps on Thursday, how long do you think it will take him? Write and explain how you made your prediction.

Writing a Math Explanation

- Make sure your prediction is clearly stated.
- Use steps to make your explanation clear.
- Show and explain carefully how you used the numbers to make your prediction.

Example

I predict it will take him 32 min. Below is how I made my prediction.

1. I looked at how long it took him to run 4 laps, which was 16 min. That means it took him 4 min to run each lap, because $16 \div 4 = 4$.
2. I did the same for how long it took him to run 6 laps. I saw that it also took him 4 min per lap. I saw the pattern.
3. Since it always takes him 4 min to run 1 lap, I multiplied $8 \times 4 = 32$.

Write to explain. Write the answer in a complete sentence.

1. The football team is playing a game away. There are 22 players on the team and 8 cheerleaders. The band will be playing a show at halftime. There are 16 band members. There will be 6 adults that will be riding on buses with the students. The school is using buses that can each carry 16 people. How many buses will the school need?

____

____

____

____

____

Name________________________________

PROBLEM-SOLVING SKILL **P 11-7**

Writing to Explain

Write to explain.

1. Use the juice prices to predict how much a 64 oz container of juice will cost.

2. Isabel took 20 min to run around the track 6 times. John took 3 min to run around the track once. Which student was running faster?

3. Nancy is saving $2 from her allowance every week. Marco is saving $1 the first week, $2 the second week, $3 the third week, and so on. At the end of 10 weeks, who will have saved more money? How much more?

4. **Reasonableness** For every 3 cans of vegetables purchased, you get 1 free can. Tessie went home with 32 cans of vegetables, but only had to pay for 16. Is this correct? Explain.

Name ______________________

Understanding Percent

R 11-8

What fraction of the grid is shaded?

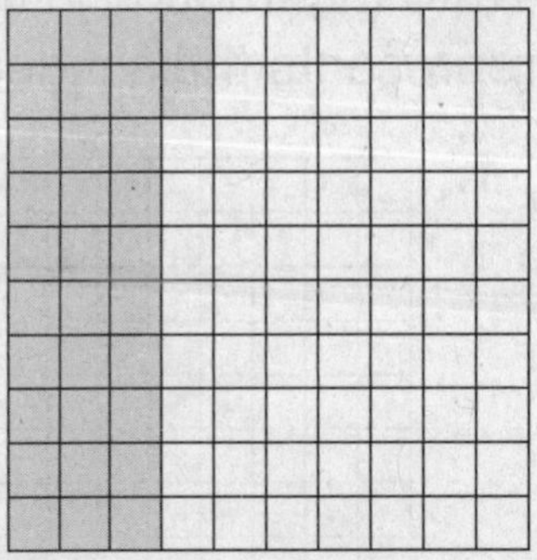

Since 32 of the hundred units are shaded, the fraction is $\frac{32}{100}$. In simplest form that is $\frac{8}{25}$.

What percent of the grid is shaded?

32 of the hundred units are shaded.

$\frac{32}{100} = 32\%$

It may be helpful to think of the percent sign (%) as having the same meaning as "out of 100."

Write a fraction in lowest terms and the percent that represents the shaded part of each figure.

1.

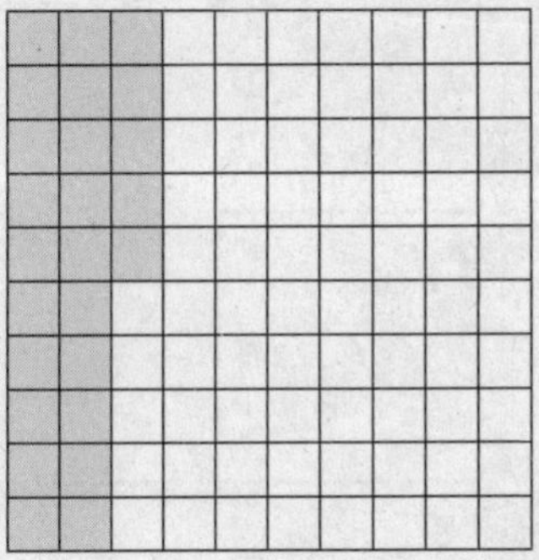

____

2.

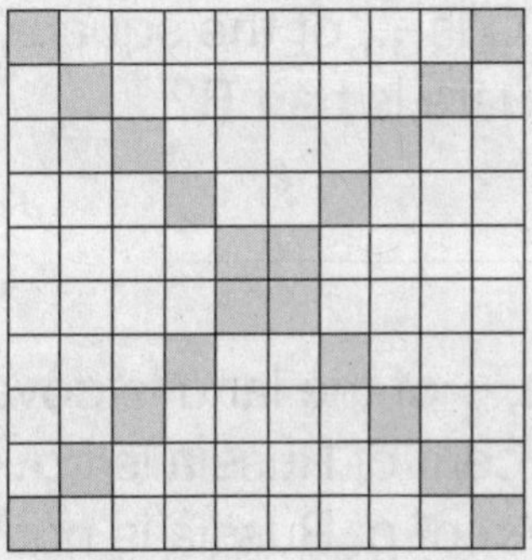

____

3.

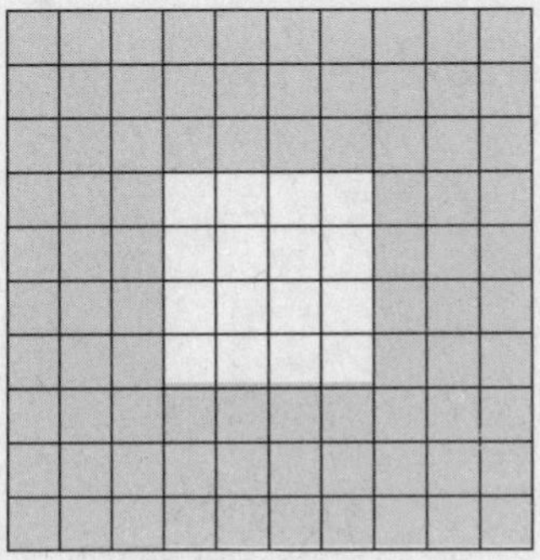

____

4.

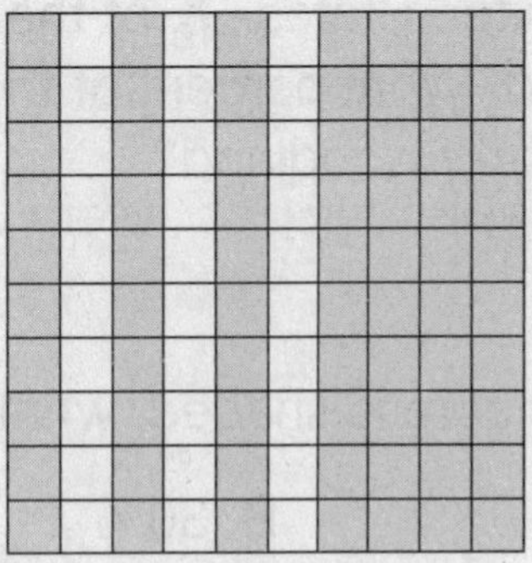

____

5. Number Sense What is "eighty-two percent" written as a fraction in simplest form? ______________

Name ___________________________________

Understanding Percent

Write the fraction in lowest terms and the percent that represents the shaded part of each figure.

1. 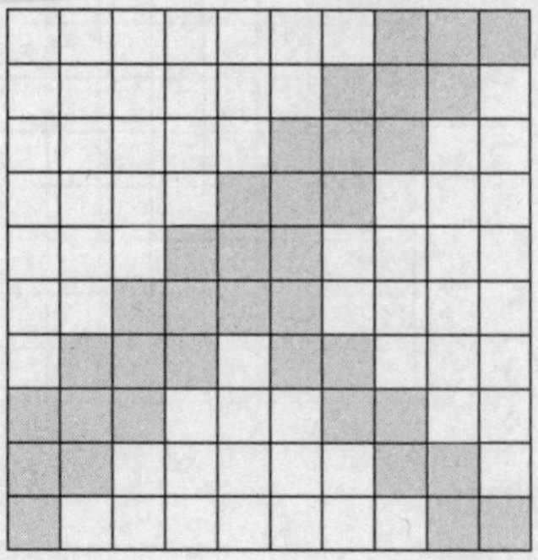

____

2. 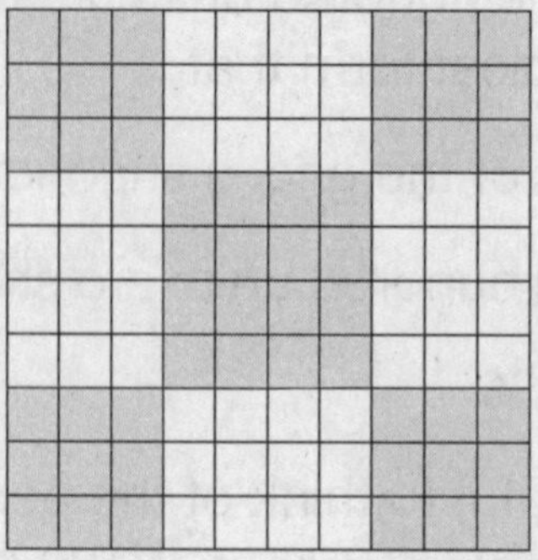

____

3. In the square, if part A is $\frac{1}{4}$ of the square and part C is $\frac{1}{10}$ of the square, what percent of the square is part B?

____

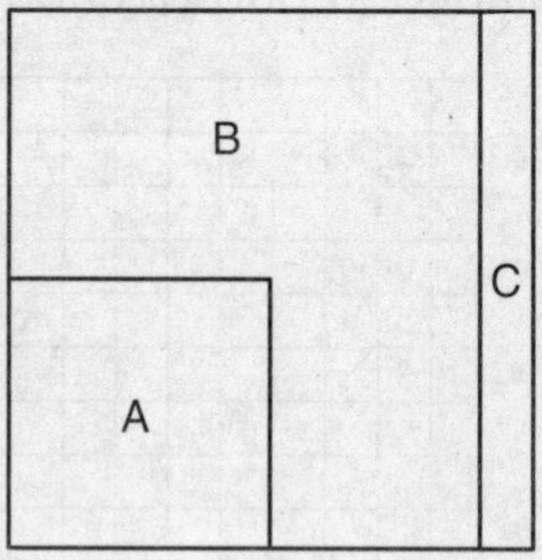

4. In Russia, $\frac{1}{4}$ of the land is covered by forests. What percent of Russia is covered by forest? What percent of Russia is not covered by forest?

____

5. In the United States, $\frac{3}{10}$ of the land is forests and woodland. What percent of the United States is forest and woodland?

____

Test Prep

6. If $\frac{2}{5}$ of a figure is shaded, what percent is not shaded?

A. 20% **B.** 30% **C.** 50% **D.** 60%

7. **Writing in Math** Explain how a decimal is related to a percent.

____

____

Name ____________________

Mental Math: Finding a Percent of a Number

R 11-9

You can use the table below to help you find the percent of a number mentally.

Percent	10%	20%	25%	$33\frac{1}{3}$%	40%	50%	60%	$66\frac{2}{3}$%	75%	80%
Fraction	$\frac{1}{10}$	$\frac{1}{5}$	$\frac{1}{4}$	$\frac{1}{3}$	$\frac{2}{5}$	$\frac{1}{2}$	$\frac{3}{5}$	$\frac{2}{3}$	$\frac{3}{4}$	$\frac{4}{5}$
Decimal	0.1	0.2	0.25	$0.33\frac{1}{3}$	0.4	0.5	0.6	$0.66\frac{2}{3}$	0.75	0.8

How to find a percent of a number:

Find $66\frac{2}{3}$% of 33.

$66\frac{2}{3}\% \times 33 = \frac{2}{3} \times 33$

$\frac{2}{3} \times 33 = 22$

So, $66\frac{2}{3}$% of 33 is 22.

Find 40% of 25.

40% is the same as $\frac{2}{5}$ or 0.4.

$\frac{2}{5} \times 25 = 10$

So, 40% of 25 is 10.

Find each using mental math.

1. 25% of 200 ________

2. 50% of 16 ________

3. 30% of 60 ________

4. 10% of 370 ________

5. Reasoning Order these numbers from least to greatest.

$\frac{3}{4}$, 0.91, 50%, $\frac{2}{5}$, 0.3

____

6. To be labeled a juice drink, only 10% of a drink must be real fruit juice. How many ounces of a 64 oz juice drink must be real juice?

____

Name ____________________

Mental Math: Finding a Percent of a Number

P 11-9

Find each using mental math.

1. 20% of 60 ________
2. 30% of 500 ________
3. 25% of 88 ________
4. 70% of 30 ________
5. **Reasoning** Order these numbers from least to greatest.
   0.85, $\frac{1}{4}$, 72%, $\frac{5}{8}$, 20%, 0.3

   ____

	Rural	Urban
Bermuda	0%	100%
Cuba	25%	75%
Guatemala	60%	40%

The table shows the percent of the population that live in rural and urban areas of each country.

6. Out of every 300 people in Cuba, how many of them live in a rural area? ________
7. Out of every 1,000 people in Guatemala, how many live in urban areas? ________

Test Prep

8. What is 40% of 240?

   A. 48 **B.** 96 **C.** 128 **D.** 960

9. **Writing in Math** If there are 1,241,356 people who live in Bermuda, how many residents of Bermuda live in urban areas? How many live in rural areas? Explain your answer.

   ____

   ____

   ____

Name ____________________

Estimating Percents

There are some percents that are easy to find mentally, such as 25%, 10%, 20%, 50%, 75%, and 100%.

To find an estimate for a percent of a number, you can change the percent and the number to compatible numbers.

Find 62% of 190.

62% is close to 60% and 190 is close to 200.

62% of 190 is about 60% of 200.

$60\% \text{ of } 200 = \frac{6}{10} \times 200$

$= 6 \times 20$

$= 120$

So, 62% of 190 is about 120.

Find 47% of 617.

47% is close to 50% and 617 is close to 600.

47% of 617 is about 50% of 600.

$50\% \text{ of } 600 = \frac{1}{2} \times 600$

$= 300$

So, 47% of 617 is about 300.

Estimate.

1. 81% of 196 ________

2. 38% of 62 ________

3. 34% of 13 ________

4. 76% of 84 ________

5. 98% of 19 ________

6. 53% of 23 ________

7. 9% of 73 ________

8. 77% of 63 ________

9. Estimation Estimate 53% of 71. Is your estimate an underestimate or an overestimate? Explain.

Name ______________________________

Estimating Percents

P 11-10

Estimate.

1. 52% of 420 ______
2. 68% of 70 ______
3. 11% of 120 ______
4. 76% of 81 ______
5. 39% of 31 ______
6. 27% of 24 ______
7. 9% of 72 ______
8. 58% of 492 ______
9. 18% of 402 ______

10. **Algebra** Use estimation to find the value of x when 25% of x is about 30.

______

A group of students were surveyed on what they like to do after school. There were 200 students surveyed, and the results were graphed.

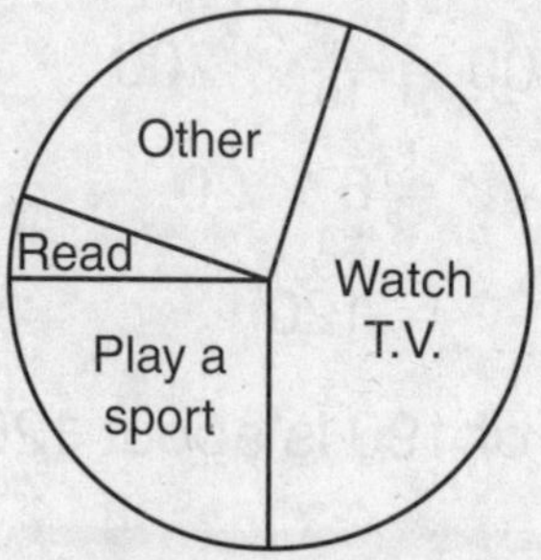

11. Estimate the number of students who prefer to play a sport after school.

______

12. Do more than or fewer than 40 students prefer to read after school?

______

Test Prep

13. Which is the best estimation for 31% of 68?

A. 20 **B.** 21 **C.** 25 **D.** 27

14. **Writing in Math** Linda says that 42 is a reasonable estimate for 34% of 119. Is she correct? Explain why or why not.

______

______

______

______

Name ______________________________

PROBLEM-SOLVING APPLICATION **R 11-11**

The Rug Maker

Kung designs rugs and carpets. Two of her latest designs are shown below. Which rug has a higher percentage of squares shaded?

Rug A

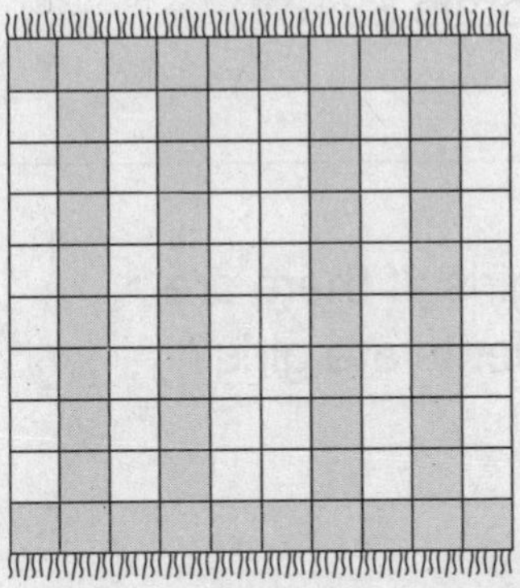

Rug B

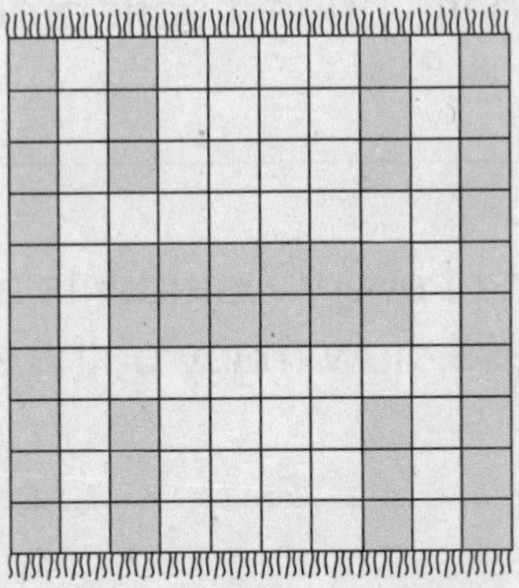

Rug A has $\frac{52}{100}$ squares shaded. That is 52% or $\frac{13}{25}$ shaded.

Rug B has $\frac{44}{100}$ squares shaded. That is 44% or $\frac{11}{25}$ shaded.

So, Rug A has a higher percentage of squares shaded.

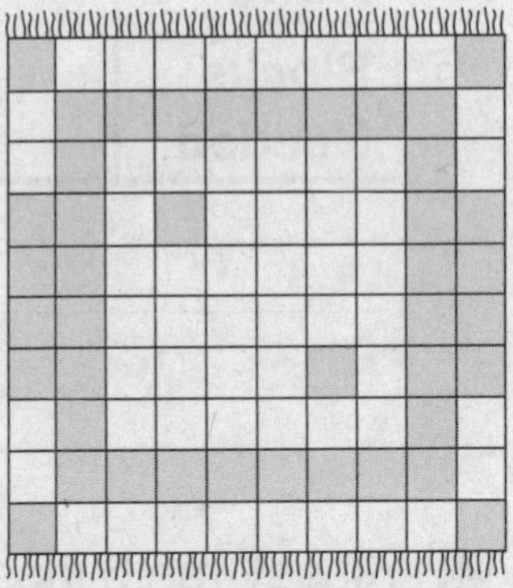

1. Kung recently made the rug at the right. Write the fraction in lowest terms and the percent that represents the shaded part of the rug.

____

2. If Kung made 12 rugs in 6 months, what is the unit rate?

____

____

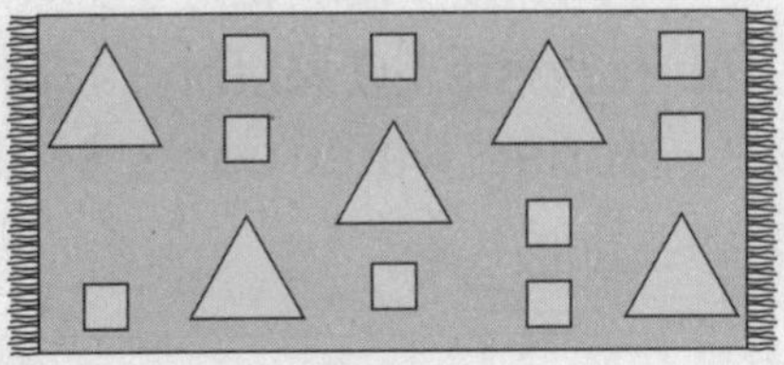

3. What is the ratio of triangles to squares? Write the ratio in three ways.

____

____

Name ____________________

PROBLEM-SOLVING APPLICATION **P 11-11**

A Pack of Percents

Solve. Write your answer to each in a complete sentence.

1. A bookstore charges 12% of your purchase price to cover sales tax and shipping and handling. About how much will be added to your purchase price if your order totals $216?

____

2. In Derreck's class, 3 out of every 7 students are girls. If there are 16 boys in Derreck's class, how many of the students are girls?

____

3. Complete the table to help you find how many blocks are needed if a tower is built of blocks where each row has one less block than the one below it. The tower is 8 rows high, and the bottom row has 20 blocks in it.

Rows	1	2	3	4	5	6	7	8
Blocks Needed								

____

____

4. Kinsey ran 3 laps around the track in 12 min yesterday. Today she ran 5 laps, and it took her 19 min 20 sec. Which day did Kinsey run faster?

____

5. It costs $0.89 for 1 L of spring water, and a 5 L jug of spring water costs $4.95. Which is the better buy?

____

____

Name

Properties of Equality

R 12-1

Property

Addition: You can add the same number to both sides of an equation and the sides remain equal.	Subtraction: You can subtract the same number from both sides of an equation and the sides remain equal.	Multiplication: You can multiply both sides of an equation by the same number and the sides remain equal.	Division: You can divide both sides of an equation by the same number (except 0) and the sides remain equal.
Example:	Example:	Example:	Example:
$4 + 8 = 8 + 4$	$12 + 6 = 18$	$3 \times 8 = 4 \times 6$	$14 + 10 = 24$
$2 + 4 + 8 = 8 + 4 + 2$	$(12 + 6) - 3 = 18 - 3$	$3 \times 8 \times 4 = 4 \times 6 \times 4$	$(14 + 10) \div 3 = 24 \div 3$

You can use inverse operations to solve equations.

Subtraction can undo addition.	Addition can undo subtraction.	Division can undo multiplication.	Multiplication can undo division.
$(6 + 8) - 8 = 6$	$(7 - 3) + 3 = 7$	$(12 \times 3) \div 3 = 12$	$(56 \div 8) \times 8 = 56$
$14 - 8 = 6$	$4 + 3 = 7$	$36 \div 3 = 12$	$7 \times 8 = 56$
$6 = 6$	$7 = 7$	$12 = 12$	$56 = 56$

Which property of equality is illustrated by each pair of equations?

1. $30 - 6 = 24$

So, $(30 - 6) + 2 = 24 + 2$.

____

2. $21 \div 7 = 3$

So, $(21 \div 7) \times 2 = 3 \times 2$.

____

Tell what inverse operation and what number must be used to get *n* alone.

3. $n \div 2$ ______________

4. $14 + n$ ______________

Evaluate each expression.

5. $6 \times 10 = (2 + 4) \times \bigcirc$ ______

6. $(15 - 5) \div 2 = 10 \div \bigcirc$ ______

Name ______________________________

Properties of Equality

P 12-1

What property of equality is illustrated by each pair of equations?

1. $12 \times 2 = 24$
So, $(12 \times 2) \div 6 = 24 \div 6$. ______________

2. $19 - 4 = 15$
So, $(19 - 4) + 6 = 15 + 6$. ______________

3. $21 + 7 = 28$
So, $(21 + 7) - 18 = 28 - 18$. ______________

Tell what inverse operation and what number you would use to get *n* alone.

4. $n - 9$ ______________

5. $14 + n$ ______________

6. $n \times 17$ ______________

7. $n \div 3$ ______________

8. $41n$ ______________

9. $n + 7$ ______________

10. Jerry has a paper route on Sundays. He started with 64 deliveries, but lost 6 accounts. Then he got 6 new accounts. How many papers does Jerry now deliver on Sundays?

____

Test Prep

11. Which operation should be used to get *y* alone in 16*y*?

A. Add 16 **B.** Subtract 16 **C.** Multiply by 16 **D.** Divide by 16

12. Writing in Math Explain how to get *j* alone in 12*j*.

____

____

____

Name ____________________

Solving Addition and Subtraction Equations

R 12-2

You can use inverse operations to solve addition and subtraction equations.

$n - 8 = 6$

8 has been subtracted from *n*. The inverse of subtraction is addition, so you can add 8 to both sides of the equation.

$n - 8 + \mathbf{8} = 6 + \mathbf{8}$

$n = 6 + 8$ The $+ 8$ undoes the $- 8$.

$n = 14$

Check your solution by substituting it into the original equation.

$n - 8 = 6$ Replace the *n* with 14.

$14 - 8 = 6$

$6 = 6$ The solution checks.

$n + 13 = 40$

13 has been added to *n*. The inverse of addition is subtraction, so you can subtract 13 from both sides of the equation.

$n + 13 - \mathbf{13} = 40 - \mathbf{13}$

$n = 40 - 13$ The $- 13$ undoes the $+ 13$.

$n = 27$

Check your solution by substituting it into the original equation.

$n + 13 = 40$ Replace the *n* with 27.

$27 + 13 = 40$

$40 = 40$ The solution checks.

Solve and check each equation.

1. $x + 14 = 21$ ________

2. $b - 7 = 13$ ________

3. $22 + m = 39$ ________

4. $21 = r - 4$ ________

5. Mary's sister is 4 years older than Mary. Her sister is 12. Use the equation $m + 4 = 12$ to find Mary's age. ____________

6. Stephanie had a box of pencils. She gave 13 to her sister and mother. Now she has 23 pencils. Use the equation $p - 13 = 23$ to find out how many pencils were in the box. ____________

Name ______________________________

Solving Addition and Subtraction Equations

P 12-2

Solve and check each equation.

1. $x + 4 = 16$ ________

2. $t - 8 = 15$ ________

3. $m - 9 = 81$ ________

4. $7 + y = 19$ ________

5. $k - 10 = 25$ ________

6. $15 + b = 50$ ________

7. $f + 18 = 20$ ________

8. $w - 99 = 100$ ________

9. $75 + n = 100$ ________

10. $p - 40 = 0$ ________

11. Jennifer has $14. She sold a notebook and pen, and now she has $18. Solve the equation $14 + m = 18$ to find how much money Jennifer received by selling the notebook and pen. ________

12. Kit Carson was born in 1809. He died in 1868. Use the equation $1{,}809 + x = 1{,}868$ to find how many years Kit Carson lived.

Test Prep

13. Which is the solution for y when $y - 6 = 19$?

A. 13 **B.** 15 **C.** 23 **D.** 25

14. Writing in Math Nellie solved $y - 3 = 16$. Is her answer correct? Explain and find the correct answer if she is incorrect.

$y - 3 = 16$

$y = 13$ Subtract 3

____

____

____

____

Name ____________________

R 12-3

Solving Multiplication and Division Equations

You can use inverse operations to solve multiplication and division equations.

$n \times 5 = 35$

The variable n has been multiplied by 5. The inverse of multiplication is division, so you can divide both sides of the equation by 5.

$n \times 5 \div \mathbf{5} = 35 \div \mathbf{5}$

$n = 35 \div 5$ The $\div$ 5 undoes the $\times$ 5.

$n = 7$

Check your solution by substituting it into the original equation.

$n \times 5 = 35$ Replace the n with 7.

$7 \times 5 = 35$

$35 = 35$ The solution checks.

$\frac{n}{7} = 8$

The variable n has been divided by 7. The inverse of division is multiplication, so you can multiply both sides of the equation by 7.

$\frac{n}{7} \times \mathbf{7} = 8 \times \mathbf{7}$

$n = 8 \times 7$ The $\times$ 7 undoes the $\div$ 7.

$n = 56$

Check your solution by substituting it into the original equation.

$\frac{n}{7} = 8$ Replace the n with 56.

$56 \div 7 = 8$

$8 = 8$ The solution checks.

Solve and check each equation.

1. $\frac{n}{5} = 3$ ____________

2. $7t = 84$ ____________

3. $x \div 9 = 18$ ____________

4. $66 = 6u$ ____________

5. $\frac{y}{10} = 200$ ____________

6. $7t = 49$ ____________

7. $160 = 16x$ ____________

8. $r \div 25 = 6$ ____________

9. Number Sense A carton of eggs is on sale for \$0.49. Use the equation $\$0.49x = \$2.45$ to find how many cartons of eggs you can purchase for \$2.45.

____

Name ____________________

Solving Multiplication and Division Equations

P 12-3

Solve and check each equation. Remember $\frac{n}{5}$ means $n \div 5$.

1. $\frac{x}{7} = 14$ ________

2. $15p = 75$ ________

3. $108 = 4 \times b$ ________

4. $t \div 12 = 18$ ________

5. $222 = 3a$ ________

6. $\frac{y}{3} = 18$ ________

Reasoning Use mental math to solve each equation.

7. $4j = 400$ ________

8. $n \div 9 = 1$ ________

9. Each member of a rescue team can carry 40 lb of equipment in his or her backpack. How many team members are needed to carry 280 lb of equipment? Use the equation $40x = 280$ to solve the problem.

____

10. A box of granola bars is divided between 3 boys. If each boy gets 6 granola bars, how many bars are in the box? Use the equation $\frac{b}{3} = 6$ to solve the problem.

____

Test Prep

11. Which property should you use to solve the equation for n when $\frac{n}{2} = 16$?

A. Addition Property of Equality

B. Subtraction Property of Equality

C. Multiplication Property of Equality

D. Division Property of Equality

12. Writing in Math Explain why you use division to solve a multiplication problem and multiplication to solve a division problem.

____

____

____

Name ______________________________

PROBLEM-SOLVING STRATEGY **R 12-4**

Write an Equation

Buttons Matilda decided to put her buttons into 7 jars. Each jar had 14 buttons in it. How many buttons did Matilda have?

Read and Understand

Step 1: What do you know?

There were a bunch of buttons that were put into 7 jars. Each jar ended up with 14 buttons.

Step 2: What are you trying to find?

How many buttons Matilda has

Plan and Solve

Step 3: What strategy will you use?

Strategy: Write an equation

Draw a picture to help you see the main idea.

Use a letter or variable to show what you are trying to find. Let j = the number of jars.

Write a number sentence using the variable.

$j \div 7 = 14$

Solve the number sentence.

$j \div 7 \times 7 = 14 \times 7$

$j = 98$

Look Back and Check

Step 4: Is your answer reasonable?

Yes, $98 \div 7 = 14$.

Complete the picture to show the main idea for this problem. Then write an equation and solve it.

1. A total of 54 students are going on a field trip, and 36 of the students are girls. How many of the students are boys?

____

Name ____________________

PROBLEM-SOLVING STRATEGY

Write an Equation

Solve each problem. Draw a picture to show the main idea for each problem. Then write an equation and solve it. Write the answer in a complete sentence.

1. Bobby has 3 times as many model spaceships as his friend Sylvester does. Bobby has 21 spaceships. How many model spaceships does Sylvester have?

____

____

2. Dan saved \$463 over the 12 weeks of summer break. He saved \$297 of it during the last 4 weeks. How much did he save during the first 8 weeks?

____

____

3. A box of peanut butter crackers was divided between 6 children. Each child got 9 crackers. How many crackers were in the box?

____

____

Name ____

Understanding Integers

R 12-5

You can write integers for word descriptions.

Word Description	Integer
A gain of 15 yd	+15
8 steps backward	−8

You can use a number line to compare and order integers.

Compare −2 ◯ −5.

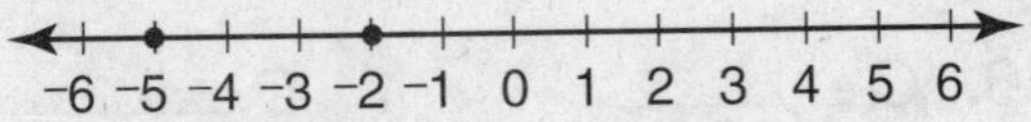

The integer −5 is farther to the left on the number line than the integer −2.

So, −5 < −2.

Write an integer for each word description.

1. 84 ft below sea level ________ **2.** A gain of 500 points ________

Use the number line for 3–5. Write the integer for each point.

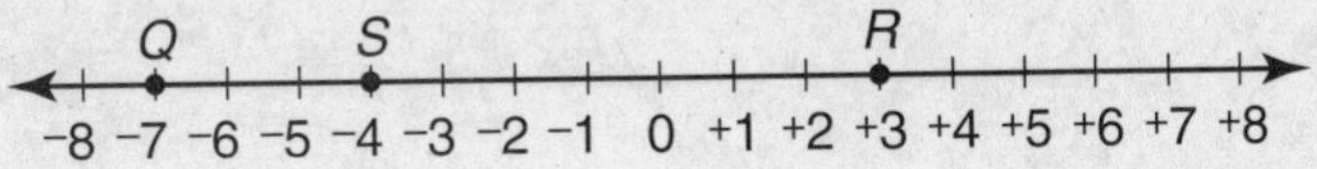

3. *Q* ________ **4.** *R* ________ **5.** *S* ________

Compare. Use >, <, or = for each ◯.

6. −1 ◯ +1 **7.** +8 ◯ +3

8. −2 ◯ −16 **9.** +6 ◯ −8

Write in order from least to greatest.

10. +6, −6, 0, −12 ________________

11. +4, −6, −5, +2 ________________

12. **Number Sense** Which is less, −9 or −4? ________________

Name ____________________

Understanding Integers

Write an integer for each word description.

1. a withdrawal of $50 ________
2. a temperature rise of 14° ________
3. 10° below zero ________

Use the number line for 4–7. Write the integer for each point.

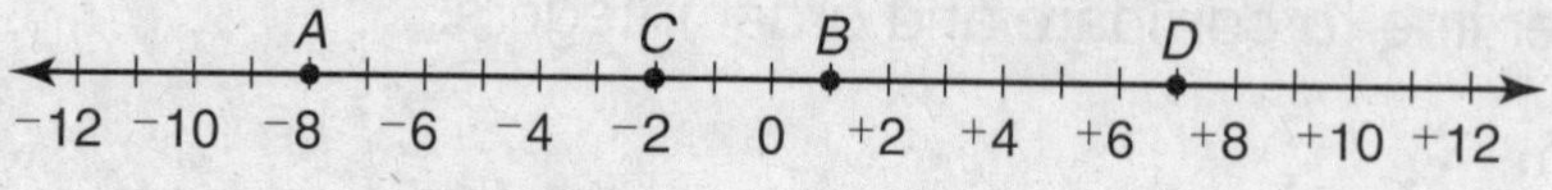

4. *A* ________
5. *B* ________
6. *C* ________
7. *D* ________

Compare. Use >, <, or = for each ◯.

8. −5 ◯ −9
9. +8 ◯ −12
10. +21 ◯ −26

Write in order from least to greatest.

11. −4, +11, −11, +4 ____, ____, ____, ____
12. −6, +6, 0, −14 ____, ____, ____, ____
13. +11, −8, +7, −4 ____, ____, ____, ____

Test Prep

14. Which point is farthest to the right on a number line?

A. −6 **B.** −2 **C.** 0 **D.** 2

15. **Writing in Math** In Fenland, U.K., the elevation from sea level is −4 m. In San Diego, U.S., it is +40 ft. The elevations are given in different units. Explain how to tell which location has a greater elevation.

____

____

____

Name ____________________

Adding Integers

Rules for adding integers on the number line:

Always start at 0 and face the positive integers. Walk forward for positive integers and backward for negative integers. The number you stop at is the answer.

Find −1 + (−4).

Start at 0 and face the positive integers. Move backward 1 unit. Then move backward 4 more units.

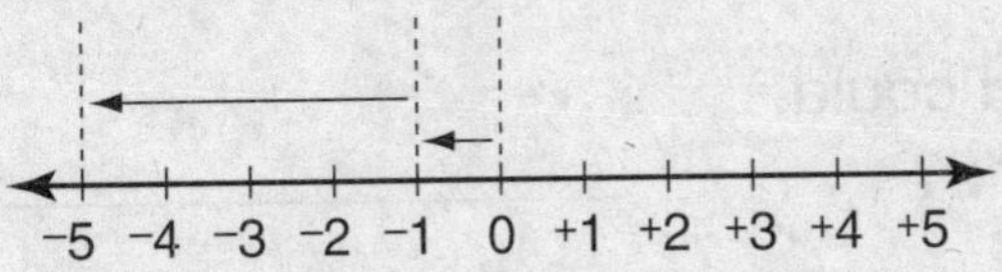

So, −1 + (−4) = −5

Find +3 + (−5).

Start at 0 and face the positive integers. Move forward 3 units. Then move backward 5 units.

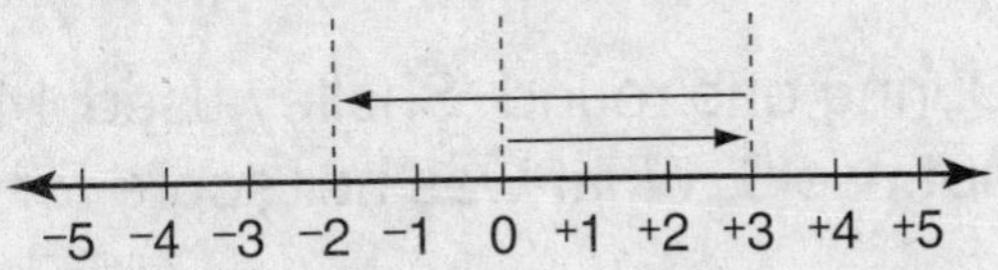

So, +3 + (−5) = −2

Add. Use a number line.

1. −3 + (−3) = ________

2. −1 + (+4) = ________

3. −7 + (+7) = ________

4. +4 + (−9) = ________

5. −5 + (−4) = ________

6. +9 + (−2) = ________

7. −11 + (+12) = ________

8. −2 + (−4) = ________

9. Mental Math What is the sum of +5 + (−3) + (−5)? Explain how you found your answer.

____

____

____

____

____

Name ________________________________

Adding Integers

P 12-6

Add. Use a number line.

1. $^{+}1 + {}^{+}3 =$ ________
2. $^{+}4 + {}^{-}7 =$ ________
3. $^{-}4 + {}^{-}2 =$ ________
4. $^{-}3 + {}^{+}1 =$ ________
5. $^{+}6 + {}^{-}6 =$ ________
6. $^{-}1 + {}^{-}4 =$ ________
7. $^{+}9 + {}^{-}7 =$ ________
8. $^{-}6 + {}^{+}12 =$ ________
9. $^{-}3 + {}^{-}8 =$ ________

In a word tile game, you score one positive point for each letter tile that you use and one negative point for each tile that you have left.

10. During one round, Shelley used 14 tiles and could not use 6. What was her score for that round? ________

11. Pete used 4 tiles, but he could not use 8. What was his score that round? ________

12. **Reasoning** In the game, if you have 18 tiles and you cannot use 3 of them, what will your score be for that round? Explain how you found the answer.

____

Test Prep

13. Which is the sum of $^{-}8 + {}^{+}5$?

A. $^{-}13$ **B.** $^{-}3$ **C.** $^{+}3$ **D.** $^{+}13$

14. **Writing in Math** During a week at camp, Tom started with a zero balance in his account at the camp store. On Monday he deposited $15. He withdrew $6 on Tuesday and $3 on Thursday. What was his account balance after Thursday's withdrawal? Explain.

____

____

____

Name ______________________________

Subtracting Integers

As when adding, always start at 0 and face the positive integers. Walk forward for positive integers and backward for negative integers. The subtraction sign signals you to turn around and face the negative integers. The number you stop at is the answer.

Find $-1 - (-4)$.

Start at 0 and face the positive integers. Move backward 1 unit. Then turn around and move backward 4 units.

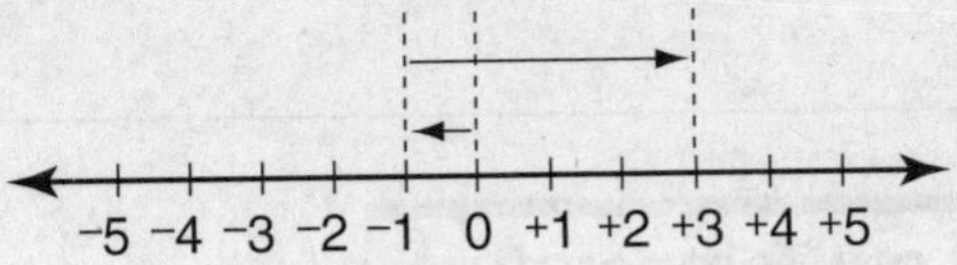

So, $-1 - (-4) = +3$.

Find $+3 - (+5)$.

Start at 0 and face the positive integers. Move forward 3 units. Then turn around and move forward 5 units.

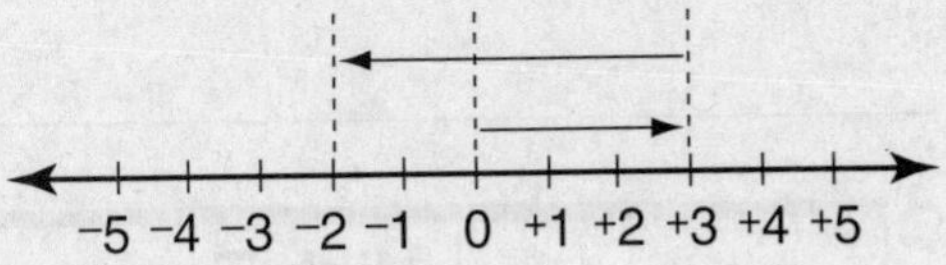

So, $+3 - (+5) = -2$.

Subtracting an integer is the same as adding its opposite. So, $-10 - (-2)$ can be written as $-10 + (+2)$.

Rewrite each subtraction using addition. Then find the answer. Use a number line to check.

1. $-16 - (+2)$ ____________

2. $+4 - (-4)$ ____________

3. $+8 - (+9)$ ____________

4. $-13 - (-6)$ ____________

5. $+5 - (+11)$ ____________

6. $-2 - (-4)$ ____________

7. $+6 - (-13)$ ____________

8. **Reasoning** Which is greater, $+6 - (-3)$ or $+6 + (-3)$? ____________

Name ______________________

Subtracting Integers

Rewrite each subtraction using addition. Then find the answer. Use a number line to check.

1. −9 − +1 ______

2. +6 − −3 ______

3. +8 − +4 ______

4. −11 − −16 ______

5. −6 − −1 ______

6. −3 − +4 ______

	High Temperature	Low Temperature
January 1	−1°F	−16°F
February 1	27°F	18°F
March 1	51°F	42°F

7. How much greater was the high temperature than the low temperature on January 1? ______

8. How much less was the low temperature on January 1 than the low temperature on February 1? ______

9. How much greater was the high temperature than the low temperature on March 1? ______

Test Prep

10. Which of the following is the same as +4 − −9?

A. −4 + −9 **B.** +4 + −9 **C.** −4 − −9 **D.** +4 + +9

11. **Writing in Math** Use the information from Exercises 7–9. Which date had the greatest difference between the high and low temperatures? Explain.

______

______

Name ____________________

PROBLEM-SOLVING SKILL

R 12-8

Writing to Explain

Backpackers A group of backpackers is hiking a trail that is 10 mi long. The table below shows how the amount of time it takes to hike each mile changes as the hikers continue on the trail.

Number of miles hiked	2	4	6	8	10
Minutes to hike each mile	10	12	14	16	18

Explain how the amount of time it takes to hike each mile changes as the number of miles hiked changes.

Writing a Math Explanation

- Identify the quantities shown in the table.
- Tell how one quantity changes as the other quantity changes. Be specific. This is an explanation of the pattern.

Example

The table shows how many miles the backpackers hiked and how long it took them to hike each mile.

As the number of miles hiked increases by 2, the number of minutes it takes to hike each mile increases by 2. This means that it takes longer and longer for the backpackers to hike the trail.

1. At a banquet, each table received 80 oz of water. Different numbers of people sat at the tables. Use the pattern to complete the table for 16 diners.

Number of diners	1	2	4	8	16
Ounces per diner	80	40	20		

Explain how the number of ounces per diner changes as the number of diners changes.

____

____

____

Name ______________________________

PROBLEM-SOLVING SKILL **P 12-8**

Writing to Explain

Write to explain.

1. In a game, you score points for each space you move your token. Complete the table and use the pattern to extend it to 7 spaces.

Number of spaces	1	2	3				
Number of points	1	3	5				

Explain how the number of points scored changes as the number of spaces moved changes.

____

____

____

2. A 4 oz jar of olives costs $1.40. An 8 oz jar of olives costs $2.50. A 16 oz jar of olives costs $3.60. Predict how much a 32 oz jar of olives will cost. Explain your prediction.

____

____

____

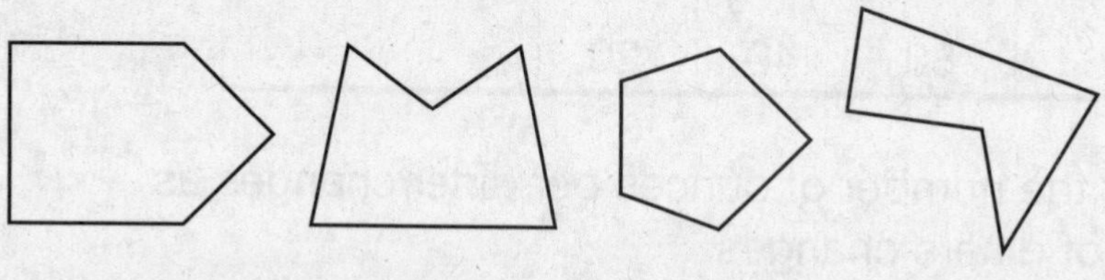

3. Explain how the figures are alike and different.

____

____

Name ______________________

The Coordinate Plane

Naming a point:

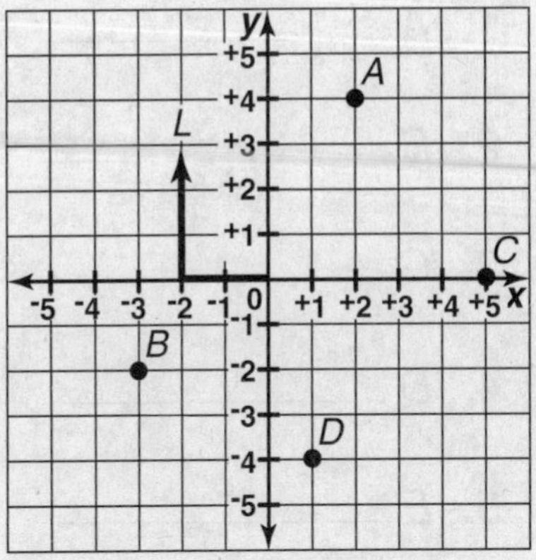

The ordered pair for point *A* is (+2, +4). It is 2 units to the right of the origin (0, 0) and 4 units above the origin.

The ordered pair for point *B* is (−3, −2), which means 3 units to the left of the origin and 2 units below the origin.

Point *C* is at (+5, 0). Point *D* is at (+1, −4).

Graphing a point:

To graph a point when you are given an ordered pair, always begin at the origin. Move left for negative *x*-values and right for positive *x*-values. Move down for negative *y*-values and up for positive *y*-values.

Graph point *L* at (−2, +3).

Move 2 units to the left and then 3 units up.

Write the ordered pair for each point.

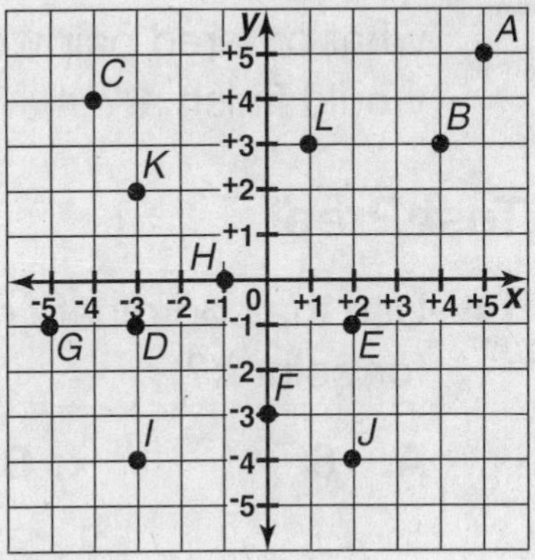

1. *A* ________ **2.** *B* ________

3. *D* ________ **4.** *E* ________

5. *C* ________ **6.** *F* ________

Name the point for each ordered pair.

7. (+2, −4) ______ **8.** (+1, +3) ______ **9.** (−5, −1) ______

10. (−3, −4) ______ **11.** (−1, 0) ______ **12.** (−3, +2) ______

13. Representation What is the ordered pair for the origin? ________

Name ____________________

The Coordinate Plane

P 12-9

Write the ordered pair for each point.

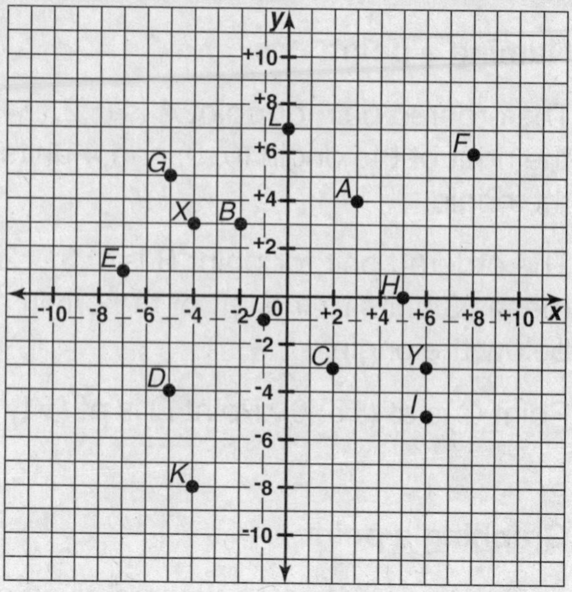

1. *A* ____________
2. *B* ____________
3. *C* ____________
4. *D* ____________
5. *E* ____________
6. *F* ____________

Name the point for each ordered pair.

7. (+5, 0) ______ 8. (−1, −1) ______ 9. (0, +7) ______

10. (+6, −5) ______ 11. (−4, −8) ______ 12. (−5, +5) ______

13. If a taxi cab were to start at the point (0, 0) and drive 6 units left, 3 units down, 1 unit right, and 9 units up, what ordered pair would name the point the cab would finish at? ____________

Test Prep

14. Use the coordinate graph above. Which is the *y*-coordinate for point *X*?

A. +6 **B.** +3 **C.** −3 **D.** −6

15. **Writing in Math** Explain how to graph the ordered pair (−2, +3).

____

____

____

____

Name ______________________________

Graphing Equations

Find the values for y when $x = -2$, 0, and 2.

Put -2 where the x is in the equation.

$y = x + {}^{+}2$

$y = ({}^{-}2) + {}^{+}2$

$y = 0$

The ordered pair, then, is $({}^{-}2, 0)$.

The other ordered pairs would be $(0, {}^{+}2)$ and $({}^{+}2, {}^{+}4)$.

Now you can plot each of the points and connect the points with a solid line. The line formed is the graph of the equation, and all of the points on the line are solutions to the equation.

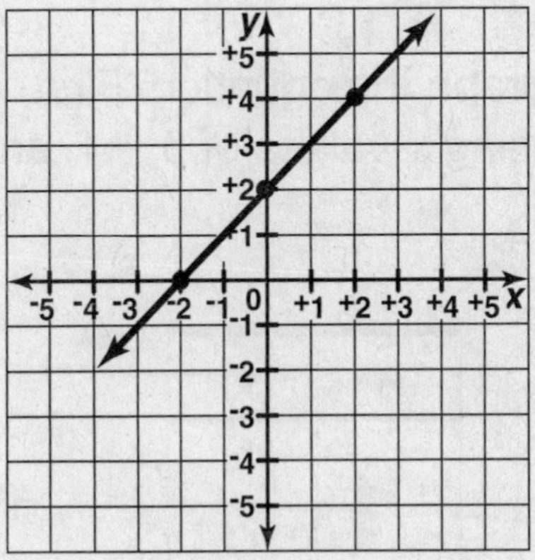

Find the values of y when $x = {}^{-}2$, $x = 0$, and $x = {}^{+}2$, then name the ordered pairs.

1. $y = x$ ______________________________

Complete the table using x-values of $^{-}2$, 0, and $^{+}2$. Graph the equation using your table.

2. $y = x - ({}^{-}3)$

x	y

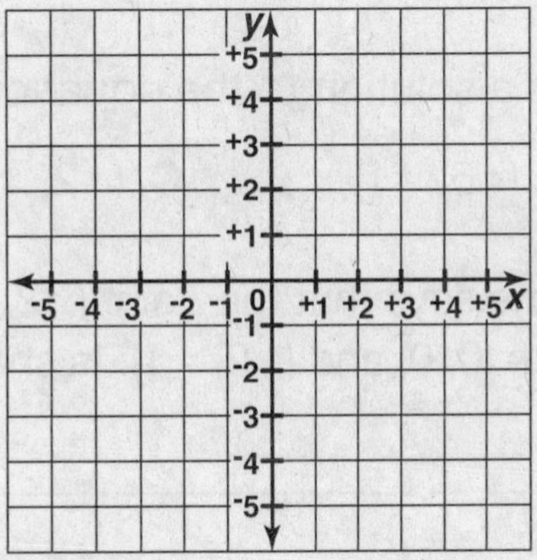

Name ______________________________

Graphing Equations

P 12-10

For each equation, find the values of y when $x = {}^{-}1$, when $x = 0$, and when $x = {}^{+}1$. Then name the ordered pairs.

1. $y = x - 1$ ____________, ____________, ____________

2. $y = 3x$ ____________, ____________, ____________

3. $y = x + {}^{-}2$ ____________, ____________, ____________

Graph the equation. First, make a table using x-values of 0, $^{+}1$, and $^{+}2$.

4. $y = x + 4$

x	y

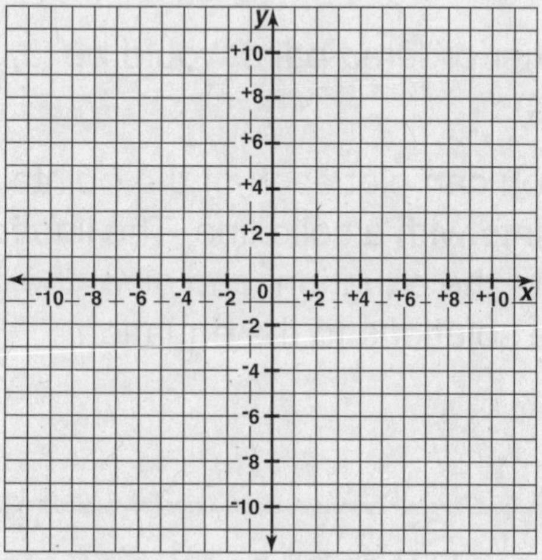

Bob earns $4 every week he takes out the trash. Use $y = 4x$, where x is the number of times Bob takes out the trash, to find how much Bob makes for taking out the trash.

5. How much will Bob have earned when he takes out the trash for 6 weeks? ____________

Test Prep

6. Which ordered pair is a solution to the equation $y = 6x$?

A. (0, 0) **B.** ($^{+}6$, $^{+}1$) **C.** ($^{+}2$, $^{+}6$) **D.** ($^{+}6$, 0)

7. Writing in Math Jolene says that the point ($^{-}2$, $^{-}1$) is on the same line as the points (0, 0) and ($^{+}2$, $^{-}1$). Is she correct? Explain.

____

____

____

Name ______________________

PROBLEM-SOLVING APPLICATION **R 12-11**

Weather in Romantown

Winter in Romantown is often cold. On December 12, the temperature at 10 A.M. was +8°F. A cold front came through, and the temperature dropped throughout the day. By 3 P.M. the temperature was 19°F lower than it was at 10 A.M. What was the temperature at 3 P.M.?

The temperature at 10 A.M. + the change in temperature = the temperature at 3 P.M.

$$^{+}8 + (^{-}19) = n$$

$$^{+}8 + (^{-}19) = {}^{-}11$$

So, the temperature at 3 P.M. was $^{-}11$°F.

1. On January 4, the temperature was $^{-}6$°F in the early morning. By 4:00 P.M. that afternoon, the temperature had risen 31°F. What was the temperature at 4:00 P.M.? ______________

2. In mid-January, members of a Romantown fire station attempted to build an ice skating rink at a local park. In the afternoon, when the temperature was +35°F, the firemen sprayed hundreds of gallons of water on the field. By how many degrees would the temperature have to drop for the water to turn to ice? ______________

The month of March in Romantown can be very wintry and cold but can also have some warmer, springlike days. Below are word descriptions for the temperatures on several days in March. Write an integer for each description.

3. 7 degrees below zero ______________

4. 49 degrees above zero ______________

5. 2 degrees below zero ______________

6. 51 degrees above zero ______________

Name ____________________

PROBLEM-SOLVING APPLICATION **P 12-11**

Equations and Graphs

Solve.

1. Today's high temperature was +15°F, and the low temperature was x degrees lower. If the low temperature was −5°F, how much less was the low temperature than the high temperature? Write an equation and solve it to find the answer.

2. Solve the problem $5x = 125$. Explain which property you needed to use.

3. Graph the points with ordered pairs $A(0, +3)$, $B(+3, -3)$, and $C(-3, -3)$. Connect the points and tell what type of figure is formed.

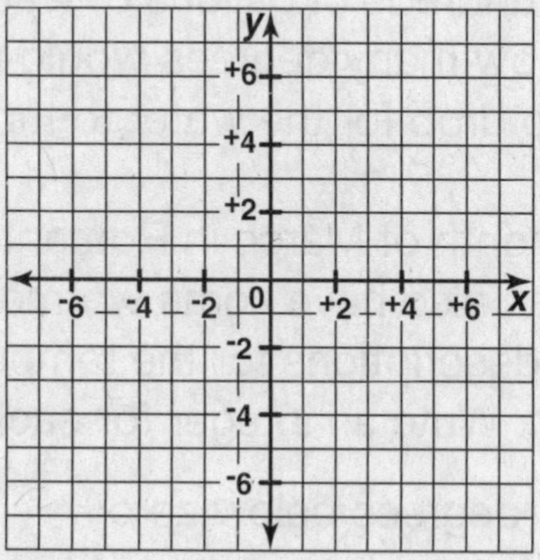

4. Martha saved the same amount of money every week for 52 weeks. At the end of the 52 weeks, she had saved $754. How much money did Martha save each week? Draw a picture and write an equation to solve.